FARM

A Multimodal Reader

Joyce Kinkead

Evelyn Funda

Lynne S. McNeill

Utah State University Press
Logan

USU
PRESS

Published by Utah State University Press
An imprint of University Press of Colorado
245 Century Circle, Suite 202
Louisville, Colorado 80027

ASSOCIATION
of UNIVERSITY
PRESSES

The University Press of Colorado is a proud member of
the Association of University Presses.

The University Press of Colorado is a cooperative publishing enterprise supported, in part, by Adams State
University, Colorado State University, Fort Lewis College, Metropolitan State University of Denver,
Regis University, University of Colorado, University of Northern Colorado, University of Wyoming, Utah
State University, and Western Colorado University.

∞ This paper meets the requirements of the ANSI/NISO Z39.48-1992 (Permanence of Paper)

ISBN: 978-1-60732-987-9 (paperback)
ISBN: 978-1-60732-988-6 (ebook)
https://doi.org/10.7330/9781607329886

Library of Congress Cataloging-in-Publication Data
Names: Kinkead, Joyce A., 1954– author. | Funda, Evelyn I., author. | McNeill, Lynne S., author.
Title: Farm : a multimodal reader / Joyce Kinkead, Evelyn Funda, Lynne S. McNeill.
Description: Logan : Utah State University Press, [2019]
Identifiers: LCCN 2019053419 (print) | LCCN 2019053420 (ebook) | ISBN 9781607329879 (paperback) |
   ISBN 9781607329886 (ebook)
Subjects: LCSH: Agriculture—History. | Farms—History.
Classification: LCC S419 .K56 2019 (print) | LCC S419 (ebook) | DDC 630—dc23
LC record available at https://lccn.loc.gov/2019053419
LC ebook record available at https://lccn.loc.gov/2019053420

Cover image: Cache Valley Barn by Jon Anderson. Cover and text design: Ellie Moore

Credits

Page	Image	Permission/Credit cine
11	Fig. 2.1	Figure 2.1. Sumerian cuneiform tablet, probably from Erech (Uruk), Mesopotamia, ca. 3100–2900 BCE. Clay, Metropolitan Museum of Art, New York City.
137	Fig. 6.2	Dorothea Lange, *Thirteen-Year-Old Sharecropper Boy near Americus, Georgia,* July 1937. Library of Congress Prints & Photographs Division Washington, D.C., LC-USF34- 017915-C [P&P] LOT 1544 (corresponding photographic print), Reproduction Number: LC-DIG-fsa-8b32269 (digital file from original neg.)
154	n/a	This promotional pamphlet from a local World's Fair association was issued in 1893 in advance of the Chicago fair. The figure is Pomona, the goddess of fruit and namesake of the eastern Los Angeles County town. [From "Greater Los Angeles and the World's Fair of 1893," posted July 7, 2017 on *The Homestead Blog,* by the Homestead Museum, Los Angeles, https://homesteadmuseum.wordpress.com/2017/07/07/greater-los-angeles-and-the-worlds-fair-of-1893/
171	Text	William Kittredge, excerpt from "Owning It All" from *The Next Rodeo: New and Selected Essays.* Copyright © 1987 by William Kittredge. Reprinted with the permission of The Permissions Company, LLC on behalf of Graywolf Press, Minneapolis, Minnesota, https://www.graywolfpress.org.
191	Text	Copyright ©1997 by Wendell Berry, from *The Unsettling of America.* Reprinted with permission of Counterpoint Press.
209–211	Text	Permission for "Breakfast" and "Snow at the Farm" is courtesy of Sutphen and permission for "The Farm" and "My Father Comes to the City" is courtesy of Beacon Press.
239	Text	Excerpted from David Fooks, "The History of Pennsylvania's Barn Stars and Hex Signs," *Material Culture* 36.2 (Fall 2004)
241	Text	Michael L. Doherty, "The Folklore of Cattle Diseases: A Veterinary Perspective," *Béaloideas* 69 (January 2001), 41–75. CODECS: online database and e-resources for Celtic studies, Online: Stichting A. G. van Hamel voor Keltische Studies. URL: https://www.vanhamel.nl/codecs/.
253	Fig. 10.2	A dowser at work, from Pierre le Brun, Histoire critique des pratiques superstitieuses (1733–1736)." —After that, please add on the original caption: Dowsing (whether for water, metal, precious gems, or even people) dates back to at least the early 1500s. While there is no scientific explanation for it, many people swear by it as a technique for understanding the landscape.
257	Text	Reprinted from https://www.factcheck.org/2009/03/illegal-backyard-garden/.
262	Text	Wendell Berry, "The Pleasures of Eating," from *What Are People For?* Copyright ©1990, 2010. Reproduced by permission of Counterpoint Press.
281	Text	Missouri Corn Palace display in the Palace of Agriculture at the 1904 World's Fair. The "corn temple" structure was 65 ft tall with a dome that was 125 ft in circumference. The temple used 1,000 bushels and consisted of 50 different shades of corn and was often used as a lounge and a meeting place. Photograph by the Official Photographic Company, 1904. Missouri Historical Society Photographs and Prints Collections. NS 20614. Courtesy of the Missouri Historical Society, St. Louis. https://mohistory.org/collections/item/resource:146833

continued on next page

Page	Image	Permission/Credit cine
286	Text	Jennifer Meta Robinson and J. A. Hartenfeld, *The Farmers' Market Book: Growing Food, Cultivating Community*, Quarry Books, 2007. Reprinted with permission of Indiana University Press.
287	n/a	Poster from Salt Lake City Farmers Market, 2002. Illustration by Greg Newbold— https://illoz.com/newbold/.
291	n/a	The Peterson Brothers' truck features the lyric that made them famous. In front of the tractor, pictured from left to right: Greg, Nathan, and Kendal Peterson.
302	Fig. 13.5	Fig. 13.5. "Sow the seeds of Victory!" Artist James Montgomery Flagg (1877–1960), lithograph, 1917. Library of Congress.
302	Fig. 13.6	Fig. 13.6. "Helping Hoover in Our U.S. School Garden," American Lithographic Co., 1919. Library of Congress, Prints & Photographs Division, Washington, DC.
302	Fig. 13.7	Fig. 13.7. Uncle Sam says, Garden to Cut Food Costs." Lithograph, A. Hoen & Co., Baltimore, 1917. Courtesy LOC.
302	Fig. 13.8	Fig. 13.8. "War Gardens for Victory—Grow Vitamins at Your Kitchen Door." Published between 1939 and 1945. Copyright by J. H. Burdett, director, National Garden Bureau.
302	Fig. 13.9	Fig. 13.9. "Join the United States School Garden Army—Enlist Now." Artist Edward Penfield. Published by American Lithographic Co., New York, ca. 1918.
304	Fig. 13.10a	Fig. 13.10A. The Woman's Land Army of America—Training School, University of Virginia, ca. 1918. Artist Herbert Paus. Library of Congress, Prints & Photographs Division, Washington, DC.
304	Fig. 13.10b	Fig. 13.10B: Pitch in and Help!—Join the Women's Land Army of the U.S. Crop Corps. 1944. Artist Hubert Morley. Courtesy of Hennepin County Library. Women wearing overalls with the insignia of the Woman's Land Army work on a farm, milking a cow, weeding, harvesting, and feeding chickens.
305		Crate label, "Princess Brand." Grown on Orange Heights in Queen Colony. Call Fruit Company. Corona, Riverside Co., Calif. Stecher Litho. Co., Rochester, N.Y. Ca. 1895–1910. 34 x 24 cm. Riverside Public Library Label Citrus Collection. Identifier: http://ark.cdlib.org/ark:/13030/kt4r29q8wd, CRIV_121, Loc Hist Lock 769.4 CIT.
		Crate label for Old Mission Brand oranges picked and packaged by the Placentia Orange Company, which was owned and managed by Charles C. Chapman. Color lithograph, 11" x 10". Old Mission Brand: https://digitalcommons.chapman.edu/chapman_family/107/
		Charles C. Chapman, ca. 1920.
		Crate label, "Golden Sceptre Brand." Washington Navels. Rialto Orange Co. Rialto, San Bernardino Co., Calif., ca. 1925, 27.5 x 27.5 cm, Riverside Public Library, Identifier: CRIV_135, Loc Hist Lock 769.4 CIT. Copyright status unknown. Golden Sceptre: https://calisphere.org/item/ark:/13030/kt8m3nd7d1/
		Crate label, "Victoria Brand." Grown and packed on Arlington Heights by Victoria Avenue Citrus Assn. Riverside, Calif., ca. 1930s, 28 x 25.5 cm. Creator: Schmidt Litho. Co., Los Angeles, Calif. Riverside Public Library, CRIV_105. Loc Hist Lock 769.4 CIT. Copyright unknown. Victoria: https://calisphere.org/item/ark:/13030/kt92903077/
		Crate label, "Lincoln Brand." Grown and packed on Arlington Heights by Victoria Avenue Citrus Association. Ca. 1930s. 28 x 25.5 cm. Riverside Public Library, Calif., CRIV_175, Loc Hist Lock 769.4 CIT
		Creator/Contributor: Schmidt, Los Angeles (?). Lincoln: https://calisphere.org/item/ark:/13030/kt4f59r013/
		Arlington Heights Fruit Company, Navajo Brand, ca. 1940-1970. Schmidt Litho Co., UC Riverside, Library, Special Collections and University Archives. Navajo Brand: https://calisphere.org/item/ark:/86086/n2dz07p6/
329	Text	"Excerpt(s) from *Farm City: The Education of an Urban Farmer*, by Novella Carpenter. ©2009 by Novella Carpenter. Used by permission of Penguin Press, an imprint of Penguin Publishing Group, a division of Penguin Random House LLC. All rights reserved.

Dedication

This book was inspired by reading Thomas Jefferson, Justin Morrill, Hamlin Garland, Willa Cather, Wendell Berry, and Sue Hubbell—among others. It is dedicated to our farm families.

COVER IMAGE: Jon Anderson, *Cache Valley Barn*. Used with permission.

Brief Table of Contents

Expanded Table of Contents

Overview of FARM: A Multimodal Reader

This book focuses on the culture of agriculture. By *culture*, we mean the knowledge, beliefs, laws, customs, ethics, and art of a society. Culture is a complex concept. It is universal but is also particular to groups. Culture is especially appropriate when focusing on farming. Consider that *cultivation*, a form of culture, can refer to agricultural improvement. Cicero, one of the foremost rhetoricians of Ancient times, writes of cultivation of the soul, comparing spiritual development to agriculture. Throughout this book, you will look at a variety of texts as lenses with which to viewthe topic of farming. These texts take multiple forms: literary works, essays, recipes, menus. The interdisciplinary nature of the selections allows readers to consider what farms, farming, and farmers means to us as a culture. The texts include examples from all states in the continental United States. We also look at the art of farming: fine art, film, and photography. Take, for instance, the cover of this book—a painting by Jon Anderson of a mountain valley in spring with a barn inscribed with an ad for Woman's Tonic. This romanticized vision of farming is but one theme to be explored in the pages that follow.

While early chapters include ancient and European texts (medieval through Renaissance), the book focuses mostly on the American farm. Readers move through the Jeffersonian idealism of the yeoman farmer ("Cultivators of the earth are the chosen people of God") to literature of the 19th and 20th centuries (Thoreau's bean field, Cather's prairie novel, Steinbeck's *The Grapes of Wrath,* as well as very contemporary memoirs like *Farm City*). A considerable amount of history contextualizes the literary texts, such as discussion of sharecropping vs. plantation systems, the rise of agribusiness and chemical farming, and Teddy Roosevelt's Country Life Commission. Written, visual, and oral texts ask readers to consider the farm in music (Woody Guthrie), art (Grant Wood), ecology (Rachel Carson's *Silent Spring*), children's and young adult literature, advertising (from early boosterism to Chipotle videos), print culture (farmers' market and victory garden posters from both world wars), folklore (food culture, vintners, and veterinarian practices, for instance), popular culture (Farm Aid concerts), and much more.

Michael Pollan, author of food-themed books such as *Cooked, The Omnivore's Dilemma,* and *The Botany of Desire,* says this:

> When I began writing about agriculture in the late '80s and '90s, I quickly figured out that no editor in Manhattan thought the subject timely or worthy of his or her attention, and that I would be better off avoiding the word entirely and talking about food, something people then still had some use for and cared about, yet oddly never thought to connect to the soil or the work of farmers.

FARM: A Multi-Modal Reader connects readers back to the soil and the work of farmers and explores how agriculture is essential to everyone—even if a person has never planted a seed, hoed a row, or pulled a carrot from the earth.

A note on texts: original style conventions have been retained in texts that were written or translated in British English.

Activities and Icons Key

Each chapter includes activities that students may undertake. Icons represent these activities—images that come from the farm.

 Explore Activities are noted by a shovel and pitchfork as you'll be digging for answers.

 Writing Assignments—opportunities to compose—are noted by a hand sowing seeds as writing often plants seeds of thought to be harvested.

 Collaboration Activities are designated by two farmers.

 Research: Do you ever feel like you are looking for a needle in a haystack when undertaking a research project? The barn brings together all of the skills needed to undertake research.

 Field Trips—what could be more appropriate for a class that explores farm literature and essays than taking a field trip? The tractor icon designates possible outings to enrich understanding of both farms and texts. Some field trips may be *virtual* as the Internet offers wonderful resources to explore.

 Viewing offers suggestions for films and works of art, and is noted by the picture of the sun rising over a field.

 For Further Reading offers suggestions for novels, stories, poetry, nonfiction that enrich the chapter. A sheaf of wheat represents these titles.

References

Pollan, Michael. 2009. "Introduction." In *Bringing It to the Table: On Farming and Food* by Wendell Berry, p xii. Berkeley, CA: Counterpoint.

🐓 SECTION ONE 🐓

Exploring Our Roots

FIGURE 1.1. Egyptian Tomb Painting Featuring Plowing and Sowing
(Photo Credit: David F. Lancy)

CHAPTER ONE

Our Connections to Agriculture

What is Your Agricultural Literacy IQ?

Everyone is connected to agriculture in some way, through the food we eat, the clothes we wear, **and** the health products we use. But a very small percentage of the US population actually produce the food and fiber that we all use. In this chapter, you will explore your personal connections to agriculture. You may believe that you do not have many links to farming or know much about the subject. Let's see if that is really true.

Take the following quiz. It will provide foundational information on agriculture and farming and set the stage for our study of texts. Read each question and circle *yes* if you agree with the statement or *no* if you disagree with the statement. The answers are located at the end of this chapter.

Yes	No	1. One acre of land is about the size of a football field.
Yes	No	2. Most of us could survive without farmers.
Yes	No	3. Corn and soybeans can be dried and crushed to make oil.
Yes	No	4. Agriculture provides food, clothes, and shelter.
Yes	No	5. Half of the earth's land is suitable for growing crops.
Yes	No	6. Topsoil loss has increased in the last 15 years.
Yes	No	7. Farmers use pesticides to increase farm production.

For the following questions, circle the best choice that answers the question.

8. During the past 50 years, the number of farms in the US has:
   a. Increased
   b. Stayed about the same
   c. Decreased
   d. Fluctuated wildly

9. Which state produces the most food?
   a. Utah
   b. Wisconsin
   c. California
   d. Texas

Source: This quiz is used with the permission of the Agriculture in the Classroom (AITC) project.

10. Which of these crops is produced in the United States?
    a. Corn
    b. Rice
    c. Wheat
    d. Soybeans
    e. All of the above

11. Out of 100 people in the US, how many are farmers?
    a. 1–2 people
    b. 3–4 people
    c. 5–7 people
    d. 10 people

12. Agriculture includes food and fiber production, processing, sales, farm equipment sales, and other sectors close to farming. With that in mind, how many people out of every 100 people in the US. work in some phase of agriculture?
    a. 5%
    b. 15%
    c. 25%
    d. 50%

13. Which of the following has allowed farmers to increase production by 300% in the last 40 years?
    a. Research and Education
    b. Economics
    c. Smaller farms
    d. All of the above

14. What percent of Utah's land is in farms and ranches?
    a. 12 percent
    b. 21 percent
    c. 53 percent
    d. 78 percent

15. Three-fourths of our *nation's* wildlife lives on . . .
    a. Bureau of Land Management
    b. Private farms and ranches
    c. Wilderness areas
    d. State lands

16. What percent of the average Americans' income is spent on food?
    a. 7%
    b. 10%
    c. 15%
    d. 20%

17. Which country/countries are the best agricultural customers for the USA?
    a. Japan
    b. Canada
    c. Mexico
    d. European Union

Growing a Nation: The Story of American Agriculture
Historical Timeline—Life on the Farm

▶17th–18th Centuries

17th century
Farmers endure rough pioneer life while adapting to
new environment

18th century
Ideas of progress, human perfectibility, rationality, and
scientific improvement flourish in the New World;
small family farms predominate, except for plantations
in southern coastal areas; housing ranges from crude log cabins
to substantial frame, brick, or stone houses; farm families
manufacture many necessities

▶1800

1810–30
Transfer of manufactures from the farm and home to the shop
and factory is greatly accelerated

▶1840

1840–60
Growth in manufacturing brings many labor-saving devices to the
farm home; rural housing improves with balloon-frame construction

1844
Success of the telegraph revolutionizes communications

1845
Mail volume increases as postage rate is lowered

▶1860

1860s
Kerosene lamps become popular

1865–90
Sod houses common on the prairies

▶1880
1895
George B. Seldon is granted US patent for automobile

1896
Rural Free Delivery (RFD) started

▶1900
1900–20
Urban influences on rural life intensify

1908
Model T Ford paves way for mass production of automobiles; President Roosevelt's Country Life Commission focuses attention on the problems of farm wives and difficulty of keeping children on the farm

1908–17
Country-life movement

▶1920
1920s
Movie houses become common in rural areas
1921
Radio broadcasts begin

▶1930
1930
13% of all farms have electricity

1936
Rural Electrification Act (REA) greatly improves quality of rural life

▶1940

1940

58% of all farms have cars; 25% have phones; 33% have electricity

▶1950

1950s

Television widely accepted; many rural areas lose population as farm family members seek outside work

1954

70.9% of all farms have cars; 49% have phones; 93% have electricity; Social Security coverage extended to farm operators

▶1960

1962

REA authorized to finance education TV in rural areas

1968

83% of all farms have phones; 98.4% have electricity

▶1970

1970s

Rural areas experience prosperity and immigration

1968

90% of all farms have phones; 98.6% have electricity

▶1980

Mid-1980s

Low prices and indebtedness affect many farmers in the Midwest; many rural counties decline in population

▶1990–2000

1990–99

Farm families make up less than 10 percent of rural population but rural areas experience some growth

---

Source: An Interactive Timeline of the History of Agriculture in the United States. https://growing anation.org/.

Chapter One Activities

 EXPLORE: How does a *farm* differ from a *ranch*? Write your definition of each and then share with classmates. Decide on a definition that can be used for future class discussions of texts to be studied.

 EXPLORE: Look at the humor list, "You May be a Farmer if . . .," on http://nwdist rict.ifas.ufl.edu/phag/2016/10/14/friday-funny-you-might-be-a-farmer/. Which are the thematic message in these humorous sayings?

 WRITING: Annually in March, National Agriculture Day is celebrated to recognize the abundance provided by agriculture. And what an appropriate time with the changing of the seasons! The day includes contests for best poster and essay. Let's assume that you are entering the essay contest.

Write a one- to two-page personal essay in which you think about your relationship to agriculture. This is your story about agriculture. If you live on a farm or a ranch, discuss what you grow or raise and what you think about your relationship to the state. If you do not live on a farm or ranch, tell us what you appreciate about farmers and ranchers. You might speculate on what needs to change in agriculture. Do you have any favorite books or films that focus on farming? If so, you might draw on that background knowledge.

For more information about National Ag Day, see the following URL: http://www.agday.org/

 COLLABORATE: Martians have landed on Earth, and one approaches and asks you "What is a farmer?" Working with a partner in your class, describe a farmer to this out-of-world visitor. How do you describe what a farmer does and what she or he looks like? What does a farm look like? Why is the farmer important in our culture? As a class, make a list of these descriptions and discuss the perceptions held about farmers and farming. (As you consider these lists, be aware of your use of objective and subjective, concrete and abstract ideas).

 RESEARCH: Is your family involved in some aspect of farming either now or in the past? As we learned in the Ag Literacy quiz, agriculture includes food and fiber production, processing, sales, farm equipment sales, and other areas close to farming. Interview family members and determine if any have been involved in agriculture.

 FIELD TRIP: Do you pass farms in your daily travels? If so, consider taking a second look and think about the aspects of the farm and farming.

 COLLABORATE: According to a proverb, bread is the staff of life. Each student will bring to class <u>one of the following</u>: 1) a loaf of bread (homemade, prepackaged, artisan bread, wheat, sourdough, or gluten-free), 2) butter, or 3) jam (homemade or locally sourced is best). While you are sharing the bread and toppings you brought, discuss some or all of the following.

- Talk about the different kinds of bread people chose to bring. What are the reasons you selected that particular bread? Do you have any personal or familial connection to this type of bread? Compare and contrast the bakers of the bread that class members brought. Why did the baker choose to bake the bread in that particular way? What kind of conclusions can you draw about the culture of agriculture (motives and methods, for example) from these various loaves of bread?
- Then consider the phrase "breaking bread." Where have you heard it before, and what does it mean in that context? Talk about what that phrase means symbolically. Do the same for the phrase "staff of life" or "give us this day our daily bread."
- Discuss the metaphors and word choices Michael Pollan makes in the following quote from *The Botany of Desire*:
  - [W]heat points [us] up, to the sun and civilization" because it is as "leavened with meaning as it [is] with air. [W]heat begins in nature, it is then transformed by culture. . . . Wheat must be harvested, threshed, milled, mixed, kneaded, shaped baked, and then, in a final miracle of transubstantiation, the doughy lump of formless matter rises to become bread. This elaborate process, with its division of labor and suggestion of transcendence, symbolized civilization's mastery of raw nature. A mere food thus became the substance of human and even spiritual communion, for there was also the old identification of bread with the body of Christ.
- Discuss the significance of the two quotes in the images below. Compare and contrast their word choice and consider why the differences are important and what they mean.

FIGURE 1.2. IF YOU ATE TODAY THANK A FARMER.
Design to be printed on mugs, T-shirts, stickers, etc. by Keep Calm and Carry On, https://keepcalms.com.

What is the farmer's economic slice of a loaf of bread?

According to National Farm Union and the US Department of Agriculture's most recent data, for the average loaf of bread costing $3.59, the farmers get about $0.20 for their wheat. Their "farm share" (an individual's percentage of retail price) is about 5%. The rest of the cost of the loaf goes to processing, electricity, packaging, wholesaling, distribution, transportation, marketing, and retailing. The percentage is even worse if that farmer's wheat goes to making breakfast cereal; a typical 18 oz box of cereal retailing for $4.60 yields the farmer a mere $0.10. Because percentages of farm share calculated in the "market basket" data (that is, average household purchases for at-home consumption) varies so much, overall the farmer typically receives only 15–19 cents of every food dollar spent in retail stores.

For more information on the farm share of other crops, see http://nfu.org/images/December2012 Farmers%20Share.pdf

Answers to the Agricultural Literacy Quiz
1. Y
2. N
3. Y
4. Y
5. N
6. N
7. Y
8. C
9. C (Why? California has farm gate sales of 31.7 billion dollars!)
10. E
11. A
12. B
13. A
14. B
15. B
16. B
17. B (at the moment, the US is also its best customer)

CHAPTER TWO

Farming in Ancient Times

History of Agriculture and Literature

In this chapter, we begin exploring how farming has been an important theme in literature since ancient times.

Farming—the domestication of plants and animals—began more than 7,000 years ago as people moved from foraging and hunting. In the process, people became more settled and gathered in groups. The Sumerians, who lived in Mesopotamia (modern-day Iraq), are considered the first farmers. In fact, they are credited with writing the First Farmer's Almanac about 1500 BCE. It was found during an archaeological expedition to Iraq in 1949 and is housed in a museum at the University of Pennsylvania. How did ancient Sumerians write? They used a stylus to make impressions on damp clay tablets, which then dried so that the writing set. This form of writing became known as *cuneiform*. The clay tablet was quite small, only a few inches in height and width.

FIGURE 2.1. Sumerian cuneiform tablet, Mesopotamia(?), ca. 3100–2900 BCE. Metropolitan Museum of Art, NYC.

The 109-line almanac provided directions about how to farm, such as plowing eight furrows at about 20 feet in length. The plow was followed closely by the person sowing the seed, as depicted in the Egyptian tomb painting shown earlier. The instructions also invoked the gods for help.

First Farmer's Almanac

The following version of the Sumerian Farmer's Almanac was translated by Samuel Noah Kramer. He added words in parentheses to help with meaning.

In days of yore a farmer instructed his son:

When you are about to take hold of your field (for cultivation), keep a sharp eye on the opening of the dikes, ditches, and mounds, (so that), when you flood the field the water will not rise too high in it. When you have emptied it of water, watch the field's water-soaked ground that it stay virile ground for you. Let shod oxen (that is, oxen whose hooves are protected in one way or another) trample it for you; (and) After having its weeds ripped out (by them) (and) the field made level ground, dress it evenly with narrow axes weighing (no more than) two-thirds of a pound each. (Following which) Let the pickax wielder eradicate the ox hooves for you (and), Smooth them out; Have all crevices worked over with a drag, and have him go with the pickax all around the four edges of the field.

While the field is drying, let your obedient (household) prepare your tools for you, make fast the yoke bar, hang up your new whips on nails, and let the hanging handles of your old whips be mended by the artisans. Let the bronze . . . your tools "heed your arm"; let the leather "headbinder", goad, "mouth-opener", (and) whip uphold you (in matters requiring discipline and control); let your *bandu*-basket crackle; (all this) will make a mighty income for you.

When your field has been supplied with what is needed, keep a sharp eye on your work. After adding an extra ox to the plow-ox—when one is harnessed to another ox, their plow is larger than (an ordinary) plow—make them . . . one *bur*; they will make for you a . . . like a storm, so that three *gur* barley will be planted in that one *bur*. Sustenance is in a plow! (Thus) Having had the field worked with the *bardil*-plow—(yes) the *bardil*-plow—(and then) having had it worked over with the *shukin*-plow, repeat (the process). (After) Having had it (the field) harrowed, (and) raked three times and pulverized fine with a hammer, let the handle of your whip uphold you; brook no idleness. Stand over them (the field laborers) during their work, (and) brook no interruptions. Do not [distract] your field workers. Since they must carry on by day, (and by) Heaven's stars for ten, (days), Their strength should be spent on the field. (And) They are not to dance attendance on you. When you are about to plow your field, let your plow break up the stubble for you. Leave your "mouth-cover" of the plow . . ., (and) leave your . . . on a narrow nail. Let your moldboards spread to the side, set up your furrows—in one *garush*, set up eight furrows. Furrows which have been deeply dug—their barley will grow long.

When you are about to plow your field, keep your eye on the man who puts in the barley seed. Let him drop the grain uniformly two fingers deep, (and) Use up one <u>shekel</u> of barley for each *garush*. If the barley seed does not sink in properly, change your share, the "tongue of the plow". If the . . ., (then) plow diagonal furrows where you have plowed straight furrows, (And) Plow straight furrows where you have plowed diagonal furrows. Let your straight furrows make your borders into *tulu*-borders; let the *lu*-furrows make straight your borders; (and) Plow *ab*-furrows where . . .; (Then) Let all its clods be removed; all its high spots be made into furrows; (and) all its depressions be made into low furrows—(all this) (It) will be good for the sprout.

After the sprout has broken through (the surface of) the ground, say a prayer to the goddess <u>Ninkilim,</u> (And) <u>Shoo away the flying birds.</u> When the barley has filled the narrow bottom of the furrow, water the top seed. When the barley stands up high as (the straw of) a mat in the middle of a boat, water it (a second time). Water (a third time)—its royal barley. If the watered barley has turned red, what you say is: "It is sick with the *samana*-disease." But if it has succeeded in producing kernel-rich barley, water it (a fourth time); (and) It will yield you an extra measure of barley in every ten (+10 %).

When you are about to harvest your field, do not let the barley bend over on itself, (but) Harvest it at the moment of its (full) strength. A reaper, a man who bundles the mown barley, and a man who [sets up the sheaves] before him—these three (as a team) shall do the harvesting for you. The gleaners must do no damage; they must not tear apart the sheaves. During your daily harvesting, as in "days of need", make the earth supply the sustenance of the young and the gleaners according to their number (that is, presumably, he must leave the fallen kernels on the ground for needy children and gleaners to pick); (and) Let them sleep (in your field) as (in) the (open) marshland. After you have obtained . . ., do not . . ., (but) Roast (some of) the mown barley, (so that) the "prayer of the mown barley" will be said for you daily.

When you are about to winnow the barley, let those who weigh your barley [prepare] for you (bins of) thirty *gur*. Have your threshing floor made level, (and) the *gur* (-bins) put in order (ready for) the road. When your tools have been [readied] for you, (and) your wagons put in order for you, have your wagons climb the (barley) mounds—your "mound-threshing" (is to take) five days. When you are about to "open the mound", bake *arra*-bread.

When you "open" the barley, have the teeth of your threshing sledges fastened with leather and let bitumen cover the . . .; When you are about to hitch the oxen (to the threshing sledge), let your men who "open" the barley, stand by with food (that is, the oxen's food). (100-108) When you have heaped up the barley, say the "prayer of the (still) uncleaned barley". When you winnow the barley, pay attention to the men who lift the barley from the ground—two "barley-lifters" should lift it for you. On the day the barley is to be cleaned, have it laid on the sticks, (and) Say a prayer evening and night. (Then) Have the barley "unloosed" (from the chaff) like (with) an overpowering wind; (and) The "unloosed" barley will be stored for you.

These are the instructions of Ninurta, the son of Enlil. O Ninurta, trustworthy farmer of Enlil, your praise is good.

 EXPLORE: Why do you think the writer invoked the god Ninurta and the goddess Ninkilim for assistance? Do you see any similarities to today's farmers? This text is a set of instructions. Does it have any literary aspects, or is it simply like a manual on how to farm?

 WRITING: Notice that the writer is addressing his son on how to farm. Update the farmer's almanac. You might offer "Advice to a Daughter on Farming," for instance. The French say, *plus ça change . . . plus c'est la même chose*—the more things change, the more they remain the same. Do you find that true in comparing a work of 1500 BCE to today?

The Disputation between the Hoe and the Plow

Consider how the following poem, also Sumerian, differs from the earlier almanac. Disputations—arguments between two objects or seasons—was a popular form of rhetoric in ancient times. The writer's goal is to compare the value and usefulness of objects. Here, the plow and hoe are anthropomorphized. That is, objects are given human traits. These two farming implements have quite a debate on which is the more useful! This text comes from Herman L. J. Vanstiphout, a Dutch scholar.

Hey! Hoe, Hoe, Hoe, tied up with string;
Hoe, made from poplar, with a tooth of ash;
Hoe, made from tamarisk, with a tooth of sea-thorn;
Hoe, double-toothed, four-toothed;
Hoe, child of the poor, bereft even of a loin-cloth;
Hoe picked a quarrel with the Plow.
Hoe and Plow—this is their dispute.
Hoe cried out to Plow
"O Plow, you draw furrows—what is your furrowing to me?
You make clods—what is your clod making to me?
You cannot dam up water when it escapes.
You cannot heap up earth in the basket.
You cannot press clay or make bricks.

You cannot lay foundations or build a house.
You cannot strengthen an old wall's base.
You cannot put a roof on a man's house.
O Plow, you cannot straighten a street.
O Plow, you draw furrows—what is your furrowing to me?
You make clods—what is your clod-making to me?"
The Plow cries out to the Hoe
"I, I am Plow, I was fashioned by the great powers, assembled by noblest hands!
I am the mighty registrar of God Enlil!
I am the faithful farmer of Mankind!
At the celebration of my harvest-festival in the fields,
Even the King slaughters cattle for me, adding sheep!
He pours out libations for me, and offers the collected liquids!
Drums and tympans sound!
The king himself takes hold of my handle-bars;
My oxen he harnesses to the yoke;
Great noblemen walk at my side;
The nations gaze at me in admiration,
The Land watches me in Joy!
The furrow I draw is set upon the plain as an adornment;
Before my sheaves, erected in the fields,
Even the teeming herds of Shakan kneel down!
Before my ripened grain, ready for harvesting . . .
The shepherd's churn is filled to the brim;
With my sheaves scattered over the fields
The sheep of Dumuzi are sated.
My stacks adorning the plains
Are like so many yellow hillocks inspiring awe.
Stacks and mounds I pile up for Enlil;
Dark emmer I amass for him.
I fill the storehouses of mankind;
Even the orphans, the widows and the destitute
Take their reed baskets
And glean my scattered grains.
My straw, piled up in the fields
People even come to collect that,
While the beasts of Shakan go about.
O Hoe, miserable hole-digger, with your pathetic long tooth,
O Hoe, always burrowing in the mud,
O Hoe, whose head is always in the dust,
O Hoe-and-brickmold, you spend your days in mud, nobody ever cleans you!
Dig holes! Dig crevices! O navel-man dig!
O hoe, you of the poor man's hand, you are not fit for the hand of the noble!
The slave's hand is adorned with your head!
And you dare to insult me?

When I go out to the plains, every eye is full of admiration"
Then the Hoe cried out to the Plow:
"O Plow, my smallness—what is that to me?
My humble state—what is that to me?
My dwelling at the river bank—what is that to me?
At Enlil's place, I precede you!
In Enlil's temple, I stand in front of you!
I make ditches, I make canals;
I fill the meadows with water;
And when the water floods the canebrake,
My small baskets carry it away.
When a canal is cut, or a ditch,
And the water rushes out as a rising flood,
Making everything into a swamp,
I, the Hoe, dam it in,
So that neither southern nor northern storm can blow it away.
The fowler samples eggs;
The fisherman catches fish;
And they all empty bird-traps
Thus is wealth spread everywhere by my doing.
Moreover, after the water is drained from the meadows
And the work in the moist earth is to be taken in hand,
O Hoe, I come out to the field—I start that before you!
The opening up of the field—I start that before you!
The sides and the bottom of the dyke I clean for you!
The weeds in the field I heap up for you!
Stumps and roots I heap up for you!
Only then you work the field, you have your go!
Your oxen are six, your people four—you yourself are merely the eleventh!
The side-boards take away the field.
And you want to compare yourself with me?
When you finally come down to the field after me,
Your single furrow already gladdens your eye!
When you finally put your head to the task,
Your tongue gets caught by brambles and thorns.
Your tooth breaks, and your tooth is renewed;
You will not keep it for long.
Your plowman calls you "This Plow is broken again!"
And, again, carpenters have to be hired, people . . .
The whole chapter of workers is milling around you.
The harness-makers scrape another green hide for you,
Twisting it with pegs for you.
Without stopping they turn the tourniquet for you,
And finally a foul hide is put upon year head.
Your work is slight, though your ways are great!

My turn of duty is twelve months;
The time you are idle is eight months;
So you are absent twice as long as you are present!
And then, on the boat you make a hut;
When you are put aboard, your 'hands' sever the boards
So that your face has to be pulled out of the water like a wine-jar.
And only after I have make a pile of logs
Can my smoke and fire dry you out!
Your seeding—funnel—what is then its importance?
Your 'important ones' are thrown upon a pile
As implements to be destroyed.
But I, I am the Hoe, and live in your city!
No one is more honored than I am.
I am but a servant following his master;
I am but the one who builds the house for his king;
I am but the one who broadens the stalls, who expands the sheepfolds!
I press clay, I make bricks;
I lay foundations, I build houses;
I strengthen the base of an old wall;
I repair the roof of the honest man;
I, I am Hoe, I lay out the streets!
When I have thus gone through the city and built its solid walls,
And have made appear the temples of the great gods therein,
Embellished them with red, yellow and streaked wash,
I go to construct the royal dwelling in the city,
Where overseers and captains dwell.
When the weakened clay has been built up, the fragile clay buttressed,
They can rest because of me in a cool, well-built dwelling.
And when the fire-side makes the hoe gleam, and they lie on their side,
You are not to go to their feast!
They eat and drink;
Their wages are paid out to them Thus I enable the laborer to support his wife and children.
For the boat-man I make an oven, I heat pitch for him;
And when I have fashioned Magur and Magilum boats,
I have enabled the boatman to support his wife and children.
For the householder I plant the garden;
And when the garden has been encircled, the fences been put up, the agreements reached,
People again take up the hoe.
When wells have been dug, and poles set up,
The bucket-bar hung, I straighten the beds
And fill their ditched with water.
When the apple-tree has blossomed and the fruits appear,
These fruits are put up as an ornament in the temples of the gods.
Thus I enable the gardener to support wife and children!

When I work at the river with the plow, strengthening the banks,
Building a hut on its banks,
Those who have passed the day in the fields
And the shift which has done the same at night,
They enter their huts.
They revive themselves as in a well-built city;
The water-skins I made they use to pour water
And so they put life into their hearts again.
And you, Plow, think to insult me (by saying) 'Go, dig a hole!?'
On the plains, where no moisture is found,
When I have dug up the sweet water,
The thirsty ones come back to life at the side of my wells!
And what then says the one to the other? What do they tell one another?
'The shepherd's hoe is surely set up as an ornament on the plains!
For when An had ordered his punishment,
And the bitterness had been ordained over Sumer,
And the waters of the well-built house had collected in the swamp,
And Enlil had frowned upon the Land,
Even the shepherd's crook of Enlil had been make felt,
When great Enlil had acted thus,
Enlil did not restrain his hand.
Then the Hoe, with its single tooth, struck the dry earth!
As for us, the winter's cold, as the locust swarm, you lift!
The heavy hand of summer as of winter you take away.
O Hoe, you binder, you bind the sheaf!
O bird-trap, you binder, you bind the reed-basket!
The lone workman, even the destitute, is provided for;
The grains . . . are spread."
Then the Storm spoke a word
"The millstone lies still, while the pestle pounds!
From side-plate and foot-plate good results may be had!
Why should the sieve quarrel with the strainer?
Why make another angry?
Ashnan, can a single one reap your neck?
Ripe grain, why should you compare?"
Then Enlil spoke to the Hoe
"O hoe, do not be so angry!
Do not cry out so loud!
Of the Hoe, is not Nisaba its overseer, its captain?
Hoe, whether five or ten shekel make your price,
Or whether one-third or one half mina,
Like a maid-servant, always ready, you will fulfill your task!"
Dispute of the Hoe and the Plow.
Because the Hoe was greater than the Plow,
Praise be to Nisaba.

EXPLORE: What are the characteristics of the plow? How does the hoe differ in personality? Do you believe that this poem is about the plow and the hoe, or do these implements stand for something (or someone) else?

COLLABORATE: Divide into groups of two with one person taking the role of Plow and the other of Hoe. Mark the lines for each role in the poem. Read aloud your lines of the poem to your partner, taking turns. Discuss how you each feel in your role. How does reading aloud the poem help with its interpretation?

RESEARCH: How have disputations such as the one between the hoe and the plow changed or remained the same over time. For instance, *The Dozens* is an oral contest between two people that involves insulting one another until one surrenders. What can you discover about this game? Are there other types of two-character exchanges similar to this in contemporary culture?

WRITING: The rhetorical device of *disputation*, an argument about which is the better of two approaches or objects, was very popular in ancient times. Might the same be said to be true today? Choose two antagonists—as in the hoe and the plow—and write a contemporary version of their disputation. For instance, this might be "The Argument between the Combine and the Auger" or "Trash Talkin' Tractors" in which one brand of tractor boasts that it is better than another brand. Or it might take the form of another popular topic for the ancient disputation in which seasons of the year are played against one another. A "battle of the bugs" might pit the Praying Mantis against the Ladybug or an alarm clock and a rooster might spar.

Farming in Classical Greece and Rome

The ancient world revered the Earth Mother, and female deities and goddesses were worshiped as being essential to agricultural success. This is not surprising, as it seemed that life emanated from women. Fertility goddesses included Ninkilim, introduced in the *Farmer's First Almanac* as well as Bona-Dea, an agricultural divinity of Rome, who had her own temple cared for by women. Almost every civilization had sculptural artifacts depicting fertility goddesses.

FIGURE 2.2. Ceres

Two fertility goddesses survived for contemporary readers familiar with mythology: Ceres, the Roman goddess of agriculture, and Demeter, her Greek counterpart. Ceres taught people to farm and was said to have discovered wheat. The annual festival in her honor was known as Cerealia, and the connection to modern breakfasts is obvious. Her image is included in the official seal of New Jersey, and a statue of her stands in the Missouri State Capitol. These modern tributes acknowledge the important role of agriculture in a state's well being.

Demeter ("the mother"), goddess of the harvest, is perhaps best known for the myth in which her daughter Persephone is kidnapped by Hades, god of the underworld. In her grief,

Demeter no longer cared for the earth, and crops died as she searched in vain for her daughter. The compromise in which Persephone would spend part of each year with Hades, her husband, and part of the year with her mother resulted in the seasons: when mother and daughter are together, the earth is fruitful. After the gods struck this compromise, Demeter remembered the kindness of a mortal king who had sheltered her during her search for Persephone. In return, she taught his sons the important arts of agriculture: plowing, sowing seed, and harvesting. She also gave the king a winged chariot pulled by snakes so that he could travel the world and teach mankind what he had learned about cultivating the earth. This knowledge was considered among the greatest gifts to mankind, for it allowed mortals to end a nomadic life, rise above the beasts, and create a society.

Hesiod's *Works and Days*

Around 700 BCE, Greek poet Hesiod wrote Works and Days, *a work of 828 verses, instructing his brother Perses in farming. It is yet another farmer's almanac even though it appeared a millennium later than the Sumerian text. And like the Sumerian almanac, the gods are also invoked here. The two brothers inherit a farm, but Hesiod oversees its care while Perses goes to the city, where he squanders his wealth. He returns and wins a judgment that allows him to partake in the farm, but Hesiod worries that his brother will also ruin it. While the poem has practical advice for farming, it begins with a discussion about ethics. It ends with advice about sailing. Included here is the middle section, which focuses on farming. Notice how Demeter is invoked. (The following translation is by H. G. Evelyn-White.)*

(Lines. 383-404) When the Pleiades, daughters of Atlas, are rising (10), begin your harvest, and your ploughing when they are going to set (11). Forty nights and days they are hidden and appear again as the year moves round, when first you sharpen your sickle. This is the law of the plains, and of those who live near the sea, and who inhabit rich country, the glens and dingles far from the tossing sea,—strip to sow and strip to plough and strip to reap, if you wish to get in all Demeter's fruits in due season, and that each kind may grow in its season. Else, afterwards, you may chance to be in want, and go begging to other men's houses, but without avail; as you have already come to me. But I will give you no more nor give you further measure. Foolish Perses! Work the work which the gods ordained for men, lest in bitter anguish of spirit you with your wife and children seek your livelihood amongst your neighbours, and they do not heed you. Two or three times, may be, you will succeed, but if you trouble them further, it will not avail you, and all your talk will be in vain, and your word-play unprofitable. Nay, I bid you find a way to pay your debts and avoid hunger.

(ll. 405-413) First of all, get a house, and a woman and an ox for the plough—a slave woman and not a wife, to follow the oxen as well—and make everything ready at home, so that you may not have to ask of another, and he refuses you, and so, because you are in lack, the season pass by and your work come to nothing. Do not put your work off till to-morrow and the day after; for a sluggish worker does not fill his barn, nor one who puts off his work: industry makes work go well, but a man who putts off work is always at hand-grips with ruin.

Source: Translation by H. G. Evelyn-White (1914). Reprinted from http://www.sacred-texts.com/cla/hesiod/works.htm.

(ll. 414-447) When the piercing power and sultry heat of the sun abate, and almighty Zeus sends the autumn rains (12), and men's flesh comes to feel far easier,—for then the star Sirius passes over the heads of men, who are born to misery, only a little while by day and takes greater share of night,—then, when it showers its leaves to the ground and stops sprouting, the wood you cut with your axe is least liable to worm. Then remember to hew your timber: it is the season for that work. Cut a mortar (13) three feet wide and a pestle three cubits long, and an axle of seven feet, for it will do very well so; but if you make it eight feet long, you can cut a beetle (14) from it as well. Cut a felloe three spans across for a wagon of ten palms' width. Hew also many bent timbers, and bring home a plough-tree when you have found it, and look out on the mountain or in the field for one of holm-oak; for this is the strongest for oxen to plough with when one of Athena's handmen has fixed in the share-beam and fastened it to the pole with dowels. Get two ploughs ready work on them at home, one all of a piece, and the other jointed. It is far better to do this, for if you should break one of them, you can put the oxen to the other. Poles of laurel or elm are most free from worms, and a share-beam of oak and a plough-tree of holm-oak. Get two oxen, bulls of nine years; for their strength is unspent and they are in the prime of their age: they are best for work. They will not fight in the furrow and break the plough and then leave the work undone. Let a brisk fellow of forty years follow them, with a loaf of four quarters (15) and eight slices (16) for his dinner, one who will attend to his work and drive a straight furrow and is past the age for gaping after his fellows, but will keep his mind on his work. No younger man will be better than he at scattering the seed and avoiding double-sowing; for a man less staid gets disturbed, hankering after his fellows.

(ll. 448-457) Mark, when you hear the voice of the crane (17) who cries year by year from the clouds above, for she give the signal for ploughing and shows the season of rainy winter; but she vexes the heart of the man who has no oxen. Then is the time to feed up your horned oxen in the byre; for it is easy to say: `Give me a yoke of oxen and a wagon,' and it is easy to refuse: 'I have work for my oxen.' The man who is rich in fancy thinks his wagon as good as built already—the fool! He does not know that there are a hundred timbers to a wagon. Take care to lay these up beforehand at home.

(ll. 458-464) So soon as the time for ploughing is proclaimed to men, then make haste, you and your slaves alike, in wet and in dry, to plough in the season for ploughing, and bestir yourself early in the morning so that your fields may be full. Plough in the spring; but fallow broken up in the summer will not belie your hopes. Sow fallow land when the soil is still getting light: fallow land is a defender from harm and a soother of children.

(ll. 465-478) Pray to Zeus of the Earth and to pure Demeter to make Demeter's holy grain sound and heavy, when first you begin ploughing, when you hold in your hand the end of the plough-tail and bring down your stick on the backs of the oxen as they draw on the pole-bar by the yoke-straps. Let a slave follow a little behind with a mattock and make trouble for the birds by hiding the seed; for good management is the best for mortal men as bad management is the worst. In this way your corn-ears will bow to the ground with fullness if the Olympian himself gives a good result at the last, and you will sweep the cobwebs from your bins and you will be glad, I ween, as you take of your garnered substance. And so you will have plenty till you come to grey (18) springtime, and will not look wistfully to others, but another shall be in need of your help.

(ll. 479-492) But if you plough the good ground at the solstice (19), you will reap sitting, grasping a thin crop in your hand, binding the sheaves awry, dust-covered, not glad at all; so you will bring all home in a basket and not many will admire you. Yet the will of Zeus who holds the aegis is different at different times; and it is hard for mortal men to tell it; for if you should plough late, you may find this remedy—when the cuckoo first calls (20) in the leaves of the oak and makes men glad all over the boundless earth, if Zeus should send rain on the third day and not cease until it rises neither above an ox's hoof nor falls short of it, then the late-plougher will vie with the early. Keep all this well in mind, and fail not to mark grey spring as it comes and the season of rain.

(ll 493-501) Pass by the smithy and its crowded lounge in winter time when the cold keeps men from field work,—for then an industrious man can greatly prosper his house—lest bitter winter catch you helpless and poor and you chafe a swollen foot with a shrunk hand. The idle man who waits on empty hope, lacking a livelihood, lays to heart mischief-making; it is not an wholesome hope that accompanies a need man who lolls at ease while he has no sure livelihood.

(ll. 502-503) While it is yet midsummer command your slaves: "It will not always be summer, build barns."

(ll. 504-535) Avoid the month Lenaeon (21), wretched days, all of them fit to skin an ox, and the frosts which are cruel when Boreas blows over the earth. He blows across horse-breeding Thrace upon the wide sea and stirs it up, while earth and the forest howl. On many a high-leafed oak and thick pine he falls and brings them to the bounteous earth in mountain glens: then all the immense wood roars and the beasts shudder and put their tails between their legs, even those whose hide is covered with fur; for with his bitter blast he blows even through them although they are shaggy-breasted. He goes even through an ox's hide; it does not stop him. Also he blows through the goat's fine hair. But through the fleeces of sheep, because their wool is abundant, the keen wind Boreas pierces not at all; but it makes the old man curved as a wheel. And it does not blow through the tender maiden who stays indoors with her dear mother, unlearned as yet in the works of golden Aphrodite, and who washes her soft body and anoints herself with oil and lies down in an inner room within the house, on a winter's day when the Boneless One (22) gnaws his foot in his fireless house and wretched home; for the sun shows him no pastures to make for, but goes to and fro over the land and city of dusky men (23), and shines more sluggishly upon the whole race of the Hellenes. Then the horned and unhorned denizens of the wood, with teeth chattering pitifully, flee through the copses and glades, and all, as they seek shelter, have this one care, to gain thick coverts or some hollow rock. Then, like the Three-legged One (24) whose back is broken and whose head looks down upon the ground, like him, I say, they wander to escape the white snow.

(ll. 536-563) Then put on, as I bid you, a soft coat and a tunic to the feet to shield your body,—and you should weave thick woof on thin warp. In this clothe yourself so that your hair may keep still and not bristle and stand upon end all over your body.

Lace on your feet close-fitting boots of the hide of a slaughtered ox, thickly lined with felt inside. And when the season of frost comes on, stitch together skins of firstling kids with ox-sinew, to put over your back and to keep off the rain. On your head above wear a shaped cap of felt to keep your ears from getting wet, for the dawn is chill when Boreas has once made his onslaught, and at dawn a fruitful mist is spread over the earth from starry heaven upon the fields of blessed men: it is drawn from the ever flowing rivers and is raised high above the earth by windstorm, and sometimes it turns to rain towards evening, and sometimes to wind when Thracian Boreas huddles the thick clouds. Finish your work and return home ahead of him, and do not let the dark cloud from heaven wrap round you and make your body clammy and soak your clothes. Avoid it; for this is the hardest month, wintry, hard for sheep and hard for men. In this season let your oxen have half their usual food, but let your man have more; for the helpful nights are long. Observe all this until the year is ended and you have nights and days of equal length, and Earth, the mother of all, bears again her various fruit.

(ll. 564-570) When Zeus has finished sixty wintry days after the solstice, then the star Arcturus (25) leaves the holy stream of Ocean and first rises brilliant at dusk. After him the shrilly wailing daughter of Pandion, the swallow, appears to men when spring is just beginning. Before she comes, prune the vines, for it is best so.

(ll. 571-581) But when the House-carrier (26) climbs up the plants from the earth to escape the Pleiades, then it is no longer the season for digging vineyards, but to whet your sickles and rouse up your slaves. Avoid shady seats and sleeping until dawn in the harvest season, when the sun scorches the body. Then be busy, and bring home your fruits, getting up early to make your livelihood sure. For dawn takes away a third part of your work, dawn advances a man on his journey and advances him in his work,—dawn which appears and sets many men on their road, and puts yokes on many oxen.

(ll. 582-596) But when the artichoke flowers (27), and the chirping grasshopper sits in a tree and pours down his shrill song continually from under his wings in the season of wearisome heat, then goats are plumpest and wine sweetest; women are most wanton, but men are feeblest, because Sirius parches head and knees and the skin is dry through heat. But at that time let me have a shady rock and wine of Biblis, a clot of curds and milk of drained goats with the flesh of an heifer fed in the woods, that has never calved, and of firstling kids; then also let me drink bright wine, sitting in the shade, when my heart is satisfied with food, and so, turning my head to face the fresh Zephyr, from the everflowing spring which pours down unfouled thrice pour an offering of water, but make a fourth libation of wine.

(ll. 597-608) Set your slaves to winnow Demeter's holy grain, when strong Orion (28) first appears, on a smooth threshing-floor in an airy place. Then measure it and store it in jars. And so soon as you have safely stored all your stuff indoors, I bid you put your bondman out of doors and look out for a servant-girl with no children;—for a servant with a child to nurse is troublesome. And look after the dog with jagged teeth; do not grudge him his food, or some time the Day-sleeper (29) may take your stuff. Bring in fodder and litter so as to have enough for your oxen and mules. After that, let your men rest their poor knees and unyoke your pair of oxen.

(ll. 609-617) But when Orion and Sirius are come into mid-heaven, and rosy-fingered Dawn sees Arcturus (30), then cut off all the grape-clusters, Perses, and bring them home. Show them to the sun ten days and ten nights: then cover them over for five, and on the sixth day draw off into vessels the gifts of joyful Dionysus. But when the Pleiades and Hyades and strong Orion begin to set (31), then remember to plough in season: and so the completed year (32) will fitly pass beneath the earth.

Notes:

(10) Early in May.

(11) In November.

(12) In October.

(13) For pounding corn.

(14) A mallet for breaking clods after ploughing.

(15) The loaf is a flattish cake with two intersecting lines scored on its upper surface which divide it into four equal parts.

(16) The meaning is obscure. A scholiast renders "giving eight mouthfuls"; but the elder Philostratus uses the word in contrast to leavened "

(17) About the middle of November.

(18) Spring is so described because the buds have not yet cast their iron-grey husks.

(19) In December.

(20) In March.

(21) The latter part of January and earlier part of February.

(22) i.e. the octopus or cuttle.

(23) i.e. the darker-skinned people of Africa, the Egyptians or Aethiopians.

(24) i.e. an old man walking with a staff (the `third leg'—as in the riddle of the Sphinx).

(25) February to March.

(26) i.e. the snail. The season is the middle of May.

(27) In June.

(28) July.

(29) i.e. a robber.

(30) September.

(31) The end of October.

(32) That is, the succession of stars which make up the full year.

 EXPLORE: Shakespeare is often cited for introducing aphorisms—maxims of moral principles—particularly in the speech of Polonius in *Hamlet*, such as "Neither a borrower nor a lender be." Hesiod wrote much earlier than Shakespeare. Do you find maxims for how to live an ethical life in *Works and Days*?

 EXPLORE: Describe the clothing, food, and behavior of ancient Greece based on evidence from the poem.

 RESEARCH: Hesiod's poem refers to the roles of women and slaves. What can you discover about the role of women in ancient Greece? Who were the slaves and how were they treated?

 RESEARCH: Who are the gods and goddesses referenced in the poem, and what is their function in Greek mythology?

 WRITING: Compose an instructional letter, offering advice and wisdom, just as Hesiod gives his brother Perses on when to plant and plow. But Hesiod is also giving a guide to how to live. To whom would you write a letter, and what would you say?

 FOR FURTHER READING: Do you want to read the entire text of *Works and Days*? It is available at this site: https://chs.harvard.edu/CHS/article/display/5290.

Virgil's *Georgics*

Written in 29 BCE, *Georgics,* by Virgil, focuses on agriculture. *Georgics* comes from the Greek word that means "to farm." Virgil, a Roman poet, is better known to modern audiences for his epic poem the *Aeneid*, which follows Aeneas, a soldier who flees Troy once it falls. The following poem focuses on how to work the earth and follows in the tradition of the Farmer's First Almanac and Hesiod's *Works and Days*. This is termed *didactic* poetry—poetry that instructs. Obviously farming successfully was of immense importance to the economy and the well being of citizens. The lengthy poem is divided into four books. One focuses on raising crops, another on caring for trees, the third on animal husbandry, and a fourth on beekeeping. By this time, agriculture was becoming a science. But Virgil provides scientific information through a poetic approach that also includes philosophical reflections on how to live an ethical life. His opening line, "What makes the cornfield smile," is not a dry approach to the topic but one that makes use of poetic language. Interest in Virgil's ode to agriculture had a resurgence in eighteenth-century England, and influenced not only poets but gardeners and landscape architects.

Book One follows here. Note that Ceres is an important figure who is addressed immediately:

GEORGIC I

What makes the cornfield smile; beneath what star
Maecenas, it is meet to turn the sod
Or marry elm with vine; how tend the steer;
What pains for cattle-keeping, or what proof
Of patient trial serves for thrifty bees;-
Such are my themes.
O universal lights
Most glorious! ye that lead the gliding year
Along the sky, Liber and Ceres mild,
If by your bounty holpen earth once changed
Chaonian acorn for the plump wheat-ear,
And mingled with the grape, your new-found gift,
The draughts of Achelous; and ye Fauns
To rustics ever kind, come foot it, Fauns
And Dryad-maids together; your gifts I sing.
And thou, for whose delight the war-horse first
Sprang from earth's womb at thy great trident's stroke,
Neptune; and haunter of the groves, for whom
Three hundred snow-white heifers browse the brakes,
The fertile brakes of Ceos; and clothed in power,
Thy native forest and Lycean lawns,
Pan, shepherd-god, forsaking, as the love
Of thine own Maenalus constrains thee, hear
And help, O lord of Tegea! And thou, too,
Minerva, from whose hand the olive sprung;

And boy-discoverer of the curved plough;
And, bearing a young cypress root-uptorn,
Silvanus, and Gods all and Goddesses,
Who make the fields your care, both ye who nurse
The tender unsown increase, and from heaven
Shed on man's sowing the riches of your rain:
And thou, even thou, of whom we know not yet
What mansion of the skies shall hold thee soon,
Whether to watch o'er cities be thy will,
Great Caesar, and to take the earth in charge,
That so the mighty world may welcome thee
Lord of her increase, master of her times,
Binding thy mother's myrtle round thy brow,
Or as the boundless ocean's God thou come,
Sole dread of seamen, till far Thule bow
Before thee, and Tethys win thee to her son
With all her waves for dower; or as a star
Lend thy fresh beams our lagging months to cheer,
Where 'twixt the Maid and those pursuing Claws
A space is opening; see! red Scorpio's self
His arms draws in, yea, and hath left thee more
Than thy full meed of heaven: be what thou wilt-
For neither Tartarus hopes to call thee king,
Nor may so dire a lust of sovereignty
E'er light upon thee, how so Greece admire
Elysium's fields, and Proserpine not heed
Her mother's voice entreating to return-
Vouchsafe a prosperous voyage, and smile on this
My bold endeavour, and pitying, even as I,
These poor way-wildered swains, at once begin,
Grow timely used unto the voice of prayer.
In early spring-tide, when the icy drip
Melts from the mountains hoar, and Zephyr's breath
Unbinds the crumbling clod, even then 'is time;
Press deep your plough behind the groaning ox,
And teach the furrow-burnished share to shine.
That land the craving farmer's prayer fulfils,
Which twice the sunshine, twice the frost has felt;
Ay, that's the land whose boundless harvest-crops
Burst, see! the barns.
But ere our metal cleave
An unknown surface, heed we to forelearn
The winds and varying temper of the sky,
The lineal tilth and habits of the spot,
What every region yields, and what denies.

Here blithelier springs the corn, and here the grape,
There earth is green with tender growth of trees
And grass unbidden. See how from Tmolus comes
The saffron's fragrance, ivory from Ind,
From Saba's weakling sons their frankincense,
Iron from the naked Chalybs, castor rank
From Pontus, from Epirus the prize-palms
O' the mares of Elis.
Such the eternal bond
And such the laws by Nature's hand imposed
On clime and clime, e'er since the primal dawn
When old Deucalion on the unpeopled earth
Cast stones, whence men, a flinty race, were reared.
Up then! if fat the soil, let sturdy bulls
Upturn it from the year's first opening months,
And let the clods lie bare till baked to dust
By the ripe suns of summer; but if the earth
Less fruitful just ere Arcturus rise
With shallower trench uptilt it- 'twill suffice;
There, lest weeds choke the crop's luxuriance, here,
Lest the scant moisture fail the barren sand.
Then thou shalt suffer in alternate years
The new-reaped fields to rest, and on the plain
A crust of sloth to harden; or, when stars
Are changed in heaven, there sow the golden grain
Where erst, luxuriant with its quivering pod,
Pulse, or the slender vetch-crop, thou hast cleared,
And lupin sour, whose brittle stalks arise,
A hurtling forest. For the plain is parched
By flax-crop, parched by oats, by poppies parched
In Lethe-slumber drenched. Nathless by change
The travailing earth is lightened, but stint not
With refuse rich to soak the thirsty soil,
And shower foul ashes o'er the exhausted fields.
Thus by rotation like repose is gained,
Nor earth meanwhile uneared and thankless left.
Oft, too, 'will boot to fire the naked fields,
And the light stubble burn with crackling flames;
Whether that earth therefrom some hidden strength
And fattening food derives, or that the fire
Bakes every blemish out, and sweats away
Each useless humour, or that the heat unlocks
New passages and secret pores, whereby
Their life-juice to the tender blades may win;
Or that it hardens more and helps to bind

The gaping veins, lest penetrating showers,
Or fierce sun's ravening might, or searching blast
Of the keen north should sear them. Well, I wot,
He serves the fields who with his harrow breaks
The sluggish clods, and hurdles osier-twined
Hales o'er them; from the far Olympian height
Him golden Ceres not in vain regards;
And he, who having ploughed the fallow plain
And heaved its furrowy ridges, turns once more
Cross-wise his shattering share, with stroke on stroke
The earth assails, and makes the field his thrall.
Pray for wet summers and for winters fine,
Ye husbandmen; in winter's dust the crops
Exceedingly rejoice, the field hath joy;
No tilth makes Mysia lift her head so high,
Nor Gargarus his own harvests so admire.
Why tell of him, who, having launched his seed,
Sets on for close encounter, and rakes smooth
The dry dust hillocks, then on the tender corn
Lets in the flood, whose waters follow fain;
And when the parched field quivers, and all the blades
Are dying, from the brow of its hill-bed,
See! see! he lures the runnel; down it falls,
Waking hoarse murmurs o'er the polished stones,
And with its bubblings slakes the thirsty fields?
Or why of him, who lest the heavy ears
O'erweigh the stalk, while yet in tender blade
Feeds down the crop's luxuriance, when its growth
First tops the furrows? Why of him who drains
The marsh-land's gathered ooze through soaking sand,
Chiefly what time in treacherous moons a stream
Goes out in spate, and with its coat of slime
Holds all the country, whence the hollow dykes
Sweat steaming vapour?
But no whit the more
For all expedients tried and travail borne
By man and beast in turning oft the soil,
Do greedy goose and Strymon-haunting cranes
And succory's bitter fibres cease to harm,
Or shade not injure. The great Sire himself
No easy road to husbandry assigned,
And first was he by human skill to rouse
The slumbering glebe, whetting the minds of men
With care on care, nor suffering realm of his
In drowsy sloth to stagnate. Before Jove

Fields knew no taming hand of husbandmen;
To mark the plain or mete with boundary-line—
Even this was impious; for the common stock
They gathered, and the earth of her own will
All things more freely, no man bidding, bore.
He to black serpents gave their venom-bane,
And bade the wolf go prowl, and ocean toss;
Shook from the leaves their honey, put fire away,
And curbed the random rivers running wine,
That use by gradual dint of thought on thought
Might forge the various arts, with furrow's help
The corn-blade win, and strike out hidden fire
From the flint's heart. Then first the streams were ware
Of hollowed alder-hulls: the sailor then
Their names and numbers gave to star and star,
Pleiads and Hyads, and Lycaon's child
Bright Arctos; how with nooses then was found
To catch wild beasts, and cozen them with lime,
And hem with hounds the mighty forest-glades.
Soon one with hand-net scourges the broad stream,
Probing its depths, one drags his dripping toils
Along the main; then iron's unbending might,
And shrieking saw-blade,- for the men of old
With wedges wont to cleave the splintering log;—
Then divers arts arose; toil conquered all,
Remorseless toil, and poverty's shrewd push
In times of hardship. Ceres was the first
Set mortals on with tools to turn the sod,
When now the awful groves 'gan fail to bear
Acorns and arbutes, and her wonted food
Dodona gave no more. Soon, too, the corn
Gat sorrow's increase, that an evil blight
Ate up the stalks, and thistle reared his spines
An idler in the fields; the crops die down;
Upsprings instead a shaggy growth of burrs
And caltrops; and amid the corn-fields trim
Unfruitful darnel and wild oats have sway.
Wherefore, unless thou shalt with ceaseless rake
The weeds pursue, with shouting scare the birds,
Prune with thy hook the dark field's matted shade,
Pray down the showers, all vainly thou shalt eye,
Alack! thy neighbour's heaped-up harvest-mow,
And in the greenwood from a shaken oak
Seek solace for thine hunger.
Now to tell

The sturdy rustics' weapons, what they are,
Without which, neither can be sown nor reared
The fruits of harvest; first the bent plough's share
And heavy timber, and slow-lumbering wains
Of the Eleusinian mother, threshing-sleighs
And drags, and harrows with their crushing weight;
Then the cheap wicker-ware of Celeus old,
Hurdles of arbute, and thy mystic fan,
Iacchus; which, full tale, long ere the time
Thou must with heed lay by, if thee await
Not all unearned the country's crown divine.
While yet within the woods, the elm is tamed
And bowed with mighty force to form the stock,
And take the plough's curved shape, then nigh the root
A pole eight feet projecting, earth-boards twain,
And share-beam with its double back they fix.
For yoke is early hewn a linden light,
And a tall beech for handle, from behind
To turn the car at lowest: then o'er the hearth
The wood they hang till the smoke knows it well.
Many the precepts of the men of old
I can recount thee, so thou start not back,
And such slight cares to learn not weary thee.
And this among the first: thy threshing-floor
With ponderous roller must be levelled smooth,
And wrought by hand, and fixed with binding chalk,
Lest weeds arise, or dust a passage win
Splitting the surface, then a thousand plagues
Make sport of it: oft builds the tiny mouse
Her home, and plants her granary, underground,
Or burrow for their bed the purblind moles,
Or toad is found in hollows, and all the swarm
Of earth's unsightly creatures; or a huge
Corn-heap the weevil plunders, and the ant,
Fearful of coming age and penury.
Mark too, what time the walnut in the woods
With ample bloom shall clothe her, and bow down
Her odorous branches, if the fruit prevail,
Like store of grain will follow, and there shall come
A mighty winnowing-time with mighty heat;
But if the shade with wealth of leaves abound,
Vainly your threshing-floor will bruise the stalks
Rich but in chaff. Many myself have seen
Steep, as they sow, their pulse-seeds, drenching them
With nitre and black oil-lees, that the fruit

Might swell within the treacherous pods, and they
Make speed to boil at howso small a fire.
Yet, culled with caution, proved with patient toil,
These have I seen degenerate, did not man
Put forth his hand with power, and year by year
Choose out the largest. So, by fate impelled,
Speed all things to the worse, and backward borne
Glide from us; even as who with struggling oars
Up stream scarce pulls a shallop, if he chance
His arms to slacken, lo! with headlong force
The current sweeps him down the hurrying tide.
Us too behoves Arcturus' sign observe,
And the Kids' seasons and the shining Snake,
No less than those who o'er the windy main
Borne homeward tempt the Pontic, and the jaws
Of oyster-rife Abydos. When the Scales
Now poising fair the hours of sleep and day
Give half the world to sunshine, half to shade,
Then urge your bulls, my masters; sow the plain
Even to the verge of tameless winter's showers
With barley: then, too, time it is to hide
Your flax in earth, and poppy, Ceres' joy,
Aye, more than time to bend above the plough,
While earth, yet dry, forbids not, and the clouds
Are buoyant. With the spring comes bean-sowing;
Thee, too, Lucerne, the crumbling furrows then
Receive, and millet's annual care returns,
What time the white bull with his gilded horns
Opens the year, before whose threatening front,
Routed the dog-star sinks. But if it be
For wheaten harvest and the hardy spelt,
Thou tax the soil, to corn-ears wholly given,
Let Atlas' daughters hide them in the dawn,
The Cretan star, a crown of fire, depart,
Or e'er the furrow's claim of seed thou quit,
Or haste thee to entrust the whole year's hope
To earth that would not. Many have begun
Ere Maia's star be setting; these, I trow,
Their looked-for harvest fools with empty ears.
But if the vetch and common kidney-bean
Thou'rt fain to sow, nor scorn to make thy care
Pelusiac lentil, no uncertain sign
Bootes' fall will send thee; then begin,
Pursue thy sowing till half the frosts be done.
Therefore it is the golden sun, his course

Into fixed parts dividing, rules his way
Through the twelve constellations of the world.
Five zones the heavens contain; whereof is one
Aye red with flashing sunlight, fervent aye
From fire; on either side to left and right
Are traced the utmost twain, stiff with blue ice,
And black with scowling storm-clouds, and betwixt
These and the midmost, other twain there lie,
By the Gods' grace to heart-sick mortals given,
And a path cleft between them, where might wheel
On sloping plane the system of the Signs.
And as toward Scythia and Rhipaean heights
The world mounts upward, likewise sinks it down
Toward Libya and the south, this pole of ours
Still towering high, that other, 'neath their feet,
By dark Styx frowned on, and the abysmal shades.
Here glides the huge Snake forth with sinuous coils
'Twixt the two Bears and round them river-wise-
The Bears that fear 'neath Ocean's brim to dip.
There either, say they, reigns the eternal hush
Of night that knows no seasons, her black pall
Thick-mantling fold on fold; or thitherward
From us returning Dawn brings back the day;
And when the first breath of his panting steeds
On us the Orient flings, that hour with them
Red Vesper 'gins to trim his his 'lated fires.
Hence under doubtful skies forebode we can
The coming tempests, hence both harvest-day
And seed-time, when to smite the treacherous main
With driving oars, when launch the fair-rigged fleet,
Or in ripe hour to fell the forest-pine.
Hence, too, not idly do we watch the stars-
Their rising and their setting-and the year,
Four varying seasons to one law conformed.
If chilly showers e'er shut the farmer's door,
Much that had soon with sunshine cried for haste,
He may forestall; the ploughman batters keen
His blunted share's hard tooth, scoops from a tree
His troughs, or on the cattle stamps a brand,
Or numbers on the corn-heaps; some make sharp
The stakes and two-pronged forks, and willow-bands
Amerian for the bending vine prepare.
Now let the pliant basket plaited be
Of bramble-twigs; now set your corn to parch
Before the fire; now bruise it with the stone.

Nay even on holy days some tasks to ply
Is right and lawful: this no ban forbids,
To turn the runnel's course, fence corn-fields in,
Make springes for the birds, burn up the briars,
And plunge in wholesome stream the bleating flock.
Oft too with oil or apples plenty-cheap
The creeping ass's ribs his driver packs,
And home from town returning brings instead
A dented mill-stone or black lump of pitch.
The moon herself in various rank assigns
The days for labour lucky: fly the fifth;
Then sprang pale Orcus and the Eumenides;
Earth then in awful labour brought to light
Coeus, Iapetus, and Typhoeus fell,
And those sworn brethren banded to break down
The gates of heaven; thrice, sooth to say, they strove
Ossa on Pelion's top to heave and heap,
Aye, and on Ossa to up-roll amain
Leafy Olympus; thrice with thunderbolt
Their mountain-stair the Sire asunder smote.
Seventh after tenth is lucky both to set
The vine in earth, and take and tame the steer,
And fix the leashes to the warp; the ninth
To runagates is kinder, cross to thieves.
Many the tasks that lightlier lend themselves
In chilly night, or when the sun is young,
And Dawn bedews the world. By night 'tis best
To reap light stubble, and parched fields by night;
For nights the suppling moisture never fails.
And one will sit the long late watches out
By winter fire-light, shaping with keen blade
The torches to a point; his wife the while,
Her tedious labour soothing with a song,
Speeds the shrill comb along the warp, or else
With Vulcan's aid boils the sweet must-juice down,
And skims with leaves the quivering cauldron's wave.
But ruddy Ceres in mid heat is mown,
And in mid heat the parched ears are bruised
Upon the floor; to plough strip, strip to sow;
Winter's the lazy time for husbandmen.
In the cold season farmers wont to taste
The increase of their toil, and yield themselves
To mutual interchange of festal cheer.
Boon winter bids them, and unbinds their cares,
As laden keels, when now the port they touch,

And happy sailors crown the sterns with flowers.
Nathless then also time it is to strip
Acorns from oaks, and berries from the bay,
Olives, and bleeding myrtles, then to set
Snares for the crane, and meshes for the stag,
And hunt the long-eared hares, then pierce the doe
With whirl of hempen-thonged Balearic sling,
While snow lies deep, and streams are drifting ice.
What need to tell of autumn's storms and stars,
And wherefore men must watch, when now the day
Grows shorter, and more soft the summer's heat?
When Spring the rain-bringer comes rushing down,
Or when the beards of harvest on the plain
Bristle already, and the milky corn
On its green stalk is swelling? Many a time,
When now the farmer to his yellow fields
The reaping-hind came bringing, even in act
To lop the brittle barley stems, have I
Seen all the windy legions clash in war
Together, as to rend up far and wide
The heavy corn-crop from its lowest roots,
And toss it skyward: so might winter's flaw,
Dark-eddying, whirl light stalks and flying straws.
Oft too comes looming vast along the sky
A march of waters; mustering from above,
The clouds roll up the tempest, heaped and grim
With angry showers: down falls the height of heaven,
And with a great rain floods the smiling crops,
The oxen's labour: now the dikes fill fast,
And the void river-beds swell thunderously,
And all the panting firths of Ocean boil.
The Sire himself in midnight of the clouds
Wields with red hand the levin; through all her bulk
Earth at the hurly quakes; the beasts are fled,
And mortal hearts of every kindred sunk
In cowering terror; he with flaming brand
Athos, or Rhodope, or Ceraunian crags
Precipitates: then doubly raves the South
With shower on blinding shower, and woods and coasts
Wail fitfully beneath the mighty blast.
This fearing, mark the months and Signs of heaven,
Whither retires him Saturn's icy star,
And through what heavenly cycles wandereth
The glowing orb Cyllenian. Before all
Worship the Gods, and to great Ceres pay

Her yearly dues upon the happy sward
With sacrifice, anigh the utmost end
Of winter, and when Spring begins to smile.
Then lambs are fat, and wines are mellowest then;
Then sleep is sweet, and dark the shadows fall
Upon the mountains. Let your rustic youth
To Ceres do obeisance, one and all;
And for her pleasure thou mix honeycombs
With milk and the ripe wine-god; thrice for luck
Around the young corn let the victim go,
And all the choir, a joyful company,
Attend it, and with shouts bid Ceres come
To be their house-mate; and let no man dare
Put sickle to the ripened ears until,
With woven oak his temples chapleted,
He foot the rugged dance and chant the lay.
Aye, and that these things we might win to know
By certain tokens, heats, and showers, and winds
That bring the frost, the Sire of all himself
Ordained what warnings in her monthly round
The moon should give, what bodes the south wind's fall,
What oft-repeated sights the herdsman seeing
Should keep his cattle closer to their stalls.
No sooner are the winds at point to rise,
Than either Ocean's firths begin to toss
And swell, and a dry crackling sound is heard
Upon the heights, or one loud ferment booms
The beach afar, and through the forest goes
A murmur multitudinous. By this
Scarce can the billow spare the curved keels,
When swift the sea-gulls from the middle main
Come winging, and their shrieks are shoreward borne,
When ocean-loving cormorants on dry land
Besport them, and the hern, her marshy haunts
Forsaking, mounts above the soaring cloud.
Oft, too, when wind is toward, the stars thou'lt see
From heaven shoot headlong, and through murky night
Long trails of fire white-glistening in their wake,
Or light chaff flit in air with fallen leaves,
Or feathers on the wave-top float and play.
But when from regions of the furious North
It lightens, and when thunder fills the halls
Of Eurus and of Zephyr, all the fields
With brimming dikes are flooded, and at sea
No mariner but furls his dripping sails.

Never at unawares did shower annoy:
Or, as it rises, the high-soaring cranes
Flee to the vales before it, with face
Upturned to heaven, the heifer snuffs the gale
Through gaping nostrils, or about the meres
Shrill-twittering flits the swallow, and the frogs
Crouch in the mud and chant their dirge of old.
Oft, too, the ant from out her inmost cells,
Fretting the narrow path, her eggs conveys;
Or the huge bow sucks moisture; or a host
Of rooks from food returning in long line
Clamour with jostling wings. Now mayst thou see
The various ocean-fowl and those that pry
Round Asian meads within thy fresher-pools,
Cayster, as in eager rivalry,
About their shoulders dash the plenteous spray,
Now duck their head beneath the wave, now run
Into the billows, for sheer idle joy
Of their mad bathing-revel. Then the crow
With full voice, good-for-naught, inviting rain,
Stalks on the dry sand mateless and alone.
Nor e'en the maids, that card their nightly task,
Know not the storm-sign, when in blazing crock
They see the lamp-oil sputtering with a growth
Of mouldy snuff-clots.
So too, after rain,
Sunshine and open skies thou mayst forecast,
And learn by tokens sure, for then nor dimmed
Appear the stars' keen edges, nor the moon
As borrowing of her brother's beams to rise,
Nor fleecy films to float along the sky.
Not to the sun's warmth then upon the shore
Do halcyons dear to Thetis ope their wings,
Nor filthy swine take thought to toss on high
With scattering snout the straw-wisps. But the clouds
Seek more the vales, and rest upon the plain,
And from the roof-top the night-owl for naught
Watching the sunset plies her 'lated song.
Distinct in clearest air is Nisus seen
Towering, and Scylla for the purple lock
Pays dear; for whereso, as she flies, her wings
The light air winnow, lo! fierce, implacable,
Nisus with mighty whirr through heaven pursues;
Where Nisus heavenward soareth, there her wings
Clutch as she flies, the light air winnowing still.

Soft then the voice of rooks from indrawn throat
Thrice, four times, o'er repeated, and full oft
On their high cradles, by some hidden joy
Gladdened beyond their wont, in bustling throngs
Among the leaves they riot; so sweet it is,
When showers are spent, their own loved nests again
And tender brood to visit. Not, I deem,
That heaven some native wit to these assigned,
Or fate a larger prescience, but that when
The storm and shifting moisture of the air
Have changed their courses, and the sky-god now,
Wet with the south-wind, thickens what was rare,
And what was gross releases, then, too, change
Their spirits' fleeting phases, and their breasts
Feel other motions now, than when the wind
Was driving up the cloud-rack. Hence proceeds
That blending of the feathered choirs afield,
The cattle's exultation, and the rooks'
Deep-throated triumph.
But if the headlong sun
And moons in order following thou regard,
Ne'er will to-morrow's hour deceive thee, ne'er
Wilt thou be caught by guile of cloudless night.
When first the moon recalls her rallying fires,
If dark the air clipped by her crescent dim,
For folks afield and on the open sea
A mighty rain is brewing; but if her face
With maiden blush she mantle, 'twill be wind,
For wind turns Phoebe still to ruddier gold.
But if at her fourth rising, for 'tis that
Gives surest counsel, clear she ride thro' heaven
With horns unblunted, then shall that whole day,
And to the month's end those that spring from it,
Rainless and windless be, while safe ashore
Shall sailors pay their vows to Panope,
Glaucus, and Melicertes, Ino's child.
The sun too, both at rising, and when soon
He dives beneath the waves, shall yield thee signs;
For signs, none trustier, travel with the sun,
Both those which in their course with dawn he brings,
And those at star-rise. When his springing orb
With spots he pranketh, muffled in a cloud,
And shrinks mid-circle, then of showers beware;
For then the South comes driving from the deep,
To trees and crops and cattle bringing bane.

Or when at day-break through dark clouds his rays
Burst and are scattered, or when rising pale
Aurora quits Tithonus' saffron bed,
But sorry shelter then, alack I will yield
Vine-leaf to ripening grapes; so thick a hail
In spiky showers spins rattling on the roof.
And this yet more 'twill boot thee bear in mind,
When now, his course upon Olympus run,
He draws to his decline: for oft we see
Upon the sun's own face strange colours stray;
Dark tells of rain, of east winds fiery-red;
If spots with ruddy fire begin to mix,
Then all the heavens convulsed in wrath thou'lt see-
Storm-clouds and wind together. Me that night
Let no man bid fare forth upon the deep,
Nor rend the rope from shore. But if, when both
He brings again and hides the day's return,
Clear-orbed he shineth, idly wilt thou dread
The storm-clouds, and beneath the lustral North
See the woods waving. What late eve in fine
Bears in her bosom, whence the wind that brings
Fair-weather-clouds, or what the rain South
Is meditating, tokens of all these
The sun will give thee. Who dare charge the sun
With leasing? He it is who warneth oft
Of hidden broils at hand and treachery,
And secret swelling of the waves of war.
He too it was, when Caesar's light was quenched,
For Rome had pity, when his bright head he veiled
In iron-hued darkness, till a godless age
Trembled for night eternal; at that time
Howbeit earth also, and the ocean-plains,
And dogs obscene, and birds of evil bode
Gave tokens. Yea, how often have we seen
Etna, her furnace-walls asunder riven,
In billowy floods boil o'er the Cyclops' fields,
And roll down globes of fire and molten rocks!
A clash of arms through all the heaven was heard
By Germany; strange heavings shook the Alps.
Yea, and by many through the breathless groves
A voice was heard with power, and wondrous-pale
Phantoms were seen upon the dusk of night,
And cattle spake, portentous! streams stand still,
And the earth yawns asunder, ivory weeps
For sorrow in the shrines, and bronzes sweat.

Up-twirling forests with his eddying tide,
Madly he bears them down, that lord of floods,
Eridanus, till through all the plain are swept
Beasts and their stalls together. At that time
In gloomy entrails ceased not to appear
Dark-threatening fibres, springs to trickle blood,
And high-built cities night-long to resound
With the wolves' howling. Never more than then
From skies all cloudless fell the thunderbolts,
Nor blazed so oft the comet's fire of bale.
Therefore a second time Philippi saw
The Roman hosts with kindred weapons rush
To battle, nor did the high gods deem it hard
That twice Emathia and the wide champaign
Of Haemus should be fattening with our blood.
Ay, and the time will come when there anigh,
Heaving the earth up with his curved plough,
Some swain will light on javelins by foul rust
Corroded, or with ponderous harrow strike
On empty helmets, while he gapes to see
Bones as of giants from the trench untombed.
Gods of my country, heroes of the soil,
And Romulus, and Mother Vesta, thou
Who Tuscan Tiber and Rome's Palatine
Preservest, this new champion at the least
Our fallen generation to repair
Forbid not. To the full and long ago
Our blood thy Trojan perjuries hath paid,
Laomedon. Long since the courts of heaven
Begrudge us thee, our Caesar, and complain
That thou regard'st the triumphs of mankind,
Here where the wrong is right, the right is wrong,
Where wars abound so many, and myriad-faced
Is crime; where no meet honour hath the plough;
The fields, their husbandmen led far away,
Rot in neglect, and curved pruning-hooks
Into the sword's stiff blade are fused and forged.
Euphrates here, here Germany new strife
Is stirring; neighbouring cities are in arms,
The laws that bound them snapped; and godless war
Rages through all the universe; as when
The four-horse chariots from the barriers poured
Still quicken o'er the course, and, idly now
Grasping the reins, the driver by his team
Is onward borne, nor heeds the car his curb.

WRITING: Compose a short parody of Virgil's *Georgics*. A *parody* imitates an original work, often in a funny way. Take a look at student Sara Andersen's parody of Book III, a portion of which is included below.

Livestock Guide for Dummies: Don't Forget the Milk
—a parody of Virgil's Georgics (Book III)
Farming is a lot of work, so much you need to do.
From cows to sheep to goats and steeds—your own rural zoo.
And don't forget the finest milk comes from the healthiest of your flock.
I offer you a lesson on how to raise livestock.

First you need to think about what goods you want to produce,
Whether for food, furs, sport, or labor, your selection you must deduce.
Once you make your choice, hopefully it was two.
It must be one male, one female; not just any two will do.

 FOR FURTHER READING: Do you wish to read the entire text of the *Georgics*? It can be found online at this site: http://www.gutenberg.org/ebooks/232. Project Gutenberg has as its mission unrestricted access to important texts.

 FOR FURTHER READING: The term *georgics* is not widely familiar to contemporary readers. In his eco-critical book, *American Georgics* (2002) Timothy Sweet focuses on early environmentally oriented literature from the sixteenth century to Thoreau. What is human's place in nature? Did environmental literature exist before *Walden*?

 VIEWING: The artist Judy Chicago portrayed a history of women in her massive ceramic and textile installation *The Dinner Party* (1979), which is on permanent exhibition at the Brooklyn Museum of Art. The first section focuses on prehistory and the role of primordial goddesses such as the earth mother and fertility goddesses. The work of art features a dinner place setting—complete with a customized plate and placemat for each woman. For instance, the first place setting has a placemat of skin decorated with shells, suitable for prehistoric times. To decide on the 39 women to be featured, Judy Chicago undertook an enormous amount of research. In doing so, she provides an "also ran" list of goddesses that is illuminating in demonstrating the pervasive influence of female deities. See the work online at this site: https://www.brooklynmuseum.org/exhibitions/dinner_party.

Why do you think female deities were so pervasive in prehistory? And why do you think they eventually lost ground?

CHAPTER THREE

The European Agricultural Tradition from the Feudal Period to the Eighteenth Century

In this chapter, you will explore how work written before Colonial America is crucial for understanding texts by Thomas Jefferson and Crèvecoeur.

Historical Overview

The New Republic in America inherited a host of cultural ideas about farming and land use from Europe, especially in regards to how agriculture relates to issues of class, citizenship, and philosophical questions. The European colonialization of the North American continent was in direct response to these cultural norms in Europe.

During the early part of the Medieval Period (especially between the ninth and fourteenth centuries, there were essentially only two classes of people: the nobility and the peasant or serf class. Land ownership in Europe was largely maintained by a hereditary line of male nobility, resulting in the manorial system of large estates in which the owner did not directly work his land but used the labor of the peasant class to cultivate his crops and care for livestock. Nobles, in turn, were obligated to lease common pastureland to peasants for grazing animals and very limited plots in common fields. There, when they were not working the nobleman's larger landholdings, they produced just enough vegetables and cereal crops to feed themselves. Rather than living on the land they farmed,

FIGURE 3.1. Simon Bening, *August: Moving Wheat, Binding Sheaves,* Labors of the Months from a Flemish Book of Hours (Bruges), miniature (125mm x 172mm), ca. 1515. Original in Munich, StB (Stundenbuch), cod. lat. 23638, fol. 9v.

41

peasant farmers lived in a nucleate village and went out each day from their village homes to tend crops. Peasants did not have the opportunity to own land independently or even move to another estate or home without the nobleman's permission. When hunger was his main driving force, he often had to accept the circumstances. A popular saying at the time was that the peasant "owned nothing but his belly." Plots were limited by how much land one man could work in the course of a year and the minimum land necessary for him to feed his family. Typically, the size of individual peasant allotments within the common fields was based on the principle of "one man, one plow."; Also known as subsistence farming, this type of agriculture meant that the peasant farmer rarely had crop surpluses to sell in the marketplace or an income with which to buy goods in a market. Moreover, there was no opportunity for class mobility. A son born to a peasant would die in the peasant class, as would his children.

A shift began in Europe around the time of the plagues in the fourteenth century, and as a result of labor shortages among the peasants, a middle class began to emerge. For the first time, the gentry and freeman classes who had no aristocratic titles were allowed to own land. Gentry or "gentlemen," from which we get the term "gentlemen farmers," were the most well off of the middle class. The gentry were literate and educated, refined, ,and held a respected position in society. They were often former loyal knights who were granted land as a reward for honorable service, and their landholdings could be significant. Farming was not a financial imperative for the gentry. They did not directly engage in manual agricultural labor, which they left to the tenant farmers who leased their lands. Their economic status was based on collecting leases from tenants and selling surplus crops in the marketplace.

One step below the gentry in the freedman class was the yeoman farmer who profited from increasing opportunities from class mobility. He was either a freedman or one who was released from his service obligations, or a "reeborn (son of a freedman), who either leased or owned 100 acres of land or less. Typically, the yeoman farmer was directly involved in the cultivation of crops and care of animals; he only hired seasonal labor and was able to sell his surplus in the marketplace. Socially, he held a position of some standing in the community, like the gentry. But the yeoman was expected to be civic-minded and had an obligation to serve in some office in the society (sometimes as a mayor, justice of the peace, deputy, or constable of a parish). As a result, yeomen were known to be honest, just, skillful, trustworthy, respectable, and virtuous.

The rise of the middle class caused a decline of a village-centered life. Land use patterns began to transform as more people lived directly on the land that they farmed, and were, therefore, somewhat more remotely removed from each other. Science also began to play a bigger role in agriculture. By the eighteenth century, when the Age of Enlightenment was in full swing, farming was often called "husbandry," a term that refers to the application of scientific principles to agriculture in animal breeding and plant selection. Scientific advancements of the period also included Jethro Tull's horse-drawn hoe for weeding and the mechanical seed drill, which meant that seeds could be machine sown in straight lines for the first time. As a result, the eighteenth century marked an agricultural revolution. Farming as an occupation was elevated and no longer just seen as the task of the peasant class.

These agricultural class issues would come into play in North America with writers like Hector St. John Crèvecoeur and Thomas Jefferson.

Literary Texts

These themes play out in the following two medieval texts. The first selection, which is a description of a Plowman, is from "The General Prologue" of Geoffrey Chaucer's (1343–1400) *Cantebury Tales*; the Middle English text on the left is translated into modern English on the right.

With hym ther was a Plowman, was his broother,	With him there was a plowman, was his brother,
That hadde ylad of donge ful many a foother.	That many a load of dung, and many another Had
A trewe swynkere and a good was he,	scattered, for a good true toiler, he,
Lyvynge in pees and parfit charitee.	Living in peace and perfect charity.
God loved he best with al his hoole herte	He loved God most, and that with his whole heart
	At all times, though he played or plied his art, And
At alle tymes, thogh hym gamed or smerte,	next, his neighbour, even as himself.
And thanne his neighebore right as hymselve.	He'd thresh and dig, with never thought of pelf
He wolde thresshe, and therto dyke and delve,	[wealth]
For Cristes sake, for every povre wight,	For Christ's own sake, for every poor wight,
Withouten hyre, if it lay in his myght.	All without pay, if it lay in his might.
His tythes payde he ful faire and wel,	He paid his taxes, fully, fairly, well,
Both of his propre swynk and his catel.	Both by his own toil and by stuff he'd sell.
In a tabard he rood upon a mere.	In a tabard he rode upon a mare.

The Vision of Piers Plowman, a Middle English alliterative poem from the late fourteenth century, was attributed to William Langland (1360–1387). A lengthy poem, it follows its narrator Will on his quest for salvation, a quest that he dreams. Along the way, he encounters a humble plowman named Piers, who becomes Will's spiritual model. They travel together for a time. John Bunyan's *Pilgrim's Progress* makes use of this same journey to find redemption motif.

From *Piers Plowman* Prologue

Then began I to dream · a marvellous dream,
That I was in a wilderness · wist I not where.
As I looked to the east · right into the sun,
I saw a tower on a toft · worthily built;
A deep dale beneath · a dungeon therein,
With deep ditches and dark · and dreadful of sight
A fair field full of folk · found I in between,
Of all manner of men · the rich and the poor,
Working and wandering · as the world asketh.
Some put them to plow · and played little enough,
At setting and sowing · they sweated right hard
And won that which wasters · by gluttony destroy.

Did you know that some sources claim that the legendary figure of Robin Hood was originally a yeoman farmer who had been cheated out of and evicted from his own land?

William Shakespeare (1564–1616) consistently used farming images throughout his plays and sonnets. Most notably, the ubiquitous Ceres makes an appearance in *The Tempest* (Act VI. Scene I). To celebrate the engagement of Miranda and Ferdinand, Prospero conjures a pageant to celebrate and bless the engagement. With the assistance of his magical spirit, Ariel, he calls forth three important goddesses, Iris (goddess of the rainbow), Juno (queen of the gods), and Ceres (the queen of agriculture). Here, Iris summons Ceres.

IRIS:
Ceres, most bounteous lady, thy rich leas
Of wheat, rye, barley, vetches, oats and pease;
Thy turfy mountains, where live nibbling sheep,
And flat meads thatch'd with stover, them to keep;
Thy banks with pioned and twilled brims,
Which spongy April at thy hest betrims,
To make cold nymphs chaste crowns; and thy broom -groves,
Whose shadow the dismissed bachelor loves,
Being lass-lorn: thy pole-clipt vineyard;
And thy sea-marge, sterile and rocky-hard,
Where thou thyself dost air;—the queen o' the sky,
Whose watery arch and messenger am I,
Bids thee leave these, and with her sovereign grace,
Here on this grass-plot, in this very place,
To come and sport: her peacocks fly amain:
Approach, rich Ceres, her to entertain.

Enter CERES

CERES:
Hail, many-colour'd messenger, that ne'er
Dost disobey the wife of Jupiter;
Who with thy saffron wings upon my flowers
Diffusest honey-drops, refreshing showers,
And with each end of thy blue bow dost crown
My bosky acres and my unshrubb'd down,
Rich scarf to my proud earth; why hath thy queen
Summon'd me hither, to this short-grass'd green?

IRIS:
A contract of true love to celebrate;
And some donation freely to estate
On the blest lovers . . .

CERES:
High'st queen of state,
Great Juno, comes; I know her by her gait.

Enter JUNO

JUNO:
How does my bounteous sister? Go with me
To bless this twain, that they may prosperous be
And honour'd in their issue.

They sing:

JUNO:
Honour, riches, marriage-blessing,
Long continuance, and increasing,
Hourly joys be still upon you!
Juno sings her blessings upon you.

CERES
Earth's increase, foison plenty,
Barns and garners never empty,
Vines and clustering bunches growing,
Plants with goodly burthen bowing;
Spring come to you at the farthest
In the very end of harvest!
Scarcity and want shall shun you;
Ceres' blessing so is on you.

A Note about Terms

What's the difference between *agriculture* and *agrarian*? Agriculture is the literal process of growing crops, while agrarian is the social and political philosophy that holds rural life can shape ideal social values. Agrarianism holds farming up as morally superior, especially in comparison to urban life (see more about agrarianism in the next chapter). Meanwhile *husbandry* means the application of scientific principles to agriculture, especially in the form of domestication, natural selection, breeding, and mechanization.

    Pastoral and *bucolic* are related terms that identify a type of agriculture or farming with animals (*pastoral* refers to herding sheep while *bucolic* refers to herding cows). More broadly, these terms are used to describe perspective on rural life and a specific literary tradition in keeping with that perspective. Pastoral and bucolic depictions of agricultural life show rural life in a romanticized manner (and most certainly superior to the urban life). The scene is peaceful, serene, contemplative, rustic, simple, and idyllic because the cowherd/shepherd has direct connection with the natural world that suggests a kind of purity. It is important to note, however, that authors exaggerated the beauty of the natural world in the pastoral and bucolic scenes. There, the natural world is a decidedly tamed landscape, one that suggests the long-held belief that the stamp of man's hand on the land has an orderly effect of calming the chaos of a true wilderness.

COLLABORATE: How are the land use patterns described above significantly different from American agricultural land use patterns of today, where farm families typically live on individual parcels of land. Consider nucleate villages versus remote homesteads. Partner up with other students in pairs or small groups, and designate half the group to speak from the perspective the old order described in the medieval section above and the other half should speak from the perspective of the family farm model. How are the differences significant? Discuss how they might impact cultural life. What kinds of cultures human interactions would result from these geographical distribution patterns? Consider things like attitudes about their ability to influence civic matters, self-determination, social interaction, relationship to land, even their sense of morality and authority.

RESEARCH: Investigate the farming practices or agricultural history of other civilizations and countries. For instance, how is American farming, as we know it, similar or different from agriculture on the Asian or African continent? What was unique about the development of farming along the Nile River in Egypt or in Mayan or Ancient American Indian civilizations? Perhaps you might research more specific topics, like Roman irrigation systems or the Irish potato famine.

FOR FURTHER READING: Thomas Tusser's *Five Hundred Points of Husbandry* (1557) is a long poem in rhyming couplets that records the events of a country year. It includes instructions and observations about farming and country customs of the Tudor time. Follow this link to the 1878 edition and choose one of Tusser's relevant poems or a passage of at least 20 lines for performance of a dramatic reading; choose anything from the first 59 chapters where Tusser includes a husbandry poem from each month of the year. Your reading should demonstrate the mood of the piece you have chosen. URL: http://www.archive.org/stream/fivehundredpoint08tussuoft/fivehundredpoint08tussuoft_djvu.txt

The American Farm

John Gast, *American Progress*, 1872. Library of Congress, Prints & Photographs Division, Washington, DC, digital ID ppmsca.09855.

Cultivators of the earth are the most valuable citizens. They are the most vigorous, the most independent, the most virtuous, and they are tied to their country, and wedded to its liberty and interests by the most lasting bonds.

—Thomas Jefferson

What Thomas Jefferson did for us cannot be measured. As Washington was our first hero, So Jefferson was our first *mind*.

—Richard Rhodes, *The Inland Ground*

❦ CHAPTER FOUR ❦

The Noble Farmer: Early American Writing

In this chapter, you will read from documents that lay the foundation for the cultural reverence of the farmer in America that you will see throughout the rest of the course. However, for as much as our culture lauds the work of agriculture, the earliest European settlers in the New World were far from ideal farmers.

In the first permanent European settlement of Jamestown, Virginia, established in May 1607, settlers struggled for over a decade to raise their own food. Winter famine claimed many lives; at the end of their third winter, only 12% of Jamestown colonists survived. The Virginia settlers were ill suited to farming because many were European aristocrats who had come to the colony to grow their wealth, not their own food. They planned to search for gold and had assumed that they could trade with Indians for food. Their leader, Captain John Smith, initiated a "work or starve" policy that required four hours of farm labor a day, but still people of the Virginia colony struggled to feed themselves. The most successful farming enterprise in the early years was the raising of tobacco for export, however that meant even fewer people were engaged in subsistence farming.

The northern colonies didn't fair much better. While Puritans of the Plymouth settlement (settled in 1620) had a better work ethic, and their colony was comprised of more families than single men, as was the case in Virginia, the Massachusetts soil was poor and rocky, and many of the colonists who formerly had been tradesmen in urban areas had little prior farming experience. They too suffered periods of famine before they learned from the local Native Americans how to grow corn, pumpkin, and beans together.

In 1760, the Reverend Jared Eliot of Killingworth, Connecticut published the first agricultural advice book in colonies. Based on essays he had written between 1748 to 1763, *Essays Upon Field-Husbandry in New-England, As It Is or May be Ordered* brought a scientific sensibility to the practice of farming, and one of his main principles was to advocate the practice of husbandry on small-sized farms. The essays also contained religious overtones. His ideas about farming in the harsh New England climate were not widely accepted until the 19th century, but his efforts to improve farming practices were noted by Benjamin Franklin, among others.

> By the time of the American Revolution, 93% of Americans were farmers. When the Industrial Revolution began in the early 1800s, roughly 90% of the population was employed in agriculture, and each farmer could feed three to five people.

By the start of the Revolutionary War, US farmers were exporting wheat, indigo, rice, Indian corn, and tobacco to Africa, the West Indies, the Mediterranean, and the British Isles, and they were increasing their exports of flour, beef, pork, fish, and lumber. The US economy was dependent on these exports; however, the British government was still controlling where American goods could be exported and how much the colonies would pay in duties for those goods shipped to Great Britain.

In no small part, the American Revolution was a result of Britain's tight control on farm exports and limitations on western settlements.

Crèvecoeur's *Letters from an American Farmer*

J. Hector St. John Crèvecœur was born in Normandy, France, the son of an aristocrat. He came to America in 1755 when he was 24. Setting out to reinvent himself as a simple American farmer, he married and bought a farm in Orange County, New York, near the Hudson River. In 1782, he published *Letters From an American Farmer: Describing Certain Provincial Situations, Manners, and Customs, Not Generally Known; and Conveying Some Idea of the Late and Present Interior Circumstances of the British Colonies of North America*, which poses the important question: "What is an American?" In answer, Crèvecoeur's book offers a series of letters written by the fictional character James, a humble farmer from Pennsylvania, to "Mr. F.B.," a learned and worldly English gentleman who visited James's farm and upon his return to England asked James to write him his impressions of America. James hesitates because, as he says, "I am neither a philosopher, politician, divine, nor naturalist, but a simple farmer." In James, Crèvecœur creates the first truly "American" character in literature, a product of his environment. He does this at precisely the moment when, as a nation recovering from the Revolution, we were trying to discover what was our national identity. As James himself would say, "Men are like plants; the goodness and flavour of the fruit proceeds from the peculiar soil and exposition in which they grow. We are nothing but what we derive from the air we breathe, the climate we inhabit, the government we obey, the system of religion we profess, and the nature of our employment."

From Letter I, Introduction

In the following letter, Farmer James recounts a conversation with his minister about why such a sophisticated man as Mr. F. B. might want to know about the life of a simple farmer.

Minister: Although he is a man of learning and taste, yet I am sure he will read your letters with pleasure: if they be not elegant, they will smell of the woods, and be a little wild; I know your turn, they will contain some matters which he never knew before. . . . . Don't you think, neighbour James, that the mind of a good and enlightened Englishman would be more improved in remarking throughout these provinces the causes which render so many people happy? In delineating the unnoticed means by which we daily increase the extent of our settlements? How we convert huge forests into pleasing fields, and exhibit through these thirteen provinces so singular a display of easy subsistence and political felicity.

In Italy all the objects of contemplation, all the reveries of the traveller, must have a reference to ancient generations, and to very distant periods, clouded with the mist of ages.—Here, on the contrary, everything is modern, peaceful, and benign. Here we have had no war to desolate our fields: our religion does not oppress the cultivators: we are strangers to those feudal institutions which have enslaved so many. Here nature opens her broad lap to receive the perpetual accession of new comers, and to supply them with food. I am sure I cannot be called a partial American when I say that the spectacle afforded by these pleasing scenes must be more entertaining and more philosophical than that which arises from beholding the musty ruins of Rome. . . . For my part I had rather admire the ample barn of one of our opulent farmers, who himself felled the first tree in his plantation, and was the first founder of his settlement, than study the dimensions of the temple of Ceres. I had rather record the progressive steps of this industrious farmer, throughout all the stages of his labours and other operations, than examine how modern Italian convents can be supported without doing anything but singing and praying. . . .

Nature hath given you a tolerable share of sense, and that is one of her best gifts let me tell you. She has given you besides some perspicuity, which qualifies you to distinguish interesting objects; a warmth of imagination which enables you to think with quickness; you often extract useful reflections from objects which presented none to my mind: you have a tender and a well meaning heart, you love description, and your pencil, assure yourself, is not a bad one for the pencil of a farmer; it seems to be held without any labour; your mind is what we called at Yale college a Tabula rasa, where spontaneous and strong impressions are delineated with facility. Ah, neighbour! had you received but half the education of Mr. F. B. you had been a worthy correspondent indeed. But perhaps you will be a more entertaining one dressed in your simple American garb, than if you were clad in all the gowns of Cambridge. You will appear to him something like one of our wild American plants, irregularly luxuriant in its various branches, which an European scholar may probably think ill placed and useless. If our soil is not remarkable as yet for the excellence of its fruits, this exuberance is however a strong proof of fertility, which wants nothing but the progressive knowledge acquired by time to amend and to correct. It is easier to retrench than it is to add; I do not mean to flatter you, neighbour James, adulation would ill become my character, you may therefore believe what your pastor says. Were I in Europe I should be tired with perpetually seeing espaliers, plashed hedges, and trees dwarfed into pigmies. Do let Mr. F. B. see on paper a few American wild cherry trees, such as nature forms them here, in all her unconfined vigour, in all the amplitude of their extended limbs and spreading ramifications—let him see that we are possessed with strong vegetative embryos. After all, why should not a farmer be allowed to make use of his mental faculties as well as others; because a man works, is not he to think, and if he thinks usefully, why should not he in his leisure hours set down his thoughts? I have composed many a good sermon as I followed my plough. The eyes not being then engaged on any particular object, leaves the mind free for the introduction of many useful ideas. It is not in the noisy shop of a blacksmith or of a carpenter, that these studious moments can be enjoyed; it is as we silently till the ground, and muse along the odoriferous furrows of our low lands, uninterrupted either by stones or stumps; it is there that the salubrious effluvia of the earth animate our spirits and serve to inspire us; every other avocation of our farms are severe labours compared to this pleasing occupation: of all the tasks which mine imposes on me ploughing is the most agreeable, because I can think as I work; my mind is at leisure; my labour flows from instinct, as well as that of my horses; there is no kind of difference between us in our different shares of that operation; one of them keeps the furrow, the other avoids it; at the end of my field they turn either to the right or left as they are bid, whilst I thoughtlessly hold and guide the plough to which they are harnessed. Do therefore, neighbour, begin this correspondence.

From Letter II, On the Situation, Feelings, and Pleasures of an American Farmer

As you are the first enlightened European I have ever had the pleasure of being acquainted with, you will not be surprised that I should, according to your earnest desire and my promise, appear anxious of preserving your friendship and correspondence. By your accounts, I observe a material difference subsists between your husbandry, modes, and customs, and ours; every thing is local; could we enjoy the advantages of the English farmer, we should be much happier, indeed, but this wish, like many others, implies a contradiction; and could the English farmer have some of those privileges we possess, they would be the first of their class in the world. Good and evil I see is to be found in all societies, and it is in vain to seek for any spot where those ingredients are not mixed. I therefore rest satisfied, and thank God that my lot is to be an American farmer, instead of a Russian boor, or an Hungarian peasant. I thank you kindly for the idea, however dreadful, which you have given me of their lot and condition; your observations have confirmed me in the justness of my ideas, and I am happier now I thought myself before. It is strange that misery, when viewed in others, should become to us a sort of real good, though I am far from to hear that there are in the world men thoroughly wretched; they are no doubt as harmless, industrious, and willing to work as we are. Hard is their fate to be thus condemned to a slavery worse than that of our negroes. Yet when young I entertained some thoughts of selling my farm. I thought it afforded but a dull repetition of the same labours and pleasures. I thought the former tedious and heavy, the latter few and insipid; but when I came to consider myself as divested of my farm I then found the world so wide, and every place so full, that I began to fear lest there would be no room for me. My farm, my house, my barn, presented to my imagination, objects from which I adduced quite new ideas; they were more forcible than before. Why should not I find myself happy, said I, where my father was? He left me no good books it is true, he gave me no other education than the art of reading and writing; but he left me a good farm, and his experience; he left me free from debts, and no kind of difficulties to struggle with.—married, and this perfectly reconciled me to my situation; my wife rendered my house all at once chearful and pleasing; it no longer appeared gloomy and solitary as before; when I went to work in my fields I worked with more alacrity and sprightliness; I felt that I did not work for myself alone, and this encouraged me much. My wife would often come with her knitting in her hand, and sit under the shady trees, praising the straightness of my furrows, and the docility of my horses; this swelled my heart and made every thing light and pleasant, and I regretted that I had not married before. I felt myself happy in my new situation, and where is that station which can confer a more substantial system of felicity than that of an American farmer, possessing freedom of action, freedom of thoughts, ruled by a mode of government which requires but little from us. I owe nothing, but a pepper corn to my country, a small tribute to my king, with loyalty and due respect; I know no other landlord than the lord of all land, to whom I owe the most sincere gratitude. My father left me three hundred and seventy-one acres of land, forty-seven of which are good timothy meadow, an excellent orchard, a good house, and a substantial barn. It is my duty to think how happy I am that he lived to build and to pay for all these improvements; what are the labours which I have to undergo, what are my fatigues when compared to his, who had every thing to do, from the first tree he felled to the finishing of his house? Every year I kill from 1500 to 2,000 weight of pork, 1,200 of beef, half a dozen of good wethers in harvest: of fowls my wife has always a great stock: what can I wish more? My negroes are tolerably faithful and healthy; by along series of industry and honest dealings, my father left behind him the name of a good man; I have but to tread his paths to be happy and a good man like him. I know enough of the law to regulate my little concerns with propriety, nor do I dread its power; these are the grand outlines of my situation, but as I can feel much more than I am able to express, I hardly know how to proceed. When my first son was born, the whole train of my ideas were suddenly altered; never was there a charm that acted so quickly and powerfully; I ceased to ramble in imagination through the wide world; my excursions since have not exceeded the bounds of my farm, and all my principal pleasures are now centered within its scanty limits: but at the same time there is not an operation belonging to it in which I do not find some food for useful reflections. This is the reason, I suppose, that when you was here, you used, in your refined stile, to denominate me the farmer of feelings; how rude must those feelings be in him who daily holds the axe or the plough, how much more refined on the contrary those of the European, whose mind is improved by education, example, books, and by every acquired advantage! Those feelings, however, I will delineate as well as I can, agreeably to your earnest request. When I contemplate my wife, by my fireside, while she either spins, knits, darns, or suckles our child, I cannot describe the various emotions of love, of gratitude, of conscious pride which thrill in my heart, and often overflow in involuntary tears. I feel the necessity, the sweet pleasure of acting my part, the part of an husband and father, with an attention and propriety which may entitle me to my good fortune. It is true these pleasing images vanish with the smoke of my pipe, but though they disappear from my mind, the impression they have made on my heart is indelible. When I play with the infant, my warm imagination runs forward, and eagerly anticipates his future temper and constitution. I would willingly open the book of fate, and know in which page his destiny is delineated; alas! where is the father who in those moments of paternal ecstacy can delineate one half of the thoughts which dilate his heart? I am sure I cannot; then again I fear for the health of those who are become so dear to me, and in their sicknesses I severely pay for the joys I experienced while they were well. Whenever I go abroad it is always involuntary. I never return home without feeling some pleasing emotion, which I often suppress as useless and foolish. The instant I enter on my own land, the bright idea of property, of exclusive right, of independence exalt my mind. Precious soil, I say to myself, by what singular custom of law is it that thou wast made to constitute the riches of the freeholder? What should we American farmers be without the distinct possession of that soil? It feeds, it clothes us, from it we draw even a great exuberancy, our best meat, our richest drink, the very honey of our bees comes from this privileged spot. No wonder we should thus cherish its possession, no wonder that so many Europeans who have never been able to say that such portion of land was theirs, cross the Atlantic to realize that happiness. This formerly rude soil has been converted by my father into a pleasant farm, and in return it has established all our rights; on it is founded our rank, our freedom, our power as citizens, our importance as inhabitants of such a district. These images I must confess I always behold with pleasure, and extend them as far as my imagination can reach: for this is what may be called the true and the only philosophy of an American farmer. Pray do not laugh in thus seeing an artless countryman tracing himself through the simple modifications of his life; remember that you have required it, therefore with candor, though with diffidence, I endeavour to follow the thread of my feelings, but I cannot tell you all. Often when I plough my low ground, I place my little boy on a chair which screws to the beam of the plough–its motion and that of the horses please him, he is perfectly happy and begins to chat. As I lean over the handle, various are the thoughts which crowd into my mind. I am now doing for him, I say, what my father formerly did for me, may God enable him to live that he may perform the same operations for the same purposes when I am worn out and old! I relieve his mother of some trouble while I have him with me, the odoriferous furrow exhilarates his spirits, and seems to do the child a great deal of good, for he looks more blooming since I have adopted that practice; can more pleasure, more dignity be added to that primary occupation? The father thus ploughing with his child, and to feed his family, is inferior only to the emperor of China ploughing as an example to his kingdom. . . . I never see an egg brought on my table but I feel penetrated with the wonderful change it would have undergone but for my gluttony; it might have been a gentle useful hen leading her chickens with a care and vigilance which speaks shame to many women. A cock perhaps, arrayed with the most majestic plumes, tender to its mate, bold, courageous, endowed with an astonishing instinct, with thoughts, with memory, and every distinguishing characteristic of the reason of man. I never see my trees drop their leaves and their fruit in the autumn, and bud again in the spring, without wonder; the sagacity of those animals which have long been the tenants of my farm astonish me: some of them seem to surpass even men in memory and sagacity. I could tell you singular instances of that kind. What then is this instinct which we so debase, and of which we are taught to entertain so diminutive an idea? My bees, above any other tenants of my farm, attract my attention and respect; I am astonished to see that nothing exists but what has its enemy, one species pursue and live upon the other: unfortunately our kingbirds are the destroyers of those industrious insects; but on the other hand, these birds preserve our fields from the depredation of crows which they pursue on the wing with great vigilance and astonishing dexterity. Thus divided by two interested motives, I have long resisted the desire I had to kill them, until last year, when I thought they increased too much, and my indulgence had been carried too far; it was at the time of swarming when they all came and fixed themselves on the neighbouring trees, from whence they catched those that returned loaded from the fields. This made me resolve to kill as many as I could, and I was just ready to fire, when a bunch of bees as big as my fist, issued from one of the hives, rushed on one of the birds, and probably strung him, for he instantly screamed, and flew, not as before, in an irregular manner, but in a direct line. He was followed by the same bold phalanx, at a considerable distance, which unfortunately becoming too sure of victory, quitted their military array and disbanded themselves. By this inconsiderate step they lost all that aggregate of force which had made the bird fly off. Perceiving their disorder he immediately returned and snapped as many as he wanted; nay he had even the impudence to alight on the very twig from which the bees had drove him. I killed him and immediately opened his craw, from which I took 171 bees; I laid them all on a blanket in the sun, and to my great surprise they returned to life, licked themselves clean, and joyfully went back to the hive; where they probably informed their companions of such an adventure and escape, as I believe had never happened before to American bees! . . .

When the severities of that season have dispirited all my cattle, no farmer ever attends them with more pleasure than I do. It is one of those duties which is sweetened with the most rational satisfaction. I amuse myself in beholding their different tempers, actions, and the various effects of their instinct now powerfully impelled by the force of hunger. I trace their various inclinations, and the different effects of their passions, which are exactly the same as among men; the law is to us precisely what I am in my barn yard, a bridle and check to prevent the strong and greedy, from oppressing the timid and weak. Conscious of superiority they always strive to encroach on their neighbours; unsatisfied with their portion, they eagerly swallow it in order to have an opportunity of taking what is given to others, except they are prevented. Some I chide, others, unmindful of my admonitions, receive some blows. Could victuals thus be given to men without the assistance of any language, I am sure they would not behave better to one another, nor more philosophically than my cattle do. The same spirit prevails in the stable; but there I have to do with more generous animals, there my well known voice has immediate influence, and soon restores peace and tranquility. Thus by superior knowledge I govern all my cattle as wise men are obliged to govern fools and the ignorant. . . .

It is my bees, however, which afford me the most pleasing and extensive themes; let me look at them when I will, their government, their industry, their quarrels, their passions, always present me with something new; for which reason, when weary with labour, my commonplace of rest is under my locust-tree, close by my bee-house. By their movements I can predict the weather, and can tell the day of their swarming; but the most difficult point is, when on the wing, to know whether they want to go to the woods or not. If they have previously pitched in some hollow trees, it is not the allurements of salt and water, of fennel, hickory leaves, etc.; nor the finest box, that can induce them to stay; they will prefer those rude, rough habitations to the best polished mahogany hive. When that is the case with mine, I seldom thwart their inclinations; it is in freedom that they work: were I to confine them, they would dwindle away and quit their labour. In such excursions we only part for a while; I am generally sure to find them again the following fall. This elopement of theirs only adds to my recreations; I know how to deceive even their superlative instinct; nor do I fear losing them, though eighteen miles from my house, and lodged in the most lofty trees, in the most impervious of our forests. I once took you along with me in one of these rambles, and yet you insist on my repeating the detail of our operations it brings back into my mind many of the useful and entertaining reflections with which you so happily beguiled our tedious hours.

After I have done sowing, by way of recreation, I prepare for a week's jaunt in the woods, not to hunt either the deer or the bears, as my neighbours do, but to catch the more harmless bees. I cannot boast that this chase is so noble, or so famous among men, but I find it less fatiguing, and full as profitable; and the last consideration is the only one that moves me. I take with me my dog, as a companion, for he is useless as to this game; my gun, for no man you know ought to enter the woods without one; my blanket, some provisions, some wax, vermilion, honey, and a small pocket compass. With these implements I proceed to such woods as are at a considerable distance from any settlements. I carefully examine whether they abound with large trees, if so, I make a small fire on some flat stones, in a convenient place; on the fire I put some wax; close by this fire, on another stone, I drop honey in distinct drops, which I surround with small quantities of vermillion, laid on the stone; and then I retire carefully to watch whether any bees appear. If there are any in that neighbourhood, I rest assured that the smell of the burnt wax will unavoidably attract them; they will soon find out the honey, for they are fond of preying on that which is not their own; and in their approach they will necessarily tinge themselves with some particles of vermillion, which will adhere long to their bodies. I next fix my compass, to find out their course, which they keep invariably strait, when they are returning home loaded. By the assistance of my watch, I observe how long those are returning which are marked with vermillion. Thus possessed of the course, and, in some measure, of the distance, which I can easily guess at, I follow the first, and seldom fail of coming to the tree where those republics are lodged. I then mark it; and thus, with patience, I have found out sometimes eleven swarms in a season; and it is inconceivable what a quantity of honey these trees will sometimes afford. It entirely depends on the size of the hollow, as the bees never rest nor swarm till it is all replenished; for like men, it is only the want of room that induces them to quit the maternal hive. Next I proceed to some of the nearest settlements, where I procure proper assistance to cut down the trees, get all my prey secured, and then return home with my prize. The first bees I ever procured were thus found in the woods, by mere accident; for at that time I had no kind of skill in this method of tracing them. The body of the tree being perfectly sound they had lodged themselves in the hollow of one of its principal limbs, which I carefully sawed off and with a good deal of labour and industry brought it home, where I fixed it up again in the same position in which I found it growing. This was in April; I had five swarms that year, and they have been ever since very prosperous. This business generally takes up a week of my time every fall, and to me it is a week of solitary ease and relaxation. . . .

[T]hese, Sir, are the narrow circles within which I constantly revolve, and what can I wish for beyond them? I bless God for all the good he has given me; I envy no man's prosperity, and with no other portion of happiness that that I may live to teach the same philosophy to my children; and give each of them a farm, shew them how to cultivate it, and be like their father, good substantial independent American farmers—an appellation which will be the most fortunate one, a man of my class can possess, so long as our civil government continues to shed blessings on our husbandry. Adieu.

From Letter III, What Is an American?

Here are no aristocratical families, no courts, no kings, no bishops, no ecclesiastical dominion, no invisible power giving to a few a very visible one; no great manufacturers employing thousands, no great refinements of luxury. The rich and the poor are not so far removed from each other as they are in Europe. Some few towns excepted, we are all tillers of the earth, from Nova Scotia to West Florida. We are a people of cultivators, scattered over an immense territory communicating with each other by means of good roads and navigable rivers, united by the silken bands of mild government, all respecting the laws, without dreading their power, because they are equitable. We are all animated with the spirit of an industry which is unfettered and unrestrained, because each person works for himself. If he travels through our rural districts he views not the hostile castle, and the haughty mansion, contrasted with the clay-built hut and miserable cabbin, where cattle and men help to keep each other warm, and dwell in meanness, smoke, and indigence. A pleasing uniformity of decent competence appears throughout our habitations. The meanest of our log-houses is a dry and comfortable habitation. Lawyer or merchant are the fairest titles our towns afford; that of a farmer is the only appellation of the rural inhabitants of our country. It must take some time ere he can reconcile himself to our dictionary, which is but short in words of dignity, and names of honour. (There, on a Sunday, he sees a congregation of respectable farmers and their wives, all clad in neat homespun, well mounted, or riding in their own humble waggons. There is not among them an esquire, saving the unlettered magistrate. There he sees a parson as simple as his flock, a farmer who does not riot on the labour of others. We have no princes, for whom we toil, starve, and bleed: we are the most perfect society now existing in the world. Here man is free; as he ought to be; nor is this pleasing equality so transitory as many others are. Many ages will not see the shores of our great lakes replenished with inland nations, nor the unknown bounds of North America entirely peopled. Who can tell how far it extends? Who can tell the millions of men whom it will feed and contain? for no European foot has as yet travelled half the extent of this mighty continent!...

In this great American asylum, the poor of Europe have by some means met together, and in consequence of various causes; to what purpose should they ask one another what countrymen they are? Alas, two thirds of them had no country. Can a wretch who wanders about, who works and starves, whose life is a continual scene of sore affliction or pinching penury; can that man call England or any other kingdom his country? A country that had no bread for him, whose fields procured him no harvest, who met with nothing but the frowns of the rich, the severity of the laws, with jails and punishments; who owned not a single foot of the extensive surface of this planet? No! urged by a variety of motives, here they came. Every thing has tended to regenerate them; new laws, a new mode of living, a new social system; here they are become men: in Europe they were as so many useless plants, wanting vegitative mould, and refreshing showers; they withered, and were mowed down by want, hunger, and war; but now by the power of transplantation, like all other plants they have taken root and flourished! Formerly they were not numbered in any civil lists of their country, except in those of the poor; here they rank as citizens. By what invisible power has this surprising metamorphosis been performed? By that of the laws and that of their industry. The laws, the indulgent laws, protect them as they arrive, stamping on them the symbol of adoption; they receive ample rewards for their labours; these accumulated rewards procure them lands; those lands confer on them the title of freemen, and to that title every benefit is affixed which men can possibly require. This is the great operation daily performed by our laws. . . .

I wish to see men cut down the first trees, erect their new buildings, till their first fields, reap their first crops, and say for the first time in their lives, "This is our own grain, raised from American soil—on it we shall feed and grow fat, and convert the rest into gold and silver."

 EXPLORE: Watch for new world/old world comparisons. You may want to refer back to the previous chapter. Note that these "Letters" were written before the revolution. How does that affect the story? Crèvecœur uses the discussion of the natural world to offer symbols for the American character; for instance, consider how the bees are symbolic. Are there other places where Crèvecœur uses this literary technique?

Thomas Jefferson

Although Thomas Jefferson was the author of the Declaration of Independence and a two-term president, he was a reluctant statesman. When his presidency was over, he was eager to return to the Virginia plantation he had named Monticello (meaning *little hillock* in Italian). There, he was able to pursue his passion of farming, which he said was "the employment of our first parents in Eden." "No occupation," he wrote, "is so delightful to me as the culture of the earth. . . . . But though an old man, I am but a young gardener."

Jefferson's land at Monticello became his agricultural laboratory, where he experimented with cultivating hundreds of varieties of plants, trees, and vegetables to discover which varieties grew best in the American soil. He worked out various methods of crop rotation and terraced gardening, devised a system for tilling hillsides, and designed farming implements (most notably a type of moldboard plow that was better fit to the American landscape than were the European plows). He also set up an agricultural library with the idea that American universities would eventually value agricultural science as much as training in the professions in medicine, law, and the clergy. He hoped that the University of Virginia would be a leading force in this educational transformation that would someday result in higher education recognizing agriculture as a "science of the first order." He predicted:

> Young men closing their academical education with this, as the crown of all other sciences, fascinated with its solid charms, and at a time when they are to choose an occupation, instead of crowding the other classes, would return to the farms of their fathers, their own, or those of others, and replenish and invigorate a calling, now languishing under contempt and oppression.

In essence, Jefferson was a farmer philosopher, expressing what would become the dominant thinking about American agriculture. Having inherited European ideals of the pastoral scene and yeoman farming, he insisted on a philosophical link between husbandry and citizenship in the newly formed republic. Many of his writings describe a kind of farmer-citizen: that is, someone who is a better citizen because he is a farmer and a better farmer because he is a citizen. For Jefferson, the farmer was involved in a noble endeavor that evidenced his manliness, strong work ethic, and moral superiority. The farmer became a quintessential American figure, symbolizing all the nation's best ideals because he was independent and self-reliant and therefore better equipped to understand the fundamental ideas of democracy. As a landowner, his direct relationship with the land brought him into a closer relationship to God, for like God, it was his task to bring order out of chaos. Land ownership gave him a sense of belonging to a place, which meant he had a personal stake in the nation's success.

After the Louisiana Purchase of 1802, which doubled the size of the country, Jefferson sent Lewis and Clark out to map and inventory the flora and fauna of the newly acquired land. To Jefferson, the Louisiana Purchase ensured an abundance of farmland for future

---

The following quotes about farming represent the views of Jefferson's contemporaries:

"There seem to be but three ways for a nation to acquire wealth. The first is by war, as the Romans did, in plundering their conquered neighbors. This is robbery. The second by commerce, which is generally cheating. The third by agriculture, the only honest way, wherein man receives a real increase of the seed thrown into the ground, a kind of continual miracle, wrought by the hand of God in his favor, as a reward for his innocent life and his virtuous industry." —Ben Franklin in *Positions to be Examined, Concerning National Wealth*, 1769

"I had rather be on my farm than be emperor of the world; and yet they charge me with wanting to be a king."— George Washington in response to newspaper criticisms of his presidency; in letter to *James McHenry (10 August 1798)*

"I hope, some day or another, we shall become a storehouse and granary for the world."—George Washington in a letter to Marquis de Lafayette, June 19, 1788

"Man may be civilized, in some degree, without great progress in manufactures and with little commerce with his distant neighbors. But without the cultivation of the earth, he is, in all countries, a savage. Until he gives up the chase, and fixes himself in some place and seeks a living from the earth, he is a roaming barbarian. When tillage begins, other arts follow. The farmers, therefore, are the founders of human civilization."—Daniel Webster in *On the Agriculture of England*, 1840

---

generations, which he believed, in turn, ensured a stable future for the country. His orders implied the attitude of the American Enlightenment, which valued science and the human ability to reason. Science could be used to comprehend the mysteries of the natural world and understand the natural laws of the universe. Moreover, Enlightenment thinkers believed that scientific reason could be applied to the betterment of society in both religion and politics. This worldview or belief stood in dramatic contrast to the Puritan mindset that believed much of the world was unfathomable. Puritans feared the uncharted American "wilderness" as chaos and the domain of the devil.

Jefferson thought of himself as a simple gardener, but in fact, Monticello was a 5000-acre plantation that raised wheat, cotton, hemp, hops, tobacco, bees, cattle, poultry, and sheep. Such extensive farming required a substantial number of laborers. Over the course of his lifetime, Jefferson owned over six hundred slaves, almost all of who came to him through inheritance (from both father and father-in-law) or by the natural increase of slaves over time. He purchased fewer than 20 of the 600, and many of those he purchased in order to reunite slave families. Because of Jefferson's ongoing financial difficulties, he sold 110 slaves; another 85 were gifted to his sister and daughters upon their marriages.

On this count, Jefferson was a man of paradox. He consistently advocated for abolition and called slavery a "moral depravity" and an "abomination." But, like many slave owners of the era, he was very paternalistic about his own slaves and felt that they needed his care and protection. He freed only a handful of his slaves during his lifetime and in his will. On a national level, he believed that in a democratic country emancipation could not be legislated by the federal government without the cooperation of slave owners taking part in the decision. He feared, however, that such a debate would threaten to divide the new nation. Slavery, he wrote, was like holding "a wolf by the ear, and we can neither hold him, nor safely let him go."

The following selections are from Jefferson's history *Notes on the State of Virginia* and from his extensive correspondence on the subject of agriculture.

Selections from *Notes on the State of Virginia (1785)*

The political economists of Europe have established it as a principle that every State should endeavour to manufacture for itself; and this principle, like many others, we transfer to America, without calculating the difference of circumstance which should often produce a difference of result. In Europe the lands are either cultivated, or locked up against the cultivator. Manufacture must therefore be resorted to of necessity not of choice, to support the surplus of their people. But we have an immensity of land courting the industry of the husbandman. Is it best then that all our citizens should be employed in its improvement, or that one half should be called off from that to exercise manufactures and handicraft arts for the other? Those who labour in the earth are the chosen people of God, if ever he had a chosen people, whose breasts he has made his peculiar deposit for substantial and genuine virtue. It is the focus in which he keeps alive that sacred fire, which otherwise might escape from the face of the earth. Corruption of morals in the mass of cultivators is a phenomenon of which no age nor nation has furnished an example. It is the mark set on those, who not looking up to heaven, to their own soil and industry, as does the husbandman, for their subsistence, depend for it on casualties and caprice of customers. Dependence begets subservience and venality, suffocates the germ of virtue, and prepares fit tools for the designs of ambition. This, the natural progress and consequence of the arts, has sometimes perhaps been retarded by accidental circumstances: but, generally speaking, the proportion which the aggregate of the other classes of citizens bears in any state to that of its husbandmen, is the proportion of its unsound to its healthy parts, and is a good enough barometer whereby to measure its degree of corruption. While we have land to labour then, let us never wish to see our citizens occupied at a workbench, or twirling a distaff. Carpenters, masons, smiths, are wanting in husbandry: but, for the general operations of manufacture, let our workshops remain in Europe. It is better to carry provisions and materials to workmen there, than bring them to the provisions and materials, and with them their manners and principles. The loss by the transportation of commodities across the Atlantic will be made up in happiness and permanence of government. The mobs of great cities add just so much to the support of pure government, as sores do to the strength of the human body. It is the manners, and spirit of a people which preserve a republic in vigour. A degeneracy in these is a canker which soon eats to the heart of its laws and constitution.

Jefferson's letters:

Letter to John Jay (First Chief Justice of the United States) Written in Paris on Aug. 23, 1785:

DEAR SIR,—I shall sometimes ask your permission to write you letters, not official but private. The present is of this kind, and is occasioned by the question proposed in yours of June 14. "whether Whether it would be useful to us to carry all our own productions, or none?" Were we perfectly free to decide this question, I should reason as follows. We have now lands enough to employ an infinite number of people in their cultivation. Cultivators of the earth are the most valuable citizens. They are the most vigorous, the most independent, the most virtuous, & they are tied to their country & to its liberty & interests by the most lasting bonds. As long therefore as they can find employment in this line, I would not convert them into mariners, artisans or anything else. But our citizens will find employment in this line till their numbers, & of course their productions, become too great for the demand both internal & foreign. This is not the case as yet, & probably will not be for a considerable time. As soon as it is, the surplus of hands must be turned to something else. I should then perhaps wish to turn them to the sea in preference to manufactures, because comparing the characters of the two classes I find the former the most valuable citizens. I consider the class of artificers as the panders of vice & the instruments by which the liberties of a country are generally overturned.

Letter to James Madison (Jefferson's presidential successor). Written at Fontainebleau, France, a community outside of Paris, on October 28, 1785

DEAR SIR,—Seven o'clock, and retired to my fireside, I have determined to enter into conversation with you. This is a village of about 15,000 inhabitants when the court is not here, and 20,000 when they are, occupying a valley through which runs a brook and on each side of it a ridge of small mountains, most of which are naked rock. The King comes here, in the fall always, to hunt. His court attend him, as do also the foreign diplomatic corps; but as this is not indispensably required and my finances do not admit the expense of a continued residence here, I propose to come occasionally to attend the King's levees, returning again to Paris, distant forty miles. This being the first trip, I set out yesterday morning to take a view of the place. For this purpose I shaped my course towards the highest of the mountains in sight, to the top of which was about a league.

As soon as I had got clear of the town I fell in with a poor woman walking at the same rate with myself and going the same course. Wishing to know the condition of the laboring poor I entered into conversation with her, which I began by enquiries for the path which would lead me into the mountain: and thence proceeded to enquiries into her vocation, condition and circumstances. She told me she was a day laborer at 8 sous or 4 d. sterling the day: that she had two children to maintain, and to pay a rent of 30 livres for her house (which would consume the hire of 75 days), that often she could get no employment and of course was without bread. As we had walked together near a mile and she had so far served me as a guide, I gave her, on parting, 24 sous. She burst into tears of a gratitude which could perceive was unfeigned because she was unable to utter a word. She had probably never before received so great an aid. This little *attendrissement*, with the solitude of my walk, led me into a train of reflections on that unequal division of property which occasions the numberless instances of wretchedness which I had observed in this country and is to be observed all over Europe.

The property of this country is absolutely concentrated in a very few hands, having revenues of from half a million of guineas a year downwards. These employ the flower of the country as servants, some of them having as many as 200 domestics, not laboring. They employ also a great number of manufacturers and tradesmen, and lastly the class of laboring husbandmen. But after all there comes the most numerous of all classes, that is, the poor who cannot find work. I asked myself what could be the reason so many should be permitted to beg who are willing to work, in a country where there is a very considerable proportion of uncultivated lands? These lands are undisturbed only for the sake of game. It should seem then that it must be because of the enormous wealth of the proprietors which places them above attention to the increase of their revenues by permitting these lands to be labored. I am conscious that an equal division of property is impracticable, but the consequences of this enormous inequality producing so much misery to the bulk of mankind, legislators cannot invent too many devices for subdividing property, only taking care to let their subdivisions go hand in hand with the natural affections of the human mind. The descent of property of every kind therefore to all the children, or to all the brothers and sisters, or other relations in equal degree, is a politic measure and a practicable one. Another means of silently lessening the inequality of property is to exempt all from taxation below a certain point, and to tax the higher portions or property in geometrical progression as they rise. Whenever there are in any country uncultivated lands and unemployed poor, it is clear that the laws of property have been so far extended as to violate natural right. The earth is given as a common stock for man to labor and live on. If for the encouragement of industry we allow it to be appropriated, we must take care that other employment be provided to those excluded from the appropriation. If we do not, the fundamental right to labor the earth returns to the unemployed. It is too soon yet in our country to say that every man who cannot find employment, but who can find uncultivated land, shall be at liberty to cultivate it, paying a moderate rent. But it is not too soon to provide by every possible means that as few as possible shall be without a little portion of land. The small landholders are the most precious part of a state.

 EXPLORE: Jefferson insists on the link between farming and citizenship in the New Republic. Make a list of passages where he does this. Consider why he makes that link. Does Jefferson address other cultural issues that we associate with the United States (for instance, the "classless society")? Reread the earlier section on "The European Agricultural Tradition" in the previous chapter and then write an essay on how one or more of these traditions influenced Jefferson's concept of farming and citizenship in the United States.

 EXPLORE: Consider Jefferson's rhetoric. Are there times when you were surprised by *how* he said things? Identify places where he uses exaggeration and hyperbole or where he seems to be making an intentionally provocative statement.

 WRITE: Is Jefferson an *agrarian* or a *pastoralist*? Compose an essay in which you argue for one viewpoint or the other, or put forth an alternate view.

 VIRTUAL FIELD TRIP: Visit http://www.monticello.org to see Jefferson's historic home and gardens and to get a sense of the life of slaves on his plantation. Search under the "House and Garden" and "Plantation and Slavery" tabs to find at least three things that surprised, pleased, or shocked you about Jefferson's plantation.

FOR FURTHER READING: Early American novelist James Fenimore Cooper created a trilogy, termed the Leather-Stocking Tales, that includes *The Pioneers* (1823), in which each of the characters presents a position about the role of the environment and nature. Are natural resources to be exploited? Is the wilderness to be protected? What is the result of the pioneers' relentless westward march to cultivate more land and displace Native Americans?

Horace Greeley

Founding editor of *The New York Tribune*, the country's most influential newspaper of its time, Horace Greeley was considered America's leading newspaper editor from 1840–1880. He was also a reformer, a staunch abolitionist, and a politician (he ran and lost a bid for the presidency to Ulysses S. Grant in 1872). Greeley—who famously said, "Go West, young man, go West"—favored westward expansion and the policy of Manifest Destiny, which was the belief that American society and institutions were especially virtuous and that white settlers from the East were ordained by God to redeem the western lands, civilize the native population, and turn the West into a productive agricultural paradise.

As you read the following excerpt from Greeley's 1871 book *What I Know of Farming: A Series of Brief and Plain Expositions of Practical Agriculture as an Art Based upon Science*, consider how his views compare and contrast with those of Jefferson.

The Farmer's Calling

If any one fancies that he ever heard *me* flattering farmers as a class, or saying anything which implied that they were more virtuous, upright, unselfish, or deserving, than other people, I am sure he must have misunderstood or that he now misrecollects me. I do not even join in the cant, which speaks of farmers as supporting everybody else—of farming as the only indispensable vocation. You may say if you will that mankind could not subsist if there were no tillers of the soil; but the same is true of house-builders, and of some other classes. A thoroughly good farmer is a useful, valuable citizen: so is a good merchant, doctor, or lawyer. It is not essential to the true nobility and genuine worth of the farmer's calling that any other should be assailed or disparaged.

Still, if one of my three sons had been spared to attain manhood, I should have advised him to try to make himself a good farmer; and this without any romantic or poetic notions of Agriculture as a pursuit. I know well, from personal though youthful experience, that the farmer's life is one of labor, anxiety, and care; that hail, and flood, and hurricane, and untimely frosts, over which he can exert no control, will often destroy in an hour the net results of months of his persistent, well-directed toil; that disease will sometimes sweep away his animals, in spite of the most judicious treatment, the most thoughtful providence, on his part; and that insects, blight, and rust, will often blast his well-grounded hopes of a generous harvest, when they seem on the very point of realization. I know that he is necessarily exposed, more than most other men, to the caprices and inclemencies of weather and climate; and that, if he begins responsible life without other means than those he finds in his own clear head and strong arms, with those of his helpmeet, he must expect to struggle through years of poverty, frugality, and resolute, persistent, industry, before he can reasonably hope to attain a position of independence, comfort, and comparative leisure. I know that much of his work is rugged, and some of it absolutely repulsive; I know that he will seem, even with unbroken good fortune, to be making money much more slowly than his neighbor, the merchant, the broker, or eloquent lawyer, who fills the general eye while he prospers, and, when he fails, sinks out of sight and is soon forgotten; and yet, I should have advised my sons to choose farming as their vocation, for these among other reasons:

I. There is no other business in which success is so nearly certain as in this. Of one hundred men who embark in trade, a careful observer reports that ninety-five fail; and, while I think this proportion too large, I am sure that a large majority do, and must fail, because competition is so eager and traffic so enormously overdone. If ten men endeavor to support their families by merchandise in a township which affords adequate business for but three, it is certain that a majority must fail; no matter how judicious their management or how frugal their living. But you may double the number of farmers in any agricultural county I ever traversed, without necessarily dooming one to failure, or even abridging his gains. If half the traders and professional men in this country were to betake themselves to farming to-morrow, they would not render that pursuit one whit less profitable, while they would largely increase the comfort and wealth of the entire community; and, while a good merchant, lawyer, or doctor, may be starved out of any township, simply because the work he could do well is already confided to others, I never yet heard of a temperate, industrious, intelligent, frugal, and energetic farmer who failed to make a living, or who, unless prostrated by disease or disabled by casualty, was precluded from securing a modest independence before age and decrepitude divested him of the ability to labor.

II. I regard farming as that vocation which conduces most directly and palpably to a reverence for Honesty and Truth. The young lawyer is often constrained, or at least tempted, by his necessities, to do the dirty professional work of a rascal intent on cheating his neighbor out of his righteous dues. The young doctor may be likewise incited to resort to a quackery he despises in order to secure instant bread; the unknown author is often impelled to write what will sell rather than what the public ought to buy; but the young farmer, acting *as* a farmer, must realize that his success depends upon his absolute verity and integrity. He deals directly with Nature, which never was and never will be cheated. He has no temptation to sow beach sand for plaster, dockseed for clover, or stoop to any trick or juggle whatever. "Whatsoever a man soweth that shall he also reap," while true, in the long run, of all men, is instantly and palpably true as to him. When he, having grown his crop, shall attempt to sell it—in other words, when he ceases to be a farmer and becomes a trader—he may possibly be tempted into one of the many devious ways of rascality; but, so long as he is acting simply as a farmer, he can hardly be lured from the broad, straight highway of integrity and righteousness.

III. The farmer's calling seems to me that most conducive to thorough manliness of character. Nobody expects him to cringe, or smirk, or curry favor, in order to sell his produce. No merchant refuses to buy it because his politics are detested or his religious opinions heterodox. He may be a Mormon, a Rebel, a Millerite, or a Communist, yet his Grain or his Pork will sell for exactly what it is worth—not a fraction less or more than the price commanded by the kindred product of like quality and intrinsic value of his neighbor, whose opinions on all points are faultlessly orthodox and popular. On the other hand, the merchant, the lawyer, the doctor, especially if young and still struggling dubiously for a position, are continually tempted to sacrifice or suppress their profoundest convictions in deference to the vehement and often irrational prepossessions of the community, whose favor is to them the breath of life.

VIEW: The nineteenth-century idea of Manifest Destiny said that successful western expansion across the North American continent hinged on settlers taming the West with agriculture. Greeley believed this, and the idea can also be seen in American art of the period. Search online and view the 1872 painting by John Gast titled *American Progress* (also fronting this section of *Farm*), Emanuel Gottlieb Leutze's 1862 mural commissioned for the US capital and entitled *Westward the Course of Empire Takes Its Way*, and the similarly named lithograph *Across the Continent Westward the Course of Empire Takes Its Way*, published by Currier and Ives in 1868 and painted by Frances F. Palmer.

Ralph Waldo Emerson

During the course of his life, Ralph Waldo Emerson worked as a Unitarian minister, a poet and essayist, and as an orator—but never as a farmer. Still, he thought highly of farming as an occupation. A leading figure in the American Transcendentalist movement, Emerson urged people to recognize the symbolic and essential truths that nature had to teach that they might rise above the corrupting effects of society. He associated farming with the Transcendentalist principles of instinct, individualism, and self-reliance, as well as the inherent divinity of the natural world. "Nature ministers to us," he wrote in "Nature," the 1836 essay that marked the beginning of the intellectual movement. "What is a farm but a mute gospel?" he asked; "The chaff and the wheat, weeds and plants, blight, rain, insects, sun,—it is a sacred emblem from the first furrow of spring to the last stack which the snow of winter overtakes in the fields."

"Agriculture of Massachusetts" from The Dial *(1842)*

In an afternoon in April, after a long walk, I traversed an orchard where two boys were grafting apple trees, and found the Farmer in his corn field. He was holding the plough, and his son driving the oxen. This man always impresses me with respect, he is so manly, so sweet-tempered, so faithful, so disdainful of all appearances, excellent and reverable in his old weather-worn cap and blue frock bedaubed with the soil of the field, so honest withal, that he always needs to be watched lest he should cheat himself. I still remember with some shame, that in some dealing we had together a long time ago, I found that he had been looking to my interest in the affair, and I had been looking to my interest, and nobody had looked to his part. As I drew near this brave laborer in the midst of his own acres, I could not help feeling for him the highest respect. Here is the Caesar, the Alexander of the soil, conquering and to conquer, after how many and many a hard-fought summer's day and winter's day, not like Napoleon hero of sixty battles only, but of six thousand, and out of every one he has come victor; and here he stands, with Atlantic strength and cheer, invincible still. These slight and useless city-limbs of ours will come to shame before this strong soldier, for his have done their own work and ours too. What good this man has, or has had, he has earned. No rich father or father-in-law left him any inheritance of land or money. He borrowed the money with which he bought his farm, and has bred up a large family, given them a good education, and improved his land in every way year by year, and this without prejudice to himself the landlord, for here he is, a man every inch of him, and reminds us of the hero of the Robin Hood ballad,

"Much, the miller's son,
There was no inch of his body
But it was worth a groom."

Innocence and justice have written their names on his brow. Toil has not broken his spirit. His laugh rings with the sweetness and hilarity of a child; yet he is a man of a strongly intellectual taste, of much reading, and of an erect good sense and independent spirit which can neither brook usurpation nor falsehood in any shape. I walked up and down the field, as he ploughed his furrow, and we talked as we walked. Our conversation naturally turned on the season and its new labors. He had been reading the Report of the Agricultural Survey of the Commonwealth, and had found good things in it; but it was easy to see that he felt towards the author much as soldiers do towards the historiographer who follows the camp, more good nature than reverence for the gownsman.

The First Report, he said, is better than the last, as I observe the first sermon of a minister is often his best, for every man has one thing which he specially wishes to say, and that comes out at first. But who is this book written for? Not for farmers; no pains are taken to send it to them; it was by accident that this copy came into my hands for a few days. And it is not for them. They could not afford to follow such advice as is given here; they have sterner teachers; their own business teaches them better. No; this was written for the literary men. But in that case, the State should not be taxed to pay for it. Let us see. The account of the maple sugar,—that is very good and entertaining, and, I suppose, true. The story of the farmer's daughter, whom education had spoiled for everything useful on a farm,—that is good too, and we have much that is like it in Thomas's Almanack. But why this recommendation of stone houses? They are not so cheap, not so dry, and not so fit for us. Our roads are always changing their direction, and after a man has built at great cost a stone house, a new road is opened, and he finds himself a mile or two from the highway. Then our people are not stationary, like those of old countries, but always alert to better themselves, and will remove from town to town as a new market opens, or a better farm is to be had, and do not wish to spend too much on their buildings.

The Commissioner advises the farmers to sell their cattle and their hay in the fall, and buy again in the spring. But we farmers always know what our interest dictates, and do accordingly. We have no choice in this matter; our way is but too plain. Down below, where manure is cheap, and hay dear, they will sell their oxen in November; but for me to sell my cattle and my produce in the fall, would be to sell my farm, for I should have no manure to renew a crop in the spring. And thus Necessity farms it, necessity finds out when to go to Brighton, and when to feed in the stall, better than Mr. Colman can tell us.

But especially observe what is said throughout these Reports of the model farms and model farmers. One would think that Mr. D. and Major S. were the pillars of the Commonwealth. The good Commissioner takes off his hat when he approaches them, distrusts the value of "his feeble praise," and repeats his compliments as often as their names are introduced. And yet, in my opinion, Mr. D. with all his knowledge and present skill, would starve in two years on any one of fifty poor farms in this neighborhood, on each of which now a farmer manages to get a good living. Mr. D. inherited a farm, and spends on it every year from other resources; other-wise his farm had ruined him long since;—and as for the Major he never got rich by his skill in making land produce, but by his skill in making men produce. The truth is, a farm will not make an honest man rich in money. I do not know of a single instance, in which a man has honestly got rich by farming alone. It cannot be done. The way in which men who have farms grow rich, is either by other resources; or by trade; or by getting their labor for nothing; or by other methods of which I could tell you many sad anecdotes. What does the Agricultural Surveyor know of all this? What can he know? He is the victim of the "Reports," that are sent him of particular farms. He cannot go behind the estimates to know how the contracts were made, and how the sales were affected. The true men of skill, the poor farmers who by the sweat of their face, without an inheritance, and without offence to their conscience, have reared a family of valuable citizens and matrons to the state, reduced a stubborn soil to a good farm, although their buildings are many of them shabby, are the only right subjects of this Report; yet these make no figure in it. These should be holden up to imitation, and their methods detailed; yet their houses are very uninviting and inconspicuous to State Commissioners. . . .

In this strain the Farmer proceeded, adding many special criticisms. . . . I believe that my friend is a little stiff and inconvertible in his own opinions, and that there is another side to be heard; but so much wisdom seemed to lie under his statement, that it deserved a record.

Farming from Society and Solitude *(1870)*

The glory of the farmer is that, in the division of labors, it is his part to create. All trade rests at last on his primitive activity. He stands close to nature; he obtains from the earth the bread and the meat. The food which was not, he causes to be. The first farmer was the first man, and all historic nobility rests on possession and use of land. Men do not like hard work, but every man has an exceptional respect for tillage, and a feeling that this is the original calling of his race, that he himself is only excused from it by some circumstance which made him delegate it for a time to other hands. If he have not some skill which recommends him to the farmer, some product for which the farmer will give him corn, he must himself return into his due place among the planters. And the profession has in all eyes its ancient charm, as standing nearest to God, the first cause.

Then the beauty of nature, the tranquility and innocence of the countryman, his independence, and his pleasing arts,—the care of bees, of poultry, of sheep, of cows, the dairy, the care of hay, of fruits, of orchards and forests, and the reaction of these on the workman, in giving him a strength and plain dignity like the face and manners of nature,—all men acknowledge. All men keep the farm in reserve as an asylum where, in ease of mischance, to hide their poverty,—or a solitude, if they do not succeed in society. And who knows how many glances of remorse are turned this way from the bankrupts of trade, from mortified pleaders in courts and senates, or from the victims of idleness and pleasure? Poisoned by town life and town vices, the sufferer resolves: "Well, my children, whom I have injured, shall go back to the land, to be recruited and cured by that which should have been my nursery, and now shall be their hospital."

The farmer's office is precise and important, but you must not try to paint him in rose-color; you cannot make pretty compliments to fate and gravitation, whose minister he is. He represents the necessities. It is the beauty of the great economy of the world that makes his comeliness. He bends to the order of the seasons, the weather, the soils and crops, as the sails of a ship bend to the wind. He represents continuous hard labor, year in, year out, and small gains. He is a slow person, timed to nature, and not to city watches. He takes the pace of seasons, plants, and chemistry. Nature never hurries: atom by atom, little by little, she achieves her work. The lesson one learns in fishing, yachting, hunting, or planting, is the manners of Nature; patience with the delays of wind and sun, delays of the seasons, bad weather, excess or lack of water,—patience with the slowness of our feet, with the parsimony of our strength, with the largeness of sea and land we must traverse, etc. The farmer times himself to Nature, and acquires that livelong patience which belongs to her. Slow, narrow man, his rule is that the earth shall feed and clothe him; and he must wait for his crop to grow. His entertainments, his liberties and his spending must be on a farmer's scale, and not on a merchant's. It were as false for farmers to use a wholesale and massy expense, as for states to use a minute economy. But if thus pinched on one side, he has compensatory advantages. He is permanent, clings to his land as the rocks do.

In the town where I live, farms remain in the same families for seven and eight generations; and most of the first settlers (in 1635), should they reappear on the farms to-day, would find their own blood and names still in possession. And the like fact holds in the surrounding towns.

This hard work will always be done by one kind of man; not by scheming speculators, nor by soldiers, nor professors, nor readers of Tennyson; but by men of endurance—deep-chested, long-winded, tough, slow and sure, and timely. The farmer has a great health, and the appetite of health, and means to his end; he has broad lands for his home, wood to burn great fires, plenty of plain food; his milk at least is unwatered; and for sleep, he has cheaper and better and more of it than citizens.

He has grave trusts confided to him. In the great household of Nature, the farmer stands at the door of the bread-room, and weighs to each his loaf. It is for him to say whether men shall marry or not. Early marriages and the number of births are indissolubly connected with abundance of food; or, as Burke said, "Man breeds at the mouth." . . .

We see the farmer with pleasure and respect when we think what powers and utilities are so meekly worn. He knows every secret of labor; he changes the face of the landscape. Put him on a new planet and he would know where to begin; yet there is no arrogance in his bearing, but a perfect gentleness. The farmer stands well on the world. Plain in manners as in dress, he would not shine in palaces; he is absolutely unknown and inadmissible therein; living or dying, he never shall be heard of in them; yet the drawing-room heroes put down beside him would shrivel in his presence; he solid and unexpressive, they expressed to gold-leaf. But he stands well on the world,—as Adam did, as an Indian does, as Homer's heroes, Agamemnon or Achilles, do.

 EXPLORE: In the margins of these passages, mark where Emerson draws upon the basic Transcendentalist principles of instinct, self-reliance or individualism, the corrupting effects of society, and the inherent divinity of the natural world. Consider if he associates agriculture more often with one principle, and if so, why. Focus on one of these principles and discuss the significance; for instance, do you see patterns in the way he uses the notion of divinity in nature?

 EXPLORE: Describe the kind of person Emerson sees as the main audience of these essays. Is he speaking to farmers themselves or to someone else? Be prepared to discuss your reasoning.

 RESEARCH: Emerson compares the farmer to a number of mythological and historical heroes. How many of these references can you find? Choose one of these references and research that figure and consider how that information might enrich our reading of Emerson's essays.

Henry David Thoreau

For two years, Henry David Thoreau conducted a personal experiment and spiritual quest at Walden Pond, less than two miles outside of Concord, Massachusetts. There, he "squatted" on a piece of land that belonged to his friend and mentor, Ralph Waldo Emerson. In 1854, his account of those two years was published in his book *Walden (Or Life in the Woods)*. His goals for his time at Walden were to discover "what are the gross necessaries of life," reject society's growing interest in technology and materialism, question society's notion of success, live as close to nature as possible, and lead a contemplative life. Urging his readers to "Simplify, Simplify, Simplify," he sets out to consider the benefits of stripping away all but the essentials. While society might consider his life in the tiny cabin he built for $28.12 ½ as impoverished, he believes that living simply greatly enriched his spiritual life. During his time at Walden, Thoreau observed how farmers can become "owned" by their farms, if they get caught up in the belief that they need bigger and better farms. The result, he feared, was that "The mass of men lead lives of quiet desperation." Thoreau also spent a good deal of time tending some meager crops of his own. Agreeing with Emerson's statement that, "Every natural fact is a symbol of some spiritual fact," Thoreau considers farming a symbolic act. He writes "Some must work in fields if only for the sake of tropes and expression, to serve a parable-maker one day." As you read the following selections from chapters in *Walden*, watch for ways that Thoreau is suggests significant spiritual truths that go beyond the simple stories he tells.

From "Economy"

I see young men, my townsmen, whose misfortune it is to have inherited farms, houses, barns, cattle, and farming tools; for these are more easily acquired than got rid of. Better if they had been born in the open pasture and suckled by a wolf, that they might have seen with clearer eyes what field they were called to labor in. Who made them serfs of the soil? Why should they eat their sixty acres, when man is condemned to eat only his peck of dirt? Why should they begin digging their graves as soon as they are born? They have got to live a man's life, pushing all these things before them, and get on as well as they can. How many a poor immortal soul have I met well-nigh crushed and smothered under its load, creeping down the road of life, pushing before it a barn seventy-five feet by forty, its Augean stables never cleansed, and one hundred acres of land, tillage, mowing, pasture, and woodlot! The portionless, who struggle with no such unnecessary inherited encumbrances, find it labor enough to subdue and cultivate a few cubic feet of flesh. . . .

One farmer says to me, "You cannot live on vegetable food solely, for it furnishes nothing to make bones with"; and so he religiously devotes a part of his day to supplying his system with the raw material of bones; walking all the while he talks behind his oxen, which, with vegetable-made bones, jerk him and his lumbering plow along in spite of every obstacle. . . .

[I]f one designs to construct a dwelling-house, it behooves him to exercise a little Yankee shrewdness, lest after all he find himself in a workhouse, a labyrinth without a clue, a museum, an almshouse, a prison, or a splendid mausoleum instead. Consider first how slight a shelter is absolutely necessary. I have seen Penobscot Indians, in this town, living in tents of thin cotton cloth, while the snow was nearly a foot deep around them, and I thought that they would be glad to have it deeper to keep out the wind. Formerly, when how to get my living honestly, with freedom left for my proper pursuits, was a question which vexed me even more than it does now, for unfortunately I am become somewhat callous, I used to see a large box by the railroad, six feet long by three wide, in which the laborers locked up their tools at night; and it suggested to me that every man who was hard pushed might get such a one for a dollar, and, having bored a few auger holes in it, to admit the air at least, get into it when it rained and at night, and hook down the lid, and so have freedom in his love, and in his soul be free. This did not appear the worst, nor by any means a despicable alternative. You could sit up as late as you pleased, and, whenever you got up, go abroad without any landlord or house-lord dogging you for rent. Many a man is harassed to death to pay the rent of a larger and more luxurious box who would not have frozen to death in such a box as this. I am far from jesting. Economy is a subject which admits of being treated with levity, but it cannot so be disposed of. A comfortable house for a rude and hardy race, that lived mostly out of doors, was once made here almost entirely of such materials as Nature furnished ready to their hands. . . .

Before I finished my house, wishing to earn ten or twelve dollars by some honest and agreeable method, in order to meet my unusual expenses, I planted about two acres and a half of light and sandy soil near it chiefly with beans, but also a small part with potatoes, corn, peas, and turnips. The whole lot contains eleven acres, mostly growing up to pines and hickories, and was sold the preceding season for eight dollars and eight cents an acre. One farmer said that it was "good for nothing but to raise cheeping squirrels on." I put no manure whatever on this land, not being the owner, but merely a squatter, and not expecting to cultivate so much again, and I did not quite hoe it all once. I got out several cords of stumps in plowing, which supplied me with fuel for a long time, and left small circles of virgin mould, easily distinguishable through the summer by the greater luxuriance of the beans there. The dead and for the most part unmerchantable wood behind my house, and the driftwood from the pond, have supplied the remainder of my fuel. I was obliged to hire a team and a man for the plowing, though I held the plow myself. My farm outgoes for the first season were, for implements, seed, work, etc., $14.72 1/2. The seed corn was given me. This never costs anything to speak of, unless you plant more than enough. I got twelve bushels of beans, and eighteen bushels of potatoes, beside some peas and sweet corn. The yellow corn and turnips were too late to come to anything. My whole income from the farm was $ 23.44 Deducting the outgoes............. 14.72 1/2 - There are left............................$ 8.71 ½ beside produce consumed and on hand at the time this estimate was made of the value of $4.50— the amount on hand much more than balancing a little grass which I did not raise. All things considered, that is, considering the importance of a man's soul and of today, notwithstanding the short time occupied by my experiment, nay, partly even because of its transient character, I believe that that was doing better than any farmer in Concord did that year. The next year I did better still, for I spaded up all the land which I required, about a third of an acre, and I learned from the experience of both years, not being in the least awed by many celebrated works on husbandry, Arthur Young among the rest, that if one would live simply and eat only the crop which he raised, and raise no more than he ate, and not exchange it for an insufficient quantity of more luxurious and expensive things, he would need to cultivate only a few rods of ground, and that it would be cheaper to spade up that than to use oxen to plow it, and to select a fresh spot from time to time than to manure the old, and he could do all his necessary farm work as it were with his left hand at odd hours in the summer; and thus he would not be tied to an ox, or horse, or cow, or pig, as at present. I desire to speak impartially on this point, and as one not interested in the success or failure of the present economical and social arrangements. I was more independent than any farmer in Concord, for I was not anchored to a house or farm, but could follow the bent of my genius, which is a very crooked one, every moment. Besides being better off than they already, if my house had been burned or my crops had failed, I should have been nearly as well off as before.

From "Where I lived, and What I Lived For"

I went to the woods because I wished to live deliberately, to front only the essential facts of life, and see if I could not learn what it had to teach, and not, when I came to die, discover that I had not lived. I did not wish to live what was not life, living is so dear; nor did I wish to practice resignation, unless it was quite necessary. I wanted to live deep and suck out all the marrow of life, to live so sturdily and Spartan—like as to put to rout all that was not life, to cut a broad swath and shave close, to drive life into a corner, and reduce it to its lowest terms, and, if it proved to be mean, why then to get the whole and genuine meanness of it, and publish its meanness to the world; or if it were sublime, to know it by experience, and be able to give a true account of it in my next excursion. For most men, it appears to me, are in a strange uncertainty about it, whether it is of the devil or of God, and have somewhat hastily concluded that it is the chief end of man here to "glorify God and enjoy him forever."

From "The Bean-Field"

Meanwhile my beans, the length of whose rows, added together, was seven miles already planted, were impatient to be hoed, for the earliest had grown considerably before the latest were in the ground; indeed they were not easily to be put off. What was the meaning of this so steady and self-respecting, this small Herculean labor, I knew not. I came to love my rows, my beans, though so many more than I wanted. They attached me to the earth, and so I got strength like Antæus. But why should I raise them? Only Heaven knows. This was my curious labor all summer—to make this portion of the earth's surface, which had yielded only cinquefoil, blackberries, johnswort, and the like, before, sweet wild fruits and pleasant flowers, produce instead this pulse. What shall I learn of beans or beans of me? I cherish them, I hoe them, early and late I have an eye to them; and this is my day's work. It is a fine broad leaf to look on. My auxiliaries are the dews and rains which water this dry soil, and what fertility is in the soil itself, which for the most part is lean and effete. My enemies are worms, cool days, and most of all woodchucks. The last have nibbled for me a quarter of an acre clean. But what right had I to oust johnswort and the rest, and break up their ancient herb garden? Soon, however, the remaining beans will be too tough for them, and go forward to meet new foes....

I planted about two acres and a half of upland; and as it was only about fifteen years since the land was cleared, and I myself had got out two or three cords of stumps, I did not give it any manure; but in the course of the summer it appeared by the arrowheads which I turned up in hoeing, that an extinct nation had anciently dwelt here and planted corn and beans ere white men came to clear the land, and so, to some extent, had exhausted the soil for this very crop.

Before yet any woodchuck or squirrel had run across the road, or the sun had got above the shrub oaks, while all the dew was on, though the farmers warned me against it—I would advise you to do all your work if possible while the dew is on—I began to level the ranks of haughty weeds in my bean-field and throw dust upon their heads. Early in the morning I worked barefooted, dabbling like a plastic artist in the dewy and crumbling sand, but later in the day the sun blistered my feet. There the sun lighted me to hoe beans, pacing slowly backward and forward over that yellow gravelly upland, between the long green rows, fifteen rods, the one end terminating in a shrub oak copse where I could rest in the shade, the other in a blackberry field where the green berries deepened their tints by the time I had made another bout. Removing the weeds, putting fresh soil about the bean stems, and encouraging this weed which I had sown, making the yellow soil express its summer thought in bean leaves and blossoms rather than in wormwood and piper and millet grass, making the earth say beans instead of grass—this was my daily work. As I had little aid from horses or cattle, or hired men or boys, or improved implements of husbandry, I was much slower, and became much more intimate with my beans than usual. But labor of the hands, even when pursued to the verge of drudgery, is perhaps never the worst form of idleness. It has a constant and imperishable moral, and to the scholar it yields a classic result. A very *agricola laboriosus* was I to travellers bound westward through Lincoln and Wayland to nobody knows where; they sitting at their ease in gigs, with elbows on knees, and reins loosely hanging in festoons; I the home-staying, laborious native of the soil. But soon my homestead was out of their sight and thought. It was the only open and cultivated field for a great distance on either side of the road, so they made the most of it; and sometimes the man in the field heard more of travellers' gossip and comment than was meant for his ear: "Beans so late! peas so late!"—for I continued to plant when others had begun to hoe—the ministerial husbandman had not suspected it. "Corn, my boy, for fodder; corn for fodder." "Does he *live* there?" asks the black bonnet of the gray coat; and the hard-featured farmer reins up his grateful dobbin to inquire what you are doing where he sees no manure in the furrow, and recommends a little chip dirt, or any little waste stuff, or it may be ashes or plaster. But here were two acres and a half of furrows, and only a hoe for cart and two hands to draw it—there being an aversion to other carts and horses—and chip dirt far away. Fellow-travellers as they rattled by compared it aloud with the fields which they had passed, so that I came to know how I stood in the agricultural world. This was one field not in Mr. Coleman's report. And, by the way, who estimates the value of the crop which nature yields in the still wilder fields unimproved by man? The crop of *English* hay is carefully weighed, the moisture calculated, the silicates and the potash; but in all dells and pond-holes in the woods and pastures and swamps grows a rich and various crop only unreaped by man. Mine was, as it were, the connecting link between wild and cultivated fields; as some states are civilized, and others half-civilized, and others savage or barbarous, so my field was, though not in a bad sense, a half-cultivated field. They were beans cheerfully returning to their wild and primitive state that I cultivated, and my hoe played the *Rans des Vaches* for them.

Near at hand, upon the topmost spray of a birch, sings the brown thrasher—or red mavis, as some love to call him—all the morning, glad of your society, that would find out another farmer's field if yours were not here. While you are planting the seed, he cries—"Drop it, drop it—cover it up, cover it up—pull it up, pull it up, pull it up." But this was not corn, and so it was safe from such enemies as he. You may wonder what his rigmarole, his amateur Paganini performances on one string or on twenty, have to do with your planting, and yet prefer it to leached ashes or plaster. It was a cheap sort of top dressing in which I had entire faith. As I drew a still fresher soil about the rows with my hoe, I disturbed the ashes of unchronicled nations who in primeval years lived under these heavens, and their small implements of war and hunting were brought to the light of this modern day. They lay mingled with other natural stones, some of which bore the marks of having been burned by Indian fires, and some by the sun, and also bits of pottery and glass brought hither by the recent cultivators of the soil. When my hoe tinkled against the stones, that music echoed to the woods and the sky, and was an accompaniment to my labor which yielded an instant and immeasurable crop. It was no longer beans that I hoed, nor I that hoed beans;

and I remembered with as much pity as pride, if I remembered at all, my acquaintances who had gone to the city to attend the oratorios. . . .

It was a singular experience that long acquaintance which I cultivated with beans, what with planting, and hoeing, and harvesting, and threshing, and picking over and selling them—the last was the hardest of all—I might add eating, for I did taste. I was determined to know beans. When they were growing, I used to hoe from five o'clock in the morning till noon, and commonly spent the rest of the day about other affairs. Consider the intimate and curious acquaintance one makes with various kinds of weeds—it will bear some iteration in the account, for there was no little iteration in the labor—disturbing their delicate organizations so ruthlessly, and making such invidious distinctions with his hoe, levelling whole ranks of one species, and sedulously cultivating another. That's Roman wormwood—that's pigweed—that's sorrel—that's piper-grass—have at him, chop him up, turn his roots upward to the sun, don't let him have a fibre in the shade, if you do he'll turn himself t'other side up and be as green as a leek in two days. A long war, not with cranes, but with weeds, those Trojans who had sun and rain and dews on their side. Daily the beans saw me come to their rescue armed with a hoe, and thin the ranks of their enemies, filling up the trenches with weedy dead. Many a lusty crest-waving Hector, that towered a whole foot above his crowding comrades, fell before my weapon and rolled in the dust.

Those summer days which some of my contemporaries devoted to the fine arts in Boston or Rome, and others to contemplation in India, and others to trade in London or New York, I thus, with the other farmers of New England, devoted to husbandry. Not that I wanted beans to eat, for I am by nature a Pythagorean, so far as beans are concerned, whether they mean porridge or voting, and exchanged them for rice; but, perchance, as some must work in fields if only for the sake of tropes and expression, to serve a parable-maker one day. It was on the whole a rare amusement, which, continued too long, might have become a dissipation. Though I gave them no manure, and did not hoe them all once, I hoed them unusually well as far as I went, and was paid for it in the end. . . .

This is the result of my experience in raising beans: Plant the common small white bush bean about the first of June, in rows three feet by eighteen inches apart, being careful to select fresh round and unmixed seed. First look out for worms, and supply vacancies by planting anew. Then look out for woodchucks, if it is an exposed place, for they will nibble off the earliest tender leaves almost clean as they go; and again, when the young tendrils make their appearance, they have notice of it, and will shear them off with both buds and young pods, sitting erect like a squirrel. But above all harvest as early as possible, if you would escape frosts and have a fair and salable crop; you may save much loss by this means.

This further experience also I gained: I said to myself, I will not plant beans and corn with so much industry another summer, but such seeds, if the seed is not lost, as sincerity, truth, simplicity, faith, innocence, and the like, and see if they will not grow in this soil, even with less toil and manurance, and sustain me, for surely it has not been exhausted for these crops. Alas! I said this to myself; but now another summer is gone, and another, and another, and I am obliged to say to you, Reader, that the seeds which I planted, if indeed they *were* the seeds of those virtues, were wormeaten or had lost their vitality, and so did not come up. Commonly men will only be brave as their fathers were brave, or timid. This generation is very sure to plant corn and beans each new year precisely as the Indians did centuries ago and taught the first settlers to do, as if there were a fate in it. I saw an old man the other day, to my astonishment, making the holes with a hoe for the seventieth time at least, and not for himself to lie down in! But why should not the

New Englander try new adventures, and not lay so much stress on his grain, his potato and grass crop, and his orchards—raise other crops than these? Why concern ourselves so much about our beans for seed, and not be concerned at all about a new generation of men? We should really be fed and cheered if when we met a man we were sure to see that some of the qualities which I have named, which we all prize more than those other productions, but which are for the most part broadcast and floating in the air, had taken root and grown in him. . . .

Ancient poetry and mythology suggest, at least, that husbandry was once a sacred art; but it is pursued with irreverent haste and heedlessness by us, our object being to have large farms and large crops merely. We have no festival, nor procession, nor ceremony, not excepting our cattle-shows and so-called Thanksgivings, by which the farmer expresses a sense of the sacredness of his calling, or is reminded of its sacred origin. It is the premium and the feast which tempt him. He sacrifices not to Ceres and the Terrestrial Jove, but to the infernal Plutus rather. By avarice and selfishness, and a grovelling habit, from which none of us is free, of regarding the soil as property, or the means of acquiring property chiefly, the landscape is deformed, husbandry is degraded with us, and the farmer leads the meanest of lives. He knows Nature but as a robber. Cato says that the profits of agriculture are particularly pious or just (*maximeque pius quæstus*), and according to Varro the old Romans "called the same earth Mother and Ceres, and thought that they who cultivated it led a pious and useful life, and that they alone were left of the race of King Saturn."

We are wont to forget that the sun looks on our cultivated fields and on the prairies and forests without distinction. They all reflect and absorb his rays alike, and the former make but a small part of the glorious picture which he beholds in his daily course. In his view the earth is all equally cultivated like a garden. Therefore we should receive the benefit of his light and heat with a corresponding trust and magnanimity. What though I value the seed of these beans, and harvest that in the fall of the year? This broad field which I have looked at so long looks not to me as the principal cultivator, but away from me to influences more genial to it, which water and make it green. These beans have results which are not harvested by me. Do they not grow for woodchucks partly? The ear of wheat (in Latin *spica*, obsoletely *speca*, from *spe*, hope) should not be the only hope of the husbandman; its kernel or grain (*granum* from *gerendo*, bearing) is not all that it bears. How, then, can our harvest fail? Shall I not rejoice also at the abundance of the weeds whose seeds are the granary of the birds? It matters little comparatively whether the fields fill the farmer's barns. The true husbandman will cease from anxiety, as the squirrels manifest no concern whether the woods will bear chestnuts this year or not, and finish his labor with every day, relinquishing all claim to the produce of his fields, and sacrificing in his mind not only his first but his last fruits also.

EXPLORE: Thoreau's view of farming is very different from Jefferson's. Outline five or more ways in which these differences seem significant. How are their individual ideas a product of their time? Are there any ways that the two writers are similar?

EXPLORE: Thoreau sees farming as a symbolic act. Where do you see this hold true? What does farming symbolize for Thoreau?

CHAPTER FIVE

The Reality of Farming: Nineteenth and Twentieth Century

In the West are "sleeping empires awaiting exploitation and development."
—C. J. Blanchard,
National Geographic, April 1910

In this chapter you will see how the nineteenth century saw dramatic changes in agriculture, including numerous scientific and technological improvements, increasing amounts of land brought under cultivation, and advancements in farm efficiency and productivity. Significant cultural changes solidify the image of the homesteader as a national icon of independence and fortitude. The first two decades of the twentieth century are often referred to as the Golden Age of agriculture because of increasing yields. But the age also had its challenges, and several of the authors in the literary section that follows will raise questions about what these "improvements" do to the culture of agriculture. Some of the main subjects of this chapter include: the importance of the Homestead Act of 1862 and emotional appeals used to promote agricultural settlement, progress and success in western migration, the role the Civil War played in that movement west, the changing concept of American landscape and the growing tension between rural and urban points of view or cultural definitions of "wild" versus "civilized," the greater role of science and technology to improve upon nature, the shift to a business model approach of running

*Important Technological Events
in US Agricultural History before 1900*

1794 Eli Whitney invents the cotton gin to mechanically remove cottonseeds

1798 Eli Whitney's concept of interchangeable parts begins to revolutionize manufacturing

1807 Robert Fulton's steamboat the Clermont is launched, marking a revolution in shipping

1811 Cumberland Road opens as the first national railroad.

1812 War of 1812 made it apparent that America needed better transportation systems and more economic independence

1831 Cyrus McCormick invents the mechanical reaper, a significant labor saving farm implement.

1837 John Deere introduces his first steel plow, which allowed settlers to break the tough virgin sod in the American Midwest.

1874 F. Glidden invented barbed wire, which helped farmers keep cattle out of their fields.

1869 Transcontinental Railroad was completed when the final spike was driven at Promontory, Utah where the east and west lines met.

1876 Alexander Graham Bell invents telephone, further revolutionizing long-distance communication.

1892 Rudolph Diesel invents the diesel engine.

farms, the role of irrigation west of the 100th Meridian, and the role of women in agricultural settlements.

Agricultural History prior to World War I

Manifest Destiny

White settlers had been encouraged to go into western lands since the expansionist sentiments that swept James K. Polk into presidency in 1844. Manifest Destiny,, the settlement policy

> In 1840, there were over 9,000,000 farmers in the US, comprising 69% of the labor force. The number of farms was over 1,000,000.

of that period, held that white Americans were divinely ordained to settle and civilize the North American continent from east to west. A popular saying of the time, repeated in newspapers, was "Go West, young man, go West! There is health in the country!" However, settlement west of the Mississippi River happened slowly, and prior to the Civil War, settlers claimed frontier land in one of two ways: either by squatter's rights or purchase from land speculators. The Mormon settlement in Utah in 1847, for instance, began when the pioneers claimed lands that legally belonged to Mexico prior to the Mexican-American War and the US annexation of the Utah territory in 1848. Other public lands in the American West were sold in huge lots to land speculators and railroad companies at public government auctions. These lands were divided up and sold to settlers, typically at a price out of reach of ordinary citizens.

VIEW: Consider the symbols in the John Gast painting "American Progress." What is the importance of light and dark? What seems to be the story Gast is telling in the painting, and how is that story related to his notion of "progress" or the nation's notion of Manifest Destiny Compare and contrast this painting with Emanuel Leutz's 1861 painting "Westward the Course of Empire Takes the Way," which you can find online. Are their messages the same or do they differ?

FIGURE 5.1. John Gast, *American Progress*, 1872. Library of Congress, Prints & Photographs Division, Washington, DC, digital ID ppmsca.09855.

The Homestead Act of 1862

In 1862, the nation was in the midst of the Civil War, and most of the country's attention was turned to the issue of slavery. Nevertheless, 1862 was a watershed year for America agriculture. President Abraham Lincoln signed into law the three most important pieces of agricultural legislation in the nation's history. First was the May 15, 1862, act to establish a US Department of Agriculture, which would professionalize farming by compiling farm statistics and testing new farming methods and machinery. Five days later on May 20, the president signed the Homestead Act of 1862, the text of which is provided below, and in July of that year he approved the Morrill Land Grant Act (discussed in Chapter 7).

> In 1860, just before the Civil War, 58% of the US labor force was engaged in agriculture. The nation had over 2,000,000 farms, with the average farm size at just under 200 acres.

Born in Kentucky in 1809 on the first of several of meager farms his family would own in the old frontier states, Lincoln never had Jefferson's passion for agriculture, yet he recognized that agriculture was the primary occupation in the country. In the fall of 1859, a year before the election, he addressed the Wisconsin State Agricultural Society Fair, saying that in the nation's future, "the most valuable of all arts will be the art of deriving a comfortable subsistence from the smallest area of soil. No community of whose every member possess this art, can ever be the victim of oppression in any of its forms. Such community will be alike independent of crowned-kings, money-kings, and land-kings." In an Independence Day address to Congress during his first year in office, Lincoln argued that the purpose of the government was "to afford all, an unfettered start, and a fair chance, in the race of life."

The Homestead Act of 1862 aimed to encourage settlement by distributing western lands under terms that made land ownership accessible to most Americans. A popular camp song of the second half of the nineteenth century encouraged people to "Come along, come along, don't be alarmed; Uncle Sam is rich enough to give us all a farm!" In exchange for a nominal filing fee, parcels of 160 acres were distributed to settlers who agreed to remain on the land and make improvements. In order to "prove up" and thus be eligible to get the "homestead patent" or deed to the land, settlers agreed to three main stipulations:

1. They would commit to staying on the land for five years and to reside on the land for a significant portion of each year.
2. They would build a dwelling and make capital improvements, such as barns and fences.
3. Within the first year, they would clear land and bring into cultivation a percentage of the claim, and they would continue to do so over the course of the five years.

Considered one of the most important pieces of legislation in United States history, the Homestead Act distributed 80 million acres of public land by 1900; that is more acres than in the whole of the state of New Mexico, and more than came under cultivation in the previous 250 years.

Although we may think of the Homestead Act as having the greatest effect on nineteenth century history, more homestead patents were filed during the 1910s than during any other decade, and by the mid-1970s, a total of 270 million acres (or 10% of the continental

> The Homestead Act was officially repealed by the Federal Land Policy and Management Act of 1976; however, a ten-year extension allowed homesteading in Alaska until 1986.

US, equivalent to the areas of Texas and California combined) had been opened up to private citizens through the Homestead Act.

Initially, fewer than half of the homesteaders filing on land proved up, due to the difficulties of clearing and bringing into cultivation 160 acres. Government officials had decided on the 160 acre homestead allotments because they believed that was the amount of land would ensure the agricultural success of a single family, specifically that the family would move beyond subsistence farming and be able to sell much of their produce in the marketplace. However, the 160 acre allotment was based upon the weather and geography of the eastern part of the country, and it did not take into account that west of the 100th Meridian (the longitude that bisects the Dakotas, Nebraska, Kansas, Oklahoma, and Texas) land is much more arid and typically gets less than twenty inches of rain per year. Therefore, over the course of the following decades several second-generation homestead acts amended the original 1862 act to ease requirements for acreage brought under cultivation, expand the acreage in homestead allotments in order to address the land productivity issue, make planting trees a part of the homesteading requirements, or encourage development of irrigation projects.

The Homestead Act May 20, 1862

AN ACT to secure homesteads to actual settlers on the public domain.

Be it enacted, That any person who is the head of a family, or who has arrived at the age of twenty-one years, and is a citizen of the United States, or who shall have filed his declaration of intention to become such, as required by the naturalization laws of the United States, and who has never borne arms against the United States Government or given aid and comfort to its enemies, shall, from and after the first of January, eighteen hundred and sixty-three, be entitled to enter one quarter-section or a less quantity of unappropriated public lands, upon which said person may have filed a pre-emption claim, or which may, at the time the application is made, be subject to pre-emption at one dollar and twenty-five cents, or less, per acre; or eighty acres or less of such unappropriated lands, at two dollars and fifty cents per acre, to

> **Graft**
>
> Because there were no government inspectors to make sure settlers fulfilled stipulations, all a settler needed do when he requested his final homestead patent was secure a witness to testify that he had made the proper improvements on his land. This meant that the various homestead acts were plagued by fraudulent claims. In some cases, settlers would pay a witness to testify that a birdhouse on his land was indeed an "erected domicile," or they would scatter seeds over the land and the witness could then confirm that they had brought the land under cultivation. Among the irrigated tracts, settlers would pay a witness to verify that he had seen the land irrigated, even though the settler had merely dumped a barrel full of water onto land in question.

be located in a body, in conformity to the legal subdivisions of the public lands, and after the same shall have been surveyed: Provided, That any person owning or residing on land may, under the provisions of this act, enter other land lying contiguous to his or her said land, which shall not, with the land so already owned and occupied, exceed in the aggregate one hundred and sixty acres. Sec. 2. That the person applying for the benefit of this act shall, upon application to the register of the land office in which he or she is about to make such entry, make affidavit before the said register or receiver that he or she is the head of a family, or is twenty-one or more years of age, or shall have performed service in the Army or Navy of the United States, and that he has never borne arms against the Government of the United States or given aid and comfort to its enemies, and that such application is made for his or her exclusive use and benefit, and that said entry is made for the purpose of actual settlement and cultivation, and not, either directly or indirectly, for the use or benefit of any other person or persons whomsoever; and upon filing the said affidavit with the register or receiver, and on payment of ten dollars, he or she shall thereupon he permitted to enter the quantity of land specified: Provided, however, That no certificate shall be given or patent issued therefor until the expiration of five years from the date of such entry; and if, at the expiration of such time, or at any time within two years thereafter, the person making such entry —or if he be dead, his widow; or in case of her death, his heirs or devisee; or in case of a widow making such entry, her heirs or devisee, in case of her death—shall prove by two credible witnesses that he, she, or they have resided upon or cultivated the same for the term of five years immediately succeeding the time of filing the affidavit aforesaid, and shall make affidavit that no part of said land has been alienated, and that he has borne true allegiance to the Government of the United States; then, in such case, he, she, or they, if at that time a citizen of the United States, shall be entitled to a patent, as in other cases provided for by law."

 EXPLORE: Consider the style and rhetoric of this legislation by listing some unique characteristics of the specialized language or sentence structure you find in the Homestead Act of 1862. How is the language different from Jefferson's historical account in *Notes on the State of Virginia*?

 VIEW: Watch the PBS documentary series *The Frontier House* (available in DVDs or on sites like Netflix). The 2002 reality series is about three modern families who agree to live as Montana homesteaders did in 1883. Discuss the factors that were essential for their success.

 RESEARCH: As a class, divide the following questions related to the Homestead Act, conduct research, and report your findings to the class.
- Were women allowed to homestead and what were the stipulations?
- What groups were originally denied access to homesteading and why? Be able to indicate the language in the Act that excludes the group(s).
- What were the other homesteading acts that came after the original 1862 act and what problems did they try to address?
- What was the Land Run of 1899?
- Who was the very first homesteader to file under the 1862 Act? Where did he homestead and what was he like?
- Who was the last homesteader and how long was the Homestead Act in effect?
- How was the Homestead Act related to Lincoln's political goals during the Civil War? Consider who was allowed to homestead and who was not. What were the political repercussions of this distinction?

Climatology, Exploration, and the Importance of Water

Early nineteenth century cartographers designated the arid, treeless, and mostly uninhabited area of the Great Plains as "The Great American Desert," and prior to the Homestead Act, many thought the land was nearly impossible to cultivate. For early settlers the plains was an obstacle to cross over as quickly as possible on their way to more fertile ground west of the Rockies. In fact, the wagons settlers used to cross the plains were often called "prairie schooners," a sea-going term signifying how desolate the plains seemed. The treeless grasslands were initially thought to be unfit for agriculture, and the numbers of settlers in the plains were limited. Starting in the 1870s, however, the region had several years of unusually high precipitation, and thus a greater number of homestead claims. Climatologists, geographers, and naturalists began to speculate that the breaking of sod allowed for more rain absorption into sponge-like dirt under the sod cover. Absorption meant evaporation that was more slow and consistent, which in turn would lead to more atmospheric moisture and thus more rain. The theory was called "Rain follows the plow." Writer and amateur scientist Charles Dana Wilber was an ardent advocate of the theory, as you can see from the excerpt below from his book *The Great Valleys and Prairies of Nebraska and the Northwest*:

> God speed the plow. . . . By this wonderful provision, which is only man's mastery over nature, the clouds are dispensing copious rains . . . [the plow] is the instrument which separates civilization from savagery; and converts a desert into a farm or garden. . . . In this miracle of progress, the plow was the unerring prophet, the procuring cause, not by any magic or enchantment, not by incantations or offerings, but instead by the sweat of his face toiling with his hands, man can persuade the heavens to yield their treasures of dew and rain upon the land he has chosen for his dwelling. . . . The raindrop never fails to fall and answer to the imploring power or prayer of labor.

Many took this as testament to man's power to profoundly change the land. Settlers had already changed how the land looked, with their neat straight rows in orderly quarter sections of the homesteads; now, some believed, cultivation was changing the climate of the plains. Planting trees was especially thought to bring rain, and one of the second generation Homestead Acts was the Timber Culture Act of 1873, which required plains settlers to plant one fourth of their claims in trees to provide wood for building materials, fuel for fires, and windbreaks for crops.

Railroad companies, which owned large tracts of land they wanted to see settled, were eager to take up the claims that more settlement would mean land becoming increasingly fertile, so they often used references to the "rain follows the plow" in their promotional materials. Commercial Clubs, which were a nineteenth-century version of small town chambers of commerce, also touted how the West was changing and becoming much more promising for settlers in the pamphlets that they distributed to factory workers and immigrants throughout the East and upper Midwest.

Although the theory of "rain follows the plow" was quickly discredited, especially when the plains suffered widespread droughts in the 1890s, what was really needed to ensure success was the development of dry land farming varieties of crops like wheat and corn. The plow may have not changed the climate, but the real and lasting transformation the theory brought about was a change in cultural attitudes. In the minds of the citizens, the Great American Desert had been transformed into the Elysian fields, an American Eden, and the "bread basket" of the nation.

Meanwhile in the regions west of the Rockies, a Civil War veteran named John Wesley Powell was the first to explore some of the major western rivers and consider what such waterways meant for agriculture in the American West. Trained as a geologist, Powell set out for his first trip down the wild rivers of the West in 1869 and soon became the most celebrated explorer since Lewis and Clark. He was the first to explore the length of the Green River from Wyoming to Utah and then at the confluence of the rivers go on to the treacherous Colorado River that led through the Grand Canyon. Powell's feat was even more remarkable given that he had lost his right arm in the war. Nevertheless, he was an able and fearless leader. He and his men lost most of their supplies when boats capsized, and the rapids were so fearsome that three of Powell's men abandoned the expedition. Powell produced the first authoritative map of the Colorado River, recorded the discovery of the flora and fauna in the canyons, and began doing ethnographic research among the native peoples who lived in the region.

In 1876, Powell published his *Report on the Lands of the Arid Region*, where he argued that most land in the West needed irrigation to adequately support agriculture and settlement. Dismissing the "Rain follows the plow" theory, he predicted that water would remain scarce and the region would some significant and unique challenges. He made the following recommendations:

- He urged government to slow the stream of homesteaders coming west and turn to a more planned settlement approach in order to avoid what he called "water wars."
- He warned against the overuse and depletion of underground watersheds.
- He argued that settlements needed to be built near water, rather than trying to bring water to settlements with complex canal systems.
- He envisioned greater cooperation in homesteading settlements and described farmers building irrigation dams and canals with their own money, so they felt a vested interest in the irrigation projects. In this, he admired the irrigation practices of the Mormons who functioned cooperatively.
- He also advocated a commons approach, in which pasturage for cattle was held by communities rather than individuals (much like the European system).
- He believed smaller homesteads were a better use of land. By his calculations, 160 acres with irrigation was too much for a single family to maintain, and 160 acres without irrigation was simply not sustainable, even when farmers used dryland farming methods.

Like the Greek goddess Cassandra, who was fated to prophesize the truth but never to be believed or heeded, Powell's predictions about water use in the West were largely ignored and dismissed. The boosters promoting western settlement trumpeted the benefits of private property rights in order to lure landless Americans and European immigrants to seek their fortunes in the West. Land rushes, in which homesteaders could claim newly opened Indian lands on a first come, first served basis, were common events. Boom towns seemingly popped up overnight, and no one talked about Powell's suggestions to take a slower, more thoughtful approach to western settlement or to create agricultural commons areas. Many of Powell's points continue to be relevant to today's westerners facing water issues in the twenty-first century.

> In 1880, there were 4 million farms in the US.

Irrigation and Reclamation Acts of the West

In Marc Reisner's history *Cadillac Desert, The American West and Its Disappearing Water*, Reisner makes the case that the history of the West is the history of water. Failing the "Rain follows the plow" theory, the American West turned to irrigation as its answer to make over "The Great American Desert" into "the garden of the world," as the promotional materials from railway companies touted. If rain could not be enticed from

> In 1900, farm population was nearly 30 million, with farmers constituting 38% of the labor force. There were over 5 million farms.

the sky by the plow, the water engineer at the turn-of-the-century was certain he could change the course of rivers instead.

Starting in 1894, irrigation legislation was enacted to amend the original Homestead Act. The Desert Land Act of 1887 gave 320 acres of land in arid regions if settlers brought the land under privately managed irrigation projects within three years. The Desert Land Act of 1894, better known as the Carey Act, allotted significant federal lands to western states; however, this act still relied upon private investment to set up the necessary canal companies. Most successful in Idaho, the Carey Act was responsible for bringing 60% of the state's farmland under cultivation.

At the turn of the twentieth century, these irrigation acts began to be called reclamation acts because they were based on the premise that irrigation would reclaim the wild desert for human use. For the first time in the West, a large-scale cooperative system of irrigation canals applied modern technology and ingenuity to the problem of the arid lands. Before this, the federal government only acted to encourage irrigation projects indirectly. The Federal Reclamation Act of 1902 committed federal money to build dams and reservoirs for water storage and better irrigation control. The act was signed into law by President Theodore Roosevelt, who was interested in the western environment and conservation; he predicted that "if the waters that now run to waste were saved and used for irrigation," the population of the West would grow to more than the population of the entire country at the turn of the century. Eventually, these reclamation acts led to huge dam-building projects that included Grand Coulee Dam and Hoover Dam.

In the 1905 *National Magazine* article entitled "Millions of New Acres for American Farmers," Califor-

> The early part of the twentieth century, from 1900 to the beginning of the First World War in 1914, is considered the "Golden Age of Agriculture." During that time the average gross income of US farms more than doubled, the value of these farms more than tripled, and farmers were using more mechanized means of farming, such as the steam tractor. By 1910, the number of farms in the nation reached its peak at 6.4 million. While the percentage of farmers in the US labor force was down to 31%, one farmer could feed 7 people.

nia booster Hamilton Wright wrote that reclamation acts would "open the way for the mightiest Anglo-Saxon civilization the world has ever known. . . . This vast, bleak desert will be completely transformed through irrigation." Wright's prose suggests a continuation of the idea that land is best when it is under the submission of human control and when mankind's improving efforts bring order out of chaos. This also echoes some of the ideas from Manifest Destiny, especially the implication that such transformation by humans is preordained by divine powers. But Reclamation Acts also evidenced a new belief about the human relationship to the land, namely that science and engineering were superior to nature and could therefore improve upon it. Such reclamation projects were often said to harness the power of mighty rivers. For instance, historian Mark Feige traces how the Carey Act offered the state of Idaho the promise of an "Industrial Eden," and a "systemized and controlled landscape" where engineers and developers were seen as "understudies of the Creator."

The April 1910 issue of *National Geographic* featured a story on the Carey Act irrigation projects. In "The Spirit of the West, Wonderful Development Since the Dawn of Irrigation," C. J. Blanchard wrote:

> Its deserts, in vastness of area, in potential wealth of soil and climate, and in rivers of constant supply, are sleeping empires awaiting exploitation and development. Here

nature offers to every man his birthright—a wide sky, the sunshine, the wind, and a sure reward for intelligent effort. . . . Irrigation has wrought its miracles. . . . Future writers will record the irrigation movement as an epoch in our history the far-reaching influence of which overshadowed in importance any other progressive movement since the opening to settlement of the Mississippi Valley. . . . The beacon of hope shines brightly in the west. It beckons the landless man to the manless land."

Carey Act Boosterism

Early community boosterism materials produced in cooperation with the railroad companies consistently relied upon appeals to *Pathos*—that is, they create an emotional response in order to convince an audience to take action. Commercial Clubs took out advertisements in newspapers, proclaiming in large letters "Plant Dimes, Harvest Dollars in Idaho. You Should go There Now!" The "Plant Dimes" campaign was used throughout the irrigated states.

 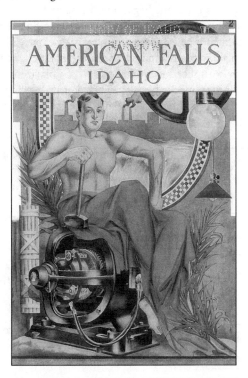

FIGURE 5.2. Idaho Commercial Club pamphlets with cover art by William Bittle Wells, Circa 1910. Courtesy of Idaho State Historical Society.

From the Commercial Club pamphlet for Buhl, Idaho *(1914)*

Why should you continue in the old rut? Are you satisfied with the opportunities you now have? Your father had the courage to settle in a new country and there make his home and possibly his fortune. But what chance would he have of making his fortune if he had to start there now? Irrigation has all the advantages of natural rainfall. The adequate supply is always there. The water is never lacking and there is never too much. The farmer controls the amount of the water for his land and by exercising reasonable judgment, may so water his crops that the maximum quantity and superior quality are obtained. Why should you take any chances in your farming operations? With irrigation the farmer knows—he does not guess. There is not watching the clouds for rain. The water is in the ditch ready for use. The results are certain. Why do you run the risk?

[Testimonial from a farmer:] When my pastures need rain, do I look anxiously at the heavens? Not on your life; I simply press the button (figuratively speaking) and can have a gentle shower or a gully washer at my option; thus my pasture is the same one month with another.

From the Commercial Club Pamphlet for Boise, Idaho *(1908)*

And this is but the beginning. In every direction the "ditch" of the irrigator is extending its potent arm and reaching out tiny life-giving fingers to reclaim the soil from the desert. . . . Entirely liberated is he from the caprice of the weather. The operation of a lever, or a few turns of a spade, and at his command is all the moisture that he requires. . . . Moreover, the farmer in the irrigated district, unlike his brother who is the plaything of the elements, is never harassed by untimely rains that impede his harvests or destroy his crops. In every way, and in a sense unknown under ordinary conditions, he is "master of the situation."

EXPLORE: Examine the prose of Charles Dana Wilber's words in the "Rain follows the plow" discussion. Underline words that are emotionally charged and especially evocative. Do you see any patterns in the kinds of images he uses?

FOR FURTHER READING: For more information, read Marc Reisner's history *Cadillac Desert, The American West and Its Disappearing Water*, and watch the documentary based on Reisner's book, available on YouTube. See especially second and third episodes, named "The American Nile" and "The Mercy of Nature." See also Mark Fiege's book *Irrigated Eden: The Making of an Agricultural Landscape in the American West*.

EXPLORE: Examine the art on the covers and the text excerpts from Idaho Commercial Club pamphlets from the Carey Act Era (1905–1915). Discuss how they appeal to emotion.

Roosevelt and the Country Life Commission

In August of 1908, as Theodore Roosevelt's second term in office was nearing its end, he appointed five men (university professors, editors of agricultural publications, and a Forest Service official) to the Country Life Commission and charged them with the responsibility of assessing the state of American agriculture in terms of the culture of rural settlements. The problem, Roo-

sevelt recognized, was that as indus-
tries in urban centers grew, increasingly strong, young workers drifted away
from the farm. Life in urban centers
seemed easier and more secure for
people making decisions about their

In 1906, President Roosevelt signed into law the Food and
Drug Act, which ensured food safety and began a program
of meat inspection. This act was in direct response to Upton
Sinclair's popular, 1906 novel *The Jungle*, which described
the unsanitary conditions in the meat packing plants.

life's occupation. For the president, however, agriculture was vital to the nation morally and socially, as well as economically. The question, then, was how to foster improvements in country life
that would ensure the continuing vitality and health of rural communities.

The following is the President's letter to Professor Bailey, appointing him and others to the Country Life Commission.

August 10, 1908

My Dear Professor Bailey:

No nation has ever achieved permanent greatness unless this greatness was based on the well being
of the great farmer class, the men who live on the soil; for it is upon their welfare, material and
moral, that the welfare of the rest of the nation ultimately rests. In the United States, disregarding
certain sections and taking the nation as a whole, I believe it to be true that the farmers in general are better off to-day than they ever were before. We Americans are making great progress in
the development of our agricultural resources. But it is equally true that the social and economic
institutions of the open country are not keeping pace with the development of the nation as a
whole. . . . In portions of the South, for example, where the Department of Agriculture, through
the farmers' cooperative demonstration work of Doctor Knapp, is directly instructing more than
30,000 farmers in better methods of farming, there is nevertheless much unnecessary suffering
and needless loss of efficiency on the farm. A physician, who is also a careful student of farm life
in the South, writing to me recently about the enormous percentage of preventable deaths of children, due to insanitary condition of southern farms, said:

"Personally, from the health point of view, I would prefer to see my own daughter, 9 years
old, at work in a cotton mill than have her live as tenant on the average southern tenant one-horse
farm. This apparently extreme statement is based upon actual life among both classes of people."

I doubt if any other nation can bear comparison with our own in the amount of attention
given by the Government, both Federal and State, to agricultural matters. But practically the
whole of this effort has hitherto been directed toward increasing the production of crops. Our attention has been concentrated almost exclusively on getting better farming. In the beginning this
was unquestionably the right thing to do. The farmer must first of all grow good crops in order
to support himself and his family. But when this has been secured the effort for better farming
should cease to stand alone, and should be accompanied by the effort for better business and better living on the farm. It is at least as important that the farmer should get the largest possible return in money, comfort, and social advantages from the crops he grows as that he should get the
largest possible return in crops from the land he farms. Agriculture is not the whole of country
life. The great rural interests are human interests, and good crops are of little value to the farmer
unless they open the door to a good kind of life on the farm. . . .

How can the life of the farm family be made less solitary, fuller of opportunity, freer from
drudgery, more comfortable, happier, and more attractive? Such a result is most earnestly to be

desired. How can life on the farm be kept on the highest level, and, where it is not already on that level, be so improved, dignified, and brightened as to awaken and keep alive the pride and loyalty of the farmer's boys and girls, of the farmer's wife, and of the farmer himself? How can a compelling desire to live on the farm be aroused in the children that are born on the farm? All these questions are of vital importance not only to the farmer but to the whole nation. . . . We hope ultimately to double the average yield of wheat and corn per acre; it will be a great achievement; but it is even more important to double the desirability, comfort, and standing of the farmer's life.

It is especially important that whatever will serve to prepare country children for life on the farm and whatever will brighten home life in the country and make it richer and more attractive for the mothers, wives, and daughters of farmers should be done promptly, thoroughly, and gladly. There is no more important person, measured in influence upon the life of the nation, than the farmer's wife, no more important home than the country home, and it is of national importance to do the best we can for both.

The farmers have hitherto had less than their full share of public attention along the lines of business and social life. There is too much belief among all our people that the prizes of life lie away from the farm. I am therefore anxious to bring before the people of the United States the question of securing better business and better living on the farm, whether by cooperation between farmers for buying, selling, and borrowing; by promoting social advantages and opportunities in the country; or by any other legitimate means that will help to make country life more gainful, more attractive, and fuller of opportunities, pleasures, and rewards for the men, women, and children of the farms. . . . .

My immediate purpose in appointing this commission is to secure from it such information and advice as will enable me to make recommendations to Congress upon this extremely important matter. I shall be glad if the commission will report to me upon the present condition of country life, upon what means are now available for supplying the deficiencies which exist, and upon the best methods of organized permanent effort in investigation and actual work along the lines I have indicated. . . .

I shall look forward with the keenest interest to your report.

Sincerely, yours, Theodore Roosevelt.

In response, the Country Life Commission devised a questionnaire that asked about the structural condition of farm homes, the sanitary conditions in the home and barnyard, the preparation for farm life that boys and girls received in schools, the rate of return farmers received from sale of their products, the services they received from railroads, road systems, United States postal service, banks, insurance agencies, and rural telephones, as well as organizations that promoted their mutual buying and selling interests. A good portion of the survey assessed the working and living conditions of farm laborers and renters, and a number of questions drew attention to family life, specifically whether farm families gathered together often enough for mutual improvement and entertainment and whether farm wives had satisfying work and adequate social support. Finally, the questionnaire asked the open-ended question: "What, in your judgment, is the most important single thing to be done for the general betterment of country life?"

Over half a million copies of the questionnaire were circulated in rural communities nationwide, and the Census Bureau tabulated the results from nearly 120,000 respondents. The

Commission also took into account numerous personal letters they received, and they held public hearings in 30 sites around the nation where farmers and their wives from 40 states and territories gathered to voice their opinions. The hearings were especially informative, according to Professor Bailey, who wrote in the final report that these events were well attended by a range of people, from rural residents to community physicians and clergy.

The Commission submitted its report to the president a little over five months later. Then, on February 9, 1909, with less than a month remaining in Roosevelt's term in office, he presented the Commission of Country Life Report to the Senate and House of Representatives with the following "Special Message."

To the Senate and House of Representatives:

I transmit herewith the report of the Commission on Country Life. At the outset I desire to point out that not a dollar of the public money has been paid to any commissioner for his work on the commission.

The report shows the general condition of farming life in the open country, and points out its larger problems; it indicates ways in which the Government, National and State, may show the people how to solve some of these problems; and it suggests a continuance of the work which the commission began. . . .

Yet farming does not yield either the profit or the satisfaction that it ought to yield and may be made to yield. There is discontent in the country, and in places discouragement. Farmers as a class do not magnify their calling, and the movement to the towns, though, I am happy say, less than formerly, is still strong.

Under our system, it is helpful to promote discussion ways in which the people can help themselves. There are three main directions in which the farmers can help themselves; namely, better farming, better business, and better living on the farm. . . . The object of the Commission on Country Life therefore is not to help the farmer raise better crops, but to call his attention to the opportunities for better business and better living on the farm. If country life is to become what it should be, and what I believe it ultimately will be—one of the most dignified, desirable, and sought-after ways of earning a living—the farmer must take advantage not only of the agricultural knowledge which is at his disposal, but of the methods which have raised and continue to raise the standards of living and of intelligence in other callings. . . . .

It would be idle to assert that life on the farm occupies as good a position in dignity, desirability, and business results as the farmers might easily give it if they chose. One of the chief difficulties is the failure of country life, as it exists at present, to satisfy the higher social and intellectual aspirations of country people. Whether the constant draining away of so much of the best elements in the rural population into the towns is due chiefly to this cause or to the superior business opportunities of city life may be open to question. But no one at all familiar with farm life throughout the United States can fail to recognize the necessity for building up the life of the farm upon its social as well as upon its productive side. . . .

For just this reason the introduction of effective agricultural cooperation throughout the United States is of the first importance. Where farmers are organized cooperatively they not only avail themselves much more readily of business opportunities and improved methods, but it is found that the organizations which bring them together in the work of their lives are used also for social and intellectual advancement. The cooperative plan . . . develops individual responsibility and has a moral as well as a financial value over any other plan. . . .

The commission has tried to help the farmers to see clearly their own problem and to see it as a whole; to distinguish clearly between what the Government can do and what the farmers must do for themselves; and it wishes to bring not only the farmers but the Nation as a whole to realize that the growing of crops, though an essential part, is only a part of country life. Crop growing is the essential foundation; but it is no less essential that the farmer shall get an adequate return for what he grows; and it is no less essential—indeed it is literally vital—that he and his wife and his children shall lead the right kind of life. . . .

From all that has been done and learned three great general and immediate needs of country life stand out:

First, effective cooperation among farmers, to put them on a level with the organized interests with which they do business.

Second, a new kind of schools in the country, which shall teach the children as much outdoors as indoors and perhaps more, so that they will prepare for country life, and not as at present, mainly for life in town.

Third, better means of communication, including good roads and a parcels post, which the country people are everywhere, and rightly, unanimous in demanding.

To these may well be added better sanitation; for easily preventable diseases hold several million country people in the slavery of continuous ill health.

The commission points out, and I concur in the conclusion, that the most important help that the Government whether National or State, can give is to show the people how to go about these tasks of organization, education, and communication with the best and quickest results. . . .

Our object should be to help develop in the country community the great ideals of community life as well as of personal character. One of the most important adjuncts to this end must be the country church, and I invite your attention to what the commission says of the country church and of the need of an extension of such work as that of the Young Men's Christian Association in country communities. Let me lay special emphasis upon what the Commission says at the very end of its report on personal ideals and local leadership. . . .

Given a sufficient foundation of material well being, the influence of the farmers and farmers' wives their children becomes the factor of first importance determining the attitude of the next generation toward farm life. The farmer should realize that the person who most needs consideration on the farm is his wife. I do not in the least mean that she should purchase ease at the expense of duty. Neither man nor woman is really happy or really useful save on condition of doing his or her duty. If the woman shirks her duty as housewife, as home keeper, as the mother whose prime function it is to bear and rear a sufficient number of healthy children, then she is not entitled to our regard. But if she does her duty she is more entitled to our regard even than the man who does his duty; and the man should show special consideration for her needs.

I warn my countrymen that the great recent progress made in city life is not a full measure of our civilization; for our civilization rests at bottom on the wholesomeness, the attractiveness, and the completeness, as well as the prosperity, of life in the country. The men and women on the farms stand for what is fundamentally best and most needed in our American life. Upon the development of country life rests ultimately our ability, by methods of farming requiring the highest intelligence, to continue to feed and clothe the hungry nations; to supply the city with fresh blood, clean bodies, and clear brains that can endure the terrific strain of modern life; we need the development of men in the open country, who will be in future, as in the past, the stay and strength of the nation in time of war, and its guiding and controlling spirit in time of peace.

THEODORE ROOSEVELT
THE WHITE HOUSE, February 9, 1909.

In addressing the "deficiencies and remedies" of country life, the Commission made a number of important recommendations:

- Although the Commission admired the independence and self-reliance of the "separate man, living quietly on his land," they did believe that the farmer was "handicapped" by separateness, and they urged farmers to welcome more cooperative and organizational efforts and advised farmers to take leadership roles in such organizations.
- Calling for a significant cultural shift in thinking about farming, they urged farmers to think in terms of a business model, something that Roosevelt had emphasized in his letter of appointment to the Country Life Commission. Farmers could learn much from a more business-like approach, and they could gain power in the marketplace by working cooperatively with other farmer-businessmen.
- They advised farmers to provide their laborers "good living facilities and [help] him in every way to be a man among men," a phrase that referred to how often hired hands were found to frequent saloons.
- In keeping with the Roosevelt's conservationist ethics, they urged rural communities "to protect and develop the natural scenery and attractiveness of the open country."
- Even though the commission had believed the task of assessing religion's role in the rural community too daunting for the time they had to make an assessment, they did write that, "The forces and institutions that make for morality and spiritual ideals among rural people must be energized. We miss the heart of the problem if we neglect to foster personal character and neighborhood righteousness."
- For the first time in American agricultural history, the Commission devoted extensive discussion to the role of women on the farms, writing, "Whatever general hardships, such as poverty, isolation, lack of labor-saving devices, may exist on any given farm, the burden of these hardships falls more heavily on the farmer's wife than on the farmer himself. In general, her life is more monotonous and the more isolated, no matter what the wealth or the poverty of the family may be." They advocated "development of a cooperative spirit in the home, simplification of the diet in many cases, the building of convenient and sanitary houses, providing running water in the house and also more mechanical help, good and convenient gardens, a less exclusive ideal of money getting on the part of the farmer, providing better means of communication, as telephones, roads, and reading circles, and developing of women's organizations."

Concluding that "the work before us, therefore, is nothing more or less than the gradual rebuilding of a new agriculture and new rural life," the Commission called for changes "in full harmony with the best American ideals."

The end of Roosevelt's term in office meant that he lost the political capital to further many of the recommendations of the Country Life Commission Report, and his handpicked successor, William Howard Taft, paid little attention to the CLC's recommendations, a fact that caused an irreparable rift between the two presidents. As such, improvements in areas identified by the Country Life Commission Report were sometimes slow in coming, if they came at all.

For instance, the report did not stem the tide of rural youth moving to urban centers, and in the case of reforming school education to represent country life issues, reformers met with solid opposition. However, the following reforms can be credited to the CLC Report:

- 4-H programs were organized to better prepare youth to remain in rural occupations.
- Rural Free Delivery and general parcel post delivery programs were begun or expanded.
- Agricultural Extension programs were funded by the Smith-Lever Act of 1914.
- Telephone service to rural areas dramatically improved.
- The Rural Electrification Act of 1935 provided federal loans to establish cooperative electric power companies.
- Rural sociology was established as an academic field that would continue studying the questions raised by the CLC.
- Federal land banks were established to supply farmers with access to farm loans.

 COLLABORATE: In small groups, imagine that you have been asked to serve on the Twenty-first Century's Country Life Commission. Write an outline of your commission's report. In the first part of your outline, consider what issues from the original CLC still need to be addressed. Secondly, describe the new challenges faced by those living in rural areas. Finally, you have the option of making recommendations to "remedy" the new "deficiencies" you outlined.

 EXPLORE: What is the effect in the CLC Report of talking about the "deficiencies and remedies" of country life? Discuss the attitude and perspective those words suggest. Where else in the CLC materials do you see that attitude?

 EXPLORE: The CLC Report was the first to study the conditions, challenges, and responsibilities of women on the American farm. Identify and discuss relevant passages in these materials.

Every Farm Is a Factory

A booklet written by Charles M. Carroll and published by the International Harvester Company in 1917 includes this excerpt.

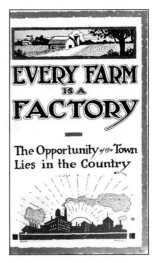

The opportunity of the town lies in the country. The country can get along without the town, but no town ever has or ever will be permanently prosperous where the land is poor. The town is built on farm profits; on what farmers produce in excess of their home needs. In fact, the towns are consumers, not real producers. Towns are the national evolution and outgrowth of necessity—places to store and distribute the world's surplus products through the channels of commerce. There is but one road to permanent city building—that road leads to the farm. . . . When the harvest fields smile, towns wax fat, and factories increase the pay roll. . . . We must not forget that every farm is a factory, and that in every state there are thousands of these factories which need our best thought and effort to make them productive.

 RESEARCH: Identify agriculturally related songs that were popular between 1865 and 1914. For instance, find songs like "Don't Leave the Farm, Boys" by Miss Clara F. Berry or the popular "How Ya Gonna Keep 'Em Down on the Farm." Lists of farm songs of the time can be found on the Internet. Choose one song and analyze the lyrics and the agricultural values they express.

 RESEARCH: The country humorist and social commentator Will Rogers was considered the leading political wit of the Progressive Era (roughly that time period discussed in this chapter) and during the Great Depression. Find and share some of Rogers's quips about farming.

 EXPLORE: As you read the literature in the next section of this chapter, be watchful for links between literary selections and history. How can the historical information help you understand the literature of the same period? Be prepared to discuss these links in class.

Literary History

In nineteenth-century American literary history, American fiction was dominated by European or eastern seaboard settings. The most popular novelist between 1870 and 1910 was Henry James, who wrote in the genre of "novel of manners" or, as it was sometimes called, "the novel of the parlor." Such works were peopled by the American upper class engaged in what one of James's dissenters called "teacup tragedies." So when these writers began to situate fiction on farms, it was—pardon the pun—groundbreaking. Recognizing the importance of this shift toward "the novel of the soil," Cather joked that her novel *O Pioneers!* was "a story concerned entirely with heavy farming people, with cornfields and pasture lands and pig yards,—set in Nebraska, of all places! As everyone knows, Nebraska is distinctly déclassé as literary background; its very name throws the delicately attuned critic into a clammy shiver of embarrassment. Kansas is almost as unpromising. Colorado, on the contrary, is considered quite possible. Wyoming really has some class, of its own kind, like well-cut riding breeches. But a New York critic voiced a very general opinion when he said [of *O Pioneers!*]: 'I simply don't care a damn what happens in Nebraska, no matter who writes about it.'"

In this section, you'll read several representative pieces that exemplify this time period in American agricultural and literary history.

Hamlin Garland, *"Under the Lion's Paw"*

This story appears in Garland's collection of semi-autobiographical stories entitled *Main-Travelled Roads* in 1891. From Garland's perspective, agriculture was undeniably a difficult life, something identified in his dedication to the book: "To my father and mother, whose half-century pilgrimage on the main travelled road of life has brought them only toil and deprivation, this book of stories is dedicated by a son to whom every day brings a deepening sense of his parents' silent heroism."

"Under the Lion's Paw"

It was the last of autumn and first day of winter coming together. All day long the plough-men on their prairie farms had moved to and fro in their wide level fields through the falling snow, which melted as it fell, wetting them to the skin all day, notwithstanding the frequent squalls of snow, the dripping, desolate clouds, and the muck of the furrows, black and tenacious as tar.

Under their dripping harness the horses swung to and fro silently with that marvelous uncomplaining patience which marks the horse. All day the wild geese, honking wildly, as they sprawled sidewise down the wind, seemed to be fleeing from an enemy behind, and with neck outthrust and wings extended, sailed down the wind, soon lost to sight.

Yet the ploughman behind his plough, though the snow lay on his ragged great-coat, and the cold clinging mud rose on his heavy boots, fettering him like gyves, whistled in the very beard of the gale. As day passed, the snow, ceasing to melt, lay along the ploughed land, and lodged in the depth of the stubble, till on each slow round the last furrow stood out black and shining as jet between the ploughed land and the gray stubble.

When night began to fall, and the geese, flying low, began to alight invisibly in the near corn-field, Stephen Council was still at work "finishing a land." He rode on his sulky plough when going with the wind, but walked when facing it. Sitting bent and cold but cheery under his slouch hat, he talked encouragingly to his four-in-hand.

"Come round there, boys! Round agin! We got t' finish this land. Come in there, Dan! Stiddy, Kate, stiddy! None o' y'r tantrums, Kittie. It's purty tuff, but got a be did. Tchk! tchk! Step along, Pete! Don't let Kate git y'r single-tree on the wheel. Once more!" They seemed to know what he meant, and that this was the last round, for they worked with greater vigor than before. "Once more, boys, an' then, sez I, oats an' a nice warm stall, an' sleep f'r all."

By the time the last furrow was turned on the land it was too dark to see the house, and the snow was changing to rain again. The tired and hungry man could see the light from the kitchen shining through the leafless hedge, and he lifted a great shout, "Supper f'r a half a dozen!"

It was nearly eight o'clock by the time he had finished his chores and started for supper. He was picking his way carefully through the mud, when the tall form of a man loomed up before him with a premonitory cough.

"Waddy ye want ?" was the rather startled question of the farmer.

"Well, ye see," began the stranger, in a deprecating tone, "we'd like t' git in f'r the night. We've tried every house f'r the last two miles, but they hadn't any room f'r us. My wife's jest about sick, 'n' the children are cold and hungry—

"Oh, y' want 'o stay all night, eh?"

"Yes, sir; it 'ud be a great accom— "

"Waal, I don't make it a practice t' turn anybuddy way hungry, not on sech nights as this. Drive right in. We ain't got much, but sech as it is—"

But the stranger had disappeared. And soon his steaming, weary team, with drooping heads and swinging single-trees, moved past the well to the block beside the path. Council stood at the side of the "schooner" and helped the children out two little half-sleeping children and then a small woman with a babe in her arms.

"There ye go!" he shouted jovially, to the children. "Now we're all right! Run right along to the house there, an' tell Mam' Council you wants sumpthin' t' eat. Right this way, Mis' keep right off t' the right there. I'll go an' git a lantern. Come," he said to the dazed and silent group at his side.

"Mother'" he shouted, as he neared the fragrant and warmly lighted kitchen, "here are some wayfarers an' folks who need sumpthin' t' eat an' a place t' snoot." He ended by pushing them all in.

Mrs. Council, a large, jolly, rather coarse-looking woman, took the children in her arms. "Come right in, you little rabbits. 'Mos asleep, hey? Now here's a drink o' milk f'r each o' ye. I'll have sam tea in a minute. Take off y'r things and set up t' the fire."

While she set the children to drinking milk, Council got out his lantern and went out to the barn to help the stranger about his team, where his loud, hearty voice could be heard as it came and went between the haymow and the stalls.

The woman came to light as a small, timid, and discouraged looking woman, but still pretty, in a thin and sorrowful way.

"Land sakes! An' you've travelled all the way from Clear Lake' t'-day in this mud! Waal! Waal! No wonder you're all tired out. Don't wait f'r the men, Mis'—" She hesitated, waiting for the name.

"Haskins."

"Mis' Haskins, set right up to the table an' take a good swig o tea whilst I make y' s'm toast. It's green tea, an' it's good. I tell Council as I git older I don't seem to enjoy Young Hyson n'r Gunpowder. I want the reel green tea, jest as it comes off'n the vines. Seems t' have more heart in it, some way. Don't s'pose it has. Council says it's all in m' eye."

Going on in this easy way, she soon had the children filled with bread and milk and the woman thoroughly at home, eating some toast and sweet-melon pickles, and sipping the tea.

"See the little rats!" she laughed at the children. "They're full as they can stick now, and they want to go to bed. Now, don't git up, Mis' Haskins; set right where you are an' let me look after 'em. I know all about young ones, though I'm all alone now. Jane went an' married last fall. But, as I tell Council, it's lucky we keep our health. Set right there, Mis' Haskins; I won't have you stir a finger."

It was an unmeasured pleasure to sit there in the warm, homely kitchen. The jovial chatter of the housewife driving out and holding at bay the growl of the impotent, cheated wind.

The little woman's eyes filled with tears which fell down upon the sleeping baby in her arms. The world was not so desolate and cold and hopeless, after all.

"Now I hope. Council won't stop out there and talk politics all night. He's the greatest man to talk politics an' read the *Tribune*.

—How old is it?"

She broke off and peered down at the face of the babe.

"Two months 'n' five days," said the mother, with a mother's exactness.

"Ye don't say! I want 'o know! The dear little pudzy-wudzy!" she went on, stirring it up in the neighborhood of the ribs with her fat forefinger.

"Pooty tough on 'oo to go gallivant'n' 'cross lots this way—"

"Yes, that's so; a man can't lift a mountain," said Council, entering the door. "Mother, this is Mr. Haskins, from Kansas. He's been eat up 'n' drove out by grasshoppers."

"Glad t' see yeh! Pa, empty that wash-basin 'n' give him a chance t' wash." Haskins was a tall man, with a thin, gloomy face. His hair was a reddish brown, like his coat, and seemed equally faded by the wind and sun, and his sallow face, though hard and set, was pathetic somehow. You would have felt that he had suffered much by the line of his mouth showing under his thin, yellow mustache.

"Hadn't Ike got home yet, Sairy?"

"Hadn't seen 'im."

"W-a-a-l, set right up, Mr. Haskins; wade right into what we've got; 'taint much, but we manage to live on it she gits fat on it," laughed Council, pointing his thumb at his wife.

After supper, while the women put the children to bed, Haskins and Council talked on, seated near the huge cooking-stove, the steam rising from their wet clothing. In the Western fashion Council told as much of his own life as he drew from his guest. He asked but few questions, but by and by the story of Haskins' struggles and defeat came out. The story was a terrible one, but he told it quietly, seated with his elbows on his knees, gazing most of the time at the hearth.

"I didn't like the looks of the country, anyhow," Haskins said, partly rising and glancing at his wife. "I was ust t' northern Ingyannie, where we have lots o' timber 'n' lots o' rain, 'n' I didn't like the looks o' that dry prairie. What galled me the worst was goin' s' far away acrosst so much fine land layin' all through here vacant.

"And the 'hoppers eat ye four years, hand runnin', did they?"

"Eat! They wiped us out. They chawed everything that was green. They jest set around waitin' f'r us to die t' eat us, too. My God! I ust t' dream of 'em sittin' 'round on the bedpost, six feet long, workin' their jaws. They eet the fork-handles. They got worse 'n' worse till they jest rolled on one another, piled up like snow in winter. Well, it ain't no use. If I was t' talk all winter I couldn't tell nawthin'. But all the while I couldn't help thinkin' of all that land back here that nobuddy was usin' that I ought 'o had 'stead o' bein' out there in that cussed country."

"Waal, why didn't ye stop an' settle here ?" asked Ike, who had come in and was eating his supper.

"Fer the simple reason that you fellers wantid ten 'r fifteen dollars an acre fer the bare land, and I hadn't no money fer that kind o' thing."

"Yes, I do my own work," Mrs. Council was heard to say in the pause which followed. "I'm a gettin' purty heavy t' be on m'laigs all day, but we can't afford t' hire, so I keep rackin' around somehow, like a foundered horse. S' lame I tell Council he can t tell how lame I am, f'r I'm jest as lame in one laig as t' other." And the good soul laughed at the joke on herself as she took a handful of flour and dusted the biscuit-board to keep the dough from sticking.

"Well, I hadn't never been very strong," said Mrs. Haskins. "Our folks was Canadians an' small-boned, and then since my last child I hadn't got up again fairly. I don't like t' complain. Tim has about all he can bear now but they was days this week when I jest wanted to lay right down an' die."

"Waal, now, I'll tell ye," said Council, from his side of the stove silencing everybody with his good-natured roar, "I'd go down and see Butler, anyway, if I was you. I guess he'd let you have his place purty cheap; the farm's all run down. He's teen anxious t' let t' somebuddy next year. It 'ud be a good chance fer you. Anyhow, you go to bed and sleep like a babe. I've got some ploughing t' do, anyhow, an' we'll see if somethin' can't be done about your case. Ike, you go out an' see if the horses is all right, an' I'll show the folks t' bed."

When the tired husband and wife were lying under the generous quilts of the spare bed, Haskins listened a moment to the wind in the eaves, and then said, with a slow and solemn tone,

"There are people in this world who are good enough t' be angels, an' only haff t' die to be angels."

Jim Butler was one of those men called in the West "land poor." Early in the history of Rock River he had come into the town and started in the grocery business in a small way, occupying a small building in a mean part of the town. At this period of his life he earned all he got, and was up early and late sorting beans, working over butter, and carting his goods to and from the station. But a change came over him at the end of the second year, when he sold a lot of land for four times what he paid for it. From that time forward he believed in land speculation as the surest way of getting rich. Every cent he could save or spare from his trade he put into land at forced sale, or mortgages on land, which were "just as good as the wheat," he was accustomed to say.

Farm after farm fell into his hands, until he was recognized as one of the leading landowners of the county. His mortgages were scattered all over Cedar County, and as they slowly but surely fell in he sought usually to retain the former owner as tenant.

He was not ready to foreclose; indeed, he had the name of being one of the "easiest" men in the town. He let the debtor off again and again, extending the time whenever possible.

"I don't want y'r land," he said. "All I'm after is the int'rest on my money that's all. Now, if y' want 'o stay on the farm, why, I'll give y' a good chance. I can't have the land layin' vacant." And in many cases the owner remained as tenant.

In the meantime he had sold his store; he couldn't spend time in it—he was mainly occupied now with sitting around town on rainy days smoking and "gassin' with the boys," or in riding to and from his farms. In fishing-time he fished a good deal. Doc Grimes, Ben Ashley, and Cal Cheatham were his cronies on these fishing excursions or hunting trips in the time of chickens or partridges. In winter they went to Northern Wisconsin to shoot deer.

In spite of all these signs of easy life Butler persisted in saying he "hadn't enough money to pay taxes on his land," and was careful to convey the impression that he was poor in spite of his twenty farms. At one time he was said to be worth fifty thousand dollars, but land had been a little slow of sale of late, so that he was not worth so much.

A fine farm, known as the Higley place, had fallen into his hands in the usual way the previous year, and he had not been able to find a tenant for it. Poor Higley, after working himself nearly to death on it in the attempt to lift the mortgage, had gone off to Dakota, leaving the farm and his curse to Butler.

This was the farm which Council advised Haskins to apply for; and the next day Council hitched up his team and drove down to see Butler.

"You jest let me do the talkin','" he said. "We'll find him wearin' out his pants on some salt barrel somew'ers; and if he thought you wanted a place he'd sock it to you hot and heavy. You jest keep quiet, I'll fix 'im."

Butler was seated in Ben Ashley's store telling fish yarns when Council sauntered in casually.

"Hello, But; lyin' agin, hey?"

"Hello, Steve! How goes it?"

"Oh, so-so. Too clang much rain these days. I thought it was goin' t freeze up f'r good last night. Tight squeak if I get m' ploughin' done. How's farmin' with you these days?"

"Bad. Ploughin' ain't half done."

"It 'ud be a religious idee f'r you t' go out an' take a hand y'rself."

"I don't haff to," said Butler, with a wink.

"Got anybody on the Higley place?"

"No. Know of anybody?"

"Waal, no; not eggsackly. I've got a relation back t' Michigan who's ben hot an' cold on the idea o' comin' West f'r some time. Might come if he could get a good lay-out. What do you talk on the farm?"

"Well, I d' know. I'll rent it on shares or I'll rent it money rent."

"Waal, how much money, say?"

"Well, say ten per cent, on the price two-fifty."

"Wall, that ain't bad. Wait on 'im till 'e thrashes?"

Haskins listened eagerly to this important question, but Council was coolly eating a dried apple which he had speared out of a barrel with his knife. Butler studied him carefully.

"Well, knocks me out of twenty-five dollars interest."

"My relation'll need all he's got t' git his crops in," said Council, in the same, indifferent way.

"Well, all right; say wait," concluded Butler.

"All right; this is the man. Haskins, this is Mr. Butler no relation to Ben the hardest-working man in Cedar County."

On the way home Haskins said: "I ain't much better off. I'd like that farm; it's a good farm, but it's all run down, an' so 'm I. I could make a good farm of it if I had half a show. But I can't stock it n'r seed it."

"Waal, now, don't you worry," roared Council in his ear. "We'll pull y' through somehow till next harvest. He's agreed t' hire it ploughed, an' you can earn a hundred dollars ploughin' an' y' c'n git the seed o' me, an' pay me back when y' can."

Haskins was silent with emotion, but at last he said, "I ain't got nothin' t' live on."

"Now, don't you worry 'bout that. You jest make your headquarters at ol' Steve Council's. Mother'll take a pile o' comfort in havin' y'r wife an' children 'round.

Y' see, Jane's married off lately, an' Ike's away a good 'eal, so we'll be darn glad t' have y' stop with us this winter. Nex' spring we'll see if y' can't git a start agin." And he chirruped to the team, which sprang forward with the rumbling, clattering wagon. "Say, looky here, Council, you can't do this. I never saw," shouted Haskins in his neighbor's ear.

Council moved about uneasily in his seat and stopped his stammering gratitude by saying: "Hold on, now; don't make such a fuss over a little thing. When I see a man down, an' things all on top of 'm, I jest like t' kick 'em off an' help 'm up. That's the kind of religion I got, an' it's about the only kind."

They rode the rest of the way home in silence. And when the red light of the lamp shone out into the darkness of the cold and windy night, and he thought of this refuge for his children and wife, Haskins could have put his arm around the neck of his burly companion and squeezed him like a lover. But he contented himself with saying, "Steve Council, you'll git y'r pay f'r this some day."

"Don't want any pay. My religion ain't run on such business principles."

The wind was growing colder, and the ground was covered with a white frost, as they turned into the gate of the Council farm, and the children came rushing out, shouting, "Papa's come!"

They hardly looked like the same children who had sat at the table the night before. Their torpidity, under the influence of sunshine and Mother Council, had given way to a sort of spasmodic cheerfulness, as insects in winter revive when laid on the hearth.

Haskins worked like a fiend, and his wife, like the heroic woman that she was, bore also uncomplainingly the most terrible burdens. They rose early and toiled without intermission till the darkness fell on the plain, then tumbled into bed, every bone and muscle aching with fatigue, to rise with the sun next morning to the same round of the same ferocity of labor.

The eldest boy drove a team all through the spring, ploughing and seeding, milked the cows, and did chores innumerable, in most ways taking the place of a man.

An infinitely pathetic but common figure this boy on the American farm, where there is no law against child labor. To see him in his coarse clothing, his huge boots, and his ragged cap, as he staggered with a pail of water from the well, or trudged in the cold and cheerless dawn out into the frosty field behind his team, gave the city-bred visitor a sharp pang of sympathetic pain. Yet Haskins loved his boy, and would have saved him from this if he could, but he could not.

By June the first year the result of such Herculean toil began to show on the farm. The yard was cleaned up and sown to grass, the garden ploughed and planted, and the house mended.

Council had given them four of his cows.

"Take 'em an' run 'em on shares. I don't want 'o milk s' many. Ike's away s' much now, Sat'd'ys an' Sund'ys, I can't stand the bother anyhow."

Other men, seeing the confidence of Council in the newcomer, had sold him tools on time; and as he was really an able farmer, he soon had round him many evidences of his care and thrift. At the advice of Council he had taken the farm for three years, with the privilege of re-renting or buying at the end of the term.

"It's a good bargain, an' y' want 'o nail it," said Council. "If you have any kind ov a crop, you c'n pay y'r debts, an' keep seed an' bread."

The new hope which now sprang up in the heart of Haskins and his wife grew almost as a pain by the time the wide field of wheat began to wave and rustle and swirl in the winds of July. Day after day he would snatch a few moments after supper to go and look at it.

"'Have ye seen the wheat t'-day, Nettie?" he asked one night as he rose from supper.

"No, Tim, I ain't had time."

"Well, take time now. Le's go look at it."

She threw an old hat on her head Tommy's hat and looking almost pretty in her thin, sad way, went out with her husband to the hedge.

"Ain't it grand, Nettie ? Just look at it."

It was grand. Level, russet here and there, heavy-headed, wide as a lake, and full of multitudinous whispers and gleams of wealth, it stretched away before the gazers like the fabled field of the cloth of gold.

"Oh, I think I hope we'll have a good crop, Tim; and oh, how good the people have been to us!"

"Yes; I don't know where we'd be t'-day if it hadn't been f'r Council and his wife."

"They're the best people in the world," said the little woman, with a great sob of gratitude.

"We'll be in the field on Monday sure," said Haskins, gripping the rail on the fences as if already at the work of the harvest.

The harvest came, bounteous, glorious, but the winds came and blew it into tangles, and the rain matted it here and there close to the ground, increasing the work of gathering it threefold.

Oh, how they toiled in those glorious days! Clothing dripping with sweat, arms aching, filled with briers, fingers raw and bleeding, backs broken with the weight of heavy bundles, Haskins and his man toiled on. Timmy drove the harvester, while his father and a hired man bound on the machine. In this way they cut ten acres every day, and almost every night after supper, when the hand went to bed, Haskins returned to the field shocking the bound grain in the light of the moon. Many a night he worked till his anxious wife came out at ten o'clock to call him in to rest and lunch. At the same time she cooked for the men, took care of the children, washed and ironed, milked the cows at night, made the butter, and sometimes fed the horses and watered them while her husband kept at the shocking.

No slave in the Roman galleys could have toiled so frightfully and lived, for this man thought himself a free man, and that he was working for his wife and babes.

When he sank into his bed with a deep groan of relief, too tired to change his grimy, dripping clothing, he felt that he was getting nearer and nearer to a home of his own, and pushing the wolf of want a little farther from his door.

There is no despair so deep as the despair of a homeless man or woman. To roam the roads of the country or the streets of the city, to feel there is no rood of ground on which the feet can rest, to halt weary and hungry outside lighted windows and hear laughter and song within, these are the hungers and rebellions that drive men to crime and women to shame.

It was the memory of this homelessness, and the fear of its coming again, that spurred Timothy Haskins and Nettie, his wife, to such ferocious labor during that first year.

"'M, yes; 'm, yes; first-rate," said Butler, as his eye took in the neat garden, the pig-pen, and the well-filled barnyard. "You're gitt'n' quite a stock around yeh. Done well, eh?" Haskins was showing Butler around the place. He had not seen it for a year, having spent the year in Washington and Boston with Ashley, his brother-in-law, who had been elected to Congress.

"Yes, I've laid out a good deal of money durin' the last three years. I've paid out three hundred dollars f'r fencin'."

"Um h'm! I see, I see," said Butler, while Haskins went on:

"The kitchen there cost two hundred; the barn ain't cost much in money, but I've put a lot o' time on it. I've dug a new well, and I— "

"Yes, yes, I see. You've done well. Stock worth a thousand dollars," said Butler, picking his teeth with a straw.

"About that," said Haskins, modestly. "We begin to feel's if we was gitt'n' a home f'r ourselves; but we've worked hard. I tell you we begin to feel it, Mr. Butler, and we're goin' t' begin to ease up purty soon. We've been kind o' plannin' a trip back t' her folks after the fall ploughin's done."

"Eggs-actly!" said Butler, who was evidently thinking of something else. "I suppose you've kind o' calc'lated on stayin' here three years more?"

"Well, yes. Fact is, I think I c'n buy the farm this fall, if you'll give me a reasonable show."

"Um m! What do you call a reasonable show?"

"Well, say a quarter down and three years' time."

Butler looked at the huge stacks of wheat, which filled the yard, over which the chickens were fluttering and crawling, catching grasshoppers, and out of which the crickets were singing innumerably. He smiled in a peculiar way as he said, "Oh, I won't be hard on yeh. But what did you expect to pay f'r the place?"

"Why, about what you offered it for before, two thousand five hundred, or possibly three thousand dollars," he added quickly, as he saw the owner shake his head.

"This farm is worth five thousand and five hundred dollars," said Butler, in a careless and decided voice.

"What!" almost shrieked the astounded Haskins. "What's that? Five thousand? Why, that's double what you offered it for three years ago."

"Of course, and it's worth it. It was all run down then—now it's in good shape. You've laid out fifteen hundred dollars in improvements, according to your own story."

"But you had nothin' t' do about that. It's my work an' my money. "

"You bet it was; but it's my land."

"But what's to pay me for all my— "

"Ain't you had the use of 'em?" replied Butler, smiling calmly into his face.

Haskins was like a man struck on the head with a sandbag; he couldn't think; he stammered as he tried to say: "But I never'd git the use. You'd rob me! More'n that: you agreed you promised that I could buy or rent at the end of three years at—"

"That's all right. But I didn't say I'd let you carry off the improvements, nor that I'd go on renting the farm at two-fifty. The land is doubled in value, it don't matter how; it don't enter into the question; an' now you can pay me five hundred dollars a year rent, or take it on your own terms at fifty-five hundred, or git out."

He was turning away when Haskins, the sweat pouring from his face, fronted him, saying again:

"But you've done nothing to make it so. You hadn't added a cent. I put it all there myself, expectin' to buy. I worked an' sweat to improve it. I was workin' for myself an' babes— "

"Well, why didn't you buy when I offered to sell? What y' kickin' about?"

"I'm kickin' about payin' you twice f'r my own things, my own fences, my own kitchen, my own garden."

Butler laughed. "You're too green t' eat, young feller. Your improvements! The law will sing another tune."

"But I trusted your word."

"Never trust anybody, my friend. Besides, I didn't promise not to do this thing. Why, man, don't look at me like that. Don't take me for a thief. It's the law. The reg'lar thing. Everybody does it."

"I don't care if they do. It's stealin' jest the same. You take three thousand dollars of my money the work o' my hands and my wife's." He broke down at this point. He was not a strong man mentally. He could face hardship, ceaseless toil, but he could not face the cold and sneering face of Butler.

"But I don't take it," said Butler, coolly "All you've got to do is to go on jest as you've been a-coin', or give me a thousand dollars down, and a mortgage at ten per cent on the rest."

Haskins sat down blindly on a bundle of oats near by, and with staring eyes and drooping head went over the situation. He was under the lion's paw. He felt a horrible numbness in his heart and limbs. He was hid in a mist, and there was no path out.

Butler walked about, looking at the huge stacks of grain, and pulling now and again a few handfuls out, shelling the heads in his hands and blowing the chaff away. He hummed a little tune as he did so. He had an accommodating air of waiting.

Haskins was in the midst of the terrible toil of the last year. He was walking again in the rain and the mud behind his plough—he felt the dust and dirt of the threshing. The ferocious husking- time, with its cutting wind and biting, clinging snows, lay hard upon him. Then he thought of his wife, how she had cheerfully cooked and baked, without holiday and without rest.

"Well, what do you think of it?" inquired the cool, mocking, insinuating voice of Butler.

"I think you're a thief and a liar!" shouted Haskins, leaping up. "A black-hearted houn'!" Butler's smile maddened him; with a sudden leap he caught a fork in his hands, and whirled it in the air. "You'll never rob another man, damn ye!" he grated through his teeth, a look of pitiless ferocity in his accusing eyes.

Butler shrank and quivered, expecting the blow; stood, held hypnotized by the eyes of the man he had a moment before despised a man transformed into an avenging demon. But in the deadly hush between the lift of the weapon and its fall there came a gush of faint, childish laughter and then across the range of his vision, far away and dim, he saw the sun-bright head of his baby girl, as, with the pretty, tottering run of a two-year-old, she moved across the grass of the dooryard. His hands relaxed: the fork fell to the ground; his head lowered.

"Make out y'r deed an' mor'gage, an' git off'n my land, an' don't ye never cross my line agin; if y' do, I'll kill ye."

Butler backed away from the man in wild haste, and climbing into his buggy with trembling limbs drove off down the road, leaving Haskins seated dumbly on the sunny pile of sheaves, his head sunk into his hands.

EXPLORE: What is the significance of the short story's title and who or what is the "lion"? Is it an appropriate title for a story about farming? Why or why not?

COLLABORATE: In small groups create a list of 3–5 ways that Hamlin's 1891 story anticipates the issues addressed in Roosevelt's Country Life Commission Report. Find passages in Hamlin's story that are related to the concerns expressed little more than a decade later by the CLC. Do you think that the recommendations from the CLC might have been able to prevent the problems at the end of the story? Discuss.

Mary E. Wilkins, "The Revolt of 'Mother'"

From *A New England Nun and Other Stories* (Harper & Brothers Publishers; New York: 1891)

"Father!"

"What is it?"

"What are them men diggin' over there in the field for?"

There was a sudden dropping and enlarging of the lower part of the old man's face, as if some heavy weight had settled therein; he shut his mouth tight, and went on harnessing the great bay mare. He hustled the collar on to her neck with a jerk.

"Father!"

The old man slapped the saddle upon the mare's back.

"Look here, father, I want to know what them men are diggin' over in the field for, an' I'm goin' to know."

"I wish you'd go into the house, mother, an' 'tend to your own affairs," the old man said then. He ran his words together, and his speech was almost as inarticulate as a growl.

But the woman understood; it was her most native tongue. "I ain't goin' into the house till you tell me what them men are doin' over there in the field," said she.

Then she stood waiting. She was a small woman, short and straight-waisted like a child in her brown cotton gown. Her forehead was mild and benevolent between the smooth curves of gray hair; there were meek downward lines about her nose and mouth; but her eyes, fixed upon the old man, looked as if the meekness had been the result of her own will, never of the will of another.

They were in the barn, standing before the wide open doors. The spring air, full of the smell of growing grass and unseen blossoms, came in their faces. The deep yard in front was littered with farm wagons and piles of wood; on the edges, close to the fence and the house, the grass was a vivid green, and there were some dandelions.

The old man glanced doggedly at his wife as he tightened the last buckles on the harness. She looked as immovable to him as one of the rocks in his pasture-land, bound to the earth with generations of blackberry vines. He slapped the reins over the horse, and started forth from the barn.

"*Father!*" said she.

The old man pulled up. "What is it?"

"I want to know what them men are diggin' over there in that field for."

"They're diggin' a cellar, I s'pose, if you've got to know."

"A cellar for what?"

"A barn."

"A barn? You ain't goin' to build a barn over there where we was goin' to have a house, father?"

The old man said not another word. He hurried the horse into the farm wagon, and clattered out of the yard, jouncing as sturdily on his seat as a boy.

The woman stood a moment looking after him, then she went out of the barn across a corner of the yard to the house. The house, standing at right angles with the great barn and a long reach of sheds and out-buildings, was infinitesimal compared with them. It was scarcely as commodious for people as the little boxes under the barn eaves were for doves.

A pretty girl's face, pink and delicate as a flower, was looking out of one of the house windows. She was watching three men who were digging over in the field which bounded the yard near the road line. She turned quietly when the woman entered.

"What are they diggin' for, mother?" said she. "Did he tell you?"

"They're diggin' for—a cellar for a new barn."

"Oh, mother, he ain't goin' to build another barn?"

"That's what he says."

A boy stood before the kitchen glass combing his hair. He combed slowly and painstakingly, arranging his brown hair in a smooth hillock over his forehead. He did not seem to pay any attention to the conversation.

"Sammy, did you know father was goin' to build a new barn?" asked the girl.

The boy combed assiduously.

"Sammy!"

He turned, and showed a face like his father's under his smooth crest of hair. "Yes, I s'pose I did," he said, reluctantly.

"How long have you known it?" asked his mother.

"'Bout three months, I guess."

"Why didn't you tell of it?"

"Didn't think 'twould do no good."

"I don't see what father wants another barn for," said the girl, in her sweet, slow voice. She turned again to the window, and stared out at the digging men in the field. Her tender, sweet face was full of a gentle distress. Her forehead was as bald and innocent as a baby's, with the light hair strained back from it in a row of curl-papers. She was quite large, but her soft curves did not look as if they covered muscles.

Her mother looked sternly at the boy. "Is he goin' to buy more cows?" said she.

The boy did not reply; he was tying his shoes.

"Sammy, I want you to tell me if he's goin' to buy more cows."

"I s'pose he is."

"How many?"

"Four, I guess."

His mother said nothing more. She went into the pantry, and there was a clatter of dishes. The boy got his cap from a nail behind the door, took an old arithmetic from the shelf, and started for school. He was lightly built, but clumsy. He went out of the yard with a curious spring in the hips, that made his loose home-made jacket tilt up in the rear.

The girl went to the sink, and began to wash the dishes that were piled up there. Her mother came promptly out of the pantry, and shoved her aside. "You wipe 'em," said she; "I'll wash. There's a good many this mornin'."

The mother plunged her hands vigorously into the water, the girl wiped the plates slowly and dreamily. "Mother," said she, "don't you think it's too bad father's goin' to build that new barn, much as we need a decent house to live in?"

Her mother scrubbed a dish fiercely. "You ain't found out yet we're women-folks, Nanny Penn," said she. "You ain't seen enough of men-folks yet to. One of these days you'll find it out, an' then you'll know that we know only what men-folks think we do, so far as any use of it goes, an' how we'd ought to reckon men-folks in with Providence, an' not complain of what they do any more than we do of the weather."

"I don't care; I don't believe George is anything like that, anyhow," said Nanny. Her delicate face flushed pink, her lips pouted softly, as if she were going to cry.

"You wait an' see. I guess George Eastman ain't no better than other men. You hadn't ought to judge father, though. He can't help it, 'cause he don't look at things jest the way we do. An' we've been pretty comfortable here, after all. The roof don't leak — ain't never but once — that's one thing. Father's kept it shingled right up."

"I do wish we had a parlor."

"I guess it won't hurt George Eastman any to come to see you in a nice clean kitchen. I guess a good many girls don't have as good a place as this. Nobody's ever heard me complain."

"I ain't complained either, mother."

"Well, I don't think you'd better, a good father an' a good home as you've got. S'pose your father made you go out an' work for your livin'? Lots of girls have to that ain't no stronger an' better able to than you be."

Sarah Penn washed the frying-pan with a conclusive air. She scrubbed the outside of it as faithfully as the inside. She was a masterly keeper of her box of a house. Her one living-room never seemed to have in it any of the dust which the friction of life with inanimate matter produces. She swept, and there seemed to be no dirt to go before the broom; she cleaned, and one could see no difference. She was like an artist so perfect that he has apparently no art. To-day she got out a mixing bowl and a board, and rolled some pies, and there was no more flour upon her than upon her daughter who was doing finer work. Nanny was to be married in the fall, and she was sewing on some white cambric and embroidery. She sewed industriously while her mother cooked, her soft milk-white hands and wrists showed whiter than her delicate work.

"We must have the stove moved out in the shed before long," said Mrs. Penn. "Talk about not havin' things, it's been a real blessin' to be able to put a stove up in that shed in hot weather. Father did one good thing when he fixed that stove-pipe out there."

Sarah Penn's face as she rolled her pies had that expression of meek vigor which might have characterized one of the New Testament saints. She was making mince-pies. Her husband, Adoniram Penn, liked them better than any other kind. She baked twice a week. Adoniram often liked a piece of pie between meals. She hurried this morning. It had been later than usual when she began, and she wanted to have a pie baked for dinner. However deep a resentment she might be forced to hold against her husband, she would never fail in sedulous attention to his wants.

Nobility of character manifests itself at loop-holes when it is not provided with large doors. Sarah Penn's showed itself to-day in flaky dishes of pastry. So she made the pies faithfully, while across the table she could see, when she glanced up from her work, the sight that rankled in her patient and steadfast soul—the digging of the cellar of the new barn in the place where Adoniram forty years ago had promised her their new house should stand.

The pies were done for dinner. Adoniram and Sammy were home a few minutes after twelve o'clock. The dinner was eaten with serious haste. There was never much conversation at the table in the Penn family. Adoniram asked a blessing, and they ate promptly, then rose up and went about their work.

Sammy went back to school, taking soft sly lopes out of the yard like a rabbit. He wanted a game of marbles before school, and feared his father would give him some chores to do. Adoniram hastened to the door and called after him, but he was out of sight.

"I don't see what you let him go for, mother," said he. "I wanted him to help me unload that wood."

Adoniram went to work out in the yard unloading wood from the wagon. Sarah put away the dinner dishes, while Nanny took down her curl-papers and changed her dress. She was going down to the store to buy some more embroidery and thread.

When Nanny was gone, Mrs. Penn went to the door. "Father!" she called.

"Well, what is it!"

"I want to see you jest a minute, father."

"I can't leave this wood nohow. I've got to git it unloaded an' go for a load of gravel afore two o'clock. Sammy had ought to helped me. You hadn't ought to let him go to school so early."

"I want to see you jest a minute."

"I tell ye I can't, nohow, mother."

"Father, you come here." Sarah Penn stood in the door like a queen; she held her head as if it bore a crown; there was that patience which makes authority royal in her voice. Adoniram went.

Mrs. Penn led the way into the kitchen, and pointed to a chair. "Sit down, father," said she; "I've got somethin' I want to say to you."

He sat down heavily; his face was quite stolid, but he looked at her with restive eyes. "Well, what is it, mother?"

"I want to know what you're buildin' that new barn for, father?"

"I ain't got nothin' to say about it."

"It can't be you think you need another barn?"

"I tell ye I ain't got nothin' to say about it, mother; an' I ain't goin' to say nothin'."

"Be you goin' to buy more cows?"

Adoniram did not reply; he shut his mouth tight.

"I know you be, as well as I want to. Now, father, look here"—Sarah Penn had not sat down; she stood before her husband in the humble fashion of a Scripture woman—"I'm goin' to talk real plain to you; I never have sence I married you, but I'm goin' to now. I ain't never complained, an' I ain't goin' to complain now, but I'm goin' to talk plain. You see this room here, father; you look at it well. You see there ain't no carpet on the floor, an' you see the paper is all dirty, an' droppin' off the walls. We ain't had no new paper on it for ten year, an' then I put it on myself, an' it didn't cost but ninepence a roll. You see this room, father; it's all the one I've had to work in an' eat in an' sit in sence we was married. There ain't another woman in the whole town whose husband ain't got half the means you have but what's got better. It's all the room Nanny's got to have her company in; an' there ain't one of her mates but what's got better, an' their fathers not so able as hers is. It's all the room she'll have to be married in. What would you have thought, father, if we had had our weddin' in a room no better than this? I was married in my mother's parlor, with a carpet on the floor, an' stuffed furniture, an' a mahogany card-table. An' this is all the room my daughter will have to be married in. Look here, father!"

Sarah Penn went across the room as though it were a tragic stage. She flung open a door and disclosed a tiny bedroom, only large enough for a bed and bureau, with a path between. "There, father," said she—"there's all the room I've had to sleep in forty year. All my children were born there—the two that died, an' the two that's livin'. I was sick with a fever there."

She stepped to another door and opened it. It led into the small, ill-lighted pantry. "Here," said she, "is all the buttery I've got—every place I've got for my dishes, to set away my victuals in, an' to keep my milk-pans in. Father, I've been takin' care of the milk of six cows in this place, an' now you're goin' to build a new barn, an' keep more cows, an' give me more to do in it."

She threw open another door. A narrow crooked flight of stairs wound upward from it. "There, father," said she, "I want you to look at the stairs that go up to them two unfinished chambers that are all the places our son an' daughter have had to sleep in all their lives. There ain't a prettier girl in town nor a more ladylike one than Nanny, an' that's the place she has to sleep in. It ain't so good as your horse's stall; it ain't so warm an' tight."

Sarah Penn went back and stood before her husband. "Now, father," said she, "I want to know if you think you're doin' right an' accordin' to what you profess. Here, when we was married, forty year ago, you promised me faithful that we should have a new house built in that lot over in the field before the year was out. You said you had money enough, an' you wouldn't ask me to live in no such place as this. It is forty year now, an' you've been makin' more money, an' I've been savin' of it for you ever since, an' you ain't built no house yet. You've built sheds an' cow-houses an' one new barn, an' now you're goin' to build another. Father, I want to know if you think it's right. You're lodgin' your dumb beasts better than you are your own flesh an' blood. I want to know if you think it's right."

"I ain't got nothin' to say."

"You can't say nothin' without ownin' it ain't right, father. An' there's another thing—I ain't complained; I've got along forty year, an' I s'pose I should forty more, if it wa'n't for that—if we don't have another house. Nanny she can't live with us after she's married. She'll have to go somewheres else to live away from us, an' it don't seem as if I could have it so, noways, father. She wa'n't ever strong. She's got considerable color, but there wa'n't never any backbone to her. I've always took the heft of everything off her, an' she ain't fit to keep house an' do everything herself. She'll be all worn out inside of a year. Think of her doin' all the washin' an' ironin' an' bakin' with them soft white hands an' arms, an' sweepin'! I can't have it so, noways, father."

Mrs. Penn's face was burning; her mild eyes gleamed. She had pleaded her little cause like a Webster; she had ranged from severity to pathos; but her opponent employed that obstinate silence which makes eloquence futile with mocking echoes. Adoniram arose clumsily.

"Father, ain't you got nothin' to say?" said Mrs. Penn.

"I've got to go off after that load of gravel. I can't stan' here talkin' all day."

"Father, won't you think it over, an' have a house built there instead of a barn?"

"I ain't got nothin' to say."

Adoniram shuffled out. Mrs. Penn went into her bedroom. When she came out, her eyes were red. She had a roll of unbleached cotton cloth. She spread it out on the kitchen table, and began cutting out some shirts for her husband. The men over in the field had a team to help them this afternoon; she could hear their halloos. She had a scanty pattern for the shirts; she had to plan and piece the sleeves.

Nanny came home with her embroidery, and sat down with her needlework. She had taken down her curl-papers, and there was a soft roll of fair hair like an aureole over her forehead; her face was as delicately fine and clear as porcelain. Suddenly she looked up, and the tender red flamed all over her face and neck. "Mother," said she.

"What say?"

"I've been thinking—I don't see how we're goin' to have any—wedding in this room. I'd be ashamed to have his folks come if we didn't have anybody else."

"Mebbe we can have some new paper before then; I can put it on. I guess you won't have no call to be ashamed of your belongin's."

"We might have the wedding in the new barn," said Nanny, with gentle pettishness. "Why, mother, what makes you look so?"

Mrs. Penn had started, and was staring at her with a curious expression. She turned again to her work, and spread out a pattern carefully on the cloth. "Nothin'," said she.

Presently Adoniram clattered out of the yard in his two-wheeled dump cart, standing as proudly upright as a Roman charioteer. Mrs. Penn opened the door and stood there a minute looking out; the halloos of the men sounded louder.

It seemed to her all through the spring months that she heard nothing but the halloos and the noises of saws and hammers. The new barn grew fast. It was a fine edifice for this little village. Men came on pleasant Sundays, in their meeting suits and clean shirt bosoms, and stood around it admiringly. Mrs. Penn did not speak of it, and Adoniram did not mention it to her, although sometimes, upon a return from inspecting it, he bore himself with injured dignity.

"It's a strange thing how your mother feels about the new barn," he said, confidentially, to Sammy one day.

Sammy only grunted after an odd fashion for a boy; he had learned it from his father.

The barn was all completed ready for use by the third week in July. Adoniram had planned to move his stock in on Wednesday; on Tuesday he received a letter which changed his plans. He came in with it early in the morning. "Sammy's been to the post-office," said he, "an' I've got a letter from Hiram." Hiram was Mrs. Penn's brother, who lived in Vermont.

"Well," said Mrs. Penn, "what does he say about the folks?"

"I guess they're all right. He says he thinks if I come up country right off there's a chance to buy jest the kind of a horse I want." He stared reflectively out of the window at the new barn.

Mrs. Penn was making pies. She went on clapping the rolling-pin into the crust, although she was very pale, and her heart beat loudly.

"I dun' know but what I'd better go," said Adoniram. "I hate to go off jest now, right in the midst of hayin', but the ten-acre lot's cut, an' I guess Rufus an' the others can git along without me three or four days. I can't get a horse round here to suit me, nohow, an' I've got to have another for all that wood-haulin' in the fall. I told Hiram to watch out, an' if he got wind of a good horse to let me know. I guess I'd better go."

"I'll get out your clean shirt an' collar," said Mrs. Penn calmly.

She laid out Adoniram's Sunday suit and his clean clothes on the bed in the little bedroom. She got his shaving-water and razor ready. At last she buttoned on his collar and fastened his black cravat.

Adoniram never wore his collar and cravat except on extra occasions. He held his head high, with a rasped dignity. When he was all ready, with his coat and hat brushed, and a lunch of pie and cheese in a paper bag, he hesitated on the threshold of the door. He looked at his wife, and his manner was defiantly apologetic. "*If* them cows come to-day, Sammy can drive 'em into the new barn," said he; "an' when they bring the hay up, they can pitch it in there."

"Well," replied Mrs. Penn.

Adoniram set his shaven face ahead and started. When he had cleared the door-step, he turned and looked back with a kind of nervous solemnity. "I shall be back by Saturday if nothin' happens," said he.

"Do be careful, father," returned his wife.

She stood in the door with Nanny at her elbow and watched him out of sight. Her eyes had a strange, doubtful expression in them; her peaceful forehead was contracted. She went in, and about her baking again. Nanny sat sewing. Her wedding-day was drawing nearer, and she was getting pale and thin with her steady sewing. Her mother kept glancing at her.

"Have you got that pain in your side this mornin'?" she asked.

"A little."

Mrs. Penn's face, as she worked, changed, her perplexed forehead smoothed, her eyes were steady, her lips firmly set. She formed a maxim for herself, although incoherently with her unlettered thoughts. "Unsolicited opportunities are the guide-posts of the Lord to the new roads of life," she repeated in effect, and she made up her mind to her course of action.

"S'posin' I *had* wrote to Hiram," she muttered once, when she was in the pantry—"s'posin' I had wrote, an' asked him if he knew of any horse? But I didn't, an' father's goin' wa'n't none of my doin'. It looks like a providence." Her voice rang out quite loud at the last.

"What you talkin' about, mother?" called Nanny.

"Nothin'."

Mrs. Penn hurried her baking; at eleven o'clock it was all done. The load of hay from the west field came slowly down the cart track, and drew up at the new barn. Mrs. Penn ran out. "Stop!" she screamed—"stop!"

The men stopped and looked; Sammy upreared from the top of the load, and stared at his mother.

"Stop!" she cried out again. "Don't you put the hay in that barn; put it in the old one."

"Why, he said to put it in here," returned one of the haymakers, wonderingly. He was a young man, a neighbor's son, whom Adoniram hired by the year to help on the farm.

"Don't you put the hay in the new barn; there's room enough in the old one, ain't there?" said Mrs. Penn.

"Room enough," returned the hired man, in his thick, rustic tones. "Didn't need the new barn, nohow, far as room's concerned. Well, I s'pose he changed his mind." He took hold of the horses' bridles.

Mrs. Penn went back to the house. Soon the kitchen windows were darkened, and a fragrance like warm honey came into the room.

Nanny laid down her work. "I thought father wanted them to put the hay into the new barn?" she said, wonderingly.

"It's all right," replied her mother.

Sammy slid down from the load of hay, and came in to see if dinner was ready.

"I ain't goin' to get a regular dinner to-day, as long as father's gone," said his mother. "I've let the fire go out. You can have some bread an' milk an' pie. I thought we could get along." She set out some bowls of milk, some bread, and a pie on the kitchen table. "You'd better eat your dinner now," said she. "You might jest as well get through with it. I want you to help me afterward."

Nanny and Sammy stared at each other. There was something strange in their mother's manner. Mrs. Penn did not eat anything herself. She went into the pantry, and they heard her moving dishes while they ate. Presently she came out with a pile of plates. She got the clothes-basket out of the shed, and packed them in it. Nanny and Sammy watched. She brought out cups and saucers, and put them in with the plates.

"What you goin' to do, mother?" inquired Nanny, in a timid voice. A sense of something unusual made her tremble, as if it were a ghost. Sammy rolled his eyes over his pie.

"You'll see what I'm goin' to do," replied Mrs. Penn. "If you're through, Nanny, I want you to go up-stairs an' pack up your things; an' I want you, Sammy, to help me take down the bed in the bedroom."

"Oh, mother, what for?" gasped Nanny.

"You'll see."

During the next few hours a feat was performed by this simple, pious New England mother which was equal in its way to Wolfe's storming of the Heights of Abraham. It took no more genius and audacity of bravery for Wolfe to cheer his wondering soldiers up those steep precipices, under the sleeping eyes of the enemy, than for Sarah Penn, at the head of her children, to move all their little household goods into the new barn while her husband was away.

Nanny and Sammy followed their mother's instructions without a murmur; indeed, they were overawed. There is a certain uncanny and superhuman quality about all such purely original undertakings as their mother's was to them. Nanny went back and forth with her light loads, and Sammy tugged with sober energy.

At five o'clock in the afternoon the little house in which the Penns had lived for forty years had emptied itself into the new barn.

Every builder builds somewhat for unknown purposes, and is in a measure a prophet. The architect of Adoniram Penn's barn, while he designed it for the comfort of four-footed animals, had planned better than he knew for the comfort of humans. Sarah Penn saw at a glance its possibilities. Those great box-stalls, with quilts hung before them, would make better bedrooms than the one she had occupied for forty years, and there was a tight carriage-room. The harness-room, with its chimney and shelves, would make a kitchen of her dreams. The great middle space would make a parlor, by-and-by, fit for a palace. Up stairs there was as much room as down. With partitions and windows, what a house would there be! Sarah looked at the row of stanchions before the allotted space for cows, and reflected that she would have her front entry there.

At six o'clock the stove was up in the harness-room, the kettle was boiling, and the table set for tea. It looked almost as home-like as the abandoned house across the yard had ever done. The young hired man milked, and Sarah directed him calmly to bring the milk to the new barn. He came gaping, dropping little blots of foam from the brimming pails on the grass. Before the next morning he had spread the story of Adoniram Penn's wife moving into the new barn all over the little village. Men assembled in the store and talked it over, women with shawls over their heads scuttled into each other's houses before their work was done. Any deviation from the ordinary course of life in this quiet town was enough to stop all progress in it. Everybody paused to look at the staid, independent figure on the side track. There was a difference of opinion with regard to her. Some held her to be insane; some, of a lawless and rebellious spirit.

Friday the minister went to see her. It was in the forenoon, and she was at the barn door shelling peas for dinner. She looked up and returned his salutation with dignity, then she went on with her work. She did not invite him in. The saintly expression of her face remained fixed, but there was an angry flush over it.

The minister stood awkwardly before her, and talked. She handled the peas as if they were bullets. At last she looked up, and her eyes showed the spirit that her meek front had covered for a lifetime.

"There ain't no use talkin', Mr. Hersey," said she. "I've thought it all over an' over, an' I believe I'm doin' what's right. I've made it the subject of prayer, an' it's betwixt me an' the Lord an' Adoniram. There ain't no call for nobody else to worry about it."

"Well, of course, if you have brought it to the Lord in prayer, and feel satisfied that you are doing right, Mrs. Penn," said the minister, helplessly. His thin gray-bearded face was pathetic. He was a sickly man; his youthful confidence had cooled; he had to scourge himself up to some of his pastoral duties as relentlessly as a Catholic ascetic, and then he was prostrated by the smart.

"I think it's right jest as much as I think it was right for our forefathers to come over from the old country 'cause they didn't have what belonged to 'em," said Mrs. Penn. She arose. The barn threshold might have been Plymouth Rock from her bearing. "I don't doubt you mean well, Mr. Hersey," said she, "but there are things people hadn't ought to interfere with. I've been a member of the church for over forty year. I've got my own mind an' my own feet, an' I'm goin' to think my own thoughts an' go my own ways, an' nobody but the Lord is goin' to dictate to me unless I've a mind to have him. Won't you come in an' set down? How is Mis' Hersey?"

"She is well, I thank you," replied the minister. He added some more perplexed apologetic remarks; then he retreated.

He could expound the intricacies of every character study in the Scriptures, he was competent to grasp the Pilgrim Fathers and all historical innovators, but Sarah Penn was beyond him. He could deal with primal cases, but parallel ones worsted him. But, after all, although it was aside from his province, he wondered more how Adoniram Penn would deal with his wife than how the Lord would. Everybody shared the wonder. When Adoniram's four new cows arrived, Sarah ordered three to be put in the old barn, the other in the house shed where the cooking-stove had stood. That added to the excitement. It was whispered that all four cows were domiciled in the house.

Toward sunset on Saturday, when Adoniram was expected home, there was a knot of men in the road near the new barn. The hired man had milked, but he still hung around the premises. Sarah Penn had supper all ready. There were brown-bread and baked beans and a custard pie; it was the supper that Adoniram loved on a Saturday night. She had on a clean calico, and she bore herself imperturbably. Nanny and Sammy kept close at her heels. Their eyes were large, and Nanny was full of nervous tremors. Still there was to them more pleasant excitement than anything else. An inborn confidence in their mother over their father asserted itself.

Sammy looked out of the harness-room window. "There he is," he announced, in an awed whisper. He and Nanny peeped around the casing. Mrs. Penn kept on about her work. The children watched Adoniram leave the new horse standing in the drive while he went to the house door. It was fastened. Then he went around to the shed. That door was seldom locked, even when the family was away. The thought how her father would be confronted by the cow flashed upon Nanny. There was a hysterical sob in her throat. Adoniram emerged from the shed and stood looking about in a dazed fashion. His lips moved; he was saying something, but they could not hear what it was. The hired man was peeping around a corner of the old barn, but nobody saw him.

Adoniram took the new horse by the bridle and led him across the yard to the new barn. Nanny and Sammy slunk close to their mother. The barn doors rolled back, and there stood Adoniram, with the long mild face of the great Canadian farm horse looking over his shoulder.

Nanny kept behind her mother, but Sammy stepped suddenly forward, and stood in front of her.

Adoniram stared at the group. "What on airth you all down here for?" said he. "What's the matter over to the house?"

"We've come here to live, father," said Sammy. His shrill voice quavered out bravely.

"What"—Adoniram sniffed—"what is it smells like cookin'?" said he. He stepped forward and looked in the open door of the harness-room. Then he turned to his wife. His old bristling face was pale and frightened. "What on airth does this mean, mother?" he gasped.

"You come in here, father," said Sarah. She led the way into the harness-room and shut the door. "Now, father," said she, "you needn't be scared. I ain't crazy. There ain't nothin' to be upset over. But we've come here to live, an' we're goin' to live here. We've got jest as good a right here as new horses an' cows. The house wa'n't fit for us to live in any longer, an' I made up my mind I wa'n't goin' to stay there. I've done my duty by you forty year, an' I'm goin' to do it now; but I'm goin' to live here. You've got to put in some windows and partitions; an' you'll have to buy some furniture."

"Why, mother!" the old man gasped.

"You'd better take your coat off an' get washed—there's the wash-basin—an' then we'll have supper."

"Why, mother!"

Sammy went past the window, leading the new horse to the old barn. The old man saw him, and shook his head speechlessly. He tried to take off his coat, but his arms seemed to lack the power. His wife helped him. She poured some water into the tin basin, and put in a piece of soap. She got the comb and brush, and smoothed his thin gray hair after he had washed. Then she put the beans, hot bread, and tea on the table. Sammy came in, and the family drew up. Adoniram sat looking dazedly at his plate, and they waited.

"Ain't you goin' to ask a blessin', father?" said Sarah.

And the old man bent his head and mumbled.

All through the meal he stopped eating at intervals, and stared furtively at his wife; but he ate well. The home food tasted good to him, and his old frame was too sturdily healthy to be affected by his mind. But after supper he went out, and sat down on the step of the smaller door at the right of the barn, through which he had meant his Jerseys to pass in stately file, but which Sarah designed for her front house door, and he leaned his head on his hands.

After the supper dishes were cleared away and the milk-pans washed, Sarah went out to him. The twilight was deepening. There was a clear green glow in the sky. Before them stretched the smooth level of field; in the distance was a cluster of hay-stacks like the huts of a village; the air was very cool and calm and sweet. The landscape might have been an ideal one of peace.

Sarah bent over and touched her husband on one of his thin, sinewy shoulders. "Father!"

The old man's shoulders heaved: he was weeping.

"Why, don't do so, father," said Sarah.

"I'll—put up the—partitions, an'—everything you—want, mother."

Sarah put her apron up to her face; she was overcome by her own triumph.

Adoniram was like a fortress whose walls had no active resistance, and went down the instant the right besieging tools were used. "Why, mother," he said, hoarsely, "I hadn't no idee you was so set on't as all this comes to."

EXPLORE: Discuss Sarah Penn's speeches during her confrontations with her husband. Consider her methods of logic and persuasion—what kind of appeals does she make? Is she convincing? What do these appeals say about her character and circumstances?

COLLABORATE: Divide the class into four small groups, one for each of the Penn family characters. In each group, your task is to plan an argument that claims your character as the most sympathetic character in the story in comparison to the others. When the class reconvenes as a larger group, hold a debate on this topic.

EXPLORE: Why is the word *mother* in quotes in the title of the story?

Mary Hallock Foote

Mary Hallock Foote was wife to Arthur Foote, a western engineer who was involved in both mining and irrigation projects in remote areas of Colorado, Idaho, South Dakota, California, and Mexico. A refined and cultured woman from a New England Quaker family, she had established herself in New York City as a writer and illustrator prior to her marriage. As she described in her autobiography *A Victorian Gentlewoman in the Far West*, she profoundly missed the East. Over time, however, she began to understand the hopes that drove settlers to these remote places. She became a western correspondent to *Century Magazine*, to which she regularly submitted illustrations, like "The Irrigating Ditch" at left and fiction, like "The Watchman," that were set in the rugged places she knew. "The Watchman," published in *The Century Magazine* (1893), is about Idaho's Snake River region in the years leading up to the Carey Act. Prior to the Carey Act, most land was held by land speculators who sold acreage to settlers at full cost, and irrigation companies were privately, not publicly, owned.

FIGURE 5.3. Mary Hallock Foote, "The Irrigation Ditch," *The Century Illustrated Monthly Magazine*, vol. 38, no. 2 (June 1889), p. 299.

"The Watchman"

The far-Eastern company was counting its Western acres under water contracts. The acres were in first crops, waiting for the water. The water was dallying down its untried channel, searching the new dry earth-banks, seeping, prying, and insinuating sly, minute forces which multiplied and insisted tremendously the moment a rift had been made. And the orders were to "watch" and "puddle;" and the watchmen were as other men, and some of them doubtless remembered they were working for a company.

Travis, the black-eyed young lumberman from the upper Columbia, had been sent down with a special word from the manager commending him as a tried hand, equal to any post or service. The ditch superintendent was looking for such a man. He gave him those five crucial miles between the head-gates and Glenn's Ferry, the notorious beat that had sifted Finlayson's force without yet finding a man who could keep the banks. Some said it was the Arc-light saloon at Glenn's Ferry; some said it was the pretty girl at Lark's.

Whatever it was, Travis raged at it in the silent hours of his one-man watch; and the report had gone up the line now, three times since he had taken hold, of breaks on his division. And the engineer would by no means "weaken" on a question of the work, nor did the loyal watchman ask that any one should weaken, to spare him. He was all eyes and ears; he watched by daylight, he listened by dark, and the sounds that he heard in his dreams were sounds of water searching the banks, swirling and sinking into holes, or of mud subsiding with a wretched flop into the insidi-ous current.

It was a queer country along the new ditch below the head-gates; as old and sun-bleached and bony as the stony valleys of Arabia Petrea; all but that strip of green that led the eye to where the river wandered, and that warm brown strip of sown land extending field by field below the ditch.

Lark's ranch was the first one below the head-gates, lying between the river and the ditch, an old homesteader's claim, sub-irrigated by means of rude dams ponding the natural sloughs. The worn-out land, never drained, was foul and sour, lapsing into swamps, the black alkali oozing and spreading from pools in its boggy pastures.

A few pioneer fruit-trees still bloomed and bore, undiscouraged by neglect, and cast home-like shadows on the weedy grass around the cabin and sheds that slouched at all angles, with nails starting and shingles warping in the sun.

Similar weather-stains and odd kicks and bulges the old rancher's person exhibited, when he came out to sun himself of a rimy morning, when cobwebs glittered on the short, late grass, and his joints reminded him that the rains were coming. And up and down the cow-trail below the ditch, morning and evening, went his dairy-herd to pasture; and after them loitered Nancy, on a strawberry pony with milk white mane and tail.

The lights and shadows chased her in and out among the willows and fleecy cottonwoods and tall swamp-grasses; but Travis rode in the glare, on the high ditch-bank, and, although they passed each other daily, he had never had a good look at the "pretty girl at Lark's." But one morn-ing the white-faced heifer broke away and bolted up the ditch-bank, and in a cloud of sun-smitten dust Nancy followed, a figure of virginal wrath with scarlet cheeks and wind-blown hair. Rein-ing her pony on the narrow bank, she called across to Travis in a voice as clear and fresh as her colors:—

"Head her off, can't you? *What* are you about!" This last to the pony, who was behaving "mean."

"Ride to the bridge and head her this way. I can drive her up the bank," Travis responded.

Nancy obeyed him, and waited at the bridge while he endeavored to persuade the heifer of the error of her ways. The heifer was not easily persuaded, and Travis was wet to the waist before he had got her out; but he lost nothing of the bright figure guarding the bridge, a slender shape all pink and blue and dark blue, with hair like the sun on brown water, and a perfect seat, and a ringing voice calling thanks and bewildering encouragement to her ally in the stream. And this was old Solomon's daughter!

But "Oh, my Nancy!" the boys would groan, with excess of appreciation beyond words, and for that Nancy heeded them not: and now Travis knew that the boys were right.

"Thank you ever so much!" her clear voice lilted, as the discomfited runaway dashed down the bank to the path she had forsaken. "I'm ever so sorry she dug all those bad tracks in the ditch. Will they do any harm?"

Travis assured her that nothing did harm if only it were known in time.

"What is the matter with it, anyhow,—the ditch? Isn't it built right?"

"The ditch is the prettiest I ever saw," Travis responded, with all the warmth of his un-requited devotion to that faithless piece of engineering. "All new ditches need watching till the banks get settled."

"Well, I should say that *you* watched! Don't you ever stir off that bank?"

"I eat and sleep sometimes."

"You must have a pretty dry camp up above. Wouldn't you like some milk once in a while?"

"Thanks; I never happened to fall in with the milkman on my beat."

"We have lots to spare, and buttermilk too, if you're not too proud to come for it. The others used to."

"I guess I don't quite catch on."

"The other watchmen, the boys who were here before you."

"Oh," said Travis coldly.

"Well, any time you choose to come down I'll save some for you," said the girl, as if that matter were settled.

"I'm afraid it is rather off my beat," Travis hesitated, "but I'm just as much obliged."

Nancy straightened herself haughtily. "Oh, it is nothing to be obliged for, if you don't care to come."

"I did not say I didn't care," Travis protested; but she was gone. The dust flew, and presently her dark blue skirt and the pony's silver tail flashed past the willows in the low grounds.

"I shall never see her again," he mourned. "So much for those other fellows spoiling her idea of a watchman's duty. Of course she thought I could come if I wanted to. Did she ask them, I wonder?"

Nancy was piqued, but not resentful. The more he did not come, as evening after evening smiled upon the level land; the more she thought of Travis, alone in his dusty camp, alone on his blinding beat; the more she dwelt upon the singularity and constancy of his refusal, the more she respected him for it.

So one day he did see her again. She was sitting on the bridge planks, leaning forward, her arms in her lap, her hat tipped back, a star of white sunlight touching her forehead. She lifted her head when she heard him coming and put her hand over her eyes, as if she were dizzy with watching the water.

"How's the ditch?" she called in a voice of sweetest cheer. She was on her feet now, and he saw how entrancing she was, in a blue muslin frock and a broad white hat with a wreath of pink roses bestrewing the tilted brim. Had they got company at the ranch? was his jealous reflection.

"How's the ditch behaving itself these days?" she repeated.

"Much as usual, thank you," Travis beamed from his saddle.

"Breaking, as usual?"

"Yes; it broke night before last."

"Well, I don't believe it's much of a ditch, anyhow. I wouldn't fret about it if I was you. Don't you think I'm very good-natured, after your snubbing me so? Here I've brought you a basket of apples, seeing you wouldn't spare time from your old ditch to come for them yourself. That in the napkin is a little pat of fresh butter." She lifted the grape-leaves that covered the basket. "I thought it might taste good in camp."

"Good! Well, I rather guess it will taste good! See here, I can't ever thank you for this—for bringing it yourself." He had few words, but his looks were moderately expressive.

Nancy blushed with pleasure. "Well, I had to—when folks are so wrapped up in their business. There, with Susan's compliments! Susan's the heifer you rounded up for me in the ditch. I know she made you a lot of work, tracking holes in your banks you're so fussy about. Do you really think it is a good ditch?"

"I am positive it is."

"Then if anything goes wrong down here they will lay the blame on you?"

"They are welcome to. That's what I am here for."

Nancy openly acknowledged her approval of a man that stood right up to his work and would take no odds of any one.

"The other boys were always complaining and saying it was the ditch. But there, I know it is mean of me to talk about them."

"I guess it won't go any further," said Travis dryly.

"Well, I hope not. They were good boys enough, but pretty trifling watchmen, I shouldn't wonder."

Travis had nothing to say to this, but he made a mental note or two.

"When will you give me a chance to return your basket?"

"Why, anytime; there's no hurry about the basket. Have you any regular times?"

He looked away, dissembling his joy in the question, and answered as if he were making an official report,—

"I leave camp at six, patrol the line to the ferry and back, lay off an hour, and down again at eleven. Back in camp at three, and two hours for dinner. On again at five, and back in camp at nine. I pass this bridge, for instance, at seven and nine of a morning, twelve and two afternoons, and six and eight in the evening."

"Six and eight," Nancy mused, with a slight increase of color. "Well, I can stop some evening after cow-time, I suppose; but it isn't any matter about the basket."

Six evenings, going and coming, Travis delayed in passing the bridge, on the watch for Nancy; six times he filled the basket with such late field-flowers as he could find, and she never came. On the seventh evening his heart announced her, from as far off as his eyes beheld her. This time she was in white, without her hat, and she wore a blue ribbon in her gold-brown braids,—a blue ribbon in her braids, and a red, red rose in either cheek; and her colors, and the colors of the sky, floated like flowers on the placid water.

"Well, where is the basket, then?" she merrily demanded.

"I left it behind, for luck." "For luck? What sort of luck?" "Six times I brought it, and you were never here; so to-night I just kicked it into the tent and came off without it. It seems to have been about the right thing to do."

"What, my basket!"

"Your basket. And it was filled with wild flowers, the prettiest I could find. It's your own fault for not coming before."

"I never set any day that I know of. I have been up to town."

Travis was not pleased to hear it.

"Yes; and I saw your company's manager. What a young man he is! I had no idea managers were ever young. And stylish—my! I'm sure I hope he'll know me when he sees me again," she added, coloring and dropping her eyes.

Travis grimly expressed the opinion that he probably would. Nancy continued to strike the wrong note with cruel precision; she could not have done better had she calculated her words; and all the while looking as innocent as the shining water under her feet,—and that last time she had been so kind!

And the ditch was as provoking as Nancy, rewarding his devotion with breaks that defied all explanation. It was not possible that the patience of the management could hold out much longer;

and when he should have been dismissed in disgrace from his post, Nancy would lightly class him as another of those "good boys enough, but trifling watchmen."

II.

The first dry moon was just past the full. At nine o'clock the sky began to whiten above the long, bare ridge of the side-hill cut. At half past, the edge of the moon's disk clove the sky-line, and the shadow of the ridge crept down among the willows and tule-beds of the bottom. At ten the shadow had shrunk; it lay black on the ditch-bank, but the whispering treetops below were turning in silver light that flickered along the cow-path and caught the still eye of a dark, shallow pool among the tules.

Nancy had chosen this night for a stroll to the bridge, where Travis might be expected to pass, any time between eight o'clock and moonrise. Instead of Travis came a man whom she recognized as one of the watchmen from a lower division. He saluted her, after the custom of the country, claiming nothing on personal grounds but the privilege to look rather hard at the girlish figure silhouetted against the water. It was yet early enough for sky-gleams to linger on still pools, or to color the wimpling reaches of the ditch.

Nancy was disappointed; she had not come out to see a strange rider passing on Travis's gray horse. Her little plans were disconcerted. She had waited for what she considered a dignified interval, before seeming to take cognizance of her watchman's hours; now it appeared that the part of dignity might be overdone. Had Travis been superseded on his beat? She was conscious of missing him already. Her walk home, through the confidential willows, struck a chill of loneliness which the aspect of the house did not dispel. All was as dark and empty as she had left it. Was her father still at work at those tedious dams? This had been his given reason for frequent absences of late, after his usual working hours; though why he should choose the dark nights for mending his dams Nancy had not asked herself. To-night she wanted him, or somebody, to drive away this queer new ache that made the moonlight too large and still for one little girl to wander in alone.

She searched for him. He was in none of the expected places; the dank fields were as empty as the house. She turned back to the ditch; from its high bank she could see farther into the shadowy places of the bottom.

Travis, meanwhile, had been leisurely pursuing his evening beat. He had overtaken one of his fellow-watchmen, on foot, walking to town, had lent him his horse for the last two miles to camp, and invited him to help himself to what he could find for supper, without waiting for his host.

"It is a still night," said Travis; "I'll mog along slowly up the ditch, and put in a little extra listening: it's at night the water talks."

Long after the rider had passed on, the tread of his horse's hoofs was heard, diminishing on the hard-tramped bank; a loosened stone rattled down and splashed into the water; the wind rustled in the tule-beds; then all surface sounds ceased, and the only talker was the ditch, chuckling and dawdling like an idle child on its errand, which it could not be persuaded to take seriously, to the desert lands.

Travis came to the ticklish spot near the bridge, and stopped to listen. Here the ditch cut through beds of clean sand, where the water might sink and work back into the old ground, the sand holding it like a sponge, till all the bottom became a bog, and the banks sank in one widespread, general wash-out. The first symptom of such deep-seated trouble would be the water's motion in the ditch,—whirling round and round as if boring a hole in the bottom.

Travis laid his ear to the current, for he could judge of the water's movement by the sound. All seemed right at the bridge, but far up the ditch he was aware of a new demonstration. He listened awhile, and then walked on with long, light steps and gained upon the sound, which persisted, defining itself as a muffled churning at marked intervals, with now and then a wait between. The prodding was of some tool at work under water, at the ditch-bank.

He crossed to the upper side, and moved forward cautiously along the ridge, crouching that his figure might not be seen against the sky.

Nancy had gone up the cow-trail, past the low grounds, and was just climbing the bank when a dark shape, of man or beast, crashed down the opposite slope and shot like a slide of rock into the water.

A half-choked cry followed the plunge, then ugly sounds of a scuffle under the ditch-bank—men breathing hard, sighing and snorting; and somebody gasped as if he were being held down till his breath was gone.

"Get in there, you old muskrat! You shall stop your own breaks if it takes your cursed carcass to do it! Now then, have you got your breath?"

Nancy stayed only to hear a voice that was her father's, convulsed with terror and the chill of his repeated duckings, begging to be spared the anguish of drowning by night in three feet of ditch-water.

"Mr. Travis," she screamed, "you let my father be, whatever you are doing to him! Father, you come right home and get on dry clothes!"

Travis was as much amazed as if Diana with the moon on her forehead had appeared on the ditch-bank to take old Solomon Lark under her maiden protection; but no less he stuck to his prize of war.

"Your father hasn't time to change his clothes just yet, Miss Nancy; he's got some work to do first."

"Who are you, to be setting my father to work? Let go of him this minute! You are drowning him; you are choking him to death!" sobbed the frantic girl. The shadow fortunately withheld the details of her father's condition, but she had seen enough. Had Travis been drinking? Was the man bereft of his senses?

He was quite himself apparently,—hideously cool, yet roused, and his voice cut like steel.

"You had better go home, Miss Nancy, and light a fire and warm a blanket for your father's bed. He'll be pretty cold before he gets through with this night's work."

After this cruel speech he took no more notice of Nancy, but leaped upon the ditch-bank and began hurling earth in great shovelfuls, patting the old man on the head with his cold tool whenever he tried to clamber up after him.

"You'd better not try *that*," he roared in a terrible voice that wounded Nancy like a blow. "Get in there, now! Puddle, puddle, or I'll have you buried to the ears in five minutes!"

It was shocking, hideous, like a horrible dream. The earth rattled down all about Solomon, and frequently upon him; the water was thick with mud, and the wretched old man tramped and puddled for dear life, helping to mend the hole which he had secretly dug where no eye could discover, till the water had fingered it and enlarged the mischief to a break.

It was the work of vermin, and as such Travis had treated his prisoner. Nancy felt the insult as keenly as she abhorred the cruelty. She fled, hysterical with wrath and despair at her own helplessness. But while she made ready the means of consolation at home, her thinking powers came back, and, between what she suspected and what she remembered, she was not wholly in the dark as to the truth between her father and Travis.

There was no one to warm Travis's blankets, when he fell back upon camp about daybreak, reeking with cold perspiration, soaked with ditch-water and sore in every muscle from his frenzy of shoveling. He had had no supper the night before; his guest had eaten all the cooked food, burned all his light-wood kindlings, and forgotten to cover the bread-pail, and his bread was full of sand. He didn't think much of those tenderfeet, who called themselves ditch-men, on that lower division where there was no work at all to speak of.

He began—worse comfort—to consider his police work from a daughter's point of view. Alas for himself and Nancy! His idyl of the ditch was shattered like the tender sky-reflections that bloomed on its still waters, and vanished when the waters were troubled. His own thoughts were as that roily pool where he had ducked the old man in the darkness. He overslept himself, after thinking he should not sleep at all, and started down his beat not until noon of the next day. Halfway to the bridge on the ditch-bank he met Nancy Lark. She gave him a note, which he dismounted to take, she vouchsafing no greeting, not even a look, and standing apart while he read it, with the air of a martyr to duty.

Mr. Travis [the letter ran],—I am a death-struck man in consequence of your outrageous treatment of me last evening. I've took a dum chill, and it has hit me in the vitals through standing in water up to my armpits. If you think your fool ditch is worth more than a Human's life, though your company's enemy, that's for you to settle as you can when the time comes you'll have to. I don't ask any favors. But if you got any decency left in you through working for that fish-livered company of bondholders coming out here to stomp us farmers into the dirt, you will call this bizness quits. I aint in no shape to fight ditches no more. You have put me where I be, and the less said on both sides the better, it looks to me. If that's so you can say so by word or writing. I should prefer writing as I aint got that confidence I might have. Yours truly, SOLOMON LARK.

"Miss Nancy," said Travis gently, "is your father very sick this morning?"

"I don't know," Nancy replied.

"Have you sent for a doctor?"

"He won't let me."

"Have you read this letter?" She flashed an indignant look at him.

"I wish you would, then."

"It is not my letter. I don't know what's in it, and I don't care to know."

"Do you know what your father was doing in the ditch last night?"

"Helping you to mend it, at the risk of his life, because you made him," Nancy answered quickly.

"Helping to mend a hole he made himself, so there would be a nice little break in the morning."

The subject rested there, till Travis, forced to take the defensive, asked:—

"Do you believe me?"

"Believe what?"

"What I have just told you about your father?"

"Oh," she said, "it makes no difference to me. I knew my father pretty well before I ever saw you. If you think he was doing that, why, I suppose you will have to think so. But even if he was, I don't call that any reason you should half drown him, and make him work himself to death beside."

"But the water was warm! And I did the work. What was it to tread dirt for an hour or so on a summer's night? Wasn't he in the ditch when I found him?"

"I don't know, I'm sure," said Nancy. "I know that you kept him there."

"Well, I hope he'll keep out of the ditch after this. Working at ditches at night isn't good for his health. But you needn't be alarmed about him this time; I think he'll recover. But remember this: last night I was the company's watchman; I had an ugly piece of work to do and I did it; but, fair play or foul, whatever may happen between your father and me, remember, it is only my work, and you are not in it."

"Well, I guess I'm in it if my father is," said Nancy, "and that is something for you to remember."

"Oh, hang the work and the ditch and all the ditches!" thought Travis; yet it was the ditch that had put color and soul and meaning into his life,—that had given him sight of Nancy. And it was not his work nor his convictions about it that stood between them now; it was her woman's contempt for justice and reason where her feelings were concerned. The case was simple as Nancy saw it; too simple, for it left him out in the cold. He would have had it complicated by a little more feeling in his direction.

"Well, have I got your answer?" she asked. "Father said I was to bring an answer, but not to let you come."

"He need not be afraid," said Travis bitterly. "If he will leave my ditch-banks alone, I shall not meddle with him. Tell him, if there are no more breaks there will be nothing to report. This break is mended—the break in the ditch, I mean."

"Then you will not tell?" Nancy stole a look at him that was half a plea.

"You would even promise to like me a little, wouldn't you, if you couldn't get the old man off any other way?" he mocked her sorrowfully. "Well, I had rather have you hate me than stoop to coax me, as I've seen girls do"—

He might be satisfied, she passionately answered; she hated him enough. She hated his work, and the hateful way he did it.

"You are an unmerciful man!" she accused him, with a sob in her voice. "You don't know the trouble my father has had; how many years he has worked, with nothing but his hands; and now your company comes and claims the water, and turns the river, that belongs to everybody, into their big ditch. I'd like to know how they came to own this river! And when they have got it all in their ditch, all the little ditches and the ponds will go dry. We were here years before any of you ever thought of coming, or knew there was a country here at all. It's claim-jumping; and not a cent will they pay, and laugh at us besides, and call us mossbacks. I don't blame my father one bit, if he did break the ditch. If you are here to watch, then watch!—watch me! Perhaps you think I've had a hand in your breaks?"

Travis turned pale. He had made the mistake of trying to reason with Nancy, and now he felt that he must go on, in justice to his case, though she was far away from all his arguments, rapt in the grief, the wrath, the conviction, of her plea.

"You talk as women talk who only hear one side," he replied. "But you people down here don't know the company's intentions; they don't ask, and when they do they won't believe what they are told. That talk against companies is an old politicians' drive. This country is too big for single men to handle; companies save years of waiting. This one will bring the railroads and the markets, and boom up the price of land. The ditch your father hates so will make him a rich man in five years, if he does nothing but sit still and let it come.

"As for water, why do you cry before you are hurt? Nobody can steal a river. That is more politicians' talk, to make out they are the settlers' friends. We are the settlers' friends, because we are the friends of the country's boom; it can't boom without us. Why should *I* believe in this company? I'm a poor man, a settler like your father. I've got land of my own, but I can see we farmers can't do everything for ourselves; it's cheaper to pay a company to help us. They are just peddlers of water, and we buy it. Who owns the other, then? Don't we own them just as much as they own us?

"Come, if you can't feel it's so, leave hating us at least till we have done all these things you accuse us of. Wait till we take all the water and ruin your land. Most of these farmers along the river have got too much water; they are ruining their own land. So I tell your father, but he thinks he knows it all."

"He is some older than you are, anyhow."

"He is too old to be working nights in ditches. Tell him so from me, will you?"

"Oh, I'll tell him! I don't think you will be troubled much with us around your ditch, after this. I went to the bridge last night because I thought you were nice, and a friend. I had a respect for you more than for any of the others. I might have come to think better of the ditch; but I've had all the ditch I want, and all the watchmen. Never, till I die, shall I forget how my father looked," she passionately returned to the charge. "An old man like him! Why didn't you put me in and make me tread dirt for you? The water was *warm*; and I'm enough better able than he was!"

"I'll get right down here and let you tread on me, and be proud to have you, if it will cure the sight of what you saw me do last night. I was mad, don't you understand? I have to answer for all this foolishness of your father's, remember. It had to be stopped."

"Was there no way to stop it but half drowning him, and insulting him besides?"

"Yes, there is another way; inform the company, and have him shut up in the Pen. *I* thought I let the old man off pretty easy. But if you prefer the other way, why, next time there's a break, we can try it."

"I'm sure we ought to thank you for your kindness," said Nancy. "And if we are Companied out of house and home, and father made a criminal, we shall thank you still more. Good-morning."

Their eyes met and hers fell. She turned away, and he remounted and rode on up the ditch, angry, as a man can be only with one he might have loved, down to those dregs of bitterness that lurk at the bottom of the soundest heart.

III.

He was but an idle watchman all that day, so sure he was that the ditch was right and Solomon the author of all his troubles; and Solomon was "fixed" at last. Weariness overcame him, and at the end of his beat he slept, under the lee of the ditch-bank, instead of returning to his camp.

Next morning he was riding along at his usual pace when it struck him how incredibly the ditch had fallen. The line of silt that marked the water's normal depth now stood exposed and dry, full two feet above its running, and the pulse of the current had weakened as though it were ebbing fast.

He put his horse to a run, and lightened ship as he went, casting off his sack of oats, then his coat and such tools as he could spare; he might have been traced to the scene of disaster by his impedimenta strewing the ditch-bank.

The water had had hours the start of him; its work was sickening to behold. A part of the bank had gone clean out, and the ditch was returning to the river by way of Solomon Lark's alfalfa fields. The homestead itself was in danger.

He cut sage-brush and tore up tules by the roots, and piled them as a wing-dam against the outer bank, and heaped dirt like mad upon the mats; and as he worked, alone, where forty men were needed, came Nancy, with glowing face, flying down the ditch-bank, calling the word of exquisite relief:—

"I've shut off the water. Was that right?"

Right! He had been wishing himself two men, nay, three: one at the bank, and one at the gates, and one carrying word to Finlayson.

"Can I do anything else?"

"Yes; make Finlayson's camp quick as you can," Travis panted over a shovelful of dirt he was heaving.

"Yes; what shall I tell him?"

"Tell him to send up everything he has got; every man and team and scraper."

Nancy was gone, but in a few moments she was back again, wringing her hands, and as white as a cherry-blossom.

"The water is all down round the house, and father is alone in bed crying like a child."

"There's nothing to cry about now. You turned off the water; see, it has almost stopped."

"Can I leave him with you?"

"Great Scott! I'll take care of him! But go, there's a blessed girl. You will save the ditch."

Nancy went, covering the desert miles as a bird flies; she exulted in this chance for reparation. But long after Finlayson's forces had arrived and gone to work, she came lagging wearily homeward, all of a color, herself and the pony, with the yellow road. She had refused a fresh horse at the ditch-camp, and, sparing the whip, reached home not until after dark.

Her father's excitement in his hours of loneliness had waxed to a pitch of childish frenzy. He wept, he cursed, he counted his losses, and when his daughter said, to comfort him, "Why, father, surely they must pay for this!" he threw himself about in his bed and gave way to lamentations in which the secret of his wildness came out. He had done the thing himself; and he dared not risk suspicion, and the investigation that would follow a heavy claim for damages.

Nancy could not believe him. "Father, do be quiet; you didn't do any such thing," she insisted. "How could you, when I know you haven't stirred out of this bed since night before last? Hush, now; you are dreaming; you are out of your head."

"I guess I know what I done. I ain't crazy, and I ain't a fool. I made this hole first, before he caught me at the upper one. I made this one to keep him busy on his way up, so's the upper one could get a good start. The upper one wouldn't 'a' hurt us. It's jest like my cussed luck! I knew it was a-comin', but I didn't think I'd get it like this. It's all his fault, the great lazy loafer, sleepin' at the bottom of his beat, 'stead o' comin' up as he'd ought to have done last evening. He wasted the whole night, —and calls himself a watchman!"

"Well, I'm glad of it," Nancy cried excitedly. "I'm just *glad* we are washed out, and I hope this will end it!" and she burst into tears, and ran out of the room.

She sat by herself, weeping and storming, in the dark little shed-room.

"Nancy!" she heard her father calling, "Nancy, child! . . . Where's that gal taken herself off to? . . . Are you a-settin' up your back on account of that ditch? If you are, you ain't no child of mine. . . . I'm dum sorry I let on a word to her about it. How do I know but she's off with it now, to that watchman feller. I'll be put in the papers—an old man informed on by his darter, and he on his last sick bed! . . . Nancy, I say, where be you a-hidin' yourself?"

Nancy returned to her forlorn charge, and after a while the old man fell asleep. She put out the lamp, for she could see to move about the room by the light of the sage-brush bonfires that flared along the ditch, lighting the men and teams, all Finlayson's force, at work upon the broken banks.

The sight was wild and alluring; she went out to watch the strange army of shadows shifting and intermingling against a wall of flame.

There was a distressful space to cross, of sand and slippery mud and drowned vegetation, including the remains of her garden; the look of everything was changed. Only the ditch-bank against the reddened sky supplied the usual landmark. Its crest was black with shovelers, and up and down in lurid light climbed the scraper-teams; climbed and dumped, and dropped over the bank to climb again, like figures in a stage procession. There was a bedlam roar and crackle of pitchy fires, rattle of harness, clank of scraper-pans, shouts of men to the cattle, oaths and words of command; and this would go forward unceasingly till the banks held water. And what was the use of contending?

Nancy felt bitterly the insignificance of such small scattered folk as her father, pitiful even in their spite. Their vengeance was like the malice of field-mice or rabbits, which the farmers fenced out of their fields into the desert where they belonged. What could such as they do either to help or hinder this invincible march of capital into the country where they, with untold hardships, had located the first claims? And some of them were ready enough, for a little temporary relief, to part with their birthright to these clever sons of Jacob.

"Out we go, to find some other wilderness for them to take away from us! We are only mossbacks," said the daughter of Esau.

As she spoke, half aloud to herself, a man rushed past her down the bank, flattened himself on his hands, laid his face to the water, and drank and paused to pant, and drank again, while she could have counted a score. Then he lifted his head, sighed, and stretched himself back with a groan of complete exhaustion.

The firelight touched his face, and showed her Travis: haggard, hollow-eyed, soaked with ditch-water, and matted with mud, looking as if he had been dragged bodily through the ditch-bank, like thread through a piece of cloth.

Nancy did not try to avoid him.

"Oh, is it you?" he marveled, softly smiling up at her. "What a splendid ride you made! Did nobody thank you? Finlayson said he couldn't find you when he was leaving camp."

Nancy answered not a word; she was trembling so that she feared to betray herself by speaking.

"I was coming to say good-by, when I had washed my face," he continued. "I got my time to-night."

"Your time?"

"My time-check. They are going to put another man in my place. So you needn't hate me any longer on account of the ditch; you can transfer all that to the next fellow."

"Isn't that just like them? They never can do anything fair!"

"Like who? Do you suppose I'm going to kick about it? The only wonder is they kept me on so long."

Every word of Travis's was a knife in Nancy's conscience, to say nothing of her pride. She hugged her arms in her shawl, and rocked herself to and fro. Travis crawled up the bank a little way further, and stretched himself humbly beside her. The dark shadows under his aching eyes started a pang of pity in the girl's heart, sore beset as she was with troubles of her own.

"I'm glad it's duskish," he remarked, "so you can't see the sweet state I'm in. I'm all over top-soil. You might rent me to a Chinaman for twenty-five dollars an acre; and I don't need any irrigating either."

An irresponsible laugh from Nancy was followed by a sob. Then she gathered herself to speak.

"See here, do you want to stay on this ditch?"

"Of course I do. I wanted to stay till I had straightened out my own record, and shown what the ditch can do. But no management under heaven could stand such work as this."

"Then stay, if you want to. You have only to say the word. You said you'd inform if there was a next time, and there is. Father did it. He made this break, too; he made them both the same night, and didn't dare to tell of this one. Now, go and clear yourself and get back your beat."

"Are you sure of this you are telling me?"

"Well, I guess so. It isn't the sort of thing I'd be likely to make up. And I say you can tell if you want to. I make you a present of the information. If father isn't willing to take the consequences, I am; and they half belong to me. I won't have anybody sheltering us, or losing by us. We have got no quarrel with you."

"That is brave of you. I wish it was something more than brave," sighed Travis. "But I want it all myself. I can't spare this information to the company. You didn't do it for them, did you?"

"When I go telling on my father to save a ditch, I guess it will be after now," said Nancy. "If that rich company, with all its men and watchmen and teams and money, can't protect itself from one poor old man"—

"Never mind the company," said Travis. "What's mine is mine. This word you gave to me, it doesn't belong to my employers. You have saved me to myself; now I shall not go kicking myself for sleeping that night on my beat. It's not so bad—oh, not half so bad—for me!"

"Then go tell them, and get the credit for it. Don't you mean to?"

She could not see him smile. "When I tell, you will hear of it."

"But you talked about your record."

"I shall have to go to work and make a new record. Ah, if you would be as kind as you are brave! Was it all just for pride you told me this? Don't you care, not the least bit, about my part— that I am down and out of everything?"

"It's your own fault, then. I have told you how you can clear yourself and stay."

"And lose my chance with you! I was thinking of coming back, some day, to tell you —what you must know already. Nancy, you do know!"

"You forget," shivered Nancy; "I am the daughter of the man you called" —

"Is that fair—to bring that up now?"

"You mustn't deceive yourself. There are some things that can't be forgotten."

"How did *I* know what I was saying? A man isn't always responsible."

"I heard you," said Nancy. "There are things we say when we are raging mad at a person, and there are things we say when we think them the dirt under our feet. You kept him down with your dirt-shovel, and you called him—what I can't ever forget."

"And is this the only hitch between us?"

"I should think it was enough. Who despises my father despises me."

"But I do not despise him," Travis did not scruple to assert. "The quarrel was not mine; and I'm not a ditch-man any longer. I will apologize to your father."

"Oh, I know it costs you nothing to apologize. You don't mind father—an old man like him! You'd take him in, and give him his meals, and pat him on the head as you would the house-dog that bites because he's old and cross. Well, I'll let you know I don't want you to forgive him, and apologize, and all that stuff. I want you to get even with him."

"Be satisfied," said Travis. "The only count I have against your father is through his daughter. There is no way for me to get even with you. And when you have spoiled a man's life just for one angry word"—

"Not angry," she interrupted. "I could have forgiven you that."

"For one word, then. And you call it square when you have given me a piece of information to use for myself, against you! I will go back now and go to work. They can't say I haven't earned my wages on this beat."

He looked down at her, longing to gather her, with all her thorny sweetness, to his breast; but her attitude forbade him.

"Can't we shake hands?" he said. They shook hands in silence, and he went back and finished the night in the ranks of the shovelers,—to work well, to love well, and to get his discharge at last. Yet Travis was not sorry that he had taken those five miles below Glenn's Ferry: he had found something to work for.

The company's officials marveled, as the weeks went by, that nothing was heard of Solomon Lark. He had ever been the sturdiest beggar for damages on the ditch. If he lacked an occasion he could invent one; he was known to be a fanatic on the subject of the small farmers' wrongs: yet now, with a veritable claim to sue for, the old protestant was dumb. Had Solomon turned the other cheek? There were jokes about it in the office; they looked to have some fun with Solomon yet.

In the early autumn the joking ceased. There was a final reason for the old man's silence,— Solomon was dead. His ranch was rented to a Chinese vegetable-gardener who bought water from the ditch.

The company, through its officials, was disposed to recognize this unspoken claim that had perished on the lips of the dead. They made an estimate, and offered Nancy Lark a fair sum in consideration of her father's losses by the ditch.

It was unusual for a company to volunteer a settlement of this kind; it was still more unusual for the indemnity to be refused. Nancy declined, by letter, first; then the manager asked her to call at the office. She did not come. He took pains to hunt her up at the house of her friends in town. He might have delegated the call, but he chose to make it in person, and was struck by an added dignity, a finer beauty in the saddened face of the girl whom he remembered as a bit of a rustic coquette.

He went over the business with her. She was perfectly intelligent in the matter; there had been no misunderstanding. Why then would she not take what belonged to her? Companies were not in the habit of paying claims that were claims of sentiment.

"I have made no claim," said Nancy.

"But you have one. You inherited one. We do not propose to rob"—

She put out her hand with a gesture of appeal.

"My father had no claim. He never made one, nor meant to make one. I am the best judge of what belongs to me. I don't want this money, and I will never take one cent of it. But there is a claim you can settle, if you are hunting up claims. It won't cost you anything," she faltered, as if some unguarded impulse had hurried her into a subject that she hardly knew how to go on with. She moved her chair back a little from the light.

"There was one of your watchmen, on the Glenn's Ferry beat, who lost his place on account of those breaks coming one after another"—

"Yes," said the manager; "there were several that did. Which man do you refer to?"

The name, she thought, was Travis. Then, blushing, she spoke out courageously:—

"It was Mr. Travis. He was discharged just after the big break. You thought it was his carelessness, but it was not. I am the only one that can say so, and I know it. You lost the best watchman you ever had on the ditch when you took his name off your pay-roll. He worked for more than just his money's worth, and it hurt him to lose that place."

"Are you aware that he made the worst record of any man on the line?"

"I don't care what his record was; he kept a good watch. It's no concern of mine to say so," she said. Trembling and red and white, the tears shining in her honest eyes, she persisted: "He had his reasons for never explaining, and they were nothing to be ashamed of. I think you might believe me!"

"I do," said the manager, willing to spare her. "I will attend to the case of Mr. Travis when I see him. I do not think he has left the country. In fact, he was inquiring about you only the other day, in the office, and he seemed very much concerned to hear of your —of the loss you have suffered. Shall I say that you spoke a good word for him?"

"You need not do that," she answered with spirit. "He knows whether he kept watch. But you may say that I ask, as a favor, that he will answer all your questions; and you need not be afraid to question him."

Travis was given back his beat, but no more explicit exoneration would he accept. The reason of his reinstatement was not made public, and naturally there was gossip about it among other discharged watchmen who had not been invited to try again.

Two of these cynic philosophers, popularly known as sore-heads, foregathered one morning at Glenn's Ferry and began to discuss the management and the ditch.

"Travis don't seem to have so much trouble with the water this year as he had last," the first ex-watchman remarked. "Used to get away with him on an average once a week, so I hear."

"He's married his girl," the other explained sarcastically. "He's got more time to look after the ditch."

There is no sand, now, in Travis's bread; the prettiest girl on the ditch makes it for him, and walks beside him when the lights are fair and the shadows long on the ditch-bank. And it is a pleasure to record that both Nancy and the ditch are behaving as dutifully as girls and water can be expected to do, when taken from their self-found paths and committed to the sober bounds of responsibility.

Flowers bloom upon its banks, heaven is reflected in its waters, fair and broad are the fertile pastures that lie beyond; but the best-trained ditch can never be a river, nor the gentlest wife a girl again.

EXPLORE: Foote personifies the water and the ditch throughout her short story. Find at least seven places where she uses personification and list them and discuss with your classmates how and why Foote uses this literary device. Then do one of the following:

- Using Foote's personifications, imagine that the water in Foote's story is a human. Create a picture, sculpture, or collage that visually represents what you think

Foote's water character could look like. You may also compose a piece of music to represent the water character or propose some other creative representation of Foote's character.

- After you have reviewed how Foote personifies the water, write a descriptive paragraph that personifies some other non-human farm thing. It could be something referenced in this textbook (for instance, a tree in Jefferson's orchard or Thoreau's beans) or it can be something else farm related (for instance, a sheepherding dog, a rooster, a tractor or plow, or a barn). Share your creative personification projects with the class.

Willa Cather

Willa Cather was born on a sheep farm in the wooded hills of Back Creek, Virginia, just fifty miles northwest of Washington, DC in 1873. In 1882 she and her family moved to a homestead on the Nebraska plains. While much of Cather's fiction expresses a deep and abiding love for that prairie landscape, she had "an unreasoning fear of being swallowed by the distances" of the plains in her early years. But, she wrote, "The country and I had it out together and by the end of the first autumn, that shaggy grass country had gripped me with a passion I have never been able to shake."

Cather's first major success came in 1913 when she published *O Pioneers!*—one of the first novels written about the West. "I had searched for books," Cather said in an interview, "telling about the beauty of the country I loved, its romance, and heroism and strength and courage of its people that had been plowed into the furrows of its soil and I did not find them. And so," she concluded, "I wrote *O Pioneers!*" A number of Cather's thirteen novels were set in the agricultural West, and if you enjoy this excerpt from *O Pioneers!*, you might also like to read her novel *My Ántonia* or her short story "Neighbour Rosicky."

The following excerpt opens as Swedish homesteader John Bergson lies on his deathbed and begins planning for the future of his family when he is gone.

O Pioneers!
"The Wild Land"

In eleven long years John Bergson had made but little impression upon the wild land he had come to tame. It was still a wild thing that had its ugly moods; and no one knew when they were likely to come, or why. Mischance hung over it. Its Genius was unfriendly to man. The sick man was feeling this as he lay looking out of the window, after the doctor had left him. . . .

Bergson went over in his mind the things that had held him back. One winter his cattle had perished in a blizzard. The next summer one of his plow horses broke its leg in a prairie-dog hole and had to be shot. Another summer he lost his hogs from cholera, and a valuable stallion died from a rattlesnake bite. Time and gain his crops had failed. He had lost two children, boys, that came between Lou and Emil, and there had been the cost of sickness and death. Now when he had at last struggled out of debt he was going to die himself. . . .

For weeks, John Bergson had been thinking about these things. . . . He often called his daughter in to talk to her about this. Before Alexandra was twelve years old she had begun to be a help to him, and as she grew older he had come to depend more and more upon her resourcefulness and good judgment. His boys were willing enough to work, but when he talked with them they usually irritated him. It was Alexandra who read the papers and followed the markets, and who learned by the mistakes of their neighbors. It was Alexandra who could always tell about what it had cost to fatten each steer, and who could guess the weight of a hog before it went on the scales closer than John Bergson himself. Lou and Oscar were industrious, but he could never teach them to use their heads about their work. . . .

"*Dotter,*" he called feebly, "*dotter!*" He heard her quick step and saw her tall figure appear in the doorway, with the light of the lamp behind her. He felt her youth and strength, how easily she moved and stooped and lifted. . . .

His daughter came and lifted him up on his pillows. She called him by an old Swedish name that she used to call him when she was little and took his dinner to him in the shipyard.

"Tell the boys to come here, daughter. I want to speak to them."

"They are feeding the horses, father. They have just come back from the Blue. Shall I call them?"

He sighed. "No, no. Wait until they come in. Alexandra, you will have to do the best you can for your brothers. Everything will come on you."

"I will do all I can, father."

"Don't let them get discouraged and go off like Uncle Otto. I want them to keep the land."

"We will, father. We will never lose the land."

There was a sound of heavy feet in the kitchen. Alexandra went to the door and beckoned to her brothers, two strapping boys of seventeen and nineteen. They came in and stood at the foot of the bed. Their father looked at them searchingly, though it was too dark to see their faces; they were just the same boys, he told himself, he had not been mistaken in them. The square head and heavy shoulders belonged to Oscar, the elder. The younger boy was quicker, but vacillating.

"Boys," said the father wearily, "I want you to keep the land together and to be guided by your sister. I have talked to her since I have been sick, and she knows all my wishes. I want no quarrels among my children, and so long as there is one house there must be one head. Alexandra is the oldest, and she knows my wishes. She will do the best she can. If she makes mistakes, she will not make so many as I have made. When you marry, and want a house of your own, the land will be divided fairly, according to the courts. But for the next few years you will have it hard, and you must all keep together. Alexandra will manage the best she can."

Oscar, who was usually the last to speak, replied because he was the older, "Yes, father. It would be so anyway, without your speaking. We will all work the place together."

"And you will be guided by your sister, boys, and be good brothers to her, and good sons to your mother? That is good. And Alexandra must not work in the fields any more. There is no necessity now. Hire a man when you need help. She can make much more with her eggs and butter than the wages of a man. It was one of my mistakes that I did not find that out sooner. Try to break a little more land every year; sod corn is good for fodder. Keep turning the land, and always put up more hay than you need. Don't grudge your mother a little time for plowing her garden and setting out fruit trees, even if it comes in a busy season. She has been a good mother to you, and she has always missed the old country."

For the first three years after John Bergson's death, the affairs of his family prospered. Then came the hard times that brought every one on the Divide to the brink of despair; three years of drouth and failure, the last struggle of a wild soil against the encroaching plowshare. The first of these fruitless summers the Bergson boys bore courageously. The failure of the corn crop made labor cheap. Lou and Oscar hired two men and put in bigger crops than ever before. They lost everything they spent. The whole country was discouraged. Farmers who were already in debt had to give up their land. A few foreclosures demoralized the county. The settlers sat about on the wooden sidewalks in the little town and told each other that the country was never meant for men to live in; the thing to do was to get back to Iowa, to Illinois, to any place that had been proved habitable. The Bergson boys, certainly, would have been happier with their uncle Otto, in the bakery shop in Chicago. Like most of their neighbors, they were meant to follow in paths already marked out for them, not to break trails in a new country. A steady job, a few holidays, nothing to think about, and they would have been very happy. It was no fault of theirs that they had been dragged into the wilderness when they were little boys. A pioneer should have imagination, should be able to enjoy the idea of things more than the things themselves. . . .

"I've been thinking, boys," Alexandra went on, "that maybe I am too set against making a change. I'm going to take Brigham and the buckboard to-morrow and drive down to the river country and a few days looking over what they've got down there. If I find anything good, you boys can go down and make a trade."

"Nobody down there will trade for anything up here," said Oscar gloomily.

"That's just what I want to find out. Maybe they are just as discontented down there as we are up here. Things away from home often look better than they are. You know what your Hans Andersen book says, Carl, about the Swedes liking to buy Danish bread and the Danes liking to buy Swedish bread, because people always think the bread of another country is better than their own. Anyway, I've heard so much about the river farms, I won't be satisfied till I've seen for myself."

Lou fidgeted. "Look out! Don't agree to anything. Don't let them fool you."

Lou was apt to be fooled himself. He had not yet learned to keep away from the shell-game wagons that followed the circus. . . .

Alexandra and Emil spent five days down among the river farms, driving up and down the valley. Alexandra talked to the men about their crops and to the women about their poultry. She spent a whole day with one young farmer who had been away at school, and who was experimenting with a new kind of clover hay. She learned a great deal. As they drove along, she and Emil talked and planned. At last, on the sixth day, Alexandra turned Brigham's head northward and left the river behind.

"There's nothing in it for us down there, Emil. There are a few fine farms, but they are owned by the rich men and couldn't be bought. Most of the land is rough and hilly. They can always scrape along down there, but they can never do anything big. Down there they have a little certainty, but up with us there is a big chance. We must have faith in the high land, Emil. I want to hold on harder than ever, and when you're a man you'll thank me." She urged Brigham forward.

When the road began to climb the first long swells of the Divide, Alexandra hummed an old Swedish hymn, and Emil wondered why his sister looked so happy. Her face was so radiant that he felt shy about asking her. For the first time, perhaps, since that land emerged from the waters of geologic ages, a human face was set toward it with love and yearning. It seemed beautiful to her, rich and strong and glorious. Her eyes drank in the breadth of it, until her tears blinded her. Then the Genius of the Divide, the great, free spirit which breathes across it, must have bent lower than it ever bent to a human will before. The history of every country begins in the heart of a man or a woman.

Alexandra reached home in the afternoon. That evening she held a family council and told her brothers all that she had seen and heard.

"I want you boys to go down yourselves and look it over. Nothing will convince you like seeing with your own eyes. The river land was settled before this, and so they are a few years ahead of us, and have learned more about farming. The land sells for three times as much as this, but in five years we will double it. The rich men down there own all the best land, and they are buying all they can get. The thing to do is to sell our cattle and what little old corn we have, and buy the Linstrum place. Then the next thing to do is to take out two loans on our half-sections, and buy Peter Crow's place; raise every dollar we can, and buy every acre we can."

"Mortgage the homestead again?" Lou cried. He sprang up and began to wind the clock furiously. "I won't slave to pay off another mortgage. I'll never do it. You'd just as soon kill us all, Alexandra, to carry out some scheme!"

Oscar rubbed his high, pale forehead. "How do you propose to pay off your mortgages?"

Alexandra looked from one to the other and bit her lip. They had never seen her so nervous. "See here," she brought out at last. "We borrow the money for six years. Well, with the money we buy a half-section from Linstrum and a half from Crow, and a quarter from Struble, maybe. That will give us upwards of fourteen hundred acres, won't it? You won't have to pay off your mortgages for six years. By that time, any of this land will be worth thirty dollars an acre—it will be worth fifty, but we'll say thirty; then you can sell a garden patch anywhere, and pay off a debt of sixteen hundred dollars. It's not the principal I'm worried about, it's the interest and taxes. We'll have to strain to meet the payments. But as sure as we are sitting here to-night, we can sit down here ten years from now independent landowners, not struggling farmers any longer. The chance that father was always looking for has come."

Lou was pacing the floor. "But how do you *know* that land is going to go up enough to pay the mortgages and—"

"And make us rich besides?" Alexandra put in firmly. "I can't explain that, Lou. You'll have to take my word for it. I *know*, that's all. When you drive about over the country you can feel it coming."

Oscar had been sitting with his head lowered, his hands hanging between his knees. "But we can't work so much land," he said dully, as if he were talking to himself. "We can't even try. It would just lie there and we'd work ourselves to death." He sighed, and laid his calloused fist on the table.

Alexandra's eyes filled with tears. She put her hand on his shoulder. "You poor boy, you won't have to work it. The men in town who are buying up other people's land don't try to farm it. They are the men to watch, in a new country. Let's try to do like the shrewd ones, and not like these stupid fellows. I don't want you boys always to have to work like this. I want you to be independent, and Emil to go to school."

Lou held his head as if it were splitting. "Everybody will say we are crazy. It must be crazy, or everybody would be doing it."

"If they were, we wouldn't have much chance. No, Lou, I was talking about that with the smart young man who is raising the new kind of clover. He says the right thing to do is usually just what everybody don't do. Why are we better fixed than any of our neighbors? Because father had more brains. Our people were better people than these in the old country. We *ought* to do more than they do, and see further ahead. Yes, mother, I'm going to clear the table now."

Alexandra rose. The boys went to the stable to see to the stock, and they were gone a long while. When they came back Lou played on his *dragharmonika* and Oscar sat figuring at his father's secretary all evening. They said nothing more about Alexandra's project, but she felt sure now that they would consent to it. Just before bedtime Oscar went out for a pail of water. When he did not come back, Alexandra threw a shawl over her head and ran down the path to the windmill. She found him sitting there with his head in his hands, and she sat down beside him.

"Don't do anything you don't want to do, Oscar," she whispered. She waited a moment, but he did not stir. "I won't say any more about it, if you'd rather not. What makes you so discouraged?"

"I dread signing my name to them pieces of paper," he said slowly. "All the time I was a boy we had a mortgage hanging over us."

"Then don't sign one. I don't want you to, if you feel that way."

Oscar shook his head. "No, I can see there's a chance that way. I've thought a good while there might be. We're in so deep now, we might as well go deeper. But it's hard work pulling out of debt. Like pulling a threshing-machine out of the mud; breaks your back. Me and Lou's worked hard, and I can't see it's got us ahead much."

"Nobody knows about that as well as I do, Oscar. That's why I want to try an easier way. I don't want you to have to grub for every dollar."

"Yes, I know what you mean. Maybe it'll come out right. But signing papers is signing papers. There ain't no maybe about that." He took his pail and trudged up the path to the house.

Alexandra drew her shawl closer about her and stood leaning against the frame of the mill, looking at the stars which glittered so keenly through the frosty autumn air. She always loved to watch them, to think of their vastness and distance, and of their ordered march. It fortified her to reflect upon the great operations of nature, and when she thought of the law that lay behind them, she felt a sense of personal security. That night she had a new consciousness of the country, felt almost a new relation to it. Even her talk with the boys had not taken away the feeling that had overwhelmed her when she drove back to the Divide that afternoon. She had never known before how much the country meant to her. The chirping of the insects down in the long grass had been like the sweetest music. She had felt as if her heart were hiding down there, somewhere, with the quail and the plover and all the little wild things that crooned or buzzed in the sun. Under the long shaggy ridges, she felt the future stirring.

 EXPLORE: Discuss Cather's portrayal of Alexandra in terms of the typical myth of male settlement in which men set out to "tame" and "conquer" a "virgin land." What kind of a shift in thinking about the land does Cather seem to portray here?

Elinore Pruitt Stewart

Elinore Pruitt Rupert Stewart was born in 1876 in central Oklahoma (then known as Indian Territory) to an impoverished couple who couldn't afford to buy shoes for her until she was six years old. Her formal education was practically nonexistent, and, according to her biographer Susanne George, she "had to teach herself to read and write from scraps of paper she found." In 1902, she married Harry Rupert and in 1906, her daughter Jerrine was born. But when the marriage failed, she and her husband divorced, and Jerrine and Elinore moved to Denver, Colorado, where she worked numerous low-paying jobs cooking, cleaning, ironing, scrubbing floors, and stoking coal furnaces. Maintaining her optimistic outlook in the face of terrible poverty, Stewart once said of this period in her life, "We haven't got any flies on the pies because we haven't got any pies!" Eventually, she went to work for two dollars a week as a nurse and housekeeper for the disabled widow Juliet Coney, a genteel woman who had been educated in Boston. In 1909 Elinore Rupert filed on a homestead in southwestern Wyoming, which she could do as a single female head of household. Shortly thereafter, she married widower Clyde Stewart, who owned adjacent land, and although initially the marriage was for the sake of convenience, they soon recognized their compatibility became devoted to each other. Stewart began a long correspondence with Mrs. Coney, writing, she says, to "bring a little of this big, clean, beautiful outdoors into your apartment for you to enjoy." At some point in their correspondence, Mrs. Coney recognized the value of Stewart's letters, and she used her influence in Boston to secure a book contract for *Letters of a Woman Homesteader*.

The book was published within the context of a national dialogue about the growing problems of workers' rights in factories. Labor protests in the cities were widespread during the time, and advocates were protesting long working hours for women, substandard working conditions in the factories, and the use of child labor in cotton mills and other manufacturing plants. The tragedy of the Triangle Shirtwaist Factory fire in New York in the spring of 1911 claimed 148 lives, mostly women, and went down in history as the largest industrial disaster in the city to that date. Keep this context in mind as you read the following selections.

Letters of a Woman Homesteader
"Proving Up"

> October 14, 1911.
>
> Dear Mrs. Coney,—

I think you must be expecting an answer to your letter by now, so I will try to answer as many of your questions as I remember. Your letter has been mislaid. We have been very much rushed all this week. We had the thresher crew two days. I was busy cooking for them two days before they came, and have been busy ever since cleaning up after them. Clyde has taken the thresher on up the valley to thresh for the neighbors, and all the men have gone along, so the children and I are alone. No, I shall not lose my land, although it will be over two years before I can get a deed to it. The five years in which I am required to "prove up" will have passed by then. I couldn't have held my homestead if Clyde had also been proving up, but he had accomplished that years ago and has his deed, so I am allowed my homestead. Also I have not yet used my desert right, so I am still entitled to one hundred and sixty acres more. I shall file on that much some day when I have sufficient money of my own earning. The law requires a cash payment of twenty-five cents per acre at the filing, and one dollar more per acre when final proof is made. I should not have married if Clyde had not promised I should meet all my land difficulties unaided. I wanted the fun and the experience. For that reason I want to earn every cent that goes into my own land and improvements myself. Sometimes I almost have a brain-storm wondering how I am going to do it, but I know I shall succeed; other women have succeeded. I know of several who are now where they can laugh at past trials. Do you know?—I am a firm believer in laughter. I am real superstitious about it. I think if Bad Luck came along, he would take to his heels if some one laughed right loudly.

I think Jerrine must be born for the law. She always threshes out questions that arise, to her own satisfaction, if to no one else's. She prayed for a long time for her brother; also she prayed for some puppies. The puppies came, but we didn't let her know they were here until they were able to walk. One morning she saw them following their mother, so she danced for joy. When her little brother came she was plainly disappointed. "Mamma," she said, "did God really make the baby?"

"Yes, dear." "Then He hasn't treated us fairly, and I should like to know why. The puppies could walk when He finished them; the calves can, too. The pigs can, and the colt, and even the chickens. What is the use of giving us a half-finished baby? He has no hair, and no teeth; he can't walk or talk, nor do anything else but squall and sleep."

After many days she got the question settled. She began right where she left off. "I know, Mamma, why God gave us such a half-finished baby; so he could learn our ways, and no one else's, since he must live with us, and so we could learn to love him. Every time I stand beside his buggy he laughs and then I love him, but I don't love Stella nor Marvin because they laugh. So that is why." Perhaps that is the reason.

Zebbie's kinsfolk have come and taken him back to Yell County. I should not be surprised if he never returned. The Lanes and the Pattersons leave shortly for Idaho, where "our Bobbie" has made some large investments.

I hope to hear from you soon and that you are enjoying every minute. With much love,
Your friend,
Elinore Stewart

"The Joys of Homesteading"

January 23, 1913.

Dear Mrs. Coney,—

I am afraid all my friends think I am very forgetful and that you think I am ungrateful as well, but I am going to plead not guilty. Right after Christmas Mr. Stewart came down with *la grippe* and was so miserable that it kept me busy trying to relieve him. Out here where we can get no physician we have to dope ourselves, so that I had to be housekeeper, nurse, doctor, and general overseer. That explains my long silence.

And now I want to thank you for your kind thought in prolonging our Christmas. The magazines were much appreciated. They relieved some weary night-watches, and the box did Jerrine more good than the medicine I was having to give her for *la grippe*. She was content to stay in bed and enjoy the contents of her box.

When I read of the hard times among the Denver poor, I feel like urging them every one to get out and file on land. I am very enthusiastic about women homesteading. It really requires less strength and labor to raise plenty to satisfy a large family than it does to go out to wash, with the added satisfaction of knowing that their job will not be lost to them if they care to keep it. Even if improving the place does go slowly, it is that much done to stay done. Whatever is raised is the homesteader's own, and there is no house-rent to pay. This year Jerrine cut and dropped enough potatoes to raise a ton of fine potatoes. She wanted to try, so we let her, and you will remember that she is but six years old. We had a man to break the ground and cover the potatoes for her and the man irrigated them once. That was all that was done until digging time, when they were ploughed out and Jerrine picked them up. Any woman strong enough to go out by the day could have done every bit of the work and put in two or three times that much, and it would have been so much more pleasant than to work so hard in the city and then be on starvation rations in the winter.

To me, homesteading is the solution of all poverty's problems, but I realize that temperament has much to do with success in any undertaking, and persons afraid of coyotes and work and loneliness had better let ranching alone. At the same time, any woman who can stand her own company, can see the beauty of the sunset, loves growing things, and is willing to put in as much time at careful labor as she does over the washtub, will certainly succeed; will have independence, plenty to eat all the time, and a home of her own in the end.

Experimenting need cost the homesteader no more than the work, because by applying to the Department of Agriculture at Washington he can get enough of any seed and as many kinds as he wants to make a thorough trial, and it doesn't even cost postage. Also one can always get bulletins from there and from the Experiment Station of one's own State concerning any problem or as many problems as may come up. I would not, for anything, allow Mr. Stewart to do anything toward improving my place, for I want the fun and the experience myself. And I want to be able to speak from experience when I tell others what they can do. Theories are very beautiful, but facts are what must be had, and what I intend to give some time.

Here I am boring you to death with things that cannot interest you! You'd think I wanted you to homestead, wouldn't you? But I am only thinking of the troops of tired, worried women, sometimes even cold and hungry, scared to death of losing their places to work, who could have plenty to eat, who could have good fires by gathering the wood, and comfortable homes of their own, if they but had the courage and determination to get them.

I must stop right now before you get so tired you will not answer. With much love to you from Jerrine and myself, I am

Yours affectionately,
Elinore Rupert Stewart

"Success"

November, 1913.

Dear Mrs. Coney,—

This is Sunday and I suppose I ought not to be writing, but I must write to you and I may not have another chance soon. Both your letters have reached me, and now that our questions are settled we can proceed to proceed.

Now, this is the letter I have been wanting to write you for a long time, but could not because until now I had not actually proven all I wanted to prove. Perhaps it will not interest you, but if you see a woman who wants to homestead and is a little afraid she will starve, you can tell her what I am telling you.

I never did like to theorize, and so this year I set out to prove that a woman could ranch if she wanted to. We like to grow potatoes on new ground, that is, newly cleared land on which no crop has been grown. Few weeds grow on new land, so it makes less work. So I selected my potato-patch, and the man ploughed it, although I could have done that if Clyde would have let me. I cut the potatoes, Jerrine helped, and we dropped them in the rows. The man covered them, and that ends the man's part. By that time the garden ground was ready, so I planted the garden. I had almost an acre in vegetables. I irrigated and I cultivated it myself.

We had all the vegetables we could possibly use, and now Jerrine and I have put in our cellar full, and this is what we have: one large bin of potatoes (more than two tons), half a ton of carrots, a large bin of beets, one of turnips, one of onions, one of parsnips, and on the other side of the cellar we have more than one hundred heads of cabbage. I have experimented and found a kind of squash that can be raised here, and that the ripe ones keep well and make good pies; also that the young tender ones make splendid pickles, quite equal to cucumbers. I was glad to stumble on to that, because pickles are hard to manufacture when you have nothing to work with. Now I have plenty. They told me when I came that I could not even raise common beans, but I tried and succeeded. And also I raised lots of green tomatoes, and, as we like them preserved, I made them all up that way. Experimenting along another line, I found that I could make catchup, as delicious as that of tomatoes, of gooseberries. I made it exactly the same as I do the tomatoes and I am delighted. Gooseberries were very fine and very plentiful this year, so I put up a great many. I milked ten cows twice a day all summer; have sold enough butter to pay for a year's supply of flour and gasoline. We use a gasoline lamp. I have raised enough chickens to completely renew my flock, and all we wanted to eat, and have some fryers to go into the winter with. I have enough turkeys for all of our birthdays and holidays.

I raised a great many flowers and I worked several days in the field. In all I have told about I have had no help but Jerrine. Clyde's mother spends each summer with us, and she

According to *Frontiers: A Short History of the American West* by Robert V. Hine and John Mack Faragher, in the early twentieth century as many as 20% of homesteads were being filed on by women (up from 5–15% during the last decades of the nineteenth century), and overall, an estimated 30,000–40,000 women gained title to lands in their own name through the one of the Homestead Acts.

The original Homestead Act of 1862 allowed women who had been widowed, deserted "without cause," divorced, or otherwise considered "head of household" and therefore "compelled to support herself and her family" to file on land; however, the act excluded married women from filing. A Government Land Office Ruling of 1864 said that a married woman is obviously "incompetent to make a homestead entry." An 1872 decision decreed that a woman who marries after filing on land "abandons her right" and would be forced to give up the land. During the next decades, these laws were challenged, and by the early 1900s some states said that a year must pass between a woman filing a claim and her marriage. When Elinore and Clyde Stewart were married, they got around this law by transferring Elinore's land under the name of Clyde's widowed mother. For more information on women homesteaders, see H. Elaine Lindgren's *Land in Her Own Name: Women as Homesteaders in North Dakota*.

helped me with the cooking and the babies. Many of my neighbors did better than I did, although I know many town people would doubt my doing so much, but I did it. I have tried every kind of work this ranch affords, and I can do any of it. Of course I *am* extra strong, but those who try know that strength and knowledge come with doing. I just love to experiment, to work, and to prove out things, so that ranch life and "roughing it" just suit me.

Your friend,
Elinore Stewart

EXPLORE: Keeping Mrs. Coney's background in mind, reread the January 23, 1913 letter, and consider Stewart's intended audience. Is this the kind of advice you would expect her to write to someone like Coney who is disabled and can afford a housekeeper? If not, what do you think accounts for Elinore's adamant "boosterism" message that "homesteading is the solution of all poverty's problems"?

EXPLORE: What character strengths make Stewart a success as a woman homesteader? Stewart uses forms of the word "prove" quite a bit. What is she trying to prove about herself?

EXPLORE: *Letters of a Woman Homesteader* is an epistolary book—that is, it is a collection of letters. What conventions of letter writing does Stewart follow, and which ones does she ignore? Think about how this book would have been different if it were a strict autobiography, if Stewart had turned her story into a work of fiction, like Mary Hallock Foote's, or if it had been a congressional report, like the Country Life Commission Report.

❦ CHAPTER SIX ❦

Farming in Hard Times

FIGURE 6.1. Diego Rivera, *The Flower Carrier*, oil and tempera on masonite, 1935. 48" x 47¾". San Francisco Museum of Modern Art, Albert M. Bender Collection, gift of Albert M. Bender in memory of Caroline Walter. ©2019 Banco de México Diego Rivera & Frida Kahlo Museums Trust, Mexico City, Mexico / Artists Rights Society (ARS), New York. Photo: Katherine Du Tiel.

American culture has a long tradition of venerating farmers and idealizing the work they do; however, there is also a long history of hard times on the American farm. This chapter pictures some of those challenges, including difficulties due to natural disasters; political and economic changes on a global level that had important consequences on farming; challenges to the mythology, especially relating to farm laborers who were forgotten and disenfranchised; the costs of modern farming methods to the environment and human health; and the changing nature of how farmers do business.

Plantation System, Sharecropping, and Tenant Farming

The Antebellum Plantation System

The plantation system of agriculture in the antebellum South created a huge disparity between the haves and the have-nots. Plantation owners, or *planters*, as they were called to distinguish them from "farmers," often had wealth, significant land holdings, the classic Georgian mansion, political influence—and, of course, slaves. According to some historians, a farmer had to own at least twenty slaves to be considered a planter and be a part of the elite planter aristocracy. Originally, the colonists had tried to use Native Americans as their agricultural slaves, but because they had no immunity to introduced diseases like measles and smallpox, this didn't prove to be feasible. The first African slaves to arrive in the colonies landed in 1619 in Virginia, and by the 1860 census, the slave states had nearly four million slaves—nearly a third of the population in the slave states.

Hierarchy of a Plantation:

White Planter/Owner makes all major decisions of management, purchasing and selling slaves, and punishment of slaves.

   White Overseer is a hired professional farmer who manages the labor force, including white indentured servants and hired laborers. He implements the orders of plantation owner, gives work assignments, allocates punishments, treats slaves who are ill, and keeps records.

   Head Driver is usually a loyal and obedient black slave who could supervise other slaves. He helps the Overseer maintain order and discipline and serves as intermediary between owner and slaves. A large plantation could have a number of drivers, all of various ranks.

Of the nation's first eighteen presidents, only six never owned slaves: the second president John Adams, John Quincy Adams (#6), Millard Filmore (#13), Franklin Pierce (#14), James Buchanan (#15, though he had two indentured servants who had formerly been slaves), and Abraham Lincoln (#16). Martin Van Buren had only own one slave during his life, a man named Tom who escaped. Of the slave-owning presidents, eight of them had slaves while holding the office of the presidency, including Thomas Jefferson, who at times was one of the largest slave owners in Virginia; 130 slaves were sold off by the estate after his death. Source: "Which US Presidents Owned Slaves?" http://tinyurl.com/slaveowningpresidents

"The plantation is a piece of machinery . . . To operate successfully, all parts should be uniform and exact, and the impelling force regular and steady. . . . No more beautiful picture of human society can be drawn than a well organized plantation." Plantation Owner, quoted in *Plantation Society and Race Relations: The Origins of Inequality*, Thomas J. Durant and J. David Knottnerus, eds.

   Artisans and House Slaves are the skilled laborers and those working most closely with the owner's family. Within this class, there is yet another caste system based on several factors, including skill level (artisans like carpenters and trained seamstresses or cooks were at the top), skin color (light-complected mulattos fared somewhat better, unless they were too fair-skinned or bore a family resemblance), and proximity to the family (for instance, the "mammy" who took care of the children was higher than the house maid).

   Field slaves directly involved in all aspects of day-to-day farm work were the largest sector of the plantation. Here too there was a caste system in which, for instance, ploughmen working with horses were above "hoe-hands," and domestically born slaves were ranked above recently imported slaves.

   For more on plantation culture, see "The Making of African American Identity" at http://www.nationalhumanitiescenter.org/pds/maai/index.htm.

The Sharecropping and Tenant Farming System

After the Civil War, the nation needed to restructure the slave-based agricultural systems that had long been the norm. Rumors circulated among the emancipated slaves that the government had promised freed slaves "forty acres and a mule" (an amount determined by the belief that forty acres was the optimal amount of land one family with one mule could tend). The rumor had some basis in fact, given that in January of 1865 General William Tecumseh Sherman ordered abandoned plantations along the Georgia and South Carolina coasts be divided up in forty-acre plots for freed blacks. However, the former plantation owners protested, saying they had been driven from their homes and now wanted their land back. President Andrew Jackson sided with the plantation owners, and an estimated 40,000 freedmen who had received grants of land via Sherman's orders were ordered to leave their land.

FIGURE 6.2. Dorothea Lange, *Thirteen-Year-Old Sharecropper Boy near Americus, Georgia,* July 1937.

The problem remained, however, of what to do with the hundreds of thousands former slaves who remained in the south but had no work and no place to live, as well as the sizable land holdings of the former planters who now had no work force to tend the fields and little money to pay wages. Thus, during the Reconstruction period farmers without farms entered a dual system of tenancy or sharecropping, which historians have called *para-slavery*, *slavery-in-kind*, or *peonage*.

Tenant farming was based on the assumptions that farmers (both freedmen and landless white men) owned their own work animals and equipment and could pay for their own seed and supplies, as well as the cost of renting the land. While the advantage here was they typically did not have to share their profits with the landowner, the clear problem was that only a few white farmers had such resources.

The other solution was a system of sharecropping in which the landowner signed an annual contract with a farmer that extended credit for seed and supplies—often by using that year's crop as collateral—and allowed the farmer 10–40 acres to farm and a small plot for a vegetable garden; in return, the owner could determine which crop would be planted in the fields and would get a sum of the profit (as much as two-thirds). In some cases where high interest rates were charged, these freedman farmers were held in *debt-bondage* because what they owed could never be paid off. In such cases, the money they received after a crop was sold was often given to the farmer with the stipulation that it could only be used in the "company store" owned by the landlord. Both black freedmen and poor white farmers (some of whom had lost farms during the hard economic times of Reconstruction) functioned under this system. Some families were able to save money and buy small farms after sharecropping, but that didn't happen often. By 1930, only one in ten African Americans who had remained in the South owned the land they farmed, and nationwide, 80% of African-American farmers and 40% of white farmers worked as sharecroppers or tenant farmers.

For more on tenant farming and sharecropping, visit "Tenant Farming and Sharecropping" at http://tinyurl.com/sharecropping-okstate, "The African American as Sharecropper" at http://tinyurl.com/sharecropping-u-houston, "Sharecropping" at http://tinyurl.com/sharecropping-georgia, and "Sharecropping" in *The Social History of the United States, The 1930s,* edited by Brian Greedberg and Linda S. Watts. For a look at the modern African-American farmer in the South, view the documentary *Homecoming: The Story of African American Farmers.*

Sharecropper's Contract between Isham G. Bailey, Cooper Hughes, and Charles Roberts
Marshall County, Mississippi, 1 January 1867.

Articles of agreement made and entered into this 1st day of January AD 1867, between IG Bailey of the first part and Cooper Hughs Freedman and Charles Roberts Freedman of the second part Witnesseth.

The said parties of the second part, have agreed and do by these presents agree and bind themselves to work for the said party of the first past during the year 1867, on the farm belonging to said party of the first part near Early Grove on said County upon the following terms and conditions to Wit the said Cooper Hughs Freedman with his wife and one other woman, and the said Charles Roberts with his wife Hannah and one boy are to work on said farm and to cultivate forty acres in corn and twenty acres in cotton, to assist in putting the fences on said farm in good order and to keep them so and to do all other work on said farm necessary to be done to keep the same in good order and to raise a good crop and to be under the control and directions of said IG Bailey and to receive for their said services one half of the cotton and one third of the corn and fodder raised by them on said farm in said year 1867 and the said Charles Roberts Freedman with his wife Hannah further agrees and binds themselves to do the washing and Ironing, and all other necessary house work for said IG Bailey and his family during said year 1867 and to receive for their said services fifty dollars in money at the expiration of said year 1867 and the said Cooper Hughs Freedman further agrees and binds himself to give the necessary attention of feeding the Stock of cattle and milking the cows twice daily belong to said IG Bailey, and do the churning when ever necessary during the said year,

And the said IG Bailey party of the first part, agrees and binds himself to furnish necessary Mules and farming implements to cultivate said crop and to feed said Mules to furnish said Cooper Hughs Freedman and his family five hundred and fifty pounds of meat, to furnish said Charles Roberts Freedman and his family four hundred and eighty seven pounds of meat and to give said parties of the second part, one half of the crop of cotton and third of the crop of corn and fodder cultivated and raised by them in said year 1867.

In witness whereof we hereto set our hands and seals the date first above written

Signed Sealed and acknowledged	{	I.G. Bailey {Seal}
My presence this 14 May AD 1865	{	Cooper [*inserted*: his mark] Hughs {Seal}
AB Conley {Seal}	{	Charles [*inserted*: his mark] Roberts {Seal}
Justice of the Peace	{	

EXPLORE: Do you think this contract is fair and reasonable? Why or why not? If not, what would make it a fair contract?

WRITE: Using the names and facts in this contract, create a story about farming in the year 1867.

Toni Morrison, Song of Solomon

In Toni Morrison's 1977 novel, she portrays a once-successful African-American farmer named Macon Dead. However, Macon is cheated out of his thriving farm and years later his grandson Milkman Dead travels to Danville, Ohio, the site where his grandfather once farmed. The following passage describes Milkman as he listens to a number of old men who knew his grandfather.

Macon Dead was the farmer they wanted to be, the clever irrigator, the peach tree grower, the hog slaughterer, the wild turkey roaster, the man who could plow forty in no time flat and sang like an angel while he did it. He had come out of nowhere, as ignorant as a hammer and as broke as a convict, with nothing but free papers, a Bible, and a pretty black haired wife, and in one year he'd leased ten acres, the next ten more. Sixteen years later he had one of the best farms in Montour County. A farm that colored their lives like a paintbrush and spoke to them like a sermon. "You see?" the farm said to them. "See? See what you can do? Never mind you can't tell one letter from another, never mind you born a slave, never mind you lose your name, never mind your daddy dead, never mind nothing. Here, this here, is what a man can do if he puts his mind to it and his back into it. Stop sniveling," it said. "Stop picking around the edges of the world. Take advantage, and if you can't take advantage, take disadvantage. We live here. On this planet, in this nation, in this country right here. Nowhere else! We got a home in this rock, don't you see! Nobody starving in my home; nobody crying in my home, and if I got a home you got one too! Grab it! Grab this land!"

Native American Farmers

American Indians found the Euro-American concept of an individual living on and farming privately held lands odd. They typically held land cooperatively in a tribal culture, or they may have been from the nomadic tribes of the Plains states who followed migrating buffalo on seasonal treks, or tended to rely on hunting more than farming for their food sources. Yet influenced by the Manifest Destiny policies of the nineteenth century, Euro-Americans believed it was important to assimilating American Indians into the national culture, and some believed the Dawes Act of 1887, also known as the "Indian Homestead Act," was the way to do that.

FIGURE 6.3. United States Department of the Interior 1911 advertisement offering Indian Land for Sale. Notes average prices of historic tribal lands per acre. Image: Wikipedia.org.

RESEARCH: As a class, divide the following questions related to the Dawes Act of 1887. Conduct research, and be prepared to report your findings to the class. A good place to start your research might be with Lawrence C. Kelly's essay "The Dawes Act and Its Failure: 1887 to 1934," available through Facts on File at http://tinyurl.com/ DawesActFailure.

1. What were the stipulations of governmental agreements regarding land with American Indians prior to 1887? (See the Northwest Ordinance of 1787, Indian Removal Act of 1830, Indian Appropriations Act of 1851, and Fort Laramie Treaty of 1868.)
2. What were the motives behind enacting the Dawes Act?
3. What did the legislators see as the benefits to the American Indians of the Dawes Act?
4. What were the benefits to non-American Indians in enacting the Dawes legislation?
5. What were the assumptions made about American Indians inherent in the Dawes Act?
6. What were the stipulations of the Dawes Act?
7. What happened to "surplus" lands?
8. How were the issues of citizenship and assimilation related to the Dawes Act?
9. What were the problems that kept the Dawes Act from working?
10. What were the unforeseen results and effects on Indian culture of the Dawes Act?

Related questions:
1. How were issues of American Indian education related to assimilation?
2. Historically, which tribal cultures in the US were involved in farming, and what kind did they practice?
3. What are modern attitudes about farming among various American Indian groups (a good place to start with this might be to look up the work of Gary Paul Nabhan)?

History of Population Shifts and the Rural-Urban Divide

Urbanization, or the move to well-populated areas, is not a new concept. The ancient cities of Rome and Baghdad had reached populations of over a million in 133 BC and 775 AD, respectively, but in both cases population declined well below those numbers by the time of the Industrial Revolution. It was London that was considered the first industrial "world city"—that is, a city involved in manufacturing and world commerce and trade. By 1700, London's population was half a million, making it the largest city in western Europe. London was also the first industrial city to reach the one-million population mark in 1810, soon to be followed by Beijing (then called Peking). The nation of Great Britain became the first truly urban society; by 1851, more than half of the population of the nation lived in cities, and by 1891 the Greater London metropolitan area was the first worldwide to reach the significant 5 million mark.

Compare these figures to numbers from the US. From 1810 to 1930, a time period roughly equivalent to the advances in the Industrial Revolution, US population statistics document the dramatic rural-to-urban shift that happened in our nation. As the Roosevelt Country Life Commission Report indicated, this shift led to serious debate about the cultural effects of a more urban society. In the year London became a "million city," the US didn't even have a city that surpassed the 100,000 mark. At that time, New York's population was just over 96,000, and it wouldn't be until 1880 that it became our nation's first city to hit that mark, with Chicago following suit in 1890.

The US Census Bureau also recognized in the 1890 census that the distribution of the population was such that there were more than 2 people per square

> **US Farm Population Figures to 1930:**
>
> **1880**: Farmers are for the first time less than half of the US population, with 49% involved in farming occupations.
> **1890**: Farmers are 43% of the labor force.
> **1900**: Farmers are 38% of the labor force.
> **1910**: Farmers are 31% of the labor force.
> **1920**: This year marked two tipping points. Total US population passed the 100 million mark, and for the first time more than half of the US population or 51.2% lived in urban communities, rather than in rural areas. Urban was defined as 2500 or more people living in incorporated towns or cities. Farmers were 27% of labor force.
> **1930**: Farmers are 21% of the labor force and have a 6.2 million population.

mile nationwide. Such data convinced the Superintendent of the Census to announce that the frontier region of the nation no longer existed and the settling of the frontier was complete. Frederick Jackson Turner would use this fact as the main catalyst for his 1893 study "The Significance of the Frontier to American History" to argue that the frontier line had been the defining factor in determining the democratic nature of the American character.

But the rural-urban shift was even more clearly demarked by the 1920 census, sometimes called the Urban Census, which documented that for the first time a greater percentage of the US population was living in urban rather than in rural areas. That year New York City was also counted as the nation's first city to reach 5 million in population, and Los Angeles was more than half a million. It would take until 1930 for Los Angeles to exceed the one million mark, making it the first city west of the Mississippi to reach that number.

For more on this topic, see the website *Growing a Nation: The Story of American Agriculture*, developed by Utah State University in cooperation with the United States Department of Agriculture. For more on the Rural-Urban demographic shift, see "Urban, Rural, and Farm Population, and Large Cities " by Campbell Gibson at http://tinyurl.com/UrbanRuralFarmPopulation.

Grant Wood, Revolt against the City

Writing to promote a sense of regionalism in all of the arts (literature, music, and drama, as well as painting), famed American painter Grant Wood wrote a pamphlet entitled *Revolt Against the City* (1934) that urged artists to move away from what he called "the domination exercised over art and letters and over much of our thinking and living by Eastern capitals of finance and politics" where, he believes, "culturally our Eastern states are still colonies of Europe" and "the whole colonial influence" is "deep-seated." "The eyes of the seaport cities," he writes, "have long been focused upon the 'mother' countries across the sea. But the colonial spirit is, of course, basically an imitative spirit, and we can have no hope of developing a culture of our own until that subservience is put in its proper historical place." On the other hand, the Depression, he said, had turned the nation "introspective" and it had "stimulated us to a re-evaluation of our resources in both art and economics." Saying that the Great Depression renewed our desire for self-reliance, he noted that "it has sent men and women back to the land; it has caused us to rediscover some of the old frontier values. In cutting us off from traditional but more artificial values, it has thrown us back upon certain true and fundamental things which are distinctively ours to use and exploit." In declaring that American art "has declared its independence from Europe, and is retreating from the cities to the more American village and country life," Wood answers those who already had "accused [him] of being a flag-waver for my own part of the country. This is no mere chauvinism. If it is patriotic, it is so because a feeling for one's own milieu and for the validity of one's own life and its surroundings is patriotic."

Revolt Against the City

The great central areas of America are coming to be evaluated more and more justly as the years pass. They are not a Hinterland for New York; they are not barbaric. . . . So many of the leaders in the arts were born in small towns and on farms that in the comments and conversations of many who have "gone East" there is today a noticeable homesickness for the scenes of their childhood. On a recent visit to New York, after seven continuous years in the Middle West, I found this attitude very striking. Seven years ago my friends had sincerely pitied me for what they called my "exile" in Iowa. They then had a vision of my going back to an uninteresting region where I could have no contact with culture and no association with kindred spirits. But now, upon my return to the East, I have found these same friends eager for news and information about the rich funds of creative material which this region holds.

I found, moreover, a determination on the part of some of the Eastern artists to visit the Middle West for the purpose of obtaining such material. I feel that, in general, such a procedure would be as false as the old one of going to Europe for subject matter, or the later fashion of going to New England fishing villages or to Mexican cities or to the mountains of our Southwest for materials. I feel that whatever virtue this new movement has lies in the necessity the painter (and the writer, too) is under, to use material which is really a part of himself. However, many New York artists and writers are more familiar, though strong childhood impressions, with village and country life than with their adopted urban environment; and for them a back-to-the-village movement is entirely feasible and defensible. But a cult or a fad for Midwestern materials is just what must be avoided. Regionalism has already suffered from a kind of cultism which is essentially false. . . .

As for my own region—the great farming section of the Middle West—I find it, quite contrary to the prevailing Eastern impression, not a drab country inhabited by peasants, but a various, rich land abounding in painting material. It does not, however furnish scenes of the picture-postcard type that one too often finds in New Mexico or further West, and sometimes in New England. Its material seems to me more sincere and honest, and to gain in depth by having to be hunted for. It is the result of analysis, and therefore is less obscured by "picturesque" surface quality. I find myself becoming rather bored by quaintness. . . .

Central and dominant in our Midwestern scene is the farmer. The depression, with its farm strikes and heroic attempts of Government to find solutions for agrarian difficulties, has emphasized for us all the fact that the farmer is basic in the economies of the country—and, further, that he is a human being. . . . Midwestern farmers are not of peasant stock. There is much variety in their ancestry, of course; but the Iowa farmer as I know him is fully as American as Boston, and has the great advantage of being farther away from European influence. He knows little of life in crowded cities, and would find such intimacies uncomfortable; it is with difficulty that he reconciles himself even to village life. He is on a little unit of his own, where he develops an extraordinary independence. The economics, geography, and psychology of his situation have always accented his comparative isolation. The farmer's reactions must be toward weather, tools, beasts, and plant to a far greater extent than those of city dwellers, and toward other human beings far less. . . .

The farmer is not articulate. Self-expression through literature and art belong not to the set of relationships with which he is familiar (those with weather, tools, and growing things), but to more socialized systems. He is almost wholly preoccupied with his struggle against the elements, with the fundamentals of life, so that he has no time . . . for the subtleties of interpretation. . . . Finally, ridicule by city folks with European ideas of the farmer as a peasant, or, as our American slang has it, a "hick," has caused a further withdrawal—a proud and disdainful answer to misunderstanding criticism.

But the very fact that the farmer is not himself vocal makes him the richest kind of material for the writer and the artist. He needs interpretation. Serious, sympathetic handling of farmer-material offers a great field for the careful worker. The life of the farmer, engaged in a constant conflict with natural forces, is essentially dramatic. The drought of last Summer provided innumerable episodes of the most gripping human interest. The nomadic movements of cattlemen in Wisconsin, in South Dakota, and in other states, the violent protests against foreclosures, the struggles against dry-year pests, the sacrifices forced upon once prosperous families—all these elements and many more are colorful, significant, and intensely dramatic.

The 1930s: Dust Bowl and the Great Depression
John Steinbeck's The Grapes of Wrath

During the 1930s, American literature began to assume a more political voice, and works like John Steinbeck's *The Grapes of Wrath* followed the sentiment of Mexican muralist painter Diego Rivera when he said in 1933 that "Art is propaganda, or it is not art." Steinbeck was deeply interested in writing the stories of laborers, farmworkers, the homeless and dispossessed, as is true of other novels like *In Dubious Battle*, *Cannery Row*, and *Of Mice and Men*. In 1940, he won the Pulitzer Prize for *The Grapes of Wrath* and in 1962, he was given Nobel Prize in literature.

While *The Grapes of Wrath* follows the Joads, a sharecropper family of "Okies" who seek a better life in California, their story is interwoven with interchapters, which compare and contrast the Joad story with that of thousands of Okies moving west and trying to adapt to a new world now run by corporate farms. The interchapters often serve as a place for Steinbeck to artfully craft his own political manifestos about the lives of the dispossessed. Sometimes they serve as juxtaposition or amplification, as intensification of the drama, and as a way of reinforcing the idea that the Joads's family story reflects a problem of national dimensions. "The causes lie deep and simple," Steinbeck writes in the book; "the causes are a hunger in the stomach, multiplied a million times; a hunger in a single soul, hunger for joy and some security, multiplied a million times." Thus, the fate of the Joads is one example of all migrant workers, who are caught up in a kind of Darwinian fight for survival.

The following excerpt is from one of the interchapters in which a family of unnamed sharecroppers is being forced off land they were born on and have worked for generations. Although the orders to clear the land completely—even if that means knocking down sharecropper shacks—may come from bank presidents or land owners, Steinbeck argues that what is really behind the displacement of these Midwestern farmers is "a monster, without thought and feeling. . . And it came about [because] owners no longer worked on their farms. They farmed on paper; and they forgot the land, the smell, the feel of it, and remembered only that they owned it."

The Grapes of Wrath

The tractors came over the roads and into the fields, great crawlers moving like insects, having the incredible strength of insects. They crawled over the ground, laying the track and rolling on it and picking it up. Diesel tractors, puttering while they stood idle; they thundered when they moved, and then settled down to a droning roar. Snub-nosed monsters raising the dust and sticking their snouts into it, straight down the country, across the country, through fences, through dooryards, in and out of gullies in straight lines. They did not run on the ground, but on their own roadbeds. They ignored hills and gulches, water courses, houses.

The man sitting in the iron seat did not look like a man; gloved, goggled, rubber dust mask over nose and mouth, he was a part of the monster, a robot in the seat. The thunder of the cylinders sounded through the country, became one with the air and the earth, so that earth and air muttered in sympathetic vibration. The driver could not control it—straight across country it went, cutting through a dozen farms and straight back. A twitch at the controls could swerve the cat, but the driver's hands could not twitch because the monster that built the tractor, the monster that sent the tractor out, had somehow got into the driver's hands, into his brain and muscle, had goggled him and muzzled him—goggled his mind, muzzled his speech, goggled his perception, muzzled his protest. He could not see the land as it was, he could not smell the land as it smelled; his feet did not stamp the clods or feel the warmth and power of the earth. He sat in an iron seat and stepped on iron pedals. He could not cheer or beat or curse or encourage the extension of his power, and because of this he could not cheer or whip or curse or encourage himself. He did not know or own or trust or beseech the land. If a seed dropped did not germinate, it was nothing. If the young thrusting plant withered in drought or drowned in a flood of rain, it was no more to the driver than to the tractor.

He loved the land no more than the bank loved the land. He could admire the tractor—its machined surfaces, its surge of power, the roar of its detonating cylinders; but it was not his tractor. Behind the tractor rolled the shining disks, cutting the earth with blades—not plowing but surgery, pushing the cut earth to the right where the second row of disks cut it and pushed it to the left; slicing blades shining, polished by the cut earth. And pulled behind the disks, the harrows combing with iron teeth so that the little clods broke up and the earth lay smooth. Behind the harrows, the long seeders—twelve curved iron penes erected in the foundry, orgasms set by gears, raping methodically, raping without passion. The driver sat in his iron seat and he was proud of the straight lines he did not will, proud of the tractor he did not own or love, proud of the power he could not control. And when that crop grew, and was harvested, no man had crumbled a hot clod in his fingers and let the earth sift past his fingertips. No man had touched the seed, or lusted for the growth. Men ate what they had not raised, had no connection with the bread.

The land bore under iron, and under iron gradually died; for it was not loved or hated, it had no prayers or curses.

 EXPLORE: How does this excerpt display one of the novel's main themes, namely, the human struggle against dehumanization? And what does Steinbeck seem to be saying about machinery and the farmer's relationship to it? What is he saying about the family farm ideal?

COLLABORATE: Sometimes passages in the novel, and especially in interchapters like these, almost sound like poetry. Critic Peter Lisca believes the novel's varying prose styles helped make it a masterpiece. Steinbeck's prose, he writes, has the "sound of passages from The Psalms," a point he makes clear by writing a passage out in poetry form ("*The Grapes of Wrath* as Fiction" in *A Casebook on The Grapes of Wrath*, A. M. Donohue, editor). The same could apply to this passage you read from Chapter 5, which is depicted here in poetic line form:

> The tractors came over the roads and into the fields,
> Great crawlers moving like insects.
> Having the incredible strength of insects. . . .
> Diesel tractors, puttering while they stood idle;
>
> They thundered when they moved,
> And then settled down to a droning roar.
> Snubnosed monsters, raising the dust
> And sticking their snouts into it,
>
> Straight down the country,
> Across the country,
> Through fences,
> Through dooryards,
> In and out of
> Gullies in
> Straight
> Lines.

Your task is to pair with a classmate and to write a "found poem." A found poem is created by taking words, phrases, and passages from one source and reframing them as poetry with changes in spacing and lines or by adding or deleting text to impart new or enhanced meaning. Select a passage that sounds like a poem to you either from the Steinbeck reading here or from the novel. Rearrange it to look like a poem by breaking it up into poetic lines. Your poem must keep thematically with what you read. Don't simply stop at breaking up the lines as above. You may rearrange sentences, use repetition of phrases or sentences, or reshape Steinbeck's language to create or enhance the metaphors and similes he uses.

Often found poetry combines words from more than one source, so you may also integrate language from other sources in this textbook or the resources the text invites you to use. For instance, you might interweave Steinbeck's language with Jefferson's, or you might show ways that Steinbeck's lines echo sentiments from Cesar Chavez's speeches or is a contrast to language from the Homestead Act.

Additionally, either discuss in class or write a paragraph describing your process and why you made the choices you made. Why did you choose the passages in Steinbeck's work for your poem? Also use this conversation to discuss the difference between prose and poetry.

Subjects Related to The Grapes of Wrath

Hoovervilles

During Herbert Hoover's presidential campaign in 1929, he made the famous campaign promise that everyone would have "a chicken in every pot." Just months after he was sworn in, the stock market crashed, and the country entered the Great Depression. At its height, one quarter of the country was jobless. Because Hoover believed that the economy would stabilize on its own and recovery was just around the corner, he provided little in relief for the needy. The growing number of homeless built shanty towns with "homes" constructed from tar paper, scrap wood, pieces of metal. Hoovervilles, as they were called by the mass of people who lived in them, sprung up from Seattle to Central Park, as well as along the migratory routes that Steinbeck describes in *The Grapes of Wrath*. People began calling the newspapers they slept under "Hoover blankets," the cardboard or cut up tires they fashioned shoes from were called "Hoover leather," and the empty pockets they wore inside out to show they were penniless were called "Hoover flags."

 VIEW: To see some of the nation's Hoovervilles, both in urban and rural areas, view this YouTube view, which is set to a famous Depression era song "Brother, Can You Spare a Dime?" sung here by Bing Crosby in 1932: http://tinyurl.com/Hoovervilles-BingCrosby.

Dorothea Lange

Documentary photographer Dorothea Lange was best known for her work during the Depression Era for the Farm Security Administration, which sent her into rural areas of America to record the plight of farmers. It was Lange who took the most iconic photograph of the Depression. "Migrant Mother" was taken in 1937 in Nipomo, California.

 VIEW: Go to the following link to watch a slide show of this and 150 more of Lange's photos: https://www.youtube.com/watch?v=Fw1AZkvdC8k

Dust Bowl: *The Plow That Broke the Plains*

The Dust Bowl experience defined a generation of American farmers. There are many resources to help you further understand the causes, effects, and scope of that ecological disaster. *The Plow That Broke the Plains* is a famous 1936 documentary about the Dust Bowl that was funded by the Farm Security Administration and the United States Department of Agriculture.

 VIEW: *The Plow That Broke the Plains*. The 25-minute video showed the severity of the problem caused by agricultural over-production and misuse of land and lack of soil conservation (http://tinyurl.com/ThePlowThatBrokeThePlains).

Dust Bowl: Ken Burns Documentary & Timothy Egan

The Ken Burns' two-part documentary *The Dust Bowl* is an excellent introduction that uses footage from the period and draws upon interviews with survivors. It was broadcast on PBS and you can view portions of it online, where you can also experiment with an interactive Dust Bowl that puts you in the position of making some of the same decisions farmers in the area had to make. The entire series is available for download on iTunes or Amazon's Prime Instant Video.

One of the people Burns interviews for his documentary was Timothy Egan, who wrote *The Worst Hard Time: The Untold Story of Those Who Survived the Great American Dust Bowl*, which was the National Book Award winner in 2006. Either read an excerpt from the book, listen to the excerpt available on Amazon, or watch Ken Burns and Tim Egan discuss the Dust Bowl (and John Steinbeck's *The Grapes of Wrath*).

VIEW: Information about Ken Burns' documentary: http://video.pbs.org/program/dust-bowl/ or find out more at http://www.pbs.org/kenburns/dustbowl/.
The Burns-Egan interview is available at http://tinyurl.com/BurnsEganDustBowl.

EXPLORE: Timothy Egan and Ken Burns are a journalist and a documentarian, respectively—both occupations that bring with them a certain expectation of objectivity and a focus on fact. Yet journalist Walter Cronkite, who had reported on the Dust Bowl during the 1930s, calls Egan's book "exciting" and says it's a "can't-put-it-down history." Reviewers have called the Burns documentary "gripping" and say it is "history brought to life." Discuss what techniques Burns and Egan use to make history so engaging, and perhaps so different from what you may think are characteristic of "history." How are these works also similar or different from the 1936 documentary *The Plow That Broke the Plains*?

Woody Guthrie and The Dust Bowl

American folk musician and activist Woody Guthrie (1912–1967) earned the nickname the "Dust Bowl Troubadour" for his numerous songs about the struggles Midwestern farmers faced during the 1930s and 1940s. He is probably best known for his song "This Land Is Your Land," which is considered one of the nation's patriotic anthems; however, even that song celebrating the beauty of the American landscape is sung from the point of view of a displaced wanderer, something highlighted in the verses that were cut for the published version (including the line "I saw my people/As they stood hungry"). Guthrie admired Steinbeck's *The Grapes of Wrath*, and he paid tribute to the novel with several songs, including "The Ballad of Tom Joad."

RESEARCH: Listen to several of Guthrie's farm songs online (available on such platforms as YouTube and Spotify). In addition to the songs listed above, also check out the songs on Guthrie's 1940 Dust Bowl Ballads album and his 1941 ballad "Pastures of Plenty." Consider Guthrie's portrayal of a farmer's relationship to the land, how Guthrie's activism is apparent, his use of Steinbeck's novel, and how the music enhances the meaning of the lyrics. You may also wish to look up Bruce Springsteen's tribute to Guthrie's song, which is called "The Ghost of Tom Joad," and consider how Springsteen's version of the story differs from Guthrie's.

Growing West in Hard Times: A Photographic Essay

"Go West," recommended Horace Greeley, the founding editor of *The New York Tribune*, the country's most influential newspaper of the mid-nineteenth century. He favored westward expansion and the philosophy of Manifest Destiny, the belief that white settlers from the East were ordained by God to redeem western lands, civilize the native population, and turn the West into a productive agricultural paradise.

Another booster, Charles Dana Wilber, advocated that rain actually follows the plow: "The plow is the instrument which separates civilization from savagery; and converts a desert into a farm or garden." Colorado River explorer and Civil War veteran John Wesley Powell disagreed. He urged the government to slow the tide of farmers taking advantage of the Homestead Act of 1862 to avoid depleting underground watersheds and prevent water wars. Boosters continued to promote the benefits of owning land, and boomtowns popped up overnight.

The Dawes Act of 1887 reduced Native American holdings to the same 160 acres as the homesteaders. That amount of acreage was based on eastern geography, not the arid lands of the West. Irrigation supposedly reduced the need to live near water. As one pamphlet from the Idaho Commercial Club (1914) proclaimed: "When my pastures need rain, do I look anxiously at the heavens? Not on your life; I simply press the button and can have a gully washer at my option."

President Teddy Roosevelt wrote that "No nation has ever achieved permanent greatness unless this greatness was based on the well being of the great farmer class; for it is upon their welfare, material and oral, that the welfare of the rest of the nation ultimately rests." His Country Life Commission (1908) was the first to address the role of women and families on farms. As a result, 4-H programs were organized, Rural Free Delivery (RFD) of mail was started, Extension Programs were funded by the Smith-Lever Act of 1914, the Rural Electrification Act (REA) of 1935 provided federal loans to establish power companies, and rural sociology was established as an academic field to continue to study the questions of the Commission.

For farmwomen, the Smith-Lever Act was particularly important. It gave land-grant colleges the chance to cooperate with the US Department of Agriculture to begin demonstration works. In this way, the information that came from research at the college was disseminated to farmers and communities. This was the birth of the Extension Homemakers, which gave women a platform to get involved with the community and civil affairs of the area. Women involved were empowered as they learned and demonstrated how to cook, preserve food, entertain, and maintain and care for clothing, a home, and their children (Figure 6.4). Jane S. McKimmon, an early extension worker in North Carolina, described the work like this: "By 1916, women had taken the bit in their teeth and were running away with the organization. They were hungry for the new experience of learning to do things through seeing them done; for the opportunity of coming together in interesting work; for the chance to produce an income which would furnish them with things they had so long desired; and for an outlet through which they could express themselves and get recognition from others for what they had done." (Source: https://www.ces.ncsu.edu/history/). The Extension Homemaker program was a tremendous help to many women, particularly getting them through hard times.

"The Worst Hard Time"—the Dust Bowl—was a direct result of drought, combined with destructive practices that failed to provide stewardship of the land. Woody Guthrie sang about Tom Joad of Steinbeck's *The Grapes of Wrath* in his "Dust Bowl Blues." Grant Wood, the painter of the iconic "American Gothic," said, "The farmer is not articulate. He needs interpreta-

FIGURE 6.4. Russell Lee, Wife of Mormon farmer with canned goods, Snowville, Utah, 1940. Gelatin silver print, 7 x 9 in. Gift of the Marie Eccles Caine Foundation. Collection of the Nora Eccles Harrison Museum of Art, Utah State University.

FIGURE 6.5. Dorothea Lange, Farm buildings in the purchase area, Widtsoe, Utah, 1936. Gelatin silver print, 7 x 9.5 in. Gift of the Marie Eccles Caine Foundation. Collection of the Nora Eccles Harrison Museum of Art, Utah State University.

FIGURE 6.6. Russell Lee, FSA (Farm Security Administration) cooperative boar, Box Elder County, Utah, 1940. Gelatin silver print, 6.5 x 9.5 in. Gift of the Marie Eccles Caine Foundation. Collection of the Nora Eccles Harrison Museum of Art, Utah State University.

FIGURE 6.7. Russell Lee, Mormon farmer shoeing a horse, Santa Clara, Utah, 1940. Gelatin silver print, 9.5 x 6.5 in. Gift of the Marie Eccles Caine Foundation. Collection of the Nora Eccles Harrison Museum of Art, Utah State University.

tion." The life of the farmer, engaged in a constant conflict with natural forces, is essentially dramatic. Photographers Dorothea Lange and Russell Lee captured these hard times as part of an initiative by the Farm Security Administration to document the plight of farm families during the Great Depression. Lange wielded her camera as a tool of social documentary. Russell Lee photographed farmers across America; his work in Utah centered on the trials and triumphs in the daily lives of farmers.

Families were displaced from their homes and farms due to a massive and long-lasting drought. The

FIGURE 6.8. Russell Lee, Farming land on outskirts of Logan, Cache County, Utah, 1940. Gelatin silver print, 7 x 9.5 in. Gift of the Marie Eccles Caine Foundation. Collection of the Nora Eccles Harrison Museum of Art, Utah State University.

FIGURE 6.9. Russell Lee, Threshing barley on a Mormon farm, Box Elder County, Utah, 1940. Gelatin silver print, 7 x 9.5 in. Gift of the Marie Eccles Caine Foundation. Collection of the Nora Eccles Harrison Museum of Art, Utah State University.

Resettlement Administration of the federal government was tasked with giving struggling farmers a fresh start, actually moving them from county to county, leaving their homes and outbuildings abandoned (Figure 6.5). Farm animals were essential. A boar might be shared among several farmers for breeding purposes (Figure 6.6). Mechanized equipment was still expensive and rare, and horses were a necessity for farm work (Figure 6.7). Although machines had been used on farms for more than fifty years, much of the work still was done with horses and rather primitive equipment. The amount of physical labor required of farmers was considerable (Figure 6.8). Communities often came together to support one another, especially during harvest (Figures 6.9 and 6.10).

Through art, farmers, farm families, and the farms themselves are brought to life in realistic photographs.

FIGURE 6.10. Russell Lee, Young town girl picking berries in Cache County, Utah. Because of diversification of crops, no migrant labor is needed or used in this section of Utah, 1940. Gelatin silver print, 9.5 x 6.5 in. Gift of the Marie Eccles Caine Foundation. Collection of the Nora Eccles Harrison Museum of Art, Utah State University.

The Californian Paradise

Steinbeck's Joad family had cause to believe that California was going to be their promised land. Certainly, California boosters had been making all kinds of agricultural promises for decades. The 1930 short travel film entitled *California The Golden* played into this rhetoric, calling the state "a land of magic at the rainbow's end" as it said that the state's citrus groves were "living gold mines." As you will see, promotional materials as far back as the 1890s also lauded California as an agricultural "paradise," a "Garden of Eden," the "land of eternal sunshine," and "the Land of Milk and Honey." Tourists were told it was the American Mediterranean and a "New Spain."

Ratcliff Hicks, Southern California: Or, The Land of the Afternoon

Successful Connecticut attorney and philanthropist Ratcliff Hicks took an extended vacation to California in 1897, and his book published the following year is a collection of letters he wrote to friends at home and pieces he published in the Connecticut newspapers. The book's effusive praise of Southern California and its efforts to associate it with the landscapes of Europe and the culture and climate of the Mediterranean countries are in keeping with much of the Californian boosterism of the turn-of-the-century.

"Vegetation Prolific"

Just think of a country where daisies, which they call here marguerites, as in France, grow on bushes as large as quince trees; rose bushes grow as large as apple trees. One I saw at Pasadena, twelve years old, was twenty-five feet in diameter and fifteen feet high. There is a rose bush in Los Angeles sixteen feet high, and has grafted onto it twelve varieties of roses. Callas that sell for one dollar each in New York, grow as turnips grow in the East, in great fields, and are set out as hedges along the roadside, or between the adjoining lots to serve as fences; their beautiful white and orange-colored stamens nowhere look so tropical and rich as against a background of perpetual green lawns. Local florists have raised lilies fourteen feet high. Wisteria and brilliant scarlet passion vines run in wild profusion, canopying many a house. Geraniums looking like trees are common. Great acres of all varieties of pinks abound. They are cut, their stems sealed in a wax solution, and are sent yearly by the tons to Easter cities. . . . You often see here squashes that weigh over three hundred pounds and measure four feet one way, potatoes weighing seven and eight pounds, onions weighing four pounds, pumpkins, ten of which will make a wagon load of a ton or over, and cabbages weighing forty-five pounds. A single grapevine near Santa Barbara covers an acre, and in 1896 bore twelve tons of grapes. The "Pride of India," the most delicate of roses, grows here as luxuriantly as any Northern weed, until it shades the whole house. No wonder this is called "The Garden Spot of the World," "The Land of the Afternoon. . . ."

The future of the olive crop of California will be fabulous, when the public are once educated to the fact that there is no olive equal for eating to the ripe, oily California olive, as compared with the green, indigestible, bitter Italian olive and that no unadulterated foreign olive oil is to be compared with the healthy doctor killing California olive oil. An olive grove is so thrifty and long lived that it is handed down from generation to generation as a valuable legacy, and some one has said that it will live on and prosper while nations rise and fall. An olive tree in Pescia, Italy, is known to be over 700 years old. The oldest olive orchard in California adjoins the Mission ruins at San Diego, and has stood for over 133 years.

The olive is the most ancient fruit tree known to history. Its leaves were woven into the laurel wreaths of the Greeks and the triumphant crowns of the Romans. It grew upon the Mount of Olives and it is intimately associated with the history of the human race all the way down from the days of Noah's Ark to the present time. It has been food and light and medicine, ever since history began. There is no olive equal to the California fruit, and it will supplant in the end all the others. It is nearly as nutritious as the best Chicago beef. Field laborers can work for days and almost indefinitely on no other diet that properly prepared olives. . . .

The atmosphere is so pure and translucent, that it transmits the rays of the sun with wonderful power. In plain view are lofty mountains covered with eternal snow, while at their base lie beautiful valleys where flowers are in perpetual bloom. . . .

This is a real heaven to any man who enjoys cultivating the land. With irrigation, crops grow here all the year. On some well watered land, the hay fed to cattle must be cut every three weeks. A good soil, abundant sunshine, and reliable water are the farmers' best friends. . . . It passes my comprehension how any intelligent farmer in New England can keep on in the old way, tilling the soil of our rugged New England hills, and leaving to his children a patrimony of hard work, hard climate, and hard times, when he might transplant them to this beautiful country, and leave them, instead, a patrimony of good soil, magnificent climate, and an independences of the times.

Charles Fletcher Lummis, editor of The Land of Sunshine: The Magazine of California and the West

The Land of Sunshine was a California booster publication contemporary to Hicks' book. The magazine, which we might say was akin to the *Sunset Magazine* or *Arizona Highways* of today, was both a tourism publication and a way to urge easterners to come settle in the peaceful valleys of the most western state. For instance, Lummis in a January 1895 article on Pomona, California tries to speak to both the tourist and settler simultaneously; to both, he is presenting California as a highbrow, cultured locale, as when he writes, "The very nature of their surroundings and occupation fosters the graces of life. Many miles of shaded avenues, roads excellent even in winter, rose gardens and lawns around the homes— all betoken love of the beautiful and consideration for the stranger. There is something in this climate that somehow tends to open the heart. The

THE LAND OF SUNSHINE— SOUTHERN CALIFORNIA. This promotional pamphlet from a local World's Fair association and covering many aspects of Southern California life was issued in 1893 in advance of the Chicago fair.

tourist who enters the fruit-growing center must be crusty indeed, if he remains long a stranger."

The magazine had articles about agriculture featured in every issue, and these emphasized California as having a natural environment that was "semi-tropical," a term the magazine used more than once in nearly every article about agriculture. Typically, one or more features focused on the success farmers had growing specific commercial crops and livestock that would seem exotic to farmers from the East: loquats, guavas, olives, ostriches, silk, walnuts and almonds, and flowers such as calla lilies, freesia, and dahlias. In January of 1895, as much of the magazine's readership was suffering in the winter cold, Lummis wrote,

If there is anything that will not grow in Southern California, it must be some plant that has escaped the catalogues, for its name is not known. The perfection attained by our fruits and flowers is as notable as the vast variety of them. This genial climate puts new character and ambition into the plant-immigrants which settle here, and they hardly know themselves, thawed out and encouraged to grow their best. Farming here is a pleasure as well as a profit. Released from the tyranny of freezes and drouths and grasshoppers, and all the other things that go to make the lot of the Eastern agriculturist a shiver of apprehension, the farmer here does his work and knows that Nature will not swindle him out of his wages. . . . He can choose the crops he would rather raise, secure that here all his harvests will be good ones, and that "whatsoever he doeth shall prosper."

As part of these regular contributions on specific crops, in March of that same year, Lummis published the following by Horace Edwards. By this time, the orange had already come to symbolize California agriculture, and for good reason, Edwards' article would suggest.

Horace Edwards, *"The Orange in Southern California"*

Orange-growing is undoubtedly the most important horticultural industry in Southern California, both as to amount invested and value of product. In a recent favorable season the output has amounted to over 6,000 car-loads, or over 2,000,000 boxes, worth not less than $3,000,000 on the trees. Whether the orange shall always rank first here, remains to be seen, as several possible rivals (such as the lemon, olive, apricot, prune and walnut) are coming to the front. At present, however, the orange is undisputed king.

To those brought up in the bleak and wintry East, orange-growing has always a deep fascination. Southern Californians of long adoption come to find it a twice-told tale; but to those residing in other portions of the United States the topic is always fresh and interesting. Newcomers manifest this by their keen delight in visiting an orange grove for the first time, and by the longing so often expressed, to pick an orange from the tree "with their own hands." Perhaps there is not another fruit in the entire domain of pomology about which is such a halo of romance as about these "golden apples of the Hesperides." They figure in tradition, song and story from time immemorial. . . .

The orange and lemon are not indigenous here. We have no native groves of the bigarade (sour orange), like those of Florida; nor thickets of sweet oranges, like those of Central America and portions of Mexico. But we have soil and climate, in certain favored sections, highly adapted to the cultivation of this fruit; and so we have very generally adopted it. The one artificial need is moisture; and this is supplied by irrigation. We have some lands perennially moist; but they are in the lowest valleys, and their atmosphere and soil have been found too cold for orange and lemon trees. Hence our cultivators have sought the high, warm lands of the interior valleys and of the foothills aligning the mountains on their southern slope; and here, with equable temperature, a genial soil, and sufficient moisture by irrigation, they have achieved the most satisfactory results.

Perhaps it is no disadvantage in the long run that this artificial condition is imposed on orange culture in California. It is thus taken out of the province of haphazard, and made one of the sciences. Without a degree of care, citrus trees cannot be grown at all here; and without good care and strict conformity to their requirements they do not become profitable. The rewards, therefore, are solely for careful culture, and the law of the survival of the fittest is always operative. . . .

Eastern readers of the *Land of Sunshine*, or those recently arrived from the East, who think of going into orange culture, should remember that while the profits are very large under favorable circumstances, there are also occasional drawbacks—such as a light frost in places, a heavy wind, the ravages of scale insects, or an unfavorable market in the East. So the average income of an orange grove for a series of years is not quite so great as might be expected by those who hear only the bright side of the story. It is true that $1000 an acre, and even more, has been made from oranges—but this was where the trees were say from twelve to twenty years old; where the greatest care had been taken in cultivating, picking, packing and shipping; and where the conditions of season and marketing were altogether favorable. An average income of one-third that amount, from trees that have been planted seven or eight years, is about as much as can be counted on in a favorable season—and is certainly enough to satisfy a reasonable man. For the product of 130 acres of orange grove, E. J. Baldwin, whose place is in the San Gabriel Valley, Los Angeles county, received this year $48,000 cash; the purchasers paying all expenses of picking and marketing.

The expense of setting out and caring for orange trees is considerable. An average estimate of the cost of a ten-acre grove, three years from planting, is $4500—including interest on the investment at 8 per cent, and reckoning the land at $250 per acre. At the expiration of three years the grove should pay at least 10 percent on the investment; and from that time on, the increase in yield is very rapid. The budded varieties begin to bear very early, and heavy yields have been obtained from trees only five years planted.

EXPLORE: Edwards cites some impressive financial figures for the citrus industry. To put those in perspective, consider the relative values below of those figures in today's economy, according to calculators at measuringworth.com. Do you believe Edwards' figures? Why or why not? Research to see if they hold true in today's citrus market.

Edwards' estimates for 1895	Today's value
California output: $3,000,000	Relative real price commodity value: $84,000,000
Potential income per acre: $1000	Relative income value: almost $250,000/acre
Baldwin's 130 acres: $48,000 cash	Real commodity price: more than $1,350,000
Expenses on 10-acre grove: $4500	Relative labor Cost: $600,000

EXPLORE: Both Edwards and Hicks associate California agriculture with places immortalized in mythology and religion. For example, Hicks mentions the Mount of Olives, the mountain above Jerusalem where Christ taught the disciples and where he reportedly ascended to heaven. Edwards mentions the golden apples of the Hesperides, which in Greek mythology were grown in a blissful garden tended by three nymphs— sometimes called the "Sunset Goddesses"— and a guarding dragon. According to myth, they were also known as "apples of joy"; eating them meant immortality. After the

FIGURE 6.11. Frederic Leighton, *The Garden of the Hesperides*, ca. 1892. Oil on canvas, diameter 66.5". Located in the Lady Lever Art Gallery, National Museums Liverpool, UK. Photo: Bridgeman Images.

Middle Ages, historians came to believe the golden apples of the Hesperides were oranges. Discuss the ways California agriculture is associated with exotic and mythological places. Why was this important in marketing California for potential farmers? Who was the audience they were appealing to?

Tomás Rivera, *And the Earth Did Not Devour Him*

Tomás Rivera was born in Texas in 1935 to a family of migrant agricultural workers, and he spent much of his childhood following the crops with his family and working in the fields. When asked what he wanted to be when he grew up, he would tell family and friends that he wanted to be a writer—a response that was met with surprise and indifference. "If people don't read," Rivera asked, "what is a writer?" In 1956, he left field work, and entered college, eventually earning multiple advanced degrees, including a PhD. In 1979, he became chancellor of University of California, Riverside, making him the first Mexican-American to hold such a position in the University of California system.

Rivera's novel, *And the Earth Did Not Devour Him*, was originally written in Spanish, published in 1971, and then translated three times, with the following from the second translation, done by Evangelina Vigil-Piñón. The novel is told in the form of numerous vignettes, and here Rivera moves into multiple and simultaneous perspectives as he describes the thoughts of individual migrant workers who are being transported to their next job. In this scene, the truck they are in breaks down in the middle of the night.

"When We Arrive"

"When we get there I'm gonna see about getting a good bed for my *vieja*. Her kidneys are really bothering her a lot nowadays. Just hope we don't end up in a chicken coop like last year, with that cement floor. Even though you cover it with straw, once the cold season sets in you just can't stand it. That was why my rheumatism got so bad, I'm sure of that."

"When we arrive, when we arrive, the real truth is that I'm tired of arriving. Arriving and leaving, it's the same thing because we no sooner arrive and . . . the real truth of the matter . . . I'm tired of arriving. I really should say when we don't arrive because that's the real truth. We never arrive."

"What a great view of the stars from here! It looks like they're coming down and touching the tarp of the truck. It's almost like there aren't any people inside. There's hardly any traffic at this hour. Every now and then a trailer passes by. The silence of the morning twilight makes everything look like it's made of satin. And now, what do I wipe myself with? Why couldn't it always be early dawn like this? We're going to be here till midday for sure. By the time they find help in the town and then by the time they fix the motor. . . . I'm going to keep my eyes on the stars till the last one disappears. I wonder how many more people are watching the same star? And how many more might there be wondering how many are looking at the same star? It's so silent it looks like it's the stars the crickets are calling to."

 EXPLORE: What is the effect and thematic significance of the structure of this chapter and its simultaneous and multiple points of view? Discuss the chapter title's significance. Rivera's novel consistently pairs the sacred with the profane. How do you see that pattern here and what is the effect?

 EXPLORE: Rivera once said the following of the novel:

> I wanted to document the spiritual strength, the concept of justice so important for the American continents. Within those migrants I saw that strength. They may be economically deprived, politically deprived, socially deprived, but they kept moving, never staying in one place to suffer or be subdued. But always searching for work; that's why they were "migrant" workers. I see that same sense of movement in the Europeans who come here and that concept of spiritual justice. It was there. And the migrant workers still have that role: to be searchers. That's an important metaphor in the Americas.

Discuss this quote and Rivera's emphasis on justice and the Europeans who migrated here—who might he be referring to? What is the effect of that? What significance does this have for American agriculture?

 EXPLORE: If you are interested in this short excerpt, read the short novel in its entirety. The following are questions to consider when you've read the whole novel.
• What is the significance of this excerpt's chapter title? How is Rivera exploring ideas of movement and settlement, dispossession and ownership? Consider this story in the context of the Jeffersonian ideal.
• What is the effect of Rivera's moments of humor? Upon what does the humor hinge?
• Make a list of what ways we as humans form our sense of identity, and then consider Rivera's characters and how they have formed their sense of identity?

 COLLABORATE: Imagine that your class is a set of film producers hired to translate this chapter of Rivera's novel into a movie. Discuss which major obstacles you would face in producing this film. What major themes do you want to emphasize? What might you have to compromise (change, ignore) from the novel for your adaptation? How would you portray the landscape and people? What kind of film and cinematography techniques would you use (such as camera angles, close-ups, music or black-and-white film)? How do you plan to create mood, and what kind of mood do you want to emphasize? How do you plan to handle questions of casting? How will you address Rivera's portrayal of American agriculture, especially in light of what you've already learned this term?

Cesar Chavez

Activist César Chàvez was born in 1927 to a poor family in Yuma, Arizona, in a region where every year tens of thousands Mexican immigrants labor on farms. The Chàvez family owned their own small farm and store in the Yuma area; however, they lost both during the Great Depression. After that, like the characters in Rivera's novel, the family survived by doing migrant farm work under difficult conditions at vegetable farms, orchards, and vineyards throughout California. In the 1950s, César Chàvez left the fields to fight for better working conditions. In 1962, he founded the National Farm Workers Association (later the United Farm Workers of America), which unionized farmworkers and used non-violent protest to force growers to improve the appalling wages and working conditions of migrant workers and ensure that they were treated with respect and dignity. Chàvez's methods of protest were influenced by Mahatma Gandhi and Martin Luther King Jr., and just a month before his death, King telegrammed Chàvez that they were "brothers in the fight for equality." Chàvez called for nationwide boycotts, nonviolent strikes, and marches, and in order to bring attention to his causes and urge farmworkers to pledge themselves to nonviolent methods of protests, Chàvez undertook several extended fasts, including the one in 1993 that led to his death.

FIGURE 6.12. César Chàvez working in the community garden in La Paz. 1975. Photo: Cathy Murphy, who was a United Farm Workers staff photographer at the time.

In addition to his work with the UFW, Chàvez was instrumental in the Supreme Court's 1975 ruling to ban the use of the short-handled hoe, which he called the fieldworkers' "symbol of suffering." The hoe forced them to work in a stooped posture all day long, which had crippling, life-long effects for the workers.

RESEARCH: Visit http://www.chavezfoundation.org to read from Chavez's speeches and writings, and view videos about his work and life. Also available online is "The Struggle in the Fields," an episode of the PBS series *Chicano!* http://tinyurl.com/ChavezStruggle. Check to see if your library has a copy of the related films *The Fight in the Fields: Cesar Chavez and the Farmworkers' Struggle* or *The Wrath of Grapes* (a film about the UFW's efforts to bring attention to the effect on farmworkers of the widespread use of dangerous pesticides and herbicides).

Post-World War II Agriculture

The Drive to Increase Yield

During World War II, American farms and farmers had to do more to feed not only our nation and our soldiers serving overseas, but also the allies who were suffering food shortages because their fields and pastures had become battlefields and their farmers were now in uniform. The war created a pressing need for higher rates of food production to make up the difference, and America was told that food could win the war.

These events caused long-lasting changes to food production rates. Because of technological and chemical advancements, as well as structural changes to how the farms operated, American farms after the war looked very different from the farms that Teddy Roosevelt's Country Life Commission had studied in the early century. Yet just as Roosevelt had worried, the exodus from country to city continued. Farm population declined, and the average age of farmers rose.

University extension agencies aimed to professionalize farming and make it more attractive to young farmers who might be tempted to follow the wide, paved road that led to the city. Chemical and implement companies urged family farmers to adopt newly developed technological and chemical practices in order to increase yields and modernize their farms. The image of the modern farmer, taking full advantage of these latest innovations, was attractive to post-war farmers who were interested in changing what an increasingly urban world thought of as the bumpkin farmer who was backward and unsophisticated.

During the 1940s, better efficiency and higher yields became the mantra of the modern farmer. For the first time, the 1940 Agricultural Census began to formally track the productivity of American farmers with estimates of how many people were fed and clothed annually by one American farmer; in 1940 that number was just 10.7, by 1960 it was 25.8, and by 1990 the number had surpassed 100. In the relative prosperity that followed the war, tractors and combines on farms were becoming more and more the norm. As availability went up, prices of the machinery came down. By 1945, there were 2.4 million tractors, according to Agricultural Census (although it would take until 1970 for mechanization to fully replace animal power). Technological advances occurred at a rapid pace, as did the changes brought on by scientific discoveries. The use of hybrid seeds, developed in the laboratories at Land Grant colleges and universities, became prevalent. So too did the use of commercial chemical fertilizers, herbicides and pesticides. By 1952, there were almost 10,000 pesticides registered for use with the USDA. Mono-cropping, the planting of a single crop rather than crop rotation of multiple crops on a farm, was now the norm; however, it exhausted the soil, and so farmers relied more on the synthetic fertilizers to increase yields.

Because nitrogen and ammonia were a key component for bombs used during the war, the government had these chemicals in large supply when the war ended, and as a result, they were diverted for agricultural use as a cheap fertilizer. By 1980, farmers were using almost 50 million tons of chemical fertilizers per year. Prior to the war the most widely used pesticides were the highly toxic arsenic and hydrogen cyanide, so when *dichlorodiphenyltrichloroethane*, known as DDT, was developed during the war to control mosquitos and malaria in the South Pacific theatre and typhus-spreading lice in the liberated concentration camps farmers were eager to put these chemicals to domestic use. Experimentations with nerve agents during the war also led to the pesticide parathion, and the herbicide 2,4-D, a synthetic hormone that controls growth in plants, was even considered at one point for use in biological warfare. Development of these synthetic biocides continued at a rapid rate after the war, resulting in a host of chemicals that included Marathon, atrazine, parquet. By 1980, commercial fertilizer use was 47,411,166 tons per year.

DDT: The "War-Born Miracle"

Advertising of pesticides and herbicides adopted the rhetoric of war and fighting. DDT, was referred to as "the war-born miracle," and in the July 6, 1946 issue of the *Nebraska Farmer* described domestic use of the chemical thusly: "After winning a glorious victory during the World War II over the insidious insect foes of G. I. Joe, DDT has shucked its military clothes, wrapped up its world-wide service bars, and come back home to take over the No. 1 spot in America's bug battle." It was also known as "the Joe Louis of insecticides." Such promotional efforts resulted in the sales of DDT jumping from $10 million in 1944 to over $110 million in 1951.

 The effectiveness of the insecticide DDT had been recognized in 1939, even though the chemical had been first synthesized in 1874. The compound was cheap, effective, and thus widely used. Paul Hermann Müller, the chemist who discovered its insecticidal properties, was awarded the Nobel Peace Prize in Medicine and Physiology in 1948.

> **Farm Census Figures:**
> **1940**: Farmers are 18% of the US labor force, and there are over 6 million farms. It takes 10–14 labor hours to produce 100 bushels (2 acres) of corn. 58% of all farms have cars; 25% have phones; 33% have electricity. Use of commercial fertilizer is more than 13 million tons per year.
>
> **1950**: Farmers are 12.2% of the labor force. One farmer supplies 15.5 people, and it requires 6.5 labor hours to produce 100 pounds (4 acres) of wheat. The use of commercial fertilizer jumps to 22 million tons per year. 70.9% of all farms have cars; 49% have phones; 93% have electricity.
>
> **1960**: Farmers are 8.3% of the labor force. Tractors have fully replaced horses and mules. Commercial fertilizer use is at 32,373,713 tons/year. One farmer supplies 25.8 people, and it requires 5 labor-hours to produce 100 bushels (3 acres) of wheat.

After World War II, DDT and similar insecticides and herbicides were touted by science and chemical companies in public health documentaries and consumer advertising as marvels of modern science that would significantly improve not only life on the farm but also in the home. For instance, DDT was impregnated into Trims DDT Children's Room Wallpaper and Ceiling Paper, which was colorfully decorated with characters from famous cartoons and fairy tales in an effort to reassure homeowners and children alike that the chemicals were harmless and beneficial. "Protect Your Children Against Disease-Carrying Insects!" the magazine caption read above the picture of a smiling mother settling an infant into her crib. Contrasting with this picture of family contentment was the threat of disease: "Medical science knows many common insects breed in filth, live in filth and carry disease. . . . Actual tests have proved that *one* fly can carry as many as 6,600,000 bacteria!" Advertised as "*Certified* to be absolutely safe for home use" and effective in killing insects for up to two years, the wallpaper had "gay new patterns that *protect* as they *beautify* a child's room" (original emphasis).

 VIEW: "Food to Win the War" was a 1941 governmental film that linked the success in the war to the success of the American farmer: http://www.agclassroom.org/gan/sources/media/food.htm.

VIEW: The ad pictured here appeared in *Time* magazine in 1947. Analyze and discuss the persuasive rhetoric used in both the text and the illustrations of this ad. The full, colored ad can be found online in a number of places; just look for the caption "DDT is Good for ME! "

VIEW: The widespread applications for DDT were emphasized in public health videos like this 1946 film called "Doomsday for Pests," which was used to advertise a DDT-based product called Destroy: http://tinyurl.com/DDT-Pestroy

A 1947 film entitled *DDT Versus Malaria: A Successful Experiment in Malaria Control,* by the Kenya Medical Department, was a black-and-white documentary that highlighted the role of DDT in fighting malaria and claimed it was "so safe you can eat it." Watch the clip at http://tinyurl.com/DDTVersusMalaria.

FIGURE 6.13. "DDT is good for me-e-e!" Pennsalt Chemicals advertisement in *Time* magazine, vol. XLIX, no. 26 (June 30, 1947).

FIELD TRIP: For more on farming during the 1940s, take a virtual field trip to the Wessel Living History Farm (York, Nebraska) by going to http://tinyurl.com/Wessels-Farminginthe40s.

Rachel Carson, *Silent Spring*

Rachel Carson's landmark book *Silent Spring,* which focuses on the agricultural application of synthetic chemicals, has been listed as one of the most significant books to have ever spurred dramatic social and political change. In that category, it keeps company with Harriet Beecher Stowe's *Uncle Tom's Cabin,* which President Lincoln said began the Civil War, and with Upton Sinclair's *The Jungle,* which directly resulted in the Pure Food and Drug Act of 1906. The Modern Library listed Carson's book as number five on their list of best nonfiction books of the twentieth century, and *Discover Magazine* named it one of the top 25 science books of all time.

Rachel Carson had significant success both as a scientist and as a writer before *Silent Spring* was published in 1962. After earning a master's degree in zoology from Johns Hopkins (where she also studied genetics and was in a doctoral program for a time until family circumstances forced her to drop out), Carson went on to become a science educator and a biologist for the Bureau of Fisheries, where she worked for 15 years. By 1962, she was already a best-selling and award-winning writer; her trilogy of books about ocean life that had earned her a National Book Award, a Burroughs Medal for natural history, and two honorary doctorates.

In 1960, the Audubon enlisted Carson's help to investigate why the eggshells of predatory birds, like the Peregrine Falcon, Osprey, Brown Pelicans, and the Bald Eagle, had become dangerously thin, which directly resulted in a high mortality rate. Widespread use of DDT on American farmlands was eventually discovered to be the cause. But the plight of the birds was only a portion of the story Carson would tell in *Silent Spring*, which exposed the long-term effects of the misuse of pesticides on American farmland. "Can anyone believe it is possible," Carson asked, "to lay down such a barrage of poisons on the surface of the earth without making it unfit for all life? They should not be called 'insecticides,' but 'biocides'" because they affected entire ecosystems. She argued that we neither fully understood nor could sufficiently control these chemicals. Such claims called into question the post-World War II belief that the future of agriculture must rely upon heavy chemical applications of pesticides and herbicides. Carson pointed out how the average human body stored potentially heavy concentrations of these "elixirs of death," she warned of how the poisons "may be passed from mother to offspring" and can "freely cross the barrier of the placenta, the traditional protective shield between the embryo and harmful substances in the mother's body." Drawing upon the well-known phrase "safe as mother's milk," Carson warned that the toxins were also transferred to infants through breast milk.

Silent Spring emphasized five key principles. First was the notion of non-selectivity—that is, the herbicides and pesticides farmers applied to their land were broad-spectrum killers that often destroyed everything they touched, both good and bad. The result was that entire ecosystems were rendered sterile. Secondly, because these chemicals did not wash away (*hydrophobic* was the term Carson used), they often had half-lives that were measured in decades or more—a notion referred to as persistence. Therefore, the contamination had long-term consequences that led to the third problem, known as biological magnification. Specifically, this means that the chemical concentration in mammals was cumulative, both over the life of the mammal itself and especially as we examine the effects of petro-chemicals on up the food chain, where Carson says the chemicals pass "from one to another in a chain of poisoning and death" and "the whole process . . . seems caught up in an endless spiral." Fourth is the notion of systemic poisoning in which the insecticide permeates all the tissues of a plant or animal and makes them toxic. In other words, the poison-*end* becomes the poison-*er* in a process Carson calls "death-by-indirection." Underlying these four principles of Carson's thesis was her belief that the real problem of contamination had its roots in human arrogance, in the belief that mankind was "intoxicated with a sense of his own power." Furthermore, she quoted Albert Schweitzer wrote, "Man can hardly even recognize the devils of his own creation."

The book contained technical diagrams of chemical atoms and detailed drawings of cellular life, along with striking illustrations of landscape and wildlife, by Lois and Louis Darling. It was this visual rhetoric that confused scientists even as it appealed to a mass audience. When it was named a Book-of-the-Month Club selection in the fall of 1962, it became a bestseller. It was even referenced on a regular basis in the *Peanuts* comics by Charles M. Schulz, who portrayed Lucy talking about Carson as her heroine.

Nevertheless, *Silent Spring* also sparked controversy, and scientists, the chemical industry, and a number of governmental leaders criticized her scientific credentials, her data, her analysis of that data, and even her character. Even though the government had been studying health concerns related to DDT since 1949, scientists undermined the book by making attacks on Carson's credentials as a marine biologist talking about biochemistry. They dismissed her because she had no university or corporate affiliation, and therefore, they believed, was a mere amateur. Then-Secretary of Agriculture Ezra Taft Benson wrote in a letter to President Eisenhower in which he wondered why an "attractive . . .

spinster was so worried about genetics." He also asserted that she was "probably a Communist"—this, in a nation that had just suffered through the McCarthy hearings a few years previously. She was accused by others of being a "hysterical woman," ill equipped to make reasoned judgments on topics of agriculture and farm chemicals. She was called a "sentimental nature lover" whose book, wrote a reviewer for *Time* magazine, was evidence of "her emotional and accurate outburst." Still others called her a fanatic and accused her of wanting to take agriculture back to the Dark Ages. In 1963 the chemical company Monsanto issued a short story parody of *Silent Spring* entitled "The Desolate Year," which portrayed a world without pesticides. Although it never mentioned Carson's work, it clearly mimicked her poetic style. (See: http://tinyurl.com/MonsantoCarson).

The tone of the book, especially with the first chapter "Fable for Tomorrow," which is excerpted below, was also controversial. Scientific critics felt this introduction was far too literary for a serious work about the chemical development of synthetic applications.

Silent Spring is credited with inspiring the environmental movement worldwide. Because of Carson's work, a number of environmental agencies were founded in the years following her death and significant environmental legislation was written, including the Endangered Species Act of 1966, which listed the bald eagle as an endangered species the following year. The Environmental Protection Agency was founded in 1970, which would be the main force behind banning DDT from use in the United States in 1972. Shortly after that, the bald eagle population began to rebound, and in 2007 it was removed from the endangered species list.

However, Carson didn't live to see these positive results of her work. She died of breast cancer in the spring of 1964, just eighteen months after the release of *Silent Spring*.

"A Fable for Tomorrow"

There was once a town in the heart of America where all life seemed to live in harmony with its surroundings. The town lay in the midst of a checkerboard of prosperous farms, with fields of grain and hillsides of orchards where, in spring, white clouds of bloom drifted above the green fields. In autumn, oak and maple and birch set up a blaze of color that flamed and flickered across a backdrop of pines. Then foxes barked in the hills and deer silently crossed the fields, half hidden in the mists of the fall mornings....

Then a strange blight crept over the area and everything began to change. Some evil spell had settled on the community: mysterious maladies swept the flocks of chickens; the cattle and sheep sickened and died. Everywhere was a shadow of death. The farmers spoke of much illness among their families. In the town the doctors had become more and more puzzled by new kinds of sickness appearing among their patients. There had been several sudden and unexplained deaths, not only among adults but even among children, who would be stricken suddenly while at play and die within a few hours. There was a strange stillness. The birds, for example—where had they gone? Many people spoke of them, puzzled and disturbed.... It was a spring without voices. On the mornings that had once throbbed with the dawn chorus of robins, catbirds, doves, jays, wrens, and scores of other bird voices there was now no sound; only silence lay over the fields and woods and marsh.

 EXPLORE: Discuss the rhetoric of this excerpt from "A Fable for Tomorrow." First, consider how this is a "fable" (a story that typically uses anthropomorphized animals to illustrate a cautionary or moral lesson; thus it is a fictitious or "fabulous" tale). Take note of any loaded terms or emotive language. For what kind of audience is Carson writing?

 EXPLORE: Locate a copy of the book *Silent Spring* and read the full chapter of "Fable for Tomorrow" and the second chapter "The Obligation to Endure"; also look through the more technical chapters like "Elixirs of Death." Then consider the following questions: How and why does Carson use the rhetoric of war in this excerpt? Where do you see her doing that? What is the effect? If you go on to read other passages from the book, consider how the tone changes from chapter to chapter. Consider the importance of Carson's audience throughout the book. Did the illustrations in the book color the way you read the book? What seems to be the message of the illustrations?

 RESEARCH: Following its publication, *Silent Spring* sparked vehement and heated debate that continues to this day. Research some of the work written in defense of and against Carson's book. Using as much of your research as possible, including quotes from the sources you found, hold a class debate. Divide the class into three groups: one group will argue in favor of Carson's argument, the second group will speak against Carson, and the third group will act as rhetoric monitors who will buzz in and identify each time they hear a debate speaker using emotive language or logical fallacies. The rhetoric monitors may want to spend their time researching how to identify logical fallacies.

"From Fence Row to Fence Row": Agriculture goes Big (1950–1990)

Agribusiness

If World War II ushered in a change in the methods farmers used in their fields by introducing more machinery and chemical applications, it also marks a change in how farmers worked when the machines were turned off, when they were looking at profits and losses or deciding whether they could buy the farm next door, or considering the purchase of a bigger and better tractor. Roosevelt's Country Life Commission had urged farmers to think more like businessmen and be progressive, and that's just what they began doing in the decades after the war. They asked themselves if the family farm really was the best model for a modern agricultural occupation or whether there was another organizational structure that might be better.

According to the Census Bureau, by 1960, farmers had dropped to 8.3% of the US labor force. That is almost a 30% drop within sixty years and a 50% drop since 1860. In the following decade the number of farmers dropped below 5%, and by the end of the 1990s farmers were just over 1% of the US population. In 1993, the US Census Bureau announced they would stop counting farmers as a separate occupational category because they were "statistically insignificant," and thereafter, farm numbers were combined with fishing and forestry numbers.

As the number of farmers continued to decline, farms began to be consolidated and enlarged well beyond the "family farmer" capacity. Farmers began to think less about farming as a patriotic act, as they had during the wars, and more about farming as a business on an industrial scale. The term "agribusiness" was coined in 1955 when a group of professors started an agribusiness program at Harvard Business School. Sometimes called corporate farming, this type of large-scale commercial farming was usually the first sector to utilize technological advances and mechanical and chemical innovations like those describe earlier. Agribusiness also brought business theories to bear on farming, and they drew upon studies done at universities in such diverse fields as horticulture, animal science, and marketing, business administration, and economics. Agribusiness succeeds due to economies of scale. The larger the company becomes, the greater the profit.

Some agribusinesses went one step further and functioned as agricultural conglomerates; in other words, the business had vested interest in various points along food's path to consumer. For instance, an apple orchard company may hold stock in a packing and distribution plant or in the truck-

In January of 1955, Secretary of Agriculture Ezra Taft Benson addressed the nation to discuss the state of agriculture. Emphasizing the progress farmers had made in the previous 25 years, he urged farmers to use new farming methods to further secure the nation's prosperity and security. Watch the speech at http://www.agclassroom.org/gan/sources/media/benson.htm

ing company that ships their produce, or a chemical company that develops pesticides for orchardists may own multiple apple orchards—these cases would be considered vertical conglomerates. A horizontal conglomerate, on the other hand, would be a company that owns multiple orchard operations. While some say these business structures create unfair monopolies that drive out small-scale family farmers, others point out that agribusiness streamlines food production and keeps food costs low. The largest conglomerates consolidate both inputs (seed companies, chemical companies, implement companies) and outputs (distribution, value-added products like processed food, advertising company, and or chain grocery stores).

Big was the watchword for farmers during the era between 1950 and 1990. President Eisenhower's Secretary of Agriculture Ezra Taft Benson had told farmers to "Get big or get out!" during the 1950s, and Benson's protégé Earl Butz, who was Secretary of Agriculture under President Nixon repeated the line often during the 1970s, adding a variation of his own: "Adapt or die!" He exhorted farmers to "plant fence row to fence row." The numbers tell the story of farms getting bigger and producing more, even as farmers themselves were becoming fewer and fewer (These numbers are based on "Growing a Nation" and USDA and American Farm Bureau statistics).

Changing size of average farm acreage:	Increasing productivity as determined by how many people one American farmer feeds and clothes:
1930: 157 acres	1840: Fewer than 2 people
1940: 175 acres	1940: 10.7
1950: 216 acres	1950: 15.5
1960: 303 acres	1960: 25.8
1970: 390 acres	1970: 47.7
1980: 426 acres	1980: 75.7
1990: 461 acres	1990: 100
	2000: Some estimate as high as 155

The Green Revolution (1945–1980)

Agriculture was responding not just to governmental advice from Benson and Butz but to warnings of the "Green Revolution," a movement that that took the message of "Get Big" worldwide. In 1961, as India was on the brink of a mass famine, the international community began to voice grave concerns about worldwide overpopulation, a problem that had become exponentially worse since 1950 and that peaked in 1964 with a growth rate of 2.1%. The problem was so worrisome that by 1968 Paul Erlich would name his study of overpopulation "The Population Bomb." That same year, the term "Green Revolution" was coined by William Gaud, Director of the United States Agency for International Development, who rhetorically situated the "Green Revolution" within the context of the "Red Revolution" (another name for the Socialist takeover of power by the Bolsheviks in Russia in 1917) and the "White Revolution" (the bloodless revolution in the early 1960s in which the Shah of Iran introduced land reforms in order to centralize the power of Pahlavi Dynasty). In so naming the movement a "revolution," then, Gaud signaled the politicization of farming on an international scale.

Henry Kissinger, Secretary of State under both Presidents Nixon and Ford was vocal about the need for national food security in our own country. Under Ford's administration in 1974, he directed a classified study with the National Security Council entitled "National Security Study Memorandum 200: Implications of Worldwide Population Growth for U.S. Security and Overseas Interests," which argued that population growth in Lesser Developed Countries constituted a serious risk to America's national security. Since declassified, the report asked, "Would food be considered an instrument of national power? . . . Is the US prepared to accept food rationing to help people who can't/won't control their population growth?" Publicly, Kissinger was known for bluntly saying, "Control oil and you control the nations; control food and you control the people."

In order to address the problem in India and other countries, The Green Revolution urged US farmers to put the technologies and scientific advancements to good use to feed the entire world. Scientists and agriculturalists developed hybrids varieties of rice with higher yields and taught third world countries about synthetic fertilizers, pesticides, and herbicides, as well as irrigation methods and mono-cropping methods.

Farm Crisis of 1980s and 1990s

The Farm Crisis that began in the 1980s was the worst financial crisis for the American family farm since The Great Depression. By the time it was over in early 1990s, farmers were nearing just 1% of total US population (down from 38% at beginning of the century), and farmers had been battered and bruised by wildly fluctuating prices, steep declines in rural population, bank closures, and high farmer foreclosure and bankruptcy rates. At the height of the crisis between 1985 and 1987, commercial banks reported an increase of 425% bankruptcies since the banks began reporting the number in 1982 (38 bankruptcies per thousand farms in 1985 and 42 per thousand in 1986); meanwhile, life insurance companies reported an increase of 1330% farm foreclosures since 1982 (27.2 foreclosures per 1000 farms in 1986 and 28.6 per thousand in 1987) (based on figures for the bankruptcy and foreclosure numbers reported in *Regulation and the Revolution in United States Farm Productivity* by Sally H. Clarke).

The Farm Crisis was caused by a perfect storm of political and economic factors, which started in the 1970s and had results that lasted on into the 1990s. Although the causes for the crisis are complex, and crossed lines of political ideologies, the following is a much-simplified outline that shows the spiraling circumstances of the Farm Crisis.

What were the Causes and Consequences of the Farm Crisis of the 1980s?

- Technology advances post-World War II. Green Revolution leads to development of higher-yield grains. That, plus exceptional weather years, mean yields go up significantly in 1970s, resulting at end of decade in a stockpile of grain.
- Farmers buy more land because of good prices, so many farms got bigger.
- Farmers buy newest equipment for these larger farms.
- Energy costs begin to rise during 1970s.
- Farmers buy more land and equipment on credit because interest rates are low and economy good.
- Many farmers begin to rely on yearly "operating loans," secured by farm land and equipment, for cost of feed, seed, fertilizers, pesticides, labor and other essential operating costs. Loans are typically repaid at end of the harvest each year, and then farmers apply for a new loan the following year.
- The government increases exports to foreign markets.
- Bad weather puts Russia on the brink of famine, and President Nixon agrees to the Russian Wheat Deal of 1972, in which US subsidizes sale of stockpiled wheat. Seemingly good news for US farmers, in the end exporters profit the most. Once stockpiles are depleted, the price of grain to US consumers is driven up, and prices for other farm products including livestock soon follow suit. Rising prices in turn cause inflation in US.
- Market is flooded with more farm products and prices plummet.
- President Carter imposes a grain embargo on Soviets in retaliation for 1980 invasion of Afghanistan. Later that year, he is defeated for reelection by Ronald Reagan.
- Embargo further cuts demand for grain and creates glut on the market.
- Farmers now have huge debt and overhead, but prices are so low that they get less than the cost to harvest a crop.
- President Reagan lifts Soviet embargo in 1981, and in 1985 signs Food Security Act, which artificially lowers prices for farmers in order to make American grain more competitive on worldwide market. Prices are down to levels not seen since end of World War I. The value of exports drop more than 50% within five years.
- Land values fall, while interest rates for operating loans go up, which means farmers are unable to sell out and pay off debts.
- The dollar is over-valued on the world market.

Gallows Humor during the Farm Crisis:

"Deere John Letters" (signs used during protests of foreclosure sales):
"Crime doesn't pay. . . Neither does farming."

Popular 1980s Bumper Sticker:
"If Dolly Parton was a Farmer, She'd be Flat-Busted, Too!"

Georgia farmer quoted during the 1980s Farm Crisis (R. Douglas Hurt's *American Agriculture, A Brief History*)
"I'd rather have two tickets on the *Titanic* than be in farming today."

- Farm wives increasingly seek off-farm jobs to keep farm solvent.
- Farm bankruptcy and foreclosure rates skyrocket (see above), and many "century farms" (those farms that had been in business under the stewardship of a single family) are sold off. Farm auctions become common, while farm activists try to rally support in protests, strikes, and tractorcades to Washington.
- Rates of closure for small banks holding debts in rural communities rises.
- Farm activists, blaming the banks for unwillingness to work with the farmers, ban together for "nickel auctions," a 1980s version of the "penny auctions" of the 1930s. Hundreds of farmers would come to the auction, intimidate serious buyers from bidding, and then only bid a nickel for farm equipment worth thousands of dollars.
- Suicide and murder rate among farmers rises dramatically, especially between 1982 and 1984, and in the grain-producing Plains states.
- First Farm Aid Concert to raise awareness about the loss of family farms takes place after harvest time in Champagne, Illinois; the concert plays to live audience of more than 80,000 and the organization raises $9,000,000 to help family farms.
- Impact of rising farm foreclosures is felt by the rural communities, which also suffer economically, leading more and more farmers to sell out and move to urban centers.

VIEW: John Mellencamp performed his 1985 song about the Farm Crisis, "Rain on the Scarecrow," at the very first Farm Aid Concert. To watch Mellencamp's original video, go to: http://tinyurl.com/RainOnTheScarecrow. For the lyrics to this song, see Chapter 12.

VIEW: Choose and watch one of the following documentaries about the Farm Crisis. Then write a film review about the documentary. (See Chapter 11 for sample film reviews.)

The Farmer's Wife is a moving PBS *Frontline* documentary that follows the farm struggles of Buschkoetter family for from 1995–1997 as they struggle to keep their farm afloat and their marriage together. Check your local library for availability or purchase it from PBS.

The Farm Crisis is an historical documentary that can serve as a good overview of the difficult economic times faced in rural areas. It is available to view online at: http://www.iptv.org/iowastories/story.cfm/farm-crisis/10632/frc_20130701/video

Troublesome Creek: A Midwestern is an award-winning documentary about an Iowa family faces the end of the farm as they know it. Faced with losing their farm because of debt, the Jordans search for a solution to hold their family farm together.

Jane Smiley, *A Thousand Acres*

Jane Smiley's 1991 novel earned her a Pulitzer Prize for Fiction. Inspired by Shakespeare's *King Lear*, this wrenching story follows Ginny, the narrator, and her two sisters, Rose and Caroline, as they cope with their tyrannical father on the family's thousand acre farm in Iowa. Although the novel is set at the beginning of the Farm Crisis, this excerpt takes the reader back in time to Ginny's childhood when the farm was successful.

A Thousand Acres

There was no way to tell by looking that the land beneath my childish feet wasn't the primeval mold I read about at school, but it was new, created by magic lines of tile my father would talk about wit pleasure and reverence. Tile "drew" the water, warmed the soil, and made it easy to work, enabled him to get into the fields with his machinery a mere twenty-four hours after the heaviest storm. Most magically, tile produced prosperity—more bushels per acre of a better crop, year after year, wet or dry. . . . It took John and Sam and, at the end, my father, a generation, twenty-five years, to lay the tile lines and dig the drainage wells and cisterns. I in my Sunday dress and hat, driving in the Buick to church, was a beneficiary of this grand effort, someone who would always have a floor to walk on. However much these acres looked like a gift of nature, or of God, they were not. We went to church to pay our respects, not to give thanks. . . .

We might as well have had a catechism:

What is a farmer?

A farmer is a man who feeds the world.

What is a farmer's first duty?

To grow more food.

What is a farmer's second duty?

To buy more land.

What are the signs of a good farm?

Clean fields, neatly painted buildings, breakfast at six, no debts, no standing water.

How will you know a good farmer when you meet him?

He will not ask you for any favors. . . .

 EXPLORE: This excerpt from Smiley's novel has a number of biblical references. Identify those references and then consider their symbolic significance. Next, consider how Smiley uses this religious rhetoric to offer some clues about the human attitudes that helped cause the economic disaster of the Farm Crisis. What does she seem to suggest is a root cause?

 EXPLORE: Read the entirety of *A Thousand Acres* and consider the Smiley's choice to set it in the 1980s. How does the Farm Crisis figure in the novel?

William Kittredge, "Owning It All"

This autobiographical essay comes from Kittredge's 1987 collection *Owning It All: Essays*. It is set in Warner Valley, in Southeastern Oregon.

A mythology can be understood as a story that contains a set of implicit instructions from a society to its members, telling them what is valuable and how to conduct themselves if they are to preserve the things they value. The teaching mythology we grew up with in the American West is a pastoral story of agricultural ownership. The story begins with a vast innocent continent, natural and almost magically alive, capable of inspiring us to reverence and awe, and yet savage, a wilderness. A good rural people come from the East, and they take the land from its native inhabitants, and tame it for agricultural purposes, bringing civilization: a notion of how to live embodied in law. The story is as old as invading armies, and at heart it is a racist, sexist, imperialist mythology of conquest; a rationale for violence—against other people and against nature.

At the same time, that mythology is a lens through which we continue to see ourselves. Many of us like to imagine ourselves as honest yeomen who sweat and work in the woods or the mines or the fields for a living. And many of us are. We live in a real family, a work centered society, and we like to see ourselves as people with the good luck and sense to live in a place where some vestige of the natural world still exists in working order. Many of us hold that natural world as sacred to some degree, just as it is in our myth. Lately, more and more of us are coming to understand our society in the American West as an exploited colony, threatened by greedy outsiders who want to take our sacred place away from us, or at least to strip and degrade it.

In short, we see ourselves as a society of mostly decent people who live with some connection to a holy wilderness, threatened by those who lust for power and property. We look for Shane to come riding out of the Tetons, and instead we see Exxon and the Sierra Club. One looks virtually as alien as the other.

And our mythology tells us we own the West, absolutely and morally—we own it because of our history. Our people brought law to this difficult place, they suffered and they shed blood and they survived, and they earned this land for us. Our efforts have surely earned us the right to absolute control over the thing we created. The myth tells us this place is ours, and will always be ours, to do with as we see fit.

That's a most troubling and enduring message, because we want to believe it, and we do believe it, so many of us, despite its implicit ironies and wrongheadedness, despite the fact that we took the land from someone else. We try to ignore a genocidal history of violence against the Native Americans.

In the American West we are struggling to revise our dominant mythology, and to find a new story to inhabit. Laws control our lives, and they are designed to preserve a model of society based on values learned from mythology. Only after re-imagining our myths can we coherently remodel our laws, and hope to keep our society in a realistic relationship to what is actual.

In Warner Valley we thought we were living the right lives, creating a great precise perfection of fields, and we found the mythology had been telling us an enormous lie. The world had proven too complex, or the myth too simpleminded. And we were mortally angered.

The truth is, we never owned all the land and water. We don't even own very much of them, privately. And we don't own anything absolutely or forever. As our society grows more and more complex and interwoven, our entitlement becomes less and less absolute, more and more likely to be legally diminished. Our rights to property will never take precedence over the needs of society. Nor should they, we all must agree in our grudging hearts. Ownership of property has always been a privilege granted by society, and revocable.

Down by the slaughterhouse my grandfather used to keep a chicken-wire cage for trapping magpies. The cage was as high as a man's head, and mounted on a sled so it could be towed off and cleaned. It worked on the same principle as a lobster trap. Those iridescent black-and-white birds could get in to feed on the intestines of butchered cows—we never butchered a fat heifer or steer for our own consumption, only aged dry cows culled from the breeding herd—but they couldn't get out.

Trapped under the noontime sun, the magpies would flutter around in futile exploration for a while, and then would give in to a great sullen presentiment of their fate, just hopping around picking at leftovers and waiting.

My grandfather was Scots-English, and a very old man by then, but his blue eyes never turned watery and lost. He was one of those cowmen we don't see so often anymore, heedless of most everything outside his playground, which was livestock and seasons and property, and, as the seasons turned, more livestock and more property, a game which could be called accumulation.

All the notes were paid off, and you would have thought my grandfather would have been secure, and released to ease back in wisdom.

But no such luck. It seemed he had to keep proving his ownership. This took various forms, like endless litigation, which I have heard described as the sport of kings, but the manifestation I recall most vividly was that of killing magpies.

In the summer the ranch hands would butcher in the after-supper cool of an evening a couple of times a week. About once a week, when a number of magpies had gathered in the trap, maybe 10 or 15, my grandfather would get out his lifetime 12-gauge shotgun and have someone drive him down to the slaughterhouse in his dusty, ancient gray Cadillac, so he could look over his catch and get down to the business at hand. Once there, the ritual was slow and dignified, and always inevitable as one shoe after another.

The old man would sit there a while in his Cadillac and gaze at the magpies with his merciless blue eyes, and the birds would stare back with their hard black eyes. The summer dust would settle around the Cadillac, and the silent confrontation would continue. It would last several minutes.

Then my grandfather would sigh, and swing open the door on his side of the Cadillac, and climb out, dragging his shotgun behind him, the pockets of his gray gabardine suit-coat like a frayed uniform bulging with shells. The stock of the shotgun had been broken sometime deep in the past, and it was wrapped with fine brass wire, which shone golden in the sunlight while the old man thumbed shells into the magazine. All this without saying a word.

In the ear of my mind I try to imagine the radio playing softly in the Cadillac, something like "Room Full of Roses" or "Candy Kisses," but there was no radio. There was just the ongoing hum of insects and the clacking of the mechanism as the old man pumped a shell into the firing chamber.

He would lift the shotgun, and from no more than 12 feet, sighting down that barrel where the bluing was mostly worn off, through the chicken wire into the eyes of those trapped magpies, he would kill them one by one, taking his time, maybe so as to prove that this was no accident.

He would fire and there would be a minor explosion of blood and feathers, the huge booming of the shotgun echoing through the flattening light of early afternoon, off the sage-covered hills and down across the hay meadows and the sloughs lined with dagger-leafed willow, frightening great flights of blackbirds from the fence lines nearby, to rise in flocks and wheel and be gone.

"Bastards," my grandfather would mutter, and then he would take his time about killing another, and finally he would be finished and turn without looking back, and climb into his side of the Cadillac, where the door still stood open. Whoever it was whose turn it was that day would drive him back up the willow-lined lane through the meadows to the ranch house beneath the Lombardy poplar, to the cool shaded living room with its faded linoleum where the old man would finish out his day playing pinochle with my grandmother and anyone else he could gather, sometimes taking a break to retune a favorite program on the Zenith Trans-Oceanic radio.

No one in our family, so far as I ever heard, knew any reason why the old man had come to hate magpies with such specific intensity in his old age. The blackbirds were endlessly worse, the way they would mass together in flocks of literally thousands, to strip and thrash in his oat and barley fields, and then feed all fall in the bins of grain stockpiled to fatten his cattle.

"Where is the difference?" I asked him once, about the magpies.

"Because they're mine," he said. I never did know exactly what he was talking about, the remnants of entrails left over from the butchering of culled stocker cows, or the magpies. But it became clear he was asserting his absolute lordship over both, and over me, too, so long as I was living on his property. For all his life and most of mine the notion of property as absolute seemed like law, even when it never was.

Most of us who grew up owning land in the West believed that any impairment of our right to absolute control of that property was a taking, forbidden by the so-called "taking clause" of the Constitution. We believed regulation of our property rights could never legally reduce the value of our property. After all, what was the point of ownership if it was not profitable? Any infringement on the control of private property was a communist perversion.

But all over the West, as in all of America, the old folkway of property as an absolute right is dying. Our mythology doesn't work anymore.

We find ourselves weathering a rough winter of discontent, snared in the uncertainties of a transitional time and urgently yearning to inhabit a story that might bring sensible order to our lives—even as we know such a story can only evolve through an almost literally infinite series of recognitions of what, individually, we hold sacred. The liberties our people came seeking are more and more constrained, and here in the West, as everywhere, we hate it.

Simple as that. And we have to live with it. There is no more running away to territory. This is it, for most of us. We have no choice but to live in community. If we're lucky we may discover a story that teaches us to abhor our old romance with conquest and possession.

My grandfather died in 1958, toppling out of his chair at the pinochle table, soon after I came back to Warner, but his vision dominated our lives until we sold the ranch in 1967. An ideal of absolute ownership that defines family as property is the perfect device for driving people away from one another. There was a rule in our family. "What's good for the property is good for you."

"Every time there was more money we bought land," my grandmother proclaimed after learning my grandfather had been elected to the Cowboy Hall of Fame. I don't know if she spoke with pride or bitterness, but I do know that, having learned to understand love as property, we were all absolutely divided at the end; relieved to escape amid a litany of divorce and settlements, our family broken in the getaway.

I cannot grieve for my grandfather. It is hard to imagine, these days, that any man could ever again think he owns the birds.

EXPLORE: How are Smiley's novel and Kittredge's autobiographical essay thematically similar? In each case, the narrators are talking about their fathers. What kind of relationships do their fathers have to the land they own? How does Smiley use Biblical references, and how does Kittredge discuss violence?

 EXPLORE: Kittredge introduces his essay with the statement, "A mythology can be understood as a story that contains a set of implicit instructions from a society to its members, telling them what is valuable and how to conduct themselves." What are the mythologies you see at work in the selections in this chapter?

Wendell Berry, "Think Little"

Wendell Berry often cites the "Get Big or Get Out!" mantra as evidence of an agricultural system gone awry. In this 1972 essay, published in *A Continuous Harmony: Essays Cultural & Agricultural,* Berry addresses the question of size and links the ongoing battle to keep the family farm to three political movements of his time: the peace movement to end the Vietnam War, the African-American Civil Rights movement, and most especially the environmental movement. In order to correct these national crises, Berry advocates for a complete paradigm shift that includes re-envisioning what it means to be a successful farmer by shifting from the "Get Big" message to a willingness to "Think Little." Presently, Berry writes, "Our model citizen is a sophisticate who before puberty understands how to produce a baby, but who at the age of thirty will not know how to produce a potato…. But the citizen who is willing to Think Little, and, accepting the discipline of that, to go ahead on his own, is already solving the problem." Berry warned that this new kind of life would be "life-harder, more laborious, poorer in luxuries and gadgets, but also, I am certain, richer in meaning and more abundant in real pleasure."

"Think Little"

Odd as I am sure it will appear to some, I can think of no better form of personal involvement in the cure of the environment than that of gardening. A person who is growing a garden, if he is growing it organically, is improving a piece of the world. He is producing something to eat, which makes him somewhat independent of the grocery business, but he is also enlarging, for himself, the meaning of food and the pleasure of eating. The food he grows will be fresher, more nutritious, less contaminated by poisons and preservatives and dyes than what he can buy at a store. He is reducing the trash problem; a garden is not a disposable container, and it will digest and re-use its own wastes. If he enjoys working in his garden, then he is less dependent on an automobile or a merchant for his pleasure. He is involving himself directly in the work of feeding people.

If you think I'm wandering off the subject, let me remind you that most of the vegetables necessary for a family of four can be grown on a plot of forty by sixty feet. I think we might see in this an economic potential of considerable importance, since we now appear to be facing the possibility of widespread famine. How much food could be grown in the dooryards of cities and suburbs? How much could be grown along the extravagant right-of-ways of the interstate system? Or how much could be grown, by the intensive practices and economics of the small farm, on so-called marginal lands? Louis Bromfield liked to point out that the people of France survived crisis after crisis because they were a nation of gardeners, who in times of want turned with great skill to their own small plots of ground. And F. H. King, an agriculture professor who traveled extensively in the Orient in 1907, talked to a Chinese farmer who supported a family of twelve, "one donkey, one cow . . . and two pigs on 2.5 acres of cultivated land"—and who did this, moreover, by agricultural methods that were sound enough organically to have maintained his land in prime fertility through several thousand years of such use. These are possibilities that are readily apparent and attractive to minds that are prepared to Think Little. To Big Thinkers—the bureaucrats and businessmen of agriculture—they are quite simply invisible. But intensive, organic agriculture kept the farms of the Orient thriving for thousands of years, whereas extensive—which is to say, exploitive or extractive—agriculture has critically reduced the fertility of American farmlands in a few centuries or even a few decades.

 EXPLORE: Compare and contrast the tone of Berry's essay "Think Little" to the tone of the other essays you have read in this book. How would you characterize the tone of his work? If you recognize dissimilarities, try to account for the differences by considering what he is arguing.

 RESEARCH: As the US has moved into the twenty-first century, the controversies over the state of the family farm continue, especially as culture began to protest the hold industrial farming had on the American food system. Research a topic from the following list of related issues (or topics from Chapter 11 or 14) and create a Power-Point or Prezi presentation that defines and introduces the topic and provides some examples of the cultural discussion about this topic.

- Factory arms
- GMO (Genetically Modified Organism)
- Biotechnology and Farming
- CAFO (Confined Animal Feeding Operation)
- Terminator Seeds or Suicide Seeds
- Rurban, Ruralesque, Exurban
- Hobby Farming
- Microfarming
- Backyard Farming
- Agricultural Sustainability
- Organic Farming
- Monsanto

The Urban Millennium: More on Rural-Urban Demographics
The 2007 United Nations Populations Fund publication "State of World Population, 2007: Unleashing the Potential of Urban Growth" announced that at some point during 2007 or 2008, the global population for the first time would reach a tipping point, in which more of the world population was living in urban centers than in rural areas. This is referred to as the arrival of the "Urban Millennium." Two years before, the International Human Dimensions Programme Report entitled "Urbanization and Global Environmental Change" said that "urbanization—both as a social phenomenon and a physical transformation of landscapes—is one of the most powerful, irreversible, and visible anthropogenic forces on Earth." A 2011 publication entitled "'We're Not in the Field Anymore': Adapting Humanitarian Efforts to an Urban World," the international humanitarian organization ALNAP (Active Learning Network for Accountability and Performance), discussed the significance of this population shift, saying, "It may well amount to the most significant change in human civilisation since the coming of agriculture. Urbanisation is a social phenomenon and a physical transformation of landscapes. . . . Much of the available data indicates that urbanisation will continue at a scale and speed that redefines our relationship with each other and with the planet."

CHAPTER SEVEN

The Farm Goes to College

History of the Land Grant College

In 2012, land grant colleges and universities celebrated the sesquicentennial of the signing of the Morrill Act by President Abraham Lincoln. The Morrill Act granted federal land to establish colleges "in order to promote the liberal education of the industrial classes." This meant that the sons and daughters of farmers had access to the kind of education offered to their wealthier counterparts at the nation's elite colleges. In essence, it was nothing less than the democratization of higher education, providing access to students who previously did not have the funds to attend college. The key text of the act (which appears shortly in its entirety) is this:

> . . . without excluding other scientific and classical studies and including military tactic, to teach such branches of learning as are related to agriculture and the mechanic arts, in such manner as the legislatures of the States may respectively prescribe, in order to promote the liberal and practical education of the industrial classes in the several pursuits and professions in life

The original mission of these new colleges included teaching agriculture, military tactics, and the mechanic arts but also classical studies, so that students could obtain both a liberal and a practical education. By *liberal education,* we mean in the classic Roman sense--education that is not only for a free human being but also education that sets a person free by imparting knowledge to think analytically. Thus, a citizen must have a liberal education in order to be a worthy participant in a democracy who is able to behave ethically, participate civically, and make decisions based on reason and logic. Studying the classics—learning Greek and Latin—and exploring the humanities make someone a liberally educated person. The land grant college also provided pragmatic education in sciences and commerce

Who was responsible for this paradigm shift in the American educational model for higher education? Justin Smith Morrill (1810–1898) was a member of Congress from Vermont when he sponsored legislation that came to bear his name. He believed that "agriculture [is] the foundation of all present and future prosperity." Iowa was the first state to act on this legislation and created the institution that came to be known as Iowa State University.

Note the date of this act: 1862. What is historically relevant about this time in U.S. History? The War Between the States. The Morrill Act in its original form did not include those states that had seceded; that came only after the conclusion of the Civil War. Although the land grant colleges were to provide access to the sons and daughters of the working class, admission was not guaranteed for black citizens in the South. As a result, a second Morrill Act of 1890 provided funding for what has

177

come to be known as historically black colleges and universities (HBCUs). In 1994, tribal colleges were added to the land grant family although for both of these latter two types of institutions, cash rather than land provided the endowment.

An important mission of the land grant colleges was to provide up-to-date research to farmers and ranchers. As a result, Congress authorized Agricultural Experiment Stations in 1887 through the Hatch Act, which was signed into law by President Grover Cleveland. The purpose of this farmers' legislation was to promote "scientific investigation and experiment respecting the principles of agricultural science." The federal-state partnership that arose from this act resulted in dramatic increases in food and fiber production. College researchers sometimes loaded train cars with animals and crops to take lectures about enhanced methods of farming directly to the people. The tripartite mission of a land-grant university—teaching, research, and service—is a result of the imperative to share knowledge with the people. Experimental farms, generally on or near college campuses, tried out new farm practices. For instance, the University of Illinois has a cornfield in the center of its campus. When there was an effort to replace it with a new library, a massive protest resulted in the new building being placed underground, leaving the Morrow Plots, which had been established in 1876, untouched.

Although some farmers looked askance at "book farming," there was no doubt that scientific understanding of farming practices helped economically and environmentally. George Washington Carver, who received much of his education at Iowa State University and its experiment station and who led Tuskegee Institute, focused on new crops, such as peanuts, that could replace the soil-depleting cotton crop, which had also been devastated by the boll weevil.

The role of the land grant college continued to evolve with Congress passing the Smith-Lever Act of 1914, authorizing cooperative extension offices at the county level in the states, with the express purpose of sharing knowledge not only with farmers but with homemakers. Extension agents had the important, if sometimes delicate, job of transmitting university knowledge to the people. In many states, women formed extension clubs for education and socializing.

FIGURE 7.1. Farmers and Homemakers Encampment (1924) at Utah State Agriculture College. A daily newspaper was distributed during the encampment. Tents numbered 164 on the Quad. (Used with permission of Special Collections & Archives, Merrill-Cazier Library, Utah State University.)

Their programs included nutrition, sewing, and gardening, but they also provided a way for women, often living in some isolation on their farms, the opportunity to come together as a community. As Wayne D. Rasmussen put it in his *Taking the University to the People: Seventy-five Years of Cooperative Extension* (1989), "No other country has focused such attention to the practical (applied) dimension of education by extending and applying the knowledge base of our land-grant universities to the laboratories of real life where people life and work, develop and lead. Extension has been copied by many countries, but is yet to be duplicated" (viii).

The national organization that brings together all land grant colleges and universities is the Association of Public and Land-grant Universities (APLU), headquartered in Washington, DC.

Enrollment in agricultural classes in colleges has steadily increased (see chart) although enrollment began declining in the 1980s in the wake of the farm crisis. Distance education became increasingly important as a way to make cooperative research and extension resources accessible, particularly to remote sites.

In this chapter, you'll explore documents from the farmers' legislation, but you'll also read an essay that asks if the land-grant college remained true to Jefferson's vision of an agrarian economy and an educated citizenry.

The first document is the actual legislation for the establishment of land-grant colleges. As you read, be particularly sensitive to how Jeffersonian influenced this legislation. And, how does it differ from Jeffersonian ideals?

Transcript of Morrill Land-Grant College Act (1862)
Chap. CXXX.--*AN ACT Donating Public Lands to the several States and Territories which may provide Colleges for the Benefit of Agriculture and Mechanic Arts.*
Be it enacted by the Senate and House of Representatives of the United States of America in Congress assembled, That there be granted to the several States, for the purposes hereinafter mentioned, an amount of public land, to be apportioned to each State a quantity equal to thirty thousand acres for each senator

and representative in Congress to which the States are respectively entitled by the apportionment under the census of eighteen hundred and sixty: *Provided,* That no mineral lands shall be selected or purchased under the provisions of this Act.

SEC. 2. *And be it further enacted,* That the land aforesaid, after being surveyed, shall be apportioned to the several States in sections or subdivisions of sections, not less than one quarter of a section; and whenever there are public lands in a State subject to sale at private entry at one dollar and twenty-five cents per acre, the quantity to which said State shall be entitled shall be selected from such lands within the limits of such State, and the Secretary of the Interior is hereby directed to issue to each of the States in which there is not the quantity of public lands subject to sale at private entry at one dollar and twenty-five cents per acre, to which said State may be entitled under the provisions of this act, land scrip to the amount in acres for the deficiency of its distributive share: said scrip to be sold by said States and the proceeds thereof applied to the uses and purposes prescribed in this act, and for no other use or purpose whatsoever: *Provided,* That in no case shall any State to which land scrip may thus be issued be allowed to locate the same within the limits of any other State, or of any Territory of the United States, but their assignees may thus locate said land scrip upon any of the unappropriated lands of the United States subject to sale at private entry at one dollar and twenty-five cents, or less, per acre: *And provided, further,* That not more than one million acres shall be located by such assignees in any one of the States: *And provided, further,* That no such location shall be made before one year from the passage of this Act.

SEC. 3. *And be it further enacted,* That all the expenses of management, superintendence, and taxes from date of selection of said lands, previous to their sales, and all expenses incurred in the management and disbursement of the moneys which may be received therefrom, shall be paid by the States to which they may belong, out of the Treasury of said States, so that the entire proceeds of the sale of said lands shall be applied without any diminution whatever to the purposes hereinafter mentioned.

SEC. 4. And be it further enacted, That all moneys derived from the sale of the lands aforesaid by the States to which the lands are apportioned, and from the sales of land scrip hereinbefore provided for, shall be invested in stocks of the United States, or of the States, or some other safe stocks, yielding not less than five per centum upon the par value of said stocks; and that the moneys so invested shall constitute a perpetual fund, the capital of which shall remain forever undiminished, (except so far as may be provided in section fifth of this act,) and the interest of which shall be inviolably appropriated, by each State which may take and claim the benefit of this act, to the endowment, support, and maintenance of at least one college where the leading object shall be, without excluding other scientific and classical studies, and including military tactics, to teach such branches of learning as are related to agriculture and the mechanic arts, in such manner as the legislatures of the States may respectively prescribe, in order to promote the liberal and practical education of the industrial classes in the several pursuits and professions in life.

SEC. 5. *And be it further enacted*, That the grant of land and land scrip hereby authorized shall be made on the following conditions, to which, as well as to the provisions hereinbefore contained, the previous assent of the several States shall be signified by legislative acts:

First. If any portion of the fund invested, as provided by the foregoing section, or any portion of the interest thereon, shall, by any action or contingency, be diminished or lost, it shall be replaced by the State to which it belongs, so that the capital of the fund shall remain forever undiminished; and the annual interest shall be regularly applied without diminution to the purposes mentioned in the fourth section of this act, except that a sum, not exceeding ten per centum upon the amount received by any State under the provisions of this act may be expended for the purchase of lands for sites or experimental farms, whenever authorized by the respective legislatures of said States.

Second. No portion of said fund, nor the interest thereon, shall be applied, directly or indirectly, under any pretence whatever, to the purchase, erection, preservation, or repair of any building or buildings.

Third. Any State which may take and claim the benefit of the provisions of this act shall provide, within five years from the time of its acceptance as provided in subdivision seven of this section, at least not less than one college, as described in the fourth section of this act, or the grant to such State shall cease; and said State shall be bound to pay the United States the amount received of any lands previously sold; and that the title to purchasers under the State shall be valid.

Fourth. An annual report shall be made regarding the progress of each college, recording any improvements and experiments made, with their cost and results, and such other matters, including State industrial and economical statistics, as may be supposed useful; one copy of which shall be transmitted by mail [free] by each, to all the other colleges which may be endowed under the provisions of this act, and also one copy to the Secretary of the Interior.

Fifth. When lands shall be selected from those which have been raised to double the minimum price, in consequence of railroad grants, they shall be computed to the States at the maximum price, and the number of acres proportionally diminished.

Sixth. No State while in a condition of rebellion or insurrection against the government of the United States shall be entitled to the benefit of this act.

Seventh. No State shall be entitled to the benefits of this act unless it shall express its acceptance thereof by its legislature within three years from July 23, 1866:

Provided, That when any Territory shall become a State and be admitted into the Union, such new State shall shall be entitled to the benefits of the said act of July two, eighteen hundred and sixty-two, by expressing the acceptance therein required within three years from the date of its admission into the Union, and providing the college or colleges within five years after such acceptance, as prescribed in this act.

SEC. 6. And be it further enacted, That land scrip issued under the provisions of this act shall not be subject to location until after the first day of January, one thousand eight hundred and sixty-three.

SEC. 7. *And be it further enacted*, That the land officers shall receive the same fees for locating land scrip issued under the provisions of this act as is now allowed for the location of military bounty land warrants under existing laws: *Provided*, their maximum compensation shall not be thereby increased.

SEC. 8. *And be it further enacted*, That the Governors of the several States to which scrip shall be issued under this act shall be required to report annually to Congress all sales made of such scrip until the whole shall be disposed of, the amount received for the same, and what appropriation has been made of the proceeds.

EXPLORE: Do the math. Is there a region of the country that benefitted from the formula to grant land?

COLLABORATE: Working with a partner, choose one of you to argue that the Morrill Act was the natural outgrowth of the Jeffersonian perspective, while the other will argue that it departed from Jefferson's beliefs. Support your argument with evidence from the text.

WRITING: It might be expected that a wartime President and Congress would be able to do little else but oversee the conflict; however, during President Lincoln's terms, western lands were opened for free settlement through the Homestead Act; the Department of Agriculture was established; the construction of a transcontinental railroad was authorized; and the National Academy of Sciences was founded. These acts indicate forward-thinking leaders. Choose one of these developments, read about its history, and then in an essay, demonstrate how it fits (along with the land-grant act) as a logical piece of a presidential vision.

VIEWING: Is there a Morrill Hall on your campus? If so, what is its architectural style and date of construction? If not, look on the Internet for examples of Morrill Halls on other college campuses. Do they have similar architectural styles? Choose three Morrill Halls, and for each one, give a description, and then offer your analysis of how they are similar and how they differ. Why is it doubtful that Morrill Halls will appear on western campuses, particularly in Utah?

RESEARCH: Land-grant colleges may feature agricultural themes for their mascots. How many colleges or universities in the USA use *Aggies* as the name for their sport teams?

Extension Homemakers Stand Strong behind Durham Extension Service
By Deborah B. McGiffin

The following is a centennial history (1911–2011) of Homemakers Clubs in Durham County, North Carolina, which reveals fascinating social and cultural changes over the decades.

It is a historical year for Cooperative Extension's Family and Consumer Sciences and the Extension and Community Association. This year marks the one-hundredth anniversary of improving the quality of families and their lives through the work and programs of Family and Consumer Sciences and Extension Homemakers, the forerunner of the Extension and Community Association. Throughout 2011, the Cooperative Extension Service will be celebrating the Family and Consumer Sciences Centennial. In 1911, Jane McKimmon, the first state Home Demonstration Agent, began to organize community "tomato" clubs as a way to educate rural women about food preservation and safety.

FIGURE 7.2. Extension Homemakers receiving sewing instructions, 1929.

Eventually the tomato clubs evolved into community Home Demonstration Clubs. Through this club system, Family and Consumer Sciences Agents and Home Demonstration Clubs or Extension Homemakers forged a partnership that provided researched based education in rural communities throughout North Carolina.

The first Home Demonstration Club in Durham County can be traced back to the Women's Betterment Society founded in 1913. Home demonstration work began in the county in 1915 after the first home agent, Mrs. Beulah Eubanks, was hired. Homemakers heeded the campaign of the United States Department of Agriculture to help supply food shipments to War World I troops in Europe. For their part in the war effort, Durham Homemakers canned 94,672 containers of fruits and vegetables that were ultimately sent to our servicemen aboard. In 1920, Miss Anna Rowe came to Durham County to assume the role as Home Demonstration Agent and she was charged with forming permanent community home demonstration clubs. During Miss Rowe's tenure in Durham, twenty clubs totaling 745 women were organized. The first new club to be organized, after the Women's Betterment Society converted to a Home Demonstration Club, was the Bahama Home Demonstration Club founded in 1919, and a year later, the Nelson Home Demonstration Club was organized. The Home Demonstration Clubs were highly structured from the beginning as they remain so today. They were each established with a governing body of annually elected officers that carried out an annual plan of work. Community officers formed the County Council and served as the supporting body to the home agent. Today, this would be equivalent to an Advisory Board. Leadership skills that members developed from their association in the Home Demonstration Clubs became significant contributions to their respective communities and to the entire county. Collectively, Extension Homemakers learned and used their Home Demonstration Clubs as a dais to interface with their local school officials and government leaders. Among the most significant accomplishments of these twenty community clubs was the eventual founding of the Durham County Home Demonstration Curb Market. The establishment of the Curb Market led to the growth of the overall Extension program in Durham County.

These early twenty demonstration clubs remained operational and met regularly through the remainder of the decade and through two more home demonstration agents who followed Anna Rowe between 1924 and 1927. In 1927, Rose Ellwood Bryan was appointed the Home Demonstration Agent for Durham County, and under her leadership, Extension Homemakers made noteworthy contributions to not only to Durham County Cooperative Extension Service, but also to the financial well being of their families. The number of home demonstration clubs grew to twenty-six.

FIGURE 7.3. Home Demonstration Club Meeting, 1930s

Just as the number of Home Demonstration Clubs grew in the late twenties, so did the clubs' community involvement. A plan of work compiled for all Durham Home Demonstration Clubs recorded monthly programmatic topics that were to be covered in each club from the years1928 to1940. The topics of interest for the women of the Home Demonstration Clubs dealt mostly with improving the quality of family life and included subjects such as food preservation, preparing school lunches, infant feeding, time management, managing household accounts, clothing construction and care, controlling household pests, gracious entertaining, and home decorating.

As the Home Demonstration Clubs became prominent community organizations, they used their status to support Extension's youth component, 4-H. They contributed to the achievements of 4-H youth by supporting their club and project work. Between 1930 and 1939, Extension Homemakers raised funds to send 75 senior 4-H members to Raleigh for 4-H State Short Courses and 120 junior 4-H members to camp. When Durham County had their first 4-H club member win a state honor and was awarded a trip to broadcast for the *National Farm and Home Hour,* Durham County Home Demonstration Clubs cooperatively raised funds to help send Pearl Nichols Williams to Washington, D.C. Then later in the midst of the depression when three other Durham 4-H members won state honors and were awarded trips to National 4-H Congress, Durham Demonstration Homemakers collectively raised more funds, and proudly sent the Durham youth to Chicago, Illinois.

Extension Homemakers in Durham County had grown in numbers and fortitude by the time the Great Depression hit. In 1930, the Durham Home Demonstration Curb Market was organized to help bring income to farm families hurt by the Depression. The Curb Market took off almost immediately. It was housed in the basement of the Farmers Mutual Exchange in downtown Durham, where the Extension offices were also housed. Homemakers came weekly on Saturday mornings to sale fruits and vegetables, poultry, eggs, butter, meats, cakes, breads, flowers, canned goods, arts and crafts, and miscellaneous items. The Curb Market opened on May 24, 1930 with about 50 sellers, but by the end of the decade there were 365 sellers. Extension reported that Durham Extension Homemakers sold $291,245.38 worth of produce during the first ten years of the Curb Market's existence. However, the impacts the Curb Market made on the families of the Homemakers were often far more substantial than the income they earned. For example, Mrs. E. A. Perry was cited in a Durham Herald-Sun article of earning enough money at the curb market from selling eggs that her family was able to wire their home with electricity and install a system of running water. Another homemaker credited the Curb Market for pulling

FIGURE 7.4. Curb Market on Opening Day, 1947

her family out of the depression. After they had lost all other sources of income, the Curb Market gave her family their last hope, and helped them survive economically. Actually, the sales at the Curb Market steadily increased during the worst years of the depression, which proved to be a lifeline for many Homemakers and their families trying to subsist through it. Durham citizens valued the Curb Market as much as Extension homemakers. By 1941, an average of 1050 citizens was shopping at the market monthly. They came for the fresh produce, meats, dairy products and the high quality of baked goods. The successfulness of the Curb Market was so astounding, according to Extension records, that homes lost in the depression were reclaimed, tenants become homeowners, boys and girls pursued college educations, and standards of living were raised for families associated with the market. Indeed the Curb Market had become such an institution in Durham that it outgrew its quarters at the Farmers' Exchange. In 1941, Durham County Extension Homemakers went before the County Board of Commissioners to request an agricultural building large enough to house the Curb Market. Eventually, after several persistent attempts and a bond referendum, the Durham County Agriculture Building was built in 1947. The building housed the Extension Service, the Durham Soil and Water Conservation District, and the USDA Farm Service Agency; it included a state of the art demonstration kitchen and an indoor pavilion large enough to house the weekly Curb Market. Extension Homemakers weathered the greatest financial storm of the twentieth century through sales generated at the Curb Market, but in doing so they also helped to bring the value of Extension Service to all of the county's citizens.

Despite Durham Farm Agent and Home Agent reports documenting substantial losses to farm families during the depression years, the County Home Demonstration Clubs between 1930 and 1940 grew in numbers and philanthropic work in addition to their clubs' monthly plans of work. Besides the phenomenal reception and exposure they received from organizing and running the Curb Market, the Home Demonstration Clubs cooperatively funded an annual Thanksgiving dinner for the Wright's Refuge beginning in 1926 and continuing through 1940. Wright's Refuge was a local Durham orphanage that housed 35 children. They contributed annually to the Jane S. McKimmon Loan Fund, a fund designed to award deserving rural girls with funds to attend an "A" grade college to study Home Economics. They collected 4,669 garments during the

1930s and distributed the clothing in 26 communities to needy families. Many of the garments were often made by hand by Extension Homemakers especially for the clothing drives. Extension Homemakers helped 166 club members by sponsoring their attendance to North Carolina Home Demonstration Short Courses in Raleigh. A 1940 county report stated the Extension Homemakers along with 4-H girls canned 3,987,493 quarts of food and distributed much of the food to the hungry. Four more Home Demonstration Clubs formed to bring the total number of clubs to 30 by 1938. Five of the clubs mobilized their communities to raise funds and built club houses. Though the depression must have been devastating to many Extension Homemakers and their families, they seemed to find strength in numbers, and thus in helping themselves, helped the greater part of Durham County.

Emerging from the depression, families were faced with the subsequent calamity facing the nation, World War II. The Durham Home Demonstration Clubs placed emphasis on food production and conservation during the war years to aid with wartime needs. Additionally, Durham Homemakers along with Home Demonstration Clubs across the state were actively supporting war efforts by collecting scrap metal, rendering fat for weapon and ammunition production, and growing victory gardens for food production. Just as Extension Homemakers were determined to endure

FIGURE 7.5. Extension Homemakers learning to can (1940s).

through the depression they took on the war years with as much zeal and determination.

Food preservation was still a major emphasis of Extension work, but by 1947, many farm families now had freezer lockers in their homes, so freezing food was practiced as well as canning. During the 1947 growing season for example, Extension Homemakers canned 40,507 quart jars of fruit, 50,914 quart jars of vegetables, and 2,040 quart jars of meat. They also froze 1,710 quarts of fruit, 2,706 quarts of vegetables and 18,607 pounds of meat. Once World War II had ended and the Durham County Extension Service had settled in their new offices at the Agricultural Building, Durham County Home Demonstration Clubs began to focus on domestic issues. The war years must have been difficult for the Extension clubs, because by 1947, the number of Home Demonstration Clubs in Durham County had dropped to sixteen clubs totaling 370 members. These were half the members and clubs prior to the War. However, the Durham County Curb Market continued its successful run in the forties, just as it had done in the thirties. During the decade of the forties, Durham County had the most prosperous of all the curb markets in the state. In 1942, the Durham Market topped sales in the state and continued to hold the state record for the highest annual sales until 1951 when Mecklenburg County passed Durham County Market sales by $105.

Durham Home Demonstration Clubs were civically involved in the late forties. Clubs raised funds to purchase community playground equipment, buy velvet curtains for a school stage, buy a freezer for another school so school food could be stored safely, and donated money for a local youth center. Since five home demonstration clubs had their own facilities, they offered their clubhouses to other community organizations that needed meeting space. When a community church burned, the Maybrook Home Demonstration Club lent its clubhouse to the church until a new church could be built. When a Glenn Club member's home was destroyed by fire, other club members rallied and obtained building materials and supplies from a local contractor to help rebuild the home. Home Demonstration Clubs all the while, continued their support of county 4-H programs and assisted with raising money whenever necessary to help send 4-H members to district, state, and national 4-H events.

Since Home Demonstrations Clubs were first organized in Durham County, members had a source and opportunity to develop leadership skills. Certainly, they took advantage of these opportunities since Extension Homemakers were the basis for Durham County having its own Agricultural Building. Extension Homemakers broadened their abilities to take on positions of leadership within their district and state organization, the North Carolina Federation of Home Demonstration Clubs.

Developing an outlet for cultural appreciation and a desire to encourage music was the inspiration that prompted Mrs. J. C. Dodson to organize the Durham County Home Demonstration Choral Group and the first Rural Church Music School in North Carolina. The success of the Rural Church Music School in organizing rural church choirs led to thirty-three such music schools forming across the state. The county music programs that resulted from the Rural Church Music School generated the development of the Julie Cuyler Foundation by Dr. W. K. Cuyler of Duke University. Through the foundation, a trust fund was created that further promoted Home Demonstration music education

FIGURE 7.6.Durham Homemakers Fairview Club Kitchen Orchestra, 1953

throughout the state. The trust fund created scholarships that were used to send Home Demonstration Club women to statewide music camps and workshops.

By 1950, club membership was up to 400, and two more Home Demonstration Clubs had formed. Locally, Extension Homemakers engaged in a variety of educational and public service activities that were often covered as news worthy stories in the local newspaper, The Durham Herald-Sun. Homemakers were interested in improving their rural roads, and started a campaign that led County Commissioners to identifying county roads and putting up road posts naming rural roads. Collectively, Durham Extension Homemakers raised funds and helped to supply county schools with athletic equipment and first aid kits. They contributed canned goods to the orphanage, the Wright Refuge. They held community educational programs that promoted Tuberculosis screenings, taught basic first aid skills, and addressed home safety issues. Extension Homemakers attended educational programs on home beautification, practical kitchen design, and clothing construction. During the fifties, Home Demonstration Clubs hosted annual fashion shows, which were a popular source of community entertainment and allowed their members to show off garments they had made during the year. Durham County Homemakers also continued their loyal support of Durham County 4-Hers. They prepared meals for summer local 4-H camps and raised funds regularly to send 4-Hers to camps, district, state and even national 4-H achievement programs. The fifties were a decade of highly visible activities and community involvement for the Home Demonstration Clubs and their members, as newspaper articles of the time document. In fact, the Raleigh News and Observer in 1954 printed that "The Home Demonstration Clubs of North Carolina are a Vital Part of Our Society." The sixties were all about change. In Durham County, it was not only the social landscape that was changing, but also the landscape in general. Urbanization began taking hold. The development of Research Triangle Park (RTP) founded in 1959 was well underway by 1965. Most of the original 4,000 acres incorporated in RTP was in Durham County. As RTP grew, so did communities neighboring the Park. Surrounding farmland gave way to development. To address the conflicting advancement of urbanization on agriculture, the Durham County Extension Service led the Agriculture and Community Improvement Committee of the Northern Central Area Development Association. Although urban development was methodical and somewhat controlled at first, it did begin to take a toll on Home Demonstrations Clubs. The Durham County clubs decreased by two to total sixteen by 1961. Clubs continued their emphasis on community service, supporting the local 4-H members and clubs, and the Wright Refuge Orphanage. They also visited known local "shut-ins" and prepared meals and holiday gift baskets for homebound citizens. Home Demonstration Clubs supported North Carolina troops and worked with the local Red Cross chapter to prepare ditty bags for American servicemen fighting in the Vietnam conflict. The more rural outlying Extension Homemaker clubs continued their interest and commitment to food preservation by preserving a total of 2,950 quarts of vegetables and fruits and freezing 3,506 pounds of garden grown produce. Homemakers displayed their interest in fashion and practicality by hosting annual community fashion shows that modeled clothing styles made by club members. Home décor still proved to be a major interest among Extension Homemakers and many home improvement projects were highlighted during monthly Home Demonstration Club meetings. Homemakers were also interested in many of the new time-saving appliances and time efficient cooking methods. Demonstrations were widely given with an emphasis of reducing time spent in the kitchen through the use of blenders and using various recipe "short-cuts."

FIGURE 7.7. Dress Revue, 1964

FIGURE 7.8. Extension Homemaker freezing vegetables (1960s)

Even though there was little to suggest how the major impact of school and social integration affected the county's Home Demonstration Clubs, the White Home Demonstration County

Council, merged and integrated with the Durham "Negro" Home Demonstration County Council in 1968. On the state level after integration of Extension offices, the North Carolina Organization of Home Demonstration Clubs became the North Carolina Extension Homemakers Association. However, the individual clubs remained segregated according to monthly newspaper club reports.

As the seventies evolved, membership in Home Demonstration clubs was in decline. The Family and Consumer Sciences traditional model for delivering Extension education to community Extension Homemaker Clubs also was shifting. To better accommodate the changing times as more women entered the work force, Family and Consumer Sciences agents began reaching non-traditional audiences in urban areas and by building collaborations with other civic groups and county agencies. Additionally, Family and Consumer Sciences curriculum began to shift in order to address issues concerning the changing social dynamics of families, as the culture evolved from an agrarian landscape to an urban one. Overall county membership totaled 240, which included sixteen clubs. Four of the original clubs formed in 1920 were still active. However, younger women were not joining Extension Homemaker clubs, primarily because they were choosing to work outside the home. With RTP in close proximity, more jobs were available. These employment opportunities apparently affected membership in the Home Demonstration Clubs, and they sought new means to attract younger women to their clubs. Several clubs began to hold night meetings and were successful in drawing some new members. But even with the declining general membership of Home Demonstration Clubs, Durham Homemakers responded to the social changes of the time. In 1970, the first integrated Home Demonstration Club was organized, the Neighborhood Actionettes. In 1973, the Durham Extension Homemaker County Council elected its first Black president, Mrs. Arthur Dennegan. Even with fewer members, Extension Homemakers stayed in the public eye and remained relevant in their communities and in the county. They kept county commissioners aware of Extension work by hosting an annual Commissioner and Extension Luncheon. Additionally, clubs presented local community programs that focused on current social issues like, drug abuse among youth, air pollution and recycling. Extension Homemakers supported the new federal initiative the Expanded Food and Nutrition Education Program referred to as EFNEP. From 1971 until 1980, Extension Homemakers provided food and served as volunteer music and craft instructors for summer EFNEP day camps. In 1975, Extension Homemakers published a cookbook titled "From the Kitchens of Durham County Extension Homemakers." Sales from the cookbooks were used to fund county 4-H programs, and in 1976, Extension Homemakers held a bicentennial field day to raise funds for the 4-H Development Fund.

Although the Curb Market had been active throughout the fifties and sixties, local interest gradually waned during the seventies. Market sellers steadily dropped as the decade wore on. The last market account entries were made in 1976. The last Extension Homemaker to sell at the Curb Market was Mrs. Linda Keith. After a 48 year run, the Durham County Curb Market closed in 1976.

The early eighties saw a slight bump in membership. Durham County Homemakers comprised of 21 clubs and a county membership enrollment of 321. Still membership slowly decreased during the nineteen-eighties. To stay in tune with times in lieu of dwindling membership, Extension Homemakers emphasized automobile restraint systems for children, programs in family resource management and decision-making, nutrition, and emergency preparedness. Extension Homemakers continued to support Durham 4-H as an on-going mission. Cooperatively, as a statewide organization, they consistently backed the education of North Carolina youth and awarded twenty annual scholarships to college students attending North Carolina colleges.

Urban sprawl eventually over took many Durham County communities as new housing and shopping developments were built. Today, many of the original communities that Home Demonstration Clubs represented new longer exist. Communities of the nineteen-twenties faded into subdivisions or into RTP as it expanded. More Extension Homemakers entered the workforce as their children grew-up and left home. Improvements to county roads and the creation of the Durham Expressway, Highway147, paved through several traditional Black neighborhoods. Coincidently, the responsibilities of Family and Consumer Sciences Extension agents are in constant flux as they are directed to address and collaborate more and more with non-traditional audiences and instructed to tackle urban issues. In 1995, to rejuvenate their image the statewide association, the North Carolina Extension Homemakers Association, became the Extension and Community Association, commonly referred to as ECA. The decreased membership of ECA on the local as well as the state level is currently reinventing itself to maintain existing clubs and to ultimately attract new members. Consequently, the North Carolina Extension and Community Association as a whole is under-going an organizational change designed to update by-laws and the leadership structure that will engage newer members in the association. State Extension advisers and a state ECA advisory board has been working for the past several years to implement a more streamlined organization absent of prior more restrictive club guidelines. Though ECA numbers may never get to the broad numbers of membership indicative of the early beginning years, ECA anticipates to move forward offering both men and women the opportunities of leadership and community involvement that so aptly established the Extension Homemakers as viable and relevant community leaders, advocates and peer educators in their respective communities, towns and counties.

In Durham County, charter Extension Homemaker members completely died out during the last thirty years. Only two the original Home Demonstration Clubs, Rougemont and Bethesda, and two more early-on clubs, Union and Forest Hills, are currently active. Presently, eighty percent of the county's population lives in the city of Durham. Although Durham Home Demonstration Club membership, now referred to as the Extension and Community Association (ECA), is at an all-time low, Durham County Extension and Community Association is still an integral part of the Durham Cooperative Extension Service. With a strong emphasis on education and service, Durham ECA makes a difference in the lives of youth and adults by significantly impacting and improving family life through sponsoring and presenting programs that emphasize education, health, nutrition, civic engagement and community development. Durham ECA members are supportive of families who are coping and caring for aging and incapacitated parents and/or other family members in crisis. ECA Club members led the drive in Durham County to educate and sign senior citizens up for direct deposit of their social security checks, enabling seniors secure and faster access to their monthly income. Fidget aprons, mammary pillows and rag dolls are made and distributed routinely by ECA members to Durham County caregivers who care for family members suffering from Alzheimer's, Breast Cancer or childhood diseases. In supporting Durham County youth, ECA members through their volunteer efforts have held life skill classes for youth attending Durham County 4-H Summer Day Camps, and helped Durham 4-H sponsor District Activity Day by hosting concessions for 4-H judges. Durham County ECA promotes Extension health and nutrition educational objectives by offering public programs that highlight healthy living habits. Durham Public Schools have benefited from ECA outreach, through the use of eye patches made by ECA members to assist with student vision tests held in the county's elementary schools. Through their other community outreach efforts, ECA helped to encourage community engagement and volunteerism with the creation and disbursement of leader appreciation packets among community partners. Because of their leadership and active involvement in Durham County, Durham ECA is able to empower hundreds of Durham residents by promoting and providing sustainable Extension-based life solutions every day.

The Durham Extension Homemakers, both past and present, enabled the Durham County Cooperative Extension Service to carry out its mission throughout the twentieth century, into the twenty-first. Their successes helped rural families make it through the dark depression era and the turbulent years of war. They furnished a social network of rural women that generated community leaders. Extension Homemakers supported and promoted the education and welfare of their children and those less fortunate living around them. Their generosity improved the standard of living in their respective communities, and enabled families to send children to college. They graciously modeled social goodness and acceptance as social norms changed to a more divergent integrated society and as urbanization swallowed many of their rural communities. Perhaps, it is because of their successes and achievements that Extension Homemakers no longer signify the contemporary community stature and prominence of their rural past. However, as the Durham County Cooperative Extension Service continues to remain a significant local entity and resource, it must pay tribute to the strong women who have backed Extension from the beginning; to the strong women who guided the Extension mission by bringing the needs of their communities to the Extension Service; to the strong women who were and still are Extension advocates, volunteers and advisors; and to the strong women who helped create the rich Extension heritage that will prolong Extension's future in Durham County.

 EXPLORE: Using evidence from the history presented here, trace the social and cultural changes in women's roles. How have they remained the same? How have they altered?

 EXPLORE: Gender and language. Note that some women are referred to in this history by their husband's names: Mrs. E. A. Perry, Mrs. Arthur Dennegan. What is the convention for referring to women in formal terms? How is a woman's identity affected by the correct use of *Mrs.*?

 RESEARCH: Has anyone in your family been involved in agriculturallyoriented clubs? If so, interview and prepare an oral history that could be placed in the archives of a Cooperative Extension library.

 RESEARCH: Are there inherent dangers to home preservation through canning (or bottling, as it is called in regions of the United States? Do research to determine why focusing on food preservation was an appropriate objective for Cooperative Extension.

"Jefferson, Morrill, and the Upper Crust"
Wendell Berry
From *The Unsettling of America: Culture & Agriculture*

Wendell Berry is a native of Henry County, Kentucky, where he farms. A noted fiction writer and poet, he is also an essayist. He has been called the twenty-first century Thoreau. In 2012, he was selected by the National Endowment for the Humanities to deliver the prestigious Jefferson Lecture. For Berry, the American family farm is the cornerstone of society. Berry's essay in which he criticizes land-grant institutions is included in part below, focusing on the sections about Jefferson and Morrill.

Jefferson, Morrill, and the Upper Crust

THE CONVICTION OF THOMAS JEFFERSON

In the mind of Thomas Jefferson, farming, education, and democratic liberty were indissolubly linked. The great conviction of his life, which he staked his life upon and celebrated in a final letter two weeks before his death, was "that the mass of mankind has not been born with saddles on their backs, nor a favored few booted and spurred, ready to ride them legitimately, by the grace of God." But if liberty was in that sense a right, it was nevertheless also a privilege to be earned, deserved, and strenuously kept; to keep themselves free, he thought, a people must be stable, economically independent, and virtuous. He believed—on the basis, it should be remembered, of extensive experience both in this country and abroad—that these qualities were most dependably found in the farming people: "Cultivators of the earth a re the most valuable citizens. They are the most vigorous, the most independent, the most virtuous, and they are tied to their country, and wedded to its liberty and interests by the most lasting bonds." These bonds were not merely those of economics and property, but those, at once more feeling and more practical, that come from the investment in a place and a community of work, devotion, knowledge, memory, and association.

By contrast, Jefferson wrote: "I consider the class of artificers as the panders of vice, and the instruments by which the liberties of a country are generally overturned." By "artificers" he meant manufacturers, and he made no distinction between "management" and "labor." The last-quoted sentence is followed by no explanation, but its juxtaposition with the one first quoted suggests that he held manufacturers in suspicion because their values were already becoming abstract, enabling them to be "socially mobile" and therefore subject pre-eminently to the motives of self-interest.

To foster the strengths and virtues necessary to citizenship in a democracy, public education was obviously necessary, and Jefferson never ceased to be thoughtful of that necessity: " ... I do most anxiously wish to see the highest degrees of education given to the higher degrees of genius, and to all degrees of it, so much as may enable them to read and understand what is going on in the world, and to keep their part of it going on right: for nothing can keep it right but their own vigilant and distrustful superintendence."

And all these statements must be read in the light of Jefferson's apprehension of the disarray of agriculture and of agricultural communities in his time: " ... the long succession of years of stunted crops, of reduced prices, the general prostration of the farming business, under levies for the support of manufacturers, etc., with the calamitous fluctuations of value in our paper medium, have kept agriculture in a state of abject depression, which has peopled the Western States by silently breaking up those on the Atlantic ... "

JUSTIN MORRILL AND THE LAND-GRANT COLLEGE ACTS

On July 2, 1862, two days less than thirty-six years after the death of Jefferson, the first of the land-grant college acts became law. This was the Morrill Act, which granted "an amount of public land, to be apportioned to each State a quantity equal to thirty thousand acres for each Senator and Representative in Congress. ... "The interest on the money from the sale of these lands was to be applied by each state "to the endowment, support, and maintenance of at least one college where the leading object shall be . . . to teach such branches of learning as are related to agriculture and the mechanic arts...in order to promote the liberal and practical education of the industrial classes in the several pursue its and professions in life."

In 1887 Congress passed the Hatch Act, which created the state agricultural experiment stations, with the purpose, among others, of promoting a sound and prosperous agriculture and rural life as indispensable to the maintenance of maximum employment and national prosperity and security." This act states that "It is also the intent of Congress to assure agriculture a position in research *equal to that of industry*, which will aid in maintaining an equitable balance between agriculture and other segments of the economy." (Emphasis mine—to call attention to the distinction made between agriculture and industry.) The act declares, further, that "It shall be the object and duty of the State agricultural experiment stations...to conduct...researches, investigations, and experiments bearing directly on and contributing to the establishment and maintenance of a permanent and effective agricultural industry...including...such investigations as have for their purpose the development and improvement of the rural home and rural life..."

And in 1914 the Smith-Lever Act created the cooperative extension service "In order to aid in diffusing among the people...useful and practical information on subjects relating to agriculture and home economics, and to encourage the application of the same..."

Together, these acts provide for what is known as the land-grant college complex. They fulfill the intention of Justin Smith Morrill, representative and later senator from Vermont. In clarification of the historical pertinence and the aims of the language of the several bills, it is useful to have Morrill's statement of his intentions in a memoir written "apparently in 1874."

Morrill was aware, as Jefferson had been, of an agricultural disorder manifested both by soil depletion and by the unsettlement of population:"...the very cheapness of our public lands, and the facility of purchase and transfer, tended to a system of bad-farming or strip and waste of the soil, by encouraging short occupancy and a speedy search for new homes, entailing upon the first and older settlements a rapid deterioration of the soil, which would not be likely to be arrested except by more thorough and scientific knowledge of agriculture and by a higher education of those who were devoted to its pursuit."

But Morrill, unlike Jefferson, had personal reason to be generously concerned for "the class of artificers": "...being myself the son of a hard-handed blacksmith...who felt his own deprivation of schools...I could not overlook mechanics in any measure intended to aid the industrial classes in the procurement of an education that might exalt their usefulness."

And he wished to break what seemed to him "a monopoly of education":

"...most of the existing collegiate institutions and their feeders were based upon the classic plan of teaching those only destined to pursue the so-called learned professions, leaving farmers and mechanics and all those who must win their bread by labor, to the haphazard of being self-taught or not scientifically taught at all, and restricting the number of those who might be supposed to be qualified to fill places of higher consideration in private or public employments to the limited number of the graduates of the literary institutions."

THE LAND-GRANT COLLEGES

To understand what eventually became of the land-grant college complex, it will be worthwhile to consider certain significant differences between the thinking of Jefferson and that of Morrill. The most important of these is the apparent absence from Morrill's mind of Jefferson's complex sense of the dependence of democratic citizenship upon education. For Jefferson, the ideals and aims of education appear to have been defined directly by the requirements of political liberty. He envisioned a local system of education with a double purpose: to foster in the general population the critical alertness necessary to good citizenship and to seek out and prepare a "natural aristocracy" of "virtue and talents" for the duties and trusts of leadership. His plan of education for Virginia did not include any form of specialized or vocational training. He apparently assumed that if communities could be stabilized and preserved by the virtues of citizenship and leadership, then the "practical arts" would be improved as a matter of course by local example, reading, etc. Morrill, on the other hand, looked at education from a strictly practical or utilitarian viewpoint. He believed that the primary aims of education were to correct the work of farmers and mechanics and "exalt their usefulness." His wish to break the educational monopoly of the professional class was Jeffersonian only in a very limited sense: he wished to open the professional class to the children of laborers. In distinguishing among the levels of education, he did not distinguish, as Jefferson did, among "degrees of genius."

Again, whereas Jefferson regarded farmers as "the most valuable citizens," Morrill looked upon the professions as "places of higher consideration." We are thus faced with a difficulty in understanding Morrill's wish to exalt the usefulness of "those who must win their bread by labor." Would education exalt their usefulness by raising the quality of their work or by making them eligible for promotion to "places of higher consideration"?

These differences and difficulties notwithstanding, the apparent intention in regard to agriculture remains the same from Jefferson to Morrill to the land-grant college acts. That intention was to promote the stabilization of farming populations and communities and to establish in that way a "permanent" agriculture, enabled by better education to preserve both the land and the people.

The failure of this intention, and the promotion by the land-grant colleges of an *impermanent* agriculture destructive of land and people, was caused in part by the lowering of the educational standard from Jefferson's ideal of public or community responsibility to the utilitarianism of Morrill, insofar as this difference in the aims of the two men represented a shift of public value. The land-grant colleges have, in fact, been very little—and have been less and less—concerned "to promote the liberal and practical education of the industrial classes" or of any other classes. Their history has been largely that of the whittling down of this aim—from education in the broad, "liberal" sense to "practical" preparation for earning a living to various "programs" for certification. They first reduced "liberal and practical" to "practical," and then for "practical" they substituted "specialized." And the standard of their purpose has shifted from usefulness to careerism. And if this has not been caused by, it certainly accompanied a degeneration of faculty standards by which professors and teachers of disciplines become first upholders of professional standards and then careerists in pursuit of power, money, and prestige.

The land-grant college legislation obviously calls for a system of local institutions responding to local needs and local problems. What we have instead is a system of institutions, which more and more resemble one another, like airports and motels, made increasingly uniform by the transience or rootlessness of their career-oriented faculties and the consequent inability to respond to local conditions.

The professor lives in his career, in a ghetto of career-oriented fellow professors. Where he may be geographically is of little interest to him. One's career is a vehicle, not a dwelling; one is concerned less for where it is than for where it will go.

The careerist professor is by definition a specialist professor. Utterly dependent upon his institution, he blunts his critical intelligence and blurs his language so as to exist "harmoniously" within it—and so serves his school with an emasculated and fragmentary intelligence, deferring "realistically" to the redundant procedures and meaningless demands of an inflated administrative bureaucracy whose educational purpose is written on its paychecks…

But just as he is dependent on his institution, the specialist professor is also dependent on his students. In order to earn a living, he must teach; in order to teach, he must have students. And so the tendency is to make a commodity of education: package it attractively, reduce requirements, reduce homework, inflate grades, lower standards, and deal expensively in "public relations."

As self-interest, laziness, and lack of conviction augment the general confusion about what an education is or ought to be, and as standards of excellence are replaced by sliding scales of adequacy, these schools begin to depend upon, and so to institutionalize, the local problems that they were founded to solve. They begin to need, and so to promote, the mobility, careerism, and moral confusion that are victimizing the local population and destroying the local communities. The stock in trade of the "man of learning" comes to be ignorance.

The colleges of agriculture are focused somewhat more upon their whereabouts than, say, the colleges of arts and sciences because of the local exigencies of climate, soils, and crop varieties; but like the rest they tend to orient themselves within the university rather than within the communities they were intended to serve. The impression is unavoidable that the academic specialists of agriculture tend to validate their work experimentally rather than practically, that they would rather be professionally reputable than locally effective, and that they pay little attention, if any, to the social, cultural, and political consequences of their work. Indeed, it sometimes appears that they pay very little attention to its economic consequences. There is nothing more characteristic of modern agricultural research than its divorcement from the sense of consequence and from all issues of value.

This is facilitated on the one hand by the academic ideal of "objectivity" and on the other by a strange doctrine of the "inevitability" of undisciplined technological growth and change. "Objectivity" has come to be simply the academic uniform of moral cowardice: one who is "objective" never takes a stand. And in the fashionable "realism" of technological determinism, one is shed of the embarrassment of moral and intellectual standards and of any need to define what is excellent or desirable. Education is relieved of its concern for truth in order to prepare students to live in "a changing world." As soon as educational standards begin to be dictated by "a changing world" (changing, of course, to a tune called by the governmental-military-academic-industrial complex), then one is justified in teaching virtually anything in any way—for, after all, one never knows for sure what "a changing world" is going to become. The way is thus opened to run a university as a business, the main purpose of which is to sell diplomas—after a complicated but undemanding four-year ritual-and thereby give employment to professors.

COLLEGES OF "AGRIBUSINESS" AND UNSETTLEMENT

That the land-grant college complex has fulfilled its obligation "to assure agriculture a position in research equal to that of industry" simply by failing to distinguish between the two is acknowledged in the term "agribusiness." The word does not denote any real identity either of function or interest, but only an expedient confusion by which the interests of industry have subjugated those of agriculture. This confusion of agriculture with industry has utterly perverted the intent of the land-grant college acts. The case has been persuasively documented by a task force of the Agribusiness Accountability Project. In the following paragraphs, Jim Hightower and Susan DeMarco give the task force's central argument:

"Who is helped and who is hurt by this research?

"It is the largest-scale growers, the farm machinery and chemicals input companies and the processors who are the primary beneficiaries. Machinery companies such as John Deere, International Harvester, Massey-Ferguson, Allis-Chalmer and J. I. Case almost continually engage in cooperative research efforts at land grant colleges. These corporations contribute money and some of their own research personnel to help land grant scientists develop machinery. In return, they are able to incorporate technological advances in their own products. In some cases they actually receive exclusive licenses to manufacture and sell the products of tax-paid research.

"If mechanization has been a boon to agribusiness, it has been a bane to millions of rural Americans. Farmworkers have been the earliest victims. There were 4.3 million hired farm workers in 1950. Twenty years later that number had fallen to 3.5 million...

"Farmworkers have not been compensated for jobs lost to mechanized research. They were not consulted when that work was designed, and their needs were not a part of the research that resulted. They simply were left to fend on their own—no re-training, no unemployment compensation, no research to help them adjust to the changes that came out of the land grant colleges.

"Independent family farmers also have been largely ignored by the land grant colleges. Mechanization research by land grant colleges is either irrelevant or only incidentally adaptable to the needs of 87 to 99 percent of America's farmers. The public subsidy for mechanization actually has weakened the competitive position of the family farmer. Taxpayers, through the land-grant college complex, have given corporate producers a technological arsenal specifically suited to their scale of operation and designed to increase their efficiency and profits. The independent family farmer is left to strain his private resources to the breaking point in a desperate effort to clamber aboard the technological treadmill."

The task force also raised the issue of academic featherbedding—irrelevant or frivolous research or instruction carried on by colleges of agriculture, experiment stations, and extension services. Evidently, people in many states may expect to be "served" by such studies as one at Cornell that discovered that "employed homemakers have less time for housekeeping tasks than non-employed homemakers." An article in the *Louisville Courier-Journal* lately revealed, for example, that "a 20-year-old waitress...recently attended a class where she learned 'how to set a real good table.'

"She got some tips on how to save steps and give faster service by 'carrying quite a few things' on the same tray. And she learned most of the highway numbers in the area, so she could give better directions to confused tourists.

"She learned all of that from the University of Kentucky College of Agriculture. Specialists in restaurant management left the Lexington campus to give the training to waitresses…

"The UK College of Agriculture promotes tourism.

"The college also helps to plan highways, housing projects, sewer systems and industrial developments throughout the state.

"It offers training in babysitting, 'family living'…"

This sort of "agricultural" service is justified under the Smith—Lever

Act, Section 347a, inserted by amendment in 1955, and by Representative Lever's "charge" to the Extension Service in 1913. Both contain language that requires some looking at.

Section 347a is based mainly upon the following congressional insight: that "in certain agricultural areas," "there is concentration of farm families on farms either too small or too unproductive or both…" For these "disadvantaged farms" the following remedies were provided: " (1) Intensive on-the-farm educational assistance to the farm family in appraising and resolving its problems; (2) assistance and counseling to local groups in appraising resources for capability of improvement in agriculture or introduction of industry designed to supplement farm income; (3) cooperation with other agencies and groups in furnishing all possible information as to existing employment opportunities, particularly to farm families having underemployed workers; and (4) in cases where the farm family, after analysis of its opportunities and existing resources, finds it advisable to seek a new farming venture, the providing of information, advice, and counsel in connection with making such change."

The pertinent language of Representative Lever's "charge" which is apparently regarded as having the force of law, at least by the

University of Kentucky Cooperative Extension Service, places upon extension agents the responsibility to assume leadership in every movement, whatever it may be, the aim of which is better farming, better living, more happiness, more education, and better citizenship."

If Section 347a is an example—as it certainly is—of special-interest legislation, its special interest is only ostensibly and vaguely in the welfare of small, ("disadvantaged") farmers. To begin with, it introduces into law and into land-grant philosophy the startling concept that a farm can be "to small" or "too unproductive." The only standard for this judgment is implied in the clauses that follow it: the farmers of such farms "are unable to make adjustments and investments required to establish profitable operations"; such a farm "does not permit profitable employment of available labor"; and—most revealing—"many of these farm families are not able to make full use of current extension programs . . . "

The first two of these definitions of a "too small" or "too unproductive" farm are not agricultural but economic: the farm must moreover, in an economy that—in 1955, as now—favors "agribusiness." (Section 347a is a product of the era in which then Assistant Secretary of Agriculture John Davis and Earl Butz were advocating "corporate control to 'rationalize' agriculture production"; in which Mr. Davis himself invented the term "agribusiness"; in which then Secretary of Agriculture Ezra Taft Benson told farmers to "Get big or get out.") Profitability may be a standard of a sort, but a most relative sort and by no means sufficient. It leaves out of consideration, for instance, the possibility that a family might farm a small acreage, take excellent care of it, make a decent, honorable, and independent living from it, and yet fail to make what the authors of Section

347a would consider a profit. But the third definition is, if possible, even more insidious: a farm is "too small" or "too unproductive" if it cannot "make full use of current extension programs." The farm is not to be the measure of the service; the service is to be the measure of the farm.

It will be argued that Section 347a was passed in response to real conditions of economic hardship on the farm and that the aim of the law was to permit the development of new extension programs as remedies. But that is at best only half true. There certainly were economic hardships on the farm in 1955; we have proof of that in the drastic decline in the number of farms and farmers since then. But there was plenty of land-grant legislation at that time to permit the extension service to devise any program necessary to deal with agricultural problems *as such*. What is remarkable about Section 347a is that it permitted the land-grant colleges to abandon these problems as such, to accept the "agribusiness" revolution as inevitable, and to undertake non-agricultural solutions to agricultural problems. And the assistances provided for in Section 347a are so general and vague as to allow the colleges to be most inventive. After 1955, the agricultural academicians would have a vested interest, not in the welfare of farmers, but in virtually anything at all that might happen to ex-farmers, their families, and their descendants forevermore. They have, in other words, a vested interest in their own failure—foolproof job security.

But it is hard to see how the language of Section 347a, loose as it is, justifies the teaching of highway numbers to waitresses, the promotion of tourism, and the planning of industrial developments, sewer systems, and housing projects. For justification of these programs we apparently must look to the language of Representative Lever's "charge," which in effect tells the extension agents to do anything they can think of.

These new "services" seem little more than desperate maneuvers on the part of the land-grant colleges to deal with the drastic reduction in the last thirty years of their lawful clientele—a reduction for which the colleges themselves are in large part responsible because of their eager collaboration with "agribusiness." As the conversion of farming into agribusiness has depopulated the farmland, it has become necessary for the agriculture specialists to develop "programs" with which to follow their erstwhile beneficiaries into the cities either that or lose their meal ticket in the colleges. If the colleges of agriculture have so assiduously promoted the industrialization of farming and the urbanization of farmers that now "96 percent of America's manpower is freed from food production," then the necessary trick of survival is to become colleges of industrialization and urbanization—that is, colleges of "agribusiness"—which, in fact, is what they have been for a long time. Their success has been stupendous: as the number of farmers has decreased, the colleges of agriculture have grown larger.

The bad faith of the program-mongering under Section 347a may be suggested by several questions: Why did land-grant colleges not address themselves to the agricultural problems of small or "disadvantaged" farmers?

Why did they not undertake the development of small-scale technologies and methods appropriate to the small farm?

Why have they assumed that the turn to "agribusiness" and big technology was "inevitable"?

Why, if they can promote tourism and plan sewer systems, have they not promoted cooperatives to give small farmers some measure of protection against corporate suppliers and purchasers?

Why have they watched in silence the destruction of the markets of the small producers of poultry, eggs, butter, cream, and milk—once the mainstays of the small-farm economy?

Why have they never studied or questioned the necessity or the justice of the sanitation laws that have been used to destroy such markets?

Why have they not tried to calculate the real (urban and rural) costs of the migration from farm to city?

Why have they raised no questions of social, political, or cultural value?

That the colleges of agriculture should have become colleges of "agribusiness"—working, in effect, *against* the interests of the small farmers, the farm communities, and the farmland—can only be explained by the isolation of specialization.

First we have the division of the study of agriculture into specialties. And then, within the structure of the university, we have the separation of these specialties from specialties of other kinds. This problem is outlined with forceful insight by Andre Mayer and Jean Mayer in an article entitled "Agriculture, the Island Empire," published in the summer 1974 issue of *Daedalus*. Like other academic professions, agriculture has gone its separate way and aggrandized itself in its own fashion: "As it developed into an intellectual discipline in the nineteenth century, it did so in academic divisions which were isolated from the liberal arts center of the university..." It "produced ancillary disciplines parallel to those in the arts and sciences..." And it "developed its own scientific organizations; its own professional, trade, and social organizations; its own technical and popular magazines; and its own public. It even has a separate political system..."

The founding fathers, these authors point out, "placed agriculture at the center of an Enlightenment concept of science broad enough to include society, politics, and sometimes even theology." But the modern academic structure has alienated agriculture from such concerns. The result is an absurd "independence" which has produced genetic research "without attention to nutritional values," which has undertaken the so-called Green Revolution without concern for its genetic oversimplification or its social, political, and cultural dangers, and which keeps agriculture in a separate "field" from ecology.

A BETRAYAL OF TRUST

The educational *ideal* that concerns us here was held clearly in the mind of Thomas Jefferson, was somewhat diminished or obscured in the mind of Justin Morrill, but survived indisputably in the original language of the land-grant college acts. We see it in the intention that education should be " liberal" as well as " practical," in the wish to foster "a sound and prosperous agriculture and rural life," in the distinct ion between agriculture and industry, in the purpose of establishing and maintaining a "permanent" agriculture, in the implied perception that this permanence would depend on the stability of "the rural home and rural life." This ideal is simply that farmers should be educated, liberally and practically, *as farmers*; education should be given and acquired with the understanding that those so educated would return to their home communities, not merely to be farmers, corrected and improved by their learning, but also to assume the trusts and obligations of community leadership, the highest form of that "vigilant and distrustful superintendence" without which the communities could not preserve themselves. This leadership, moreover, would tend to safeguard agriculture's distinction from and competitiveness with industry. Conceivably, had it existed, this leadership might have resulted in community-imposed restraints upon technology, such as those practiced by the Amish.

Having stated the ideal, it becomes possible not merely to perceive the degeneracy and incoherence of the land-grant colleges within themselves, but to understand their degenerative influence on the farming communities. It becomes possible to see that their failure goes beyond the disintegration of intellectual and educational standards; it is the betrayal of a trust.

The land-grant acts gave to the colleges not just government funds and a commission to teach and to do research, but also a purpose which may be generally stated as the preservation of agriculture and rural life. That this purpose is a practical one is obvious from the language of the acts; no one, I dare say, would deny that this is so. It is equally clear, though far less acknowledged, that the purpose is also moral, insofar as it raises issues of value and of feeling. It may be that pure practicality can deal with agriculture so long as agriculture is defined as a set of problems that are purely technological (though such a definition is in itself a gross falsification), but it inevitably falters at the meanings of "liberal," "sound and prosperous," "permanent and effective," "development and improvement"; and it fails altogether to address the concepts of "the rural home and rural life." When the Hatch Act, for instance, imposed upon the colleges the goals of "a permanent and effective agricultural industry" and "the development and improvement of the rural home and rural life," it implicitly required of them an allegiance to the agrarian values that have constituted one of the dominant themes of American history and thought.

The tragedy of the land-grant acts is that their moral imperative came finally to have nowhere to rest except on the careers of specialists whose standards and operating procedures were amoral: the "objective" practitioners of the "science" of agriculture, whose minds have no direction other than that laid out by career necessity and the logic of experimentation. They have no apparent moral allegiances or bearings or limits. Their work thus inevitably serves whatever power is greatest. That power at present is the industrial economy, of which "agribusiness" is a part. Lacking any moral force or vision of its own, the "objective" expertise of the agriculture specialist points like a compass needle toward the greater good of the "agribusiness" corporations. The objectivity of the laboratory functions in the world as indifference; knowledge without responsibility is merchandise, and greed provides its applications. Far from developing and improving the rural home and rural life, the land-grant colleges have blindly follower the drift of virtually the whole population away from home, blindly documenting or serving the consequent disorder and blindly rationalizing this disorder as "progress" or "miraculous development."

At this point one can begin to understand the violence that has been done to the Morrill Act's provision for a "liberal and practical education." One imagines that Jefferson might have objected to the inclusion of the phrase "and practical," and indeed in retrospect the danger in it is clearly visible. Nevertheless, the law evidently sees "liberal and practical" as a description of one education, not two.

And as long as the two terms are thus associated, the combination remains thinkable: the "liberal" side, for instance, might offer necessary restraints of value to the "practical"; the "practical" interest might direct the "liberal" to crucial issues of use and effect.

In practice, however, the Morrill Act's formula has been neatly bisected and carried out as if it read "a liberal or a practical education." But though these two kinds of education may theoretically be divided and given equal importance, in fact they are no sooner divided than they are opposed. They enter into competition with one another, and by a kind of educational Gresham's Law the practical curriculum drives out the liberal.

This happens because the *standards* of the two kinds of education are fundamentally different and fundamentally opposed. The standard of liberal education is based upon definitions of excellence in the various disciplines. These definitions are in turn based upon example. One learns to order one's thoughts and to speak and write coherently by studying exemplary thinkers, speakers, and writers of the past. One studies *The Divine Comedy* and the Pythagorean theorem not to acquire something to be exchanged for something else, but to understand the orders and the kinds of thought and to furnish the mind with subjects and examples. Because the standards are rooted in examples, they do not change.

The standard of practical education, on the other hand, is based upon the question of what will work, and because the practical is by definition of the curriculum set aside from issues of value, the question tends to be resolved in the most shallow and immediate fashion: what is practical is what makes money; what is most practical is what makes the most money. Practical education is an "investment," something acquired to be exchanged for something else—a "good" job, money, prestige. It is oriented entirely toward the future, toward what *will* work in the "changing world" in which the student is supposedly being prepared to "compete." The standard of practicality, as used, is inherently a degenerative standard. There is nothing to correct it except suppositions about what the world will be like and what the student will therefore need to know. Because the future is by definition unknown, one person's supposition about the future tends to be as good, or as forceful, as another's. And so the standard of practicality tends to revise itself downward to meet, not the needs, but the desires of the student who, for instance, does not want to learn a science because he *intends* to pursue a career in which he does not think a knowledge of science will be necessary.

It could be said that a liberal education has the nature of a bequest, in that it looks upon the student as the potential heir of a cultural birthright, whereas a practical education has the nature of a commodity to be exchanged for position, status, wealth, etc., *in the future*. A liberal education rests on the assumption that nature and human nature do not change very much or very fast and that one therefore needs to understand the past. The practical educators assume that human society itself is the only significant context, that change is therefore fundamental, constant, and necessary, that the future will be wholly unlike the past, that the past is outmoded, irrelevant, and an encumbrance upon the future—the present being only a time for dividing past from future, for getting ready.

But these definitions, based on division and opposition, are too simple. It is easy, accepting the viewpoint of either side, to find fault with the other. But the wrong is on neither side; it is in their division. One of the purposes of this book is to show how the practical, divorced from the discipline of value, tends to be defined by the immediate interests of the practitioner, and so becomes destructive of value, practical and otherwise. But it must not be forgotten that, divorced from the practical, the liberal disciplines lose their sense of use and influence and become attenuated and aimless. The purity of "pure" science is then ritualized as a highly competitive intellectual game without awareness of use, responsibility, or consequence, such as that described in *The Double Helix*, James D. Watson's book about the discovery of the structure of DNA. And the so-called humanities become a world of their own, a collection of "professional" sublanguages, complicated circuitries of abstruse interpretation, feckless exercises of sensibility. Without the balance of historic value, practical education gives us that most absurd of standards: "relevance," based upon the suppositional needs of a theoretical future. But liberal education, divorced from practicality, gives something no less absurd: the specialist professor of one or another of the liberal arts, the custodian of an inheritance he has learned much about, but nothing from.

And in the face of competition from the practical curriculum, the liberal has found it impossible to maintain its own standards and so has become practical—that is, career-oriented—also. It is now widely assumed that the only good reason to study literature or philosophy is to become a teacher of literature or philosophy—in order, that is, to get an income from it. I recently received in the mail a textbook of rhetoric in which the author stated that "there is no need for anyone except a professional linguist to be able to explain language operations specifically and accurately." Maybe so, but how does one escape the implicit absurdity that linguists should study the language only to teach aspiring linguists?

The education of the student of agriculture is almost as absurd, and it is more dangerous: he is taught a course of practical knowledge and procedures for which uses do indeed exist, but these uses lie outside the purview and interest of the school. The colleges of agriculture produce agriculture specialists and "agribusinessmen" as readily as farmers, and they are producing far more of them. Public funds originally voted to provide for "the liberal and practical education" of farmers thus become, by moral default, an educational subsidy given to the farmers' competitors.

THE VAGRANT ARISTOCRACY

But in order to complete an understanding of the modern disconnection between work and value, it is necessary to see how certain "aristocratic" ideas of status and leisure have been institutionalized in this system of education. This is one of the liabilities of the social and political origins not only of our own nation, but of most of the "advanced" nations of the world. Democracy has involved more than the enfranchisement of the lower classes; it has meant also the popularization of the more superficial upper-class values: leisure, etiquette (as opposed to good manners), fashion, everyday dressing up, and a kind of dietary persnicketiness. We have given a highly inflated value to "days off" and to the wearing of a necktie; we pay an exorbitant price for the *looks* of our automobiles; we pay dearly, in both money and health, for our predilection for white bread. We attach much the same values to kinds of profession and levels of income that were once attached to hereditary classes.

It is extremely difficult to exalt the usefulness of any productive discipline as *such* in a society that is at once highly stratified and highly mobile. Both the stratification and the mobility are based upon notions of prestige, which are in turn based upon these reliquary social fashions. Thus doctors are given higher status than farmers, not because they are more necessary, more useful, more able, more talented, or more virtuous, but because they are *thought* to be "better"—one assumes because they talk a learned jargon, wear good clothes all the time, and make a lot of money. And this is true generally of "office people" as opposed to those who work with their hands. Thus an industrial worker does not aspire to become a master craftsman, but rather a foreman or manager. Thus a farmer's son does not usually think to "better" himself by becoming a better farmer than his father, but by becoming, professionally, a better kind of man than his father.

It is characteristic of our present society that one does not think to improve oneself by becoming better at what one is doing or by assuming some measure of public responsibility in order to improve local conditions; one thinks to improve oneself by becoming different, by "moving up" to a "place of higher consideration." Thinkable changes, in other words, tend to be quantitative rather than qualitative, and they tend to involve movement that is both social and geographic. The unsettlement at once of population and of values is virtually required by the only generally acceptable forms of aspiration. The typical American "success story" moves from a modest rural beginning to urban affluence, from manual labor to office work.

We must ask, then, what must be the educational effect, the influence, of a farmer's son who believes, with the absolute authorization of his society, that he has mightily improved himself by becoming a professor of agriculture. Has he not improved himself by an "upward" motivation which by its nature avoids the issue of quality—which assumes simply that an agriculture specialist is better than a farmer? And does he not exemplify to his students the proposition that "the way up" leads away from home? How could he, who has "succeeded" by earning a Ph.D. and a nice place in town, advise his best students to go home and farm, or even assume that they might find good reasons for doing so?

I am suggesting that our university-based structures of success, as they have come to be formed upon quantitative measures, virtually require the degeneration of qualitative measures and the disintegration of culture. The university accumulates information at a rate that is literally inconceivable, yet its structure and its self-esteem institutionalize the likelihood that not much of this information will ever be taken home. We do not work where we live, and if we are to hold up our heads in the presence of our teachers and classmates, we must not live where we come from.

 EXPLORE: Berry originally wrote this essay in the 1970s. Is this criticism still valid? Why or why not? What do you think has changed in the way the US views agriculture and production? What has not changed?

 EXPLORE: Describe the *tone* of Berry's essay. Having read his essay, how might you describe his character and his beliefs?

  COLLABORATE AND WRITE: What is your field of study? Is it in the sciences? In the humanities? The social sciences? Berry makes an argument that Jefferson's approach to education encompasses all fields while Morrill may seem to emphasize practical education. As a result, agricultural sciences have lost their knowledge of the humanities, which is important to being a well-educated person. In a paragraph, agree or disagree with Berry's argument; you may use your own field of study to illustrate your points. Then partner with another student who disagrees with your opinion and discuss each other's point of view.

 RESEARCH: Berry said that his motivation for writing *The Unsettling of America: Culture & Agriculture* was to criticize modern or orthodox agriculture. In the preface, he cites a 1967 presidential commission report on food and fiber that the "country's biggest farm problem is a surplus of farmers." Research this report and the follow up to it. When did the attitude toward the number of small farmers change? Or has it?

 WRITE: Wendell E. Berry held an academic appointment at the University of Kentucky, its state's land-grant institution. Write in role of an agricultural scientist (e.g., director of the agricultural experiment station; a professor; a research vice president) rebutting Berry's argument in "Jefferson, Morrill, and the Upper Crust."

 FOR FURTHER READING: In 2011, Berry was honored by the National Endowment for the Humanities when invited to deliver the annual Jefferson Lecture. That speech is available here: http://www.neh.gov/news/2012-jefferson-lecture-wendell-

<u>berry</u>. Read it. How have Berry's views changed (or not) in the forty years since he wrote "Jefferson, Morrill, and the Upper Crust"?

 FOR FURTHER READING: Wendell Berry is particularly contemptuous of former Secretary of Agriculture Earl L. Butz, who infamously said to farmers, "Get big or get out." In Jane Smiley's satiric novel, *Moo* (1995), which takes place on a land-grant university campus, Butz is a character: a hog. Smiley is also the author of *A Thousand Acres*, which won the 1992 Pulitzer Prize for Literature; it is a re-telling of the *King Lear* story on an Iowa farm. (Fun fact: *The Story of Edgar Sawtelle*, a novel about a boy growing up on a dog farm in Wisconsin, is based on the plot of *Hamlet*.)

Farms and Genres

Poster from Salt Lake City Farmers Market, 2002.
Illustration by Greg Newbold — www.gregnewbold.com

Nonfiction	Poetry	Short Story	Mythology
Essays	Fiction	Folklore	Horror
Autobiography	Fable	Legend	Supernatural
Biography	Fairy Tale	Western	Satire
Memoir	Fantasy	Tall Tale	Script
History	Science Fiction	Mystery	Thriller
Drama	Humor	Detective Story	Novel

About Genres

Genre is a French term (pronounced /ˈʒɑnrə/) used to classify types of texts and literature. The two major classifications are *poetry* and *prose*. The latter refers to essays, novels, journalistic writing, and correspondence. Poetry is a form that takes advantage of symbolic language, rhythm, and compression.

Within prose are two large categories: *fiction* and *nonfiction*. Realistic fiction may almost seem like nonfiction at times with its reliance on present-day situations and believable characters, but it is not. Likewise, a contemporary term, *creative nonfiction*, borrows from literary conventions and style but remains factual. Truman Capote is said to have created the modern nonfiction novel when he authored *In Cold Blood* (1966), which is about a farm family in Kansas brutally murdered in 1959.

Genres typically stay within defined bounds without crossover. Novels may be historical fiction, mysteries, thrillers, horror, fantasy, or science fiction, or may even have elements of magical realism. While novels are generally lengthy, the short story is fiction that is considerably shorter, and its ingredients—such as number of characters and locale—are limited. Plays and scripts are meant to be performed on stage or screen. Some authors—such as John Dos Passos (1896–1970)—have experimented with multi-genre works, embedding biography and newspaper accounts in fictional narrative as in *Manhattan Transfer* and *U.S.A.*

Poetry began as *epic poems* recounting the glories of rulers such as Gilgamesh or the quests described by Homer in *The Odyssey* in narrative format. Since that time, the types of poems written have expanded. , Popularized by Shakespeare, the *sonnet*, a 14-line poem with specific structure, rhyme, and meter known for its romantic themes. With19 lines, the *villanelle* features 5 stanzas of 3 lines, ending with a four-line quatrain. The *haiku*, which comes from Japan, contains three lines with the first having five syllables, the second seven, and the third returning to five. *Limericks*, which have five lines with the first, second, and fifth lines of the stanza rhyming, usually focus on a ribald topic and are funny. An *elegy* mourns a loss, as Walt Whitman did in "O Captain, My Captain" following President Lincoln's assassination or A. E. Housman's "To an Athlete Dying Young."

Concrete poetry actually looks like the subject of the poem. May Swenson (1913–1989) wrote many volumes of poetry, and some of her works such as "Women" and "Fountains of Aix" are examples of concrete poems. A *found poem* is derived from a text. Prose becomes poetry. For instance, here is a found poem that comes from Chapter 33 of the award-winning young adult novel, Judy Blundell's *What I Saw and How I Lied* (2008).

I rolled up the tube of Fatal Apple
Lipstick and painted my mouth.

A doll, a dish—
The dish would do it.

Their fear was in the car with us.
Didja do it, Joe?
Didja love him, Bev?   —by Kolbie Blume

While the types of poetry are numerous, perhaps most popular is *free verse,* which does not follow formal conventions of rhyme and meter and is more akin to spoken word. Free verse is poetic, making use of language—repetition, alliteration, and patterns—to communicate its message. Its lines and stanzas may break in what seem to be unusual places. While free verse is not constrained by conventions of traditional forms, it may be said to have its own constraints. In the final analysis, the poem has to convey meaning and feeling to its readers.

In this section of *FARM: A Multimodal Reader,* you will explore various genres, including poetry, children's literature, and folklore—among others. How does the particular genres chosen by the writers contribute to the theme of culture and agriculture? Do the same farm themes appear across genres?

CHAPTER EIGHT

Farms and Poetry

Perhaps it seems a bit unusual to think about farms as a theme for poetry, but one of the most famous farmer-poets, Robert Frost, probably didn't think so. He and others have found inspiration and images on the farm. His "Stopping By Woods on a Snowy Evening" was written at his farm near Shaftsbury, Vermont. Poetry about farms, beginning in ancient times, has been evident throughout this reader.

Nature is often the subject of poems, and farming can be thought of as a subset of nature poetry. Within the farm is the cycle of life: birth, death, triumph, tragedy. For some poets, the farm is also a spiritual experience, building on the Emerson's concept of "nature as the key to spirit." This communion with the land is at the heart of many farm-themed poems. While farm poems may include philosophical and metaphorical messages, they may be funny as well as serious.

Farm poets run the gamut from the Romantic writer William Wordsworth and his "The Farmer of Tilsbury Vale" to cowboy/cowgirl poetry that is performed extemporaneously. Sometimes called the "pig poet," David Lee authored *Porcine Legacy* (1974), *Porcine Canticles* (1984), and *Wayburne Pig* (1997), only three of the sixteen volumes of poetry for the man who served as Utah's first Poet Laureate (1997–2002). Through his poetry, he explores rural landscapes and the relationships of people with nature, often using regional dialect as in the following lines from "Loading a Boar" in which his neighbor John says,

> "[Y]oung feller, you aint got started yet and the reason's cause you trying to do it outside yourself and aint looking in and if you wanna by god write pomes you gotta write pomes about what you know and not about the rest and you can write about pigs and that boar and Jan and you and me and the rest and there aint no way you're gonna quit." (http://www.poets.org/viewmedia.php?prmMID/16766#sthash.RoeoXZCQ.dpuf.)

Lee believes "that the kind of poetry he creates can meet a social and cultural need." He says, "I think there is a need for an oral tradition, and a need right now to return to a narrative form in poetry, to get back to the idea of story for the sake of story, the story as art. That's where I'm aiming and betting my life, and I hope this is what people are looking for." (From http://www.raintaxi.com/online/1999fall/lee.shtml.) Lee says that he has been quoted as saying that "he writes poetry for people who don't read poetry," and even if that quote is not necessarily attributable to him, it's a fine statement of his goal.

Farm poets often find inspiration in the everyday. In Julia Shipley's "Two Eggs," this Vermont poet-farmer finds eggs in the chicken that she has just butchered. One of Robert Frost's most famous poems is "The Hired Man," which seems on the surface to be a conversation between a farm couple about an elderly farm helper who has returned to them—even though he wasn't the best hand ever and even though his own family lives close by.

Although John Clare (1793–1864) was the son of a peasant farmer in England, and a farm laborer himself with formal schooling only until the age of 11, he wanted to be a poet. Following are two of the 3,500 poems he wrote during his lifetime, of which only about 400 were published. This peasant-poet is now considered one of Great Britain's significant poets.

The Bean Field

A bean field full in blossom smells as sweet
As Araby, or groves of orange flowers;
Black-eyed and white, and feathered to one's feet,
How sweet they smell in morning's dewy hours!
When seething night is left upon the flowers,
And when morn's bright sun shines o'er the field,
The bean-bloom glitters in the gems o' showers,
And sweet the fragrance which the union yields
To battered footpaths crossing o'er the fields.

Water-Lilies

The water-lilies on the meadow stream
   Again spread out their leaves of glossy green;
And some, yet young, of a rich copper gleam,
   Scarce open, in the sunny stream are seen,
Throwing a richness upon Leisure's eye,
   That thither wanders in a vacant joy;
While on the sloping banks, luxuriantly,
   Tending of horse and cow, the chubby boy,
In self-delighted whims, will often throw
   Pebbles, to hit and splash their sunny leaves;
Yet quickly dry again, they shine and glow
   Like some rich vision that his eye deceives;
Spreading above the water, day by day,
In dangerous deeps, yet out of danger's way.

One truism about poetry is that it is meant not only to be read but also to be heard. The sound of the words and the rhythm of the lines are essential in contributing to meaning. The performance of poems also has its roots in ancient times when all poetry was oral. In contemporary times, resurgence in poetry performance has occurred with Slam Poetry, Poetry Out Loud, and other coffeehouse-style gatherings.

Four Poems by Joyce Sutphen

Poet Joyce Sutphen (born 1949) grew up on a farm in Minnesota, and she continues to live in the state. In 2011, she was named Minnesota Poet Laureate, following the tenure of Robert Bly, who has also authored farm-themed poems. She has written four volumes as poetry and has edited an anthology featuring Minnesota women poets. She has a PhD in Renaissance Drama, and her familiarity with classical forms of poetry is evident in the poems she has written about farm life. In an interview[1] following her appointment as Poet Laureate, she cited her three major influences: Shakespeare, Bob Dylan, and Elizabeth Bishop.

The Farm

My father's farm is an apple blossomer.
He keeps his hills in dandelion carpet
and weaves a lane of lilacs between the rose
and the jack-in-the-pulpits.
His sleek cows ripple in the pastures.
The dog and purple iris
keep watch at the garden's end.

His farm is rolling thunder,
a lightning bolt on the horizon.
His crops suck rain from the sky
and swallow the smoldering sun.
His fields are oceans of heat,
where waves of gold
beat the burning shore.

A red fox
pauses under the birch trees,
a shadow is in the river's bend.
When the hawk circles the land,
my father's grainfields whirl beneath it.
Owls gather together to sing in his woods,
and the deer run his golden meadow.

My father's farm is an icicle,
a hillside of white powder.
He parts the snowy sea,
and smooths away the valleys.
He cultivates his rows of starlight
and drags the crescent moon
through dark unfurrowed fields.

---

[1]http://mnartists.org/article.do?rid=296981

Breakfast

My father taught me how to eat breakfast
those mornings when it was my turn
to help him milk the cows. I loved rising up from

the darkness and coming quietly down
the stairs while the others were still sleeping.
I'd take a bowl from the cupboard, a spoon

from the drawer, and slip into the pantry
where he was already eating spoonfuls
of cornflakes covered with mashed strawberries

from our own strawberry fields forever.
Didn't talk much—except to mention how
good the strawberries tasted or the way

those clouds hung over the hay barn roof.
Simple—that's how we started up the day.

Snow at the Farm

My father gets his tractor out.
It is winter, finally—the first
big snow of the year—and

he is eighty-four. He does not leap
into the seat the way that I
remember, but once he's there

he pulls down the brim of his cap,
and all-in-one his legs and arms
work at clutches, throttles, and

levers as he pushes and loads
the snow into neat hills at
the edge of the yard. The sun

is a bright shield in the sky,
something I cannot bear to look at,
and the snow is so white that
it shows black where the plow
cuts in. From the kitchen window
I watch the red tractor moving

back and forth through the blue
and white world, my father's
hands at the wheel.

My Father Comes to the City

Tonight his airplane comes in from the West,
and he rises from his seat, a suitcoat slung
over his arm. The flight attendant smiles
and says, "Have a nice visit," and he nods
as if he has done this all before,
as if his entire life hasn't been 170 acres
of corn and oats, as if a plow isn't dragging
behind him through the sand and clay,
as if his head isn't nestling in the warm
flank of a Holstein cow.

Only his hands tell the truth:
fingers thick as ropes, nails flat
and broken in the trough of endless chores.
He steps into the city warily, breathing
metal and exhaust, bewildered by the
stampede of humanity circling around him.
I want to ask him something familiar,
something about tractors and wagons,
but he is taken by the neon night,
crossing carefully against the light.

EXPLORE: Metaphor and simile are poetic devices in which comparisons are made. For instance, "My love is like a red, red rose" is a simile, while "Jealousy is a green-eyed monster" is a metaphor. Re-read the four poems here and find instances of these poetic devices. How do they contribute to the meaning of poems

 EXPLORE: Poets deliberately choose specific formats for their writing. Even *free verse* is not particularly free. Formal poetry forms vary widely: haiku, limerick, cinquain, sonnet. The form may include a certain number of lines: sonnets have fourteen lines; the cinquain has five. The rhythm of poetry is also important, and there may be a certain meter to the lines. Look at Sutphen's poems again. What interesting structural decisions has she made?

 EXPLORE AND FOR FURTHER READING: While poems stand alone, they can also form a larger whole. Do you get the idea that Sutphen's poems may combine to form *memoir*? To see if that is true, consider reading from her poetry volumes: *Straight Out of View; First Words; Coming Back to the Body; Naming the Stars; Fourteen Sonnets.*

 FOR FURTHER READING: Robert Frost's "The Death of the Hired Man" is a classic poem that focuses on a farm couple. The aphorism "Home is the place where when you go they must take you in" comes from this poem. Read the poem and react to the three characters. Read it aloud with different people taking the dialogue parts of the poem.

 EXPLORE: Both John Clare and Henry David Thoreau write about bean fields, one in poetry and one in nonfiction. How do these texts compare? Differ? For yet another example, see John Nichols' novel *The Milagro Beanfield War* (1974).

 WRITING: Find a poem that has farming or agriculture as a theme. Examples include Jane Kenyon, "Let Evening Come," Ruth Lechlitner's "Kansas Boy," and works by Carl Sandburg, Seamus Heaney, Robert Bly, Donald Hall, and Wendell Berry. Across the pond, as the British say, poets to be investigated include poet-farmer Robert Burns, John Clare, Miceal Kearney, and Jen Hadfield. Where do you find poems? A very fine resource is at the following URL: http://poetry.org/links.htm. Also, you can simply Google "poetry farm" or something similar. "Apple Jack" is an example that came up from such a search. Practice reading this poem aloud. Then read it aloud to an audience—even if that is only one person. Then, in your essay, copy your farm poem of choice at the beginning. Please note not only the title and author but also the date of publication and the source. Then in the paragraph(s) to follow, discuss the themes in the poem. Next, include your personal response to the poem. Finally, reflect on what it meant to read it aloud to an audience.

Consider the following criteria when writing:
• The poem is a good choice, reflecting agricultural theme

- Important bibliographic information for the poem is included
- The essay is well written and includes information about reading aloud as well as personal reflection
- The essay is written in an engaging style and is interesting to readers
- Passages from the poem are quoted accurately
- Commas and periods are placed <u>inside</u> quotation.
  - o FYI: British English places commas and periods outside quotation marks—one of the many reasons that George Bernard Shaw said, "England and America are two countries separated by a common language."

 WRITING OPPORTUNITY: Do you write poetry? Annually, The Frost Farm Prize for metrical poetry honors the legacy of Robert Frost, who lived on a New Hampshire farm from 1900 to1911. Frost's barn is the site of poetry readings. For more information and to submit a poem for consideration see robertfrostfarm.org.

 RESEARCH: Does your state or city have a poet laureate? Investigate to see how long the poet laureate program has been in existence. Why should a city, state, or the nation designate a poet laureate? What do poet laureates do? (You might look at the work that former US Poet Laureate Billy Collins did in his Poetry 180 program for high schools.)

 EXPLORE AND COLLABORATE: Are song lyrics poetry or poetic? Consider these lyrics "You Plant Your Fields," performed by the group New Grass Revival (among others)--lyrics that draw on farm wisdom. Make a case that lyrics have the potential to be poetry or poetic—or take an opposing view. Partner with another student to weigh each other's arguments.

Writing Your Childhood

Star Coulbrooke, Inaugural Poet Laureate of Logan, Utah, 2018 (*artsandmuseums.utah.gov*)

Read May Swenson's "The Centaur":
http://www.babsonarabians.com/Readers_Corner/The_Centaur.htm

Also see "Little Girls Farming in the Fifties" below

Think of a childhood game, activity, or work of the imagination.
Examples: Red Rover, Jacks, Post Office, jump rope, sidewalk chalk, counting, coloring, swimming, ball games, swinging, see-sawing, marching band, dancing, playing house or playing doctor, Checkers, Chess, marbles, imaginary friends, tea time, dolls, cars, soldiers, etc.

Start by describing your part in the game or activity. Give it a specific timeframe ("that summer that I was ten") and place ("a willow grove down by the old canal").

As you compose your piece, you may consider copying Swenson's form and style (three-line stanzas in free verse), or you may choose to write a response to her poem (what happened in your own hobby-horse scenario, for instance). Try not to force any pattern, however. Relax and let the writing guide itself. Toward the beginning or near the middle of the piece, begin to incorporate details of the place in which the activity occurred. Swenson uses details such as dust, grass, fence ("paling"), porch, hall, and sink. It can be helpful to stop and draw a map at this point in the poem. Imagine yourself outside the place where the thing happened. As you picture the surroundings, remember to add sensory details—smells, sounds, the emotional feel of the place. Weather often plays a part in memory. Swenson brings the feel of summer heat into her poem with descriptions of the powdery dust on her Centaur's hoofs. Animals may enter the writing, whether fantasized or actual. If they appear, give them a place. Let the playfulness of childhood come into the writing: how might you have become the thing you were playing, or how might the other people involved seem fantastical, for instance? Describe your actions and justify them through the thought-process of childlike imagination. This will be tricky because you want to keep the child's sense of innocence while employing an adult's perspective, so the language must be sophisticated and simple at the same time.

Think of how Swenson uses bodily actions to help readers "feel" the scene and therefore see it more vividly. ("jouncing between my thighs," "my thighs hugging his ribs," spanked my own behind.") How did it feel to be in close contact with your own body, or with certain objects, or with others' bodies? This kind of intimate detail gives a piece of writing vivacity and intrigue. Add dialogue if it comes naturally, if there are particular things you might have heard over and over as a child. The speaking parts must be realistic, must fit the sense of the narrative. Above all, have fun with the writing! Revision can come later.

Little Girls Farming in the Fifties
We sit up high on rusted seats,
metal molded to fit a man's bottom, round holes for venting hot sweat
on long turns around fields
over hours of plowing and planting.
We don't know the real work,
only this imaginary traveling
on relics of a family farm, wide rake bearing rows of curved steel tines, wagon-
    sized drill with disks mounted for sowing, wooden seed boxes
lined up, sun-dried, lids curled.

CHAPTER NINE

Through a Child's Eyes

In the horror-thriller-detective film *The Silence of the Lambs* (1991), the protagonist, FBI agent Clarice Starling (played by Jodie Foster), relates the awful experience of waking up as a child on a sheep ranch and hearing the screams of lambs as they were slaughtered. As an adult, her goal is to save innocents in danger, such as the woman being held captive by a serial killer.

Any child who has grown up on a farm has no doubt learned about life and death and the birds and the bees from an early age. Farm animals die, crops are ruined, and people are maimed in accidents with equipment. In literature written for children that focuses on farm themes, these themes may or may not be evident. Perhaps most well known of all farm fiction for children is E. B. White's classic *Charlotte's Web* (1952) in which Fern, a little girl, saves a runt pig named Wilbur. The spider, Charlotte, continues to save Wilbur time after time until his future is secured—although Charlotte's is not. In contrast, Robert Newton Peck's young adult novel *A Day No Pigs Would Die* (1972) is a coming of age story in which Rob's pet pig Pinky finally has to be sacrificed when the family faces economic hardship. Although graphic in detail, the novel is true to life on a farm.

Mildred Armstrong Kalish in her memoir *Little Heathens: Hard Times and High Spirits on an Iowa Farm During the Great Depression* (2007) details the children's duty of cleaning a hog's head in preparation for making *headcheese*, an example of eating the pig from tip to tail, which is a philosophy that is replicated in some contemporary restaurants:

> Preparing the head for cooking usually fell to us Little Kids. Just as we were never permitted to see my uncle deliver the fatal sledgehammer blow to the head of the hog, we were never permitted to see him sever the head from the body of the butchered porker. Somehow it just appeared, partially submerged in cold water, in the largest dishpan we had. We children were provided with small handheld brushes, a couple of toothbrushes, several clean washcloths, and a box of baking soda: Arm & Hammer, of course. Someone had already scraped the hairs off; I have no idea how that was done. It was our job to douse the creature with baking soda, and scrub the head until it was pink and clean. The truly repulsive part of the endeavor was that we had to thoroughly clean the ears and brush the teeth with the baking soda until they were completely free from any debris or dirt. This is where the toothbrushes and washcloths came in handy. We had to turn back the lips and ears, dust with the soda, and have at the orifices with brushes and washcloths. Can you see a five- to ten-year-old child of today turning to such a task? (138–139)

The 1903 classic children's book *Rebecca of Sunnybrook Farm* or the *Anne of Green Gables* series offers romantic notions of childhood and farm life with little, if any, bloodshed. Children seem innately interested in farms, attending Baby Animal Days at historic agricultural museums or singing "The Farmer in the Dell" on the playground:

> The farmer in the dell
> The farmer in the dell
> Hi-ho, The derry-o
> The farmer in the dell
> [Roud Folk Song Index #6306]

This chapter lays out a series of books for young readers, beginning with picture books and extending through books for teens, all with a farming theme. This listing is just a small sampling of the wealth available to young readers.

Literature for Young Readers

Picture Books for Children

Children's books require expert combination of text and art. Dr. Seuss's *The Cat in the Hat* uses only 225 words and his *Green Eggs and Ham* only 54. Writing to such a specific audience—often non-readers—can be a challenge. Likewise, the artwork must be engaging. The type of art can be diverse: drawings, paintings, photographs, collages, or printmaking such as woodblock prints. Likewise, the approach to the works of art may be realistic, fantastical, imaginative, expressionistic, or even primitive. Color, line, and shape are concepts to consider when looking at artwork. Even a two-dimensional book may use texture, but in some children's books, texture becomes an important element with furry, soft, or prickly materials included in the actual book. When a children's book is reviewed, all of these elements—including the size of the book and whether or not it's hardback or paperback—must be included. With the wealth of books available, one way to distinguish among them is to look at those that have won awards. The Caldecott Prize is given for excellent illustration in children's books; the Newbery Prize honors outstanding books for children and teens; the Orbis Prize recognizes stellar picture books.

Hello, Day! by Anita Lobel offers children the opportunity to make sounds of the animals pictured, like "Moo."

Once Upon MacDonald's Farm by Stephen Gammell presents a funny tale of "Old MacDonald," who has somehow acquired zoo animals instead of farm animals.

Rosie's Walk by Pat Hutchins follows a hen that walks around the farm yard, seemingly unaware of the fox that is following her. Don't worry: the fox is outfoxed. The fox in the hen house is a theme of several books including Mem Fox's *Hattie and the Fox* and Roald Dahl's *Fantastic Mr. Fox.*

A Farmer's Alphabet by Mary Azarian features stunning woodcuts set in Vermont.

Image copyright Mary Azarian, 1980.

Heartland by Diane Siebert includes beautiful paintings by Wendell Minor in a book that celebrates the Midwest with lyrical writing such as "I am the Heartland. / On these plains / Rise elevators filled with grains."

On the Farm by David Elliott is an award-winning book that features 13 poems.

Raising Yoder's Barn by Jane Yolen (1998) is a beautifully illustrated children's book that tells the story of an Amish barn raising from a young boy's perspective.

Stanley Goes for a Drive by Craig Frazier features bold, graphic artwork and a clever story in which the seemingly simple-minded Stanley devises a way to change the weather on a day when the "pond was so dry that it couldn't even make a reflection."

Click, Clack, Moo: Cows That Type by Doreen Cronin is a children's book that adults will enjoy, too, as its humor works on multiple levels. This book was so successful that several others, including *Duck for President*, followed.

Punk Farm by Jarrett Krosoczka. And now, for something completely different: farm animals in a rock band doing a rather different rendition of "Old MacDonald Had a Farm."

Funny Farm by Mark Teague features city slicker Edward—a dog—getting his comeuppance by farm animals when he visits the country.

John Deere books. Tractor and farm equipment manufacturer John Deere provides one example of how corporations market their products to children—through books. These may be fiction—as in *Good Night, Johnny Tractor*—or informational. John Deere has also been the subject of biographies written for children, such as *Pioneer Plowmaker*. His enormous success came from developing a steel plow that "self scoured," so the farmer did not have to stop continuously to clean dirt from a wooden plow. In this same vein of the importance of farm equipment to children is *My First Tractor: Stories of Farmers and Their First Love* by Michael Farmer with a forward by farm author Jerry Apps (e.g., *Eat Rutabagas, Letters from Hillside Farm*).

A Midwestern Corn Festival: Ears Everywhere is one in a series by folklorist Lisa Gabbert, who uncovers the activities in harvest festivals; others focus on apples and maple sugar.

A Farm features the idyllic art of Carl Larsson and depicts bygone days of farm life in Sweden.

Chapter Books

A next step in farm-themed books for young readers is the chapter book, which is a story divided into section. For instance, *Charlotte's Web*'s 22 chapters follow the seasons: spring, summer, fall, winter.

Sarah, Plain and Tall by Patricia MacLachlan is the touching story of a Kansas family that has lost its mother; Sarah is a "mail order bride" come to see if she fits with the father, son, and daughter.

The *Little House* series by Laura Ingalls Wilder follows the Ingalls family from the Big Woods to the Prairie and beyond as the children encounter adventure after adventure growing up on various homesteads. As with *Charlotte's Web,* Garth Williams served as illustrator.

Strawberry Girl by Lois Lenski won the 1946 Newbery Award and tells the story of Birdie Boyer and her family on their backwoods Florida farm, complete with Hatfield-and-Mc-Coys-type feuding.

Caddie Woodlawn, published in 1935, is the story of tomboy childhood of author Carol Ryrie Brink's grandmother in 1860s Wisconsin; it, too, is a Newbery Award Medal winner.

Temple Grandin: How the Girl Who Loved Cows Embraced Autism and Changed the World is a biographical book by Sy Montgomery (with Grandin) that provides an inspiring look at a woman who became a scientist and university professor.

Seedfolks by Paul Fleischman is an inspiring story of how one young girl planting bean seeds in a vacant lot turned into a community garden. Multicultural voices abound. It's a popular read for communities, who do a common literature experience or "one book" program. This is the young people's version of urban farming book, such as *Farm City: The Education of an Urban Farmer* by Novella Carpenter.

Lily's Victory Garden (2012) by Helen L. Wilbur focuses on a young girl who finds space for a victory garden during World War II, but it is in a neighbor's yard, and they are parents to a soldier who has been killed.

The Trouble with Chickens, by *Click, Clack, Moo* author Doreen Cronin features dog detective J. J. Tully, who in a former life was a search-and-rescue dog but who has retired to a farm and investigates in a *noir* fashion.

The Wonderful Adventures of Nils is a Swedish children's book by Selma Lagerlof, the first woman to win the Nobel Prize for Literature (1909). Nils is a boy transformed to elf size due to his unkind behavior to animals, but his size allows him to mount the back of a large goose and look over the farms and land in Sweden—a painless way to learn about geography.

The Six Bullerby Children by award-winning Astrid Lindgren is but one of the titles in a group of novels set on farms; in this one, three small farmhouses are home to six lively children.

Hilda Stahl published a series focused on Elizabeth Gail, including *The Mystery at the Johnson Farm.*

The Boxcar Children Beginning: The Aldens of Fair Meadow Farm is a prequel written by Patricia MacLachlin (2012) that uncovers the origin of this classic children's story.

Huskings, Quiltings, and Barn Raising: Work-Play Parties in Early America (1992) by Victoria Sherrow contains detailed descriptions of a variety of events along with recipes.

Adolescent or Young Adult Literature

Books for teens—called junior books before the 1960s—really took off in 1967 with the publication of benchmark books such as S. E. Hinton's *The Outsiders*. But before that, there were books such as Rose Wilder Lane's *Let the Hurricane Roar* (also called *Young Pioneers*), which introduced newlyweds on a lonely homestead. Lane came by storytelling naturally as the daughter of Laura Ingalls Wilder although some suspect that Lane—a published writer—was the real writer behind the *Little House* books.

The Omnivore's Dilemma: The Secrets Behind What You Eat is the young reader's version of the adult nonfiction book by Michael Pollan. He is called a "supermarket detective," who encourages readers to reflect on their eating choices and their implications environmentally and globally.

Chew on This: Everything You Don't Want to Know about Fast Food (2007) is the children's version of *Fast Food Nation*, written by Eric Schlosser and Charles Wilson.

Black Potatoes: The Story of the Great Irish Famine, 1845–1850 by Susan Campbell Bartoletti won an award for outstanding history.

Across Five Aprils by Irene Hunt is an award-winning novel about a boy left to run an Illinois farm during the Civil war.

Long Way from Chicago and *Fair Weather* are both novels by Richard Peck that feature country versus city themes in historical settings in Illinois.

Return to Sender by Julia Alvarez focuses on the difficult situation in which farmers need hired hands, who may also be illegal immigrants. In this novel, the narration switches between two preteens, Tyler, the son of a Vermont farmer, and Mari.

Esperanza Rising by Pam Munoz Ryan spotlights an unusual immigration experience in which the daughter of a wealthy Mexican family is displaced to the USA during the Great Depression and must join other farm laborers. Magical realism is used in the narrative.

Out of the Dust by Karen Hesse won the 1998 Newbery Medal for its depiction in free verse poems of the Oklahoma Dustbowl and its effect on a farm girl.

Jip: His Story by Katherine Paterson, better known for her *Bridge to Terabithia*, is historical fiction set on a "poor farm" in Vermont.

The Beet Fields: Memories of a Sixteenth Summer is the work of ever-popular Gary Paulsen and draws on his own life story to tell the tale of a run-away boy.

Green Angel by Alice Hoffman is the first in a series of dystopian novels about a teen named Green who is the lone survivor on the family vegetable farm. Not to be confused with the vampire novel *The Farm* by Emily McKay that has nothing to do with agriculture.

"Dust Pneumonia" from *Out of the Dust* by Karen Hesse

This selection from the Newbery Award winning book is one of the free verse poems that focuses on the horrific effects of the Dust Bowl.

Dust Pneumonia

Two Fridays ago,
Pete Guymon drove in with a
truck full of produce.
He joked with Calb Hardly,
Mr. Hardly's son,
while they unloaded eggs and cream
down at the store.
Pete Guymon teased Calb Hardly about the
Wildcats
losing to Hooker.
Calb Hardly teased Pete Guymon about his
wheezy
truck sucking in dust.

Last Friday,
Pete Guymon took ill with dust pneumonia.
Nobody knew how to keep that produce truck on
the
road.
It sat,
filled with turkeys and heavy hens
waiting for delivery,
it sat out in front of Pete's drafty shack,
and sits there still,
the cream curdling
the apples going soft.

Because a couple of hours ago,
Pete Guymon died.

Mr. Hardly
was already on the phone
to a new produce
supplier
before evening.
He had people in the store
and no food to sell them.

His boy, Calb,
Slammed the basketball against the side of the
House
until Calb's ma yelled for him to quit,
and late that night a truck rattled up to the store,
with colored springs,
dozens of hens,
filthy eggs,
and a driver with no interest whatsoever in young
Calb Hardly
or his precious Wildcats.

March, 1935
(140–141)

EXPLORE: What is dust pneumonia? Is it recorded how many people died of dust pneumonia during the Dust Bowl? What are the relationships among the characters in this free verse poem?

WRITE: This free verse poem reads much like a *found poem*, which is a selection of prose put into poetic format. Find a passage in a book or story that you've read already or intend to read and put it into poetic form. How did you decide where to make line breaks?

Activities

 FOR FURTHER READING: Choose a book appropriate for a young reader that focuses on farming as a theme, or is set on a farm, or features characters that might be termed *farmers*, even if they are away from a farm setting. Read the book and be prepared to discuss or write about it. In addition to the titles listed in this chapter, there is a list of farm-themed books in the final section of this reader, and they are also found through Internet searches.

 EXPLORE: What are the common themes for children's or young adult literature on farming and agriculture? Are there taboo subjects, that is, subjects that do not occur in children's or young adult books you have found in your other reading?

 WRITE: Imagine that you are a member of Goodreads.com, a website that is a treasure trove of reviews by people who are not only knowledgeable but also passionate about reading. Choose a book for a young reader that focuses on farming as a theme or setting and write a review of that book for Goodreads. (You don't have to post it, but you certainly may do so if you wish.) Read the excerpt from Goodreads' review philosophy below (and there are more policies and examples on its website: http://www.goodreads.com/review/guidelines). Goodreads offers excellent advice on writing about books.

Our Review Philosophy

Goodreads is for expressing your honest opinions about books. Don't be afraid to say what you think about the book! We welcome your passion, as it helps the millions of other readers on Goodreads learn what a book is really about, and decide whether or not they want to read it.

We believe that Goodreads members should see the best, most relevant, thought provoking reviews (positive and negative) when they visit a book page. Our job is to show members those reviews, and not show reviews that we deem to not be appropriate or a high enough level of quality.

However we value that members trust us with your thoughts and words and take our stewardship of storing your reviews seriously. We promise to always store your reviews on your profile and in your bookshelves and will never delete or modify them – except for certain extreme situations, which are described below. Your thoughts and your words are yours, and we promise you we will always respect that.

Here are some examples of what we allow in reviews:

• Creativity! Some of the best reviews on Goodreads use the book as inspiration for a personal essay or other piece of creative writing. As long as they don't go against our guidelines in other ways, these reviews are welcome and encouraged!

• Images in reviews are fine (and sometimes hilarious) but please, no nudity or graphic violence.

• Pre-publication reviews. Many of our members receive advance copies of books to review, either through Goodreads giveaways or another source. We have no way of knowing the exact date that review copies are available. As such, each book is eligible to be reviewed as soon as it appears on the site.

• Harsh critical statements that apply to the book or the writing in it, such as "This guy can't write a lick," or "This book is absolute trash." Again, honest opinions about books are always going to be welcome and encouraged on Goodreads.

 WRITE: Write a book review for a journal for librarians and teachers that offers the essential information about the book as well as a brief summary followed by your analysis. Include helpful resources such as websites. A sample book review format appears below.

Sample Book Review Format for Writing Assignments:

Author: Kirby Larson
Title: *Hattie Big Sky*
Publication information: Delacorte, 2006 (hardback); Yearling, 2008 (paperback)
Category or genre: Historical fiction for Young Adults
Number of pages: 304 pages
Reading level: Young adult
Awards: Newbery Honor Book, 2006 Montana Book Award, and several others

Summary: Hattie Brooks, a 16-year-old orphan, has been passed around a series of relatives after her parents' death in the early twenieth century. Her current "family" overworks her with rarely a kind word. When her long-lost uncle's will reveals that she has inherited his Montana homestead, she jumps at the chance to head west, taking Mr. Whiskers, her cat, with her on the train. After all, her best friend, Charlie has enlisted to fight in WWI, so there is nothing to keep her in Iowa. When she arrives in Montana in 1918, it is not a rosy picture: the cabin is barely weatherproof; she has to build miles of fence and bring in a crop to "prove up" the place and get her land. Fortunately, kind neighbors--particularly Perilee Mueller--whose husband Karl is German-born help. Hattie can comfortably hold the paradoxical notions of Charlie killing Germans and her outrage over the persecution of the Mueller family. In addition to the narrative, letters to Charlie and articles that Hattie writes for her hometown Iowa newspaper enliven the format of the tale.

Analysis: This novel of Hattie Brooks at first might seem in the tradition of "and a little child shall lead them," with the goodness of Hattie managing to meet the almost impossible tasks of proving up, demonstrating to the citizens that their prejudice is unreasonable, and changing the vigilante Traft Martin into a better person. But, Kirby Larson does not whitewash the hardships that Hattie faces or the tragedies that can occur in such a setting. Larson had the model of her great-grandmother, who truly did homestead solo on the Montana frontier, for inspiration. The characters are well drawn and complex. The recipes at the book's end are a charming addition. I read this novel shortly after I finished *The Book Thief*, which focuses on a German family during WWII. In spite of the fact that the books had different "world wars" for settings, I found some interesting parallels, and reading them together enriched the experience. (One other recommendation: Ivan Doig writes movingly of Montana ranch life, particularly in his novel, *Dancing at the Rascal Fair*, which is part of a trilogy about Scottish immigrant families.)

From a farming perspective, this novel provided insight into the requirements of homesteading, the kinds of farm equipment and farming methods of the day, and the reality of physical labor required to manage a farm. There was a boom in homesteading in Montana in 1900, which peaked with the wheat harvest of 1917, which was important to the war effort. The drought of 1918, though, led to the bust of 1920 when many lost their land. No doubt the Influenza epidemic, which some credit as ending WWI, also did not help.

About the author: Larson writes children's books, too, including *Two Bobbies: A True Story of Hurricane Katrina, Friendship and Survival*. She lives in Washington.

Web resources: http://www.hattiebigsky.com/; http://www.kirbylarson.com/hattiebigsky.html

❦ Chapter Ten ❦

Farms and Folklore

Farm Folklore and Folklore about Farms

The word *folklore* usually brings to mind the past: traditional ways of living, stories passed down from generation to generation, old wives' tales. The truth is that folklore can be quite contemporary; it's always being generated anew as culture evolves and develops. Folklore is most easily summed up as informal traditional culture. *Traditional* means passed on (which can be over the course of generations, as with a family custom, or over the course of a few days, as with a political joke), and informal means that we learn it from the people around us rather than from an institution, so that there's rarely a single correct version.

Folklore encompasses all the informally learned expressive culture that we have in our lives: instead of published novels and poetry we have urban legends and jokes; instead of art museums we have graffiti and yard decorations; instead of symphonies we have folksongs. The main thing that distinguishes folklore from other forms of cultural expression is the way we learn it: by observation and experience from the people around us. To get a sense of what the process of folk transmission looks like, envision a giant game of telephone, where individual people pass along a story or custom or belief. This necessarily involves a lot of individual retellings and highlights the difference between folk and mass culture. In mass culture, when lots of people read the same book or see the same television show, everyone gets the same version. In folk culture, when lots of people have heard the same story or practiced the same custom, it has been retold or reenacted anew for them each time.

With this definition of folklore, you can easily see how something doesn't have to be old to be folklore—we're constantly learning new cultural forms and traditions informally from the people around us. Studying those cultural forms is a great way to understand what's important to a culture or group. Because folklore is passed on from person to person, it's typically shaped by consensus; as it's passed around it evolves to be as representative of the group as possible. Bad jokes don't get told anymore; uninteresting legends stop being shared. This means that if a joke or legend is in wide circulation, it must be expressing or reflecting something important to a lot of people. Folklorists try to discover the important message behind the folklore.

The stuff of folklore is typically divided up into four main categories: things we say, things we do, things we make, and things we believe. You'll find examples from each of these categories below. When folklorists study these types of folklore, they can produce two kinds of work: they *collect* folklore (stories, songs, customs, etc.) and thus gather and document primary sources, and then they *analyze* that folklore, producing scholarly works that become secondary sources. The examples below show this two-part process.

Farmer's Daughter Jokes

In order to find, document, and interpret folk culture, folklorists conduct fieldwork. They go out into the world to interview, observe, photograph, and record the expressive culture of everyday life. Rural cultures such as farmsteads have often been a focus of this field research, and one of the things that distinguishes folklore fieldwork from other types of research is its focus on **context**. *Folklorists know that the words of a joke don't contain the entire meaning of the joke; the teller's experiences, circumstances, personality, and worldview all shape and are reflected in the meaning of a joke. The ability to fully comprehend folklore often reveals whether a listener is an insider or an outsider to a given folk culture. Consider the following transcribed "farmer's daughter" joke and accompanying ethnographic data, collected by folklorist Jim Leary from Polish Wisconsin farmer Max Trzebiatowski.*

Joke A:

"This is an old story. It's been said a lot. One time there was a guy runnin' for county sheriff. [Leary: Was this Pete?] Yeah, coulda been Pete. This guy was runnin' for county sheriff. But this was horse and buggy days. And he went out campaigning. This was maybe a week or so before the election. And some of them, they were out quite a ways from where he lived. And the night fell on him. And he passed one place. He asked if he could stay there overnight. Yes, he could stay there, but they told him: 'You gotta sleep upstairs.' And they had a daughter. A full-grown daughter. And she slept upstairs. And, uh, they all went to bed. And their daughter couldn't fall asleep. There was a man. And she was thinkin' about the man more than she needed sleep. And then in the middle of the night she got up. And she went into the room, where that delegate was sleepin', for sheriff. And she wanted him to have a little fun with her. And, uh, he thought is case it was gave out that he would be screwin' someone else's woman, it would be a bad reputation for him. So he didn't. And she went to bed. Next morning she got up. He was still sleepin'. She got up, and she went to the barn. And there was a cow that was in heat. But the cow was outside, the bull inside. So she let the bull loose to breed the cow. And they had a manure pile there in front of the barn. And the bull went out and laid down on that manure pile. Never, never paid no attention to the cow. And the woman she kicked it in the hind end and she says: "Are you, son-of-a-bitch, runnin' for county sheriff, too?' [Max pauses as Rose and I laugh.] This is an old one. This was repeated quite a lot. Whoever made it up made it up good."

Joke A has two interconnected episodes. In the first, a sexually potent male denies a lusty female's advances because he fears social repercussions; in the second a stud bull ignores a cow in heat for, presumably, the same reason. The joke turns on the incongruity of attributing a thinking man's motives to the subsequent behavior of a dumb beast. The actors parading through farmhouse and barnyard are mostly familiar types in Max's telling and, indeed, throughout the region. The bull regularly plays aggressive suitor to a docile cow (or a boar to a sow, or a rooster to a hen); and the farmer's daughter is proverbially wanton. The object of her affection, however, is usually not the sheriff but either that buggy-riding urbanite, the traveling salesman, or her father's hired man.

More critically, this fiction called upon Max's own experience. He had ten sisters, five of them older. These young farm women were part of Andro's [their father's] work force and, besides helping with household tasks, they did nearly everything except ploughing: dragging, spreading manure with pitchforks, shocking oats, cocking hey, piling hay, milking cows, and tending cattle in unfenced pasture land. "In older days," according to Max, "the bull was loose with the cows." His sisters, consequently, were fully aware both of farm work's grime and toil, and of the cycle of beasts.

They were also aware of the presence of young men. Contrary to scenarios in traditional and popular fictions, traveling salesmen were infrequent visitors. "Some came round when cars was coming in, to sell cars," but none ever stayed the night. Andro bought farm equipment through the local implement dealer, traded at Amherst stores, and acquired work horses from nearby breeders. He also employed hired men on his expending acreage, sometimes three or four at a time. They were typically teenage farm boys, second and third or fourth sons from neighboring families "that had too much help to home." Some of these men, in Max's recollections, "didn't last long. If he wasn't a hard worker, Dad couldn't use him." Most were diligent and two, the Patoka brothers, remained for several years. Each eventually married one of Max's sisters and Andro generously set up the newlyweds on farms of their own. Max pointed out, however, that, "The kids were well watched. . . . They couldn't get out of eyesight with the hired men, or have any fun," Rose chimed in, "Not like nowdays." Their own courtship was confined to shared labor in the fields, stolen glances at mealtime, community celebrations, and Sunday afternoon "visiting." This strict code of behavior established the fact that, despite rough labor, farm folk were genteel; and it served to counter outsiders' stereotypical notions that because Polish women worked in the fields, they were little more than animals.

Within this old-fashioned world, a landless man's lot was hard. Max's cousin Pete lacked a father's bounty and, although raised on a farm, he had to find work—scant, intermittent, Depression work—in Stevens Point as an odd-job carpenter and a coal shoveler. When he had the capital, he ran a succession of taverns—one of which burned. Despite struggles, Pete was and is an engaging fellow, full of jokes and artful talk. In the 1950s he tried unsuccessfully to parlay his popularity into victory in the race for county sheriff: "There was some that voted for him, but there was more that didn't." As is often the case elsewhere in America, the sheriff is an elected official in Portage County. Candidates have long been from the rural and working classes, voting has frequently followed ethnic lines, and the practice of soliciting support through face-to-face contact with constituents is customary. Besides power and a guaranteed salary, the sheriff acquired status on par with any landholder.

Against this background, Joke A (and here I'm guessing that Max's concrete statements warrant my more abstract extrapolations) dramatizes issues which were fundamental to his generation's world. "Natural" desires for the "fun" of sexual gratification were pitted against cultural strivings for reputation and respectability—with the latter winning out. This basic theme, likewise present in jokes where farmers' daughters frolic with salesmen and hired men, was especially amplified in Max's telling. In contrast with a roving drummer or a callow farm boy, the would-be sheriff risked not only community disapproval but also economic ruin for a moment's pleasure. The daughter's physical movement from house to barnyard simultaneously involved an unmistakable symbolic shift from the world of human beings to the world of animals. There her actions, which resulted in the bull being likened to the sheriff, subtly but surely emphasized the converse point: people who act like beasts become beasts. No wonder this joke was "said a lot." No wonder Max reckoned, "Whoever made it up, made it up good."

 COLLABORATE: Folklorists often find deep meaning and significant symbolism in things people consider to be trivial (like jokes). Pair up with a classmate and share some jokes you've heard (or told) before, and consider what the context of those jokes contributes to their meaning or importance. Can you think of any jokes that rely heavily on awareness of contextual clues in order to make sense?

 EXPLORE: As noted, folklore often deals with insider versus outsider perspectives (referred to as *emic* versus *etic* perspectives, respectively). Max Trzebiatowski's joke is clearly told from an *emic* perspective, as Leary's analysis reveals. How might this joke be different, either in meaning or in delivery, if the teller had been an outsider to the Polish farming culture of Wisconsin?

 RESEARCH: Do an online search for farmer's daughter jokes, and review the results. How many jokes can you find? What information in addition to the text of the jokes is included? What kind of additional information would it be helpful to have documented? What does the widespread popularity of farmer's daughter jokes tell us about farming culture in general?

The Country Life

One genre of folklore that accompanies many different occupations is folksong. Whether setting the pace for manual labor or distracting workers from arduous tasks, song and hard work often go hand in hand. Because folklore by definition never has a single "correct" version, folksongs are extremely adaptable. Individual singers can alter or add verses to make them better fit their situations, and songs can be lengthened or shortened to match up with the time available. The following traditional song, Country Life (sometimes called Country Boy), often ends after the first two verses, the ones about spring and winter, highlighting that these are the main representative verses for most singers. But the song can go on at length, too, incorporating many more elements of the farming experience. This song highlights the importance of the seasonal round, and the way that lifestyles have to adjust accordingly to the seasonal work that needs to be done. The word "laylum," which sometimes is transcribed "layland" or "leyland" is variously defined as a tree branch or a newly seeded field.

Oh, I like to rise when the sun she rises
Early in the morning
And I like to hear them small birds singing
Merrily upon their laylum
And hurrah for the life of a country boy
And to ramble in the new-mown hay!

In spring we sow at the harvest mow
And that's how the seasons round they go
But of all the times if choose I may
'Twould be rambling through the new-mown hay

Oh, I like to rise when the sun she rises
Early in the morning

And I like to hear them small birds singing
Merrily upon their laylum
And hurrah for the life of a country boy
And to ramble in the new-mown hay!

In the winter when the sky is grey
We hedge and ditch our lives away
But in the summer when the sun shines gay
We go rambling through the new-mown hay

Oh, I like to rise when the sun she rises
Early in the morning
And I like to hear them small birds singing
Merrily upon their laylum
And hurrah for the life of a country boy
And to ramble in the new-mown hay!

In summer when the sun is hot
We sing, and we dance, and we drink a lot
We spend all night in sport and play
And go rambling in the new-mown hay

Oh, I like to rise when the sun she rises
Early in the morning
And I like to hear them small birds singing
Merrily upon their laylum
And hurrah for the life of a country boy
And to ramble in the new-mown hay!

In autumn when the oak trees turn
We gather all the wood that›s fit to burn
We cut and we stash and we stow away
And go rambling in the new-mown hay

Oh, I like to rise when the sun she rises
Early in the morning
And I like to hear them small birds singing
Merrily upon their laylum
And hurrah for the life of a country boy
And to ramble in the new-mown hay!

I like to hear the Morris dancers
Clash their sticks and drink our ale
I like to hear those bells a-play
As we ramble in the new-mown hay

Oh, I like to rise when the sun she rises
Early in the morning
And I like to hear them small birds singing
Merrily upon their laylum
And hurrah for the life of a country boy
And to ramble in the new-mown hay!

Oh, Nancy is my darling gay
And she blooms like the flowers every day
But I love her best in the month of May
When we're rambling through the new-mown hay

Oh, I like to rise when the sun she rises
Early in the morning
And I like to hear them small birds singing
Merrily upon their laylum
And hurrah for the life of a country boy
And to ramble in the new-mown hay!

EXPLORE: Search for audio or video recordings of this song online, and locate at least three different performances of it. How are the versions you find similar and how are they different?

WRITE: Create a new verse for the song "Country Life" that incorporates your own experiences of the various seasons of work or your own understandings of farm life. You can create a parody verse that plays off the themes of the original song, or you can create a genuine verse. For example, here's one common parody verse for this song, which pokes fun at the sentiment of the chorus:

Oh, I like big birds, I like small birds
I like birds of every size.
But if they wake me before the sun's up
I'll poke out their little eyes!

Food and Custom in Farming Communities

Folk customs fall under the general category of "things we do," and they emphasize action and partici-pation. Rather than simply telling or hearing a joke or singing a song, customary folklore requires ac-tive engagement, like a holiday celebration or an initiation. The custom described below is a wedding tradition that is practiced in a number of rural communities, and the focus on food highlights the larger social process that's taking place. As the writer says, "food is extraordinary in its ordinariness—it is a basic requirement of survival, and yet we attach an immense amount of meaning and importance to its acquisition, preparation, and consumption. The inclusion of certain foods can often reveal what is at the heart of a traditional custom.

Chickarees: Rural Community Festivities for Newlyweds, by Rosa Palmer Thornley

The rancher's wife could see two silhouettes against the yard light as she walked through the porch to answer the knock. Hinges squeaked as she pushed the screen door open and scowled, "What have you boys been up to?" She recognized her young neighbors as they hung their heads and kicked the gravel under their feet trying to cover up the blood that still dripped from the chickens they had just butchered. "You didn't take my laying hens did you?" she scolded. They held up the feathery bodies by the legs and repented, "No ma'am. We sorted out the poults. Now we need a pot to cook 'em. We're having a chickaree." The woman relaxed and opened the door wider, offering the boys a bucket to catch the mess made by the chickens. They followed her into the kitchen where she set a pot to boil water and positioned a cast iron frying pan on the coal stove to start heating the lard for their meal.

When I asked my uncle for more details as he related this tale, he shook his head, "Don't know anymore. It was just one of those stories that started in church one Sunday morning with 'Did you hear what happened last night?' and we all just keep passing it around." The young perpetrators in his story had used the distortion of the term *shivaree* to describe a meal in which stolen chickens were the main fare that was served during a late-night, impromptu celebration following a marriage in the rural community of Park Valley, Utah. The community is spread over 500 square miles in the northwest corner of Utah. The sheep and cattle ranches, where approximately 200 citizens live, are sometimes separated by miles of sagebrush and cedar-covered landscape. Although distance required self-reliance, the small population and isolation heightened social interaction that celebrated or honored life cycle events like birth, marriage, and death; shivarees belonged to this type of celebration. Pauline Greenhill identified through her Canadian research that shivarees (also spelled "charivaris"; "shivaree is more common west of the Mississippi) were a way to welcome brides, who were frequently outsiders, into the community. One respondent to her research query associated this phenomenon with rural societies. "In my days the community of farmers all KNEW each other and welcomed a newcomer" (175, emphasis in text). Marriage constituted a change in the social structure as it often moved a member of the community from one status to another.

Similar to historic charivaris, which had roots in the medieval courts of France, these wedding celebrations had a carnivalesque atmosphere where the norms of the community were turned upside down in a type of iconoclastic revelry (Crane 145). One fictional charivari titled *Roman de Fauvel* illustrated the obnoxious noise from clanging pot and kettles, which escalated to breaking windows, exposing naked backsides and tossing dung in people's faces (146). The only indication of food in that medieval manuscript was the cookware used to create discordant music – a component of charivaris that evolved to become synonymous with the term *rough music*, used to describe the practice throughout the British Isles.

The shivaree custom emigrated to North American from Western Europe and was used in Canada and the Deep South to show disapproval. As the custom moved west and into the twentieth century, the function became less punitive and more celebratory. Loretta Johnson described frontier shivarees as a "rowdy seal of approval" (372). Hijinks and disorderly horseplay were "traditional, expected for every marriage, and meant to be fun" (384):

Frontier shivarees often featured a dip in the horse tank or a local spring. . . . One couple, rumored to have strewn fractured hearts around them, were shivareed mercilessly. After storming the bridal suite of the hotel and demanding and receiving the traditional treats, the shivareers proceeded to the business at hand, which was to throw the couple into the horse tank at the town pump on Main Street. The groom put up a stout fight, but was eventually subdued. (Hockenhull qtd on 381)

Johnson described these types of secular celebrations as a way for the community to exercise "its self-proclaimed right to participate actively in the marriage" (380). Several elements of the European tradition were modified for the Western style of "fun." Discordant music like that in *Roman de Fauvel* continued to be a way to signal the beginning of a shivaree; this was followed by pranks described in the example above, and instead of monetary ransoms, food became the payment of choice. Rough music was absent in the shivaree practice in Park Valley, Utah. The cooking utensils were used for their true, practical purpose—to prepare a meal.

The common, individualistic act of eating became a significant element in the marriage rite of shivaree performed in that isolated ranching community in the northwest corner of Utah. Professor David Marshall argued in "Food as Ritual, Routine or Convention," that "food is extraordinary in its ordinariness," and that "while the sensual pleasures of eating are completely individualized, eating is a highly social activity and regulated by the community." More than just the nutritional function, food can have a complex meaning depending on the context surrounding a meal (70-2). Marshall's argument is confirmed when food and the communal meal are studied in the context of how the ritualized tradition of shivaree was practiced in Park Valley, Utah. The meal served at the end of the performance served to consummate a rite of passage as newlyweds were offered a hand of friendship and accepted into the community where their new household would help to sustain the rural, ranching lifestyle.

Although other researchers found that food and drink were sometimes paid as a ransom to stop shivarees, this element in the shivaree ritual performed in Park Valley served another function. Marshall reaffirmed previous research that "goods are consumed for what they come to mean, not just what they do, and become important as 'markers' of social position and indicative of social inclusion" (72). Park Valley newlyweds were transitioning from a state of adolescence to adulthood when married couples were expected to establish a new household that would help sustain the ranching culture in this community that had been diminishing since 1910. Arnold van Gennap views rites of passage as an integral part of societies:

The life of an individual in any society is a series of passages from one age to another. . . . [P]rogression from one group to the next is accompanied by special acts. . . . [E]very change in a person's life involves actions and reactions between sacred and profane—actions and reactions to be regulated and guarded so that society as a whole will suffer no discomfort or injury. . . . [A] man's life comes to be made up of a succession of stages with similar ends and beginning: birth, social puberty, marriage, fatherhood, advancement to a higher class, occupational specialization, and death. . . . [The] essential purpose is to enable the individual to pass from one defined position to another which is equally well defined (2–3).

Shivarees performed in Park Valley served as an informal celebration to mark that rite of passage from one social position to another.

Although a majority of wedding ceremonies were (and still are) performed outside of the valley, couples usually planned a reception and dance to celebrate with their hometown neighbors afterwards. This formal event was organized by the bride, groom, and family. Visser, author of *The Rituals of Dinner*, recognizes that "weddings [add receptions] are initiations into a new way of life . . . . usually celebrated with food and drink" (30). Many of the Anglo-Saxon traditions, like a tiered wedding cake, were part of the formal festivities. Park Valley bride, Bonnie Pugsley Hill remembers balancing her wedding cake on her lap for over an hour as the newlyweds traveled from Garland to Park Valley for their reception. These edible creations connect these Utah newlyweds with the broader culture of the United States. However, the informal, generally impromptu shivarees (festivities not typically taking place in all surrounding communities) that came after wedding receptions tell a better story of the subculture of this isolated ranching community.

Pranks were a recognizable element in contemporary shivarees, but were frequently merged with the food element. Shivariers in Park Valley constructed tricks to humiliate and have fun with the couple. Rud and Letitia Palmer were kicking up their heels on the dance floor on the night of their reception when one of Rud's friends turned loose a greased pig. The crowd separated and the owner of the frantic animal promised the newlyweds that if they could catch the little wiener, they could keep her, which could become the seed livestock for their new home in this rural community. Rud didn't want to soil his borrowed suit, so he stood back and let his new bride chase it. The audience waited around the edges and constantly herded the animal toward the center of the room. This was the best entertainment everyone had all night. Finally, Letitia got frustrated, put her hands on her hips and said, "For heaven's sake Rud, get over here and help me." He headed in and caught the pig by the hind legs, carried it outside, and put it in the rumble seat of his old '29 Chevy. Rituals like these elements of shivarees are what researchers see as "one manifestation of 'authoritative performance' that offer a collective sense of identity and integration among participants," and serves to "create and sustain shared traditions that link the individual and the community"; it helps "achieve a sense of community for those involved" (Arnold and Price qtd in Marshall 73). The Palmers married at the end of the Great Depression when times were hard and livestock like that little wiener pig that could supplement a couple's income was valuable. They raised the animal as a sow that produced multiple generations of offspring. Rud and Letitia's community of friends was offering them a gift that served to feed them not for just one meal, but for many years, further sustaining the society.

Ordinary rituals like eating often made difficult passages easier. Margaret Visser believes that shared meals are a way to order chaos:

> Full-dress celebrations of coming together, or *marking transitions* and recollections, almost always require food, with all the ritual politeness implied in dining—the proof that we all know how eating should be managed. We eat whenever life becomes dramatic: at weddings, birthdays, funerals, at parting and at welcoming home, or at any moment which a group decides is worthy of remark. (22, italics added)

She affirms that sharing food goes beyond just providing physical nutrition; it helps us understand "kinship systems (who belongs with whom; which people eat together) . . . . Breaking bread and sharing it with friends 'means' friendship itself, and also trust, pleasure, and gratitude in the sharing. Bread as a particular symbol, and food in general, becomes the actual bond which unites us" (1–3). Marshall supported this in his argument about this "(extra)ordinary consumption . . . Oral consumption . . . eating implies the consumption (dissolving, using up) of the food but is also simultaneously as process of production—or better, construction . . . reproducing or constructing life on all levels, from the physical to the social" (Falk quoted in Marshall 70–71). Food appropriated, prepared, and served during Park Valley shivarees mirrored the social relations of that community.

The chickens borrowed from the coop of the ranch wife are a clearer indication of the function of food served during the events held in the community. A woman's kitchen was often part of the communal "home" in the valley. When talking about Park Valley, many of those who live there (and others who haven't lived in the area for many generations), refer to the place as "out home." One young man who grew up in the area describes the solidarity between neighbors:

> There's a lot of houses out there, that I would call home, that I wouldn't be scared to walk into at three in the morning and go to their bedroom and ask them if I could sleep on their couch. There's a lot of houses out there that I wouldn't be scared to do that at. . . . [In] Park Valley, you knew everybody, and you knew what was going on in their lives. (Kunzler)

This community spirit extends to kitchens, kitchen cupboards, refrigerators, and even chicken coops, but stops short of borrowing goods that would adversely impact the financial stability of the household, shown when the young perpetrators from the first story were careful not to kill the woman's laying hen—in other words, stealing her egg money.

Because of the isolation of the rural community, those who made their homes in the area had to be self-sustaining. Large gardens, fruit trees, livestock, and smokehouses were common fixtures on almost every ranch, but the chicken coop was more accessible and generally had a reliable supply of foodstuffs. This provided a communal pantry for young men performing a shivaree—or as they called it "chickaree." Eggs and chickens were available all hours of the days and nights, which was ideal for late night events. Impromptu shivarees rarely allowed time for requests of donations.

In urban areas, a wife whose property was damaged or stolen may have called local authorities to press charges against the youth. However, the closest police officer was an hour-and-a-half away. More important than compensation for her loss was preserving the relationship the society depended on—what Devin Kunzler recognized, "you knew everybody, and you knew what was going on in their lives." The ranch wife knew that shivarees occurred on special occasion like marriages that created a liminal period—time out of time. Layne Palmer compares the suspension of social rules during shivarees to the only other time it is permitted in the community—Halloween. Shivaree pranks were the tricks, and the communal meal in Park Valley was the treat. The ingredients for the meal were confiscated from homes throughout the valley. When chicken coops didn't supply meat and eggs, shivariers raided pantries and refrigerators for their meal. In this way, the rural society controls the consumption of the community—what was served during that impromptu performance was produced or stored on the homestead.

After Rud and Letitia Palmer's escapade with the little wiener pig on the dance floor, they headed out for their little log cabin in a canyon near the Century Gold Mine. Trying to avoid further pranks, the couple turned off their headlights as they pulled away from the festivities that night, hoping darkness would cover their route up the mountain. When they reached the cabin, they looked back down and saw a string of carlights from the partiers following them up the canyon. They realized that the shivariers could hear the squeals from their new little companion in the back seat. Rud knew what was in store for the newlyweds since he had been involved (probably as the instigator) in other shivarees, which could include something as simple as being dressed up in their spouses clothes, to other more threatening pranks like kidnapping and separating the spouse to opposite ends of the valley for the night. He took his new wife by the hand and said, "C'mon, we're going to surprise those people. We're going to fool them." Still dressed in their wedding attire, they climbed the steep hill behind the cabin and hunkered down behind the sagebrush. With the pig still squealing in the back of the car, they watched the shivariers light their lanterns and search the cabin. When they realized they'd been fooled, some of the men in the group hollered up,

"Yeah, we know you're up on the side of the hill."

"We can't see ya'."

"Come on down and be good sports."

Eventually, the couple gave up and walked on down to greet the shivariers. The event wasn't considered complete until they shared a meal together. The group provided the couple with some chickens to prepare a late dinner for the party. Older members of the community remember that newlyweds on other occasions were required to butcher the chickens and pluck feathers, then the pots were brought out to either scald or fry the poultry for supper.

Items that were available for shivarees were part of the consumption process. Just as food is thought of as a "process of production—or better, construction . . . reproducing or constructing life on all levels," it has the same effect on the community (Marshall 70). Holly Carter and her husband Jay were not shivaried—they escaped. They told everybody they had to leave immediately after their wedding reception because they were going to a concert. After the show they snuck back to the valley without telling anyone and stayed in his grandfather's completely vacant home. Holly remembers that by the next day, they had to go knocking on a neighbor's door and ask her to feed them. Being newlyweds, they hadn't set up house and so, their pantry was as empty as the house. The isolation of the community prevented them from running to the store for groceries, or to McDonald's for a Big Mac. Other couples remembered that after being directed to fix the meal at the end of the shivaree, they were almost immediately invited to sit down and enjoy a little more time with their "guests" while the shivariers cooked the food. The meal served at the end of shivarees gave the community an opportunity to share the newlywed's first meal in the valley together. They were "breaking bread."

Margaret Visser offered the richest function for food found in Park Valley's shivarees. She affirms that sharing food goes beyond just providing physical nutrition; it helps us understand "kinship systems (who belongs with whom; which people eat together) . . . . Breaking bread and sharing it with friends means friendship itself, and also trust, pleasure, and gratitude in the sharing. Bread as a particular symbol, and food in general, becomes, in the actual bond which unites us" (1–3). The etymology of companion literally means "'bread fellow, messmate,' from Lain *com-* 'with' + *panis* 'bread'." Regardless of what was served in Park Valley shivarees, it represented consumption, or assimilation into the body of the community. It became an event where friends provided and shared the couple's first meal together. It functioned as a rite of incorporation into that community.

Works Cited

"Companion." *Online Etymology Dictionary.* Web. 7 May 2013.

Greenhill, Pauline. *Make the Night Hideous: Four English-Canadian Charivaries, 1881-1940.* Canada: University of Toronto Press, 2010. Print.

Johnson, Loretta T. "Charivari/Shivaree: A European Folk Ritual on the American Plains." *Journal of Interdisciplinary History* 20:3 (Winter, 1990). 371-387. *JSTOR.* 3 April 2011. Web. 3 April 2011.

Kunzler, Devin. Personal Interview. 9 August 2012.

Palmer, Layne Russell. Personal interview. 23 Oct. 2011.

Marshall, David. "Food as Ritual, Routine or Convention." *Consumption Markets and Culture* 8.1 (Mar. 2005): 69-85. Web. 18 Apr. 2013.

Visser, Margaret. *The Rituals of Dinner: The Origins, Evolution, Eccentricities, and Meaning of Table Manners.* New York: Grove Weidenfeld, 1991. Print.

EXPLORE: The shivaree is described as occurring in a *liminal* time period, meaning a time when the people involved are "betwixt and between" two states—in this case, between single and married. What other customs can you think of that also deal with liminal states of being, where people, events, or places are in between two states? How do those examples include "carnivalesque" elements?

RESEARCH: Shivarees date back to medieval times. What can you learn about the older forms of the shivaree? How, if at all, does it connect to the events described here?

VIEWING: Visit http://www.danjunot.com/SDOWN/GALLERY_page.htm and view the painting of a traditional Cajun shivaree. How does the depicted event compare to the events described as taking place in Park Valley, Utah?

WRITE: Describe the food that is traditionally present at one of your favorite holiday celebrations. (It doesn't matter whether the food is home-cooked or ordered as takeout; both can be traditional.) Remember the folklorist's interest in *context*: go beyond simply listing the foods that your chosen holiday involves and get into the deeper description of where, when, and with whom the food traditions take place (Is it *grandpa's* mashed potatoes, or can anyone make them? Who typically hosts the celebration? Does everyone cook together, or do only some people cook? What do the people who aren't cooking do while food is being prepared? Do you think these foods are unique to your experience, or does everyone eat something similar? Which food absolutely *must* be present?)

Recipe: Grandma's Ginger Crumb Cake

"The recipe originated with the James family. Min, or Menah Callahan James, apparently passed it on to Grandma—possibly through Grandpa. It traveled to Utah with one of the Mormon immigrant families from Norway or England. Min's Callahan family was some of the first settlers in the Rosette area, just a few miles from where Grandma and Grandpa ultimate built their ranch. So to say this was an old family recipe really does apply here. Those who lived and worked together shared this favorite with each other. It was evidence of their bonds and the frugal, self-reliant lifestyle they lived. It belonged to the community clan."

—Rosa Palmer Thornley

Barn Stars and Hex Signs

Artwork and yard decoration fall into a category of folklore known as material culture. Unlike the more ephemeral forms of folklore like stories, customs, and beliefs, material culture solidifies tradition, making it tangible and giving it objective presence. Even when no people are present, elements of material culture can communicate cultural and social meanings all by themselves (unlike a spoken story, which doesn't remain behind once the storyteller has left). Of course, there's a danger in reading too much into the folk art or folk objects of a group of people that we can't talk to. The short article below highlights the dangers of outsiders making interpretations about another group's expressive material culture.

FIGURE 10.1. An example of traditinal hex signs from Pennsylvania. Courtesy of Patrick J. Donmoyer, Pennsylvania German Cultural Heritage Center, Kutztown University.

David Fooks, The History of Pennsylvania's Barn Stars and Hex Signs

Barn stars and hex signs—nothing could be a more recognizable symbol of the Pennsylvania Dutch, nor be more clouded in mystery. The terms "barn star" and "hex sign" are frequently used interchangeably when describing the circular designs the Pennsylvania Dutch painted on their barns. These designs were usually about four feet in diameter and frequently contained a six, eight, or twelve-pointed star within the circle. They could be simple or elaborate designs and were almost always colorful. Frequently, designs seemed to be unique to certain geographic areas. . . .

Wallace Nutting's tour book, *Pennsylvania Beautiful*, contained the first suggestion that these barn stars had some sort of superstitious significance. This began a spate of conjecture and folktales concerning the superstitious symbolism represented by these designs. This book is also responsible for the beginning of the use of the term "hex sign" to describe the barn stars. Nowhere in historical records or extensive research has there been any credible evidence found to suggest any superstitious symbolism prior to Mr. Nutting's book. In fact, it seems the stars were painted primarily to beautify the barn, a practice the Pennsylvania Dutch exercised with most of their possessions. . . .

The oldest known graphic evidence of barn stars was a drawing in an 1872 calendar featuring a Pennsylvania Dutch farmstead complete with barn and painted stars. The earliest recorded interview relating to barn stars in search of empirical evidence was an interview with a barn star painter who had memories of painting stars just after the Civil War.

The stars have provoked much interest about their folk meanings and the superstitious power they are attributed as having. Harry Adam, the oldest living known barn painter was asked if he painted specific signs for a specific purpose, or even if he was ever requested to paint specific signs for specific reasons. Harry laughed and claimed all of the superstition concerning the stars was just nonsense. "The only times I was ever asked to do anything specific was when people would ask me to do something nicer than what was on their neighbor's barns/' . . .

Research indicates the practice of painting star designs on barns originated in Berks County, and evidence has been found dating this practice back as far as to possibly the late 1700s. The designs were painted directly onto the siding of the barn—a practice that started before paint became commercially available in the region. It was originally thought that barns of that era were not painted. Recent research, however, indicates that the farmers in the area may have been very adept at making their own linseed oil-based paints at a very early time. Frugal Pennsylvania Dutch farmers may well have been painting their barns as a preservative long before the rest of the nation picked up on this practice. As much trouble as it may have been to mix paint, it would have been much easier than replacing the barn siding every 20 to 30 years. The main ingredient was linseed oil, milled from flax. The linseed oil would then be boiled along with herbs that were thought to help with the drying. Iron oxide was an additional ingredient found in soil deposits throughout the region. This gave the paint its distinctive "Barn Red" color. Three coats were used with the final coat having varnish mixed with it. This formula created a most durable paint. Colors such as yellow, blue, black, and white were mixed in the same process with different natural coloring agents and were used not only on furniture and interiors of the houses but on barn stars as well. . . .

The hex sign has become an ambassador, so to speak, of our Pennsylvania Dutch culture. Representing the myth of Pennsylvania Dutch superstitions through the use of gaudy color, native designs, and stories of the symbolic power held within the sign, the public finds the hex sign irresistible. The interest and curiosity sparked by the hex sign stimulates hundreds of thousands of people every year to search for more information about the Pennsylvania Dutch. The superstitious stories of the hex sign are a myth, a fabrication—a joke, if you will, in an effort to market a local product by a canny Pennsylvania Dutchman. Inspired by all of the wrong reasons, they nonetheless create interest and curiosity in the outside world. It is our job to present the correct and honest story of the Pennsylvania Dutch culture to these curious people once they come to us for information.

The first hex sign was made in 1950 at the Kutztown Folk Festival. Milton Hill, a barn star painter from Berks County, was painting four foot barn stars on large wall sections built for his demonstration. Many visitors expressed the desire to be able to take these designs home with them. Dr. Alfred Shoemaker, the Festival Director, had a carpenter cut out circles of plywood, and Mr. Hill started painting his barn stars on these circles and selling them to the tourists. By the end of the 1950 Festival, he had found interest in numerous sizes as well as a variety of designs. . . .

Although hex sign painting may have begun with misleading and commercial motives, there is no doubt that it has established itself as a unique, indigenous, American folk art, exhibiting high quality workmanship and unique artistic styles. Considering the first hex sign was made in 1950, this makes hex sign painting the most recent recognized form of indigenous American Folk Art.

EXPLORE: Have you ever encountered barn stars or hex signs on local buildings? If not, what other kind of traditional decorations do people in your region use on their homes or outbuildings? What about yard art in general? Many people in rural areas create objects like bottle trees, shoe fences, and homemade mailboxes to express their individuality. Are you familiar with any examples? What can you learn about the people behind these creations simply by examining the objects or art?

FIELD TRIP: Do you have barn or yard art where you live? What does it look like? Consider photographing and then writing a description.

RESEARCH: So-called hex signs have been a source of misunderstanding for the Pennsylvania Dutch for some time now. Can you dig up any other examples of cultural iconography or customary behavior that is similarly misunderstood or misrepresented by outsiders?

Weather Lore

Superstitions often take the form of cause and effect, and can be either descriptive (meaning that they explain what *will* happen) or proscriptive (meaning that they tell you what to do to *make* something happen). In times of uncertainty, superstitions can provide a sense of control, and a reason to move forward with one decision over another.

Dew on grass in morning: :no rain today

Snapping turtle crossing road: will rain within three days

Red sky at sunset: pretty clear day tomorrow

Ring around the moon: will rain within three days

Crescent moon turned up: no rain

Crescent moon turned down: rain

Rain on Easter Sunday: will rain every Sunday for seven Sundays

Lots of nuts and acorns: bad winter, Mother Nature is providing for the animals.

Dark wooly worms crossing road in fall: bad winter

Break a ripe persimmon pit in fall: spoon means lots of snow, knife means very cold, and fork mild winter

Thunder in January, frost on that day in May

Plant corn when hickory leaves are as big as a squirrel's ear

Old blind sow found an acorn: unexpected stroke of luck

Chickens stay out in a rain if it is going to rain all day

Working with Animals

When groups of people cannot access or choose not to access institutions for their information or assistance, they rely on folk culture to get by. We do this when we suffer from the common cold and treat it with chicken soup and a day home from school or work; Irish farmers, as described by veterinarian Michael Doherty, do it when they need to identify and treat their animals' ailments. Folk medicine is often contrasted with contemporary biomedicine as a backwards way to approach "scientific" issues, but many people have had great success with their traditional beliefs and rituals as treatment for specific conditions. Ever tried to cure a wart with duct tape? It works! Even in regions and cultures where people have ready access to medical professionals, folklorists have found that traditional approaches to health and wellness are often used in conjunction with more institutional scientific methods. [Original formatting has been retained.]

The Folklore of Cattle Diseases: A Veterinary Perspective, by Michael L. Doherty

Introduction

Patrick Logan in his *Irish Country Cures*, stated, "Veterinary folklore is almost forgotten . . . today, if a farmer has a sick cow, he is certain to consult a veterinary surgeon. A review of the veterinary literature in Europe reveals that there has been little research in veterinary folklore. Only a few brief papers have been published in the area, including a communication on the folklore of animal diseases in Turley and the Balkan countries. There have been no previous studies of veterinary folklore in Ireland. The purpose of the present investigation was to establish the experience of the veterinary profession of folk custom and belief as it applies to diseases of cattle in Ireland. Its objective was to record living folklore as well as drawing on experiences of the past. There were two components to the study: information was gathered on the local terminology for diseases as well as on traditional cures for specific conditions. The terminology for an animal disease can tell us something about its place in folk memory and this terminology is inextricably linked with the history of the disease itself.

Folk Cures

Q. 1 Have you ever encountered the practice of 'turning the sod' for the treatment of interdigital necrobacillos in cattle?

Fig. 3 illustrates the regional distribution of reports by veterinarians of the folk practice of 'turning the sod' (referred to as 'turning the scraw' [Ir. *scraith*] in parts of county Offaly). Reports were received that the custom is currently practised in counties Tyrone, Cavan, Offaly, Westmeath and Meath. A Kildare veterinarian noted that the practice was widespread in that county in the 1950s but that it waned with the advent of sulphonamides in practice. Reports of 'turning the sod' being performed between 15 and 20 years ago were provided by veterinarians in counties Derry and Laois. The details of how the procedure is performed vary from region to region, as illustrated from the following selected descriptions by veterinarians of current practices that they have observed.

County Down: 'A sod is dug out or sometimes torn out with the aid of the owner's boot and turned upside down in the name of the Father, the Son and the Holy Ghost. This is done often in the south Armagh area and beyond and extends across the religious beliefs'.

Figure 3. Distribution of the custom of treating interdigital necro-
bacillosis by "turning the sod."

County Offaly: 'A animal that has foul is watched were it walks. Then, using a spade the impression made on the soil by the affected foot is dug out and turned over'

County Meath: 'The animal with foul is watched, the imprint made by the lame foot is identified, a circle is cut round this with a penknife and then the inner core of this circle cut out with the knife. The sod is then taken to the perimeter of the field and thrown out; a prayer is said, sometimes the 'Hail Mary'. The sod may be thrown onto a whitethorn bush'. Plates 4 (a) and (b) show Mr. John McDonnell 'turning the sod' on his farm at Rosnaree, Slane, county Meath in August 1997. An outer circle is initially cut in the sod (a) and then the inner core is removed (b).

Plate 4a. 'Turning the sod.'

Plate 4b. 'Turning the sod.'

Q. 2 Have you ever encountered the practice of using people with the 'the cure for bleeding' in cases of haemorrhage/babesiosis in cattle? Do you know of any prayers or charms which were/are used to cure 'bleeding'?

Fig. 5 illustrates the widespread regional distribution of reports by veterinarians of the folk cures for bleeding. Reports revealed the practice to be still in use in counties Antrim, Tyrone, Cavan, Fermanagh, Armagh, Monaghan, Donegal, Sligo, Offaly, Westmeath, Meath, Carlow and Wicklow. Reports were also received that this practice was used in counties Tipperary and Kildare up to 20 years ago. Details of how the procedure was and is performed vary from region to region, as illustrated by the following descriptions:

Counties Armagh, Fermanagh: 'I don't think prayers were involved, just notification of the person with the cure in the following cases:

    (i)   after dehorning cattle—mention the incident to the person with the cure (county Armagh)

    (ii)   Redwater cases: send for the vet but also tell the neighbor with the cure (county Armagh)

    (iii) Very large haematoma in dairy cows: neighbour with cure was informed-cattle improved (county Fermanagh)'.

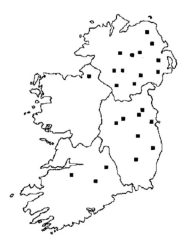

Figure 5. Distribution of the custom of curing bleeding in cattle by distance-healing.

County Tyrone: 'I was working in the Cookstown area of county Tyrone in 1989–1990. On getting a call to a haemorrhage case usually after calving, the farmer would ring a local woman immediately who was said to have the cure for bleeding. She required some description of the cow, colour, breed, location etc. By the time the vet arrived at the farm the bleeding was invariably under control'.

'Like most things in Northern Ireland, there are both Protestant and Catholic charms. However, in an urgent case, the religion of the charmer is deemed irrelevant!'

County Antrim: 'The person with the charm requires to know the sex of the animal and its colour only. If the animal is bi-coloured, the predominant colour must be given first'. . .

'A progressive pedigree beef breeder always calls the 'charmer' to resolve any bleeding problems'.

County Down: 'The person with the gift was contacted either by telegram or phone or word of mouth . . . I knew of a man, now dead in whose house a trunk was found filled with telegrams giving descriptions of animals with redwater and bleeding due to numerous causes'.

County Westmeath: 'The prayer for the cure for bleeding was "Christ was born of the Virgin Mary in a poor stable in Bethlehem and was brought to river Jordan to be baptized. The water was sweet and the water was good. He commanded the water and the water stopped. By his word and in his name, I command this blood to do the same." Three Hail Marys must be said in honour of the Precious Blood'.

County Monaghan: A cure for redwater from Carrickmacross, was based on the following prayer: 'By the blood of Adam's sin was bought, By the blood of Christ's sin was bought, By this prayer you will understand, That this (animal/pet name if any). Will stop passing blood and Nine Hail Marys'.

County Louth: The identity of the animal and the townland in which it was located were regarded as essential information to the healer with the cure for bleeding. These cures although applicable to redwater are also used for any bleeding problem such as bleeding after dehorning, castration, abomasal ulceration, and post-parturient haemorrhage.

Q. 3 Have you ever encountered the use of garlic in the treatment of recumbency in post-parturient cows?

The majority of reports were of witnessing this practice some 30 to 40 years ago in counties Donegal, Tyrone, Dublin, Mayo and Galway. Reports that this folk cure is still practised were received from counties Derry, Antrim and Armagh. Details of how the procedure is performed vary from region to region as illustrated by the following descriptions:

County Armagh: A clove of garlic is inserted under the skin in the tail region, done in bad winters when animals went down. A man from Carrickmacross still does it in the South Armagh area charging £10-£20 for his services and travelling about in an old red tractor'.

County Antrim: 'The soft part of the tail at the 3rd and 4th coccygeal vertebrae was slit and a mixture of garlic, soot and goose dung applied and bandaged in position. A once common procedure in North Antrim'.
". . . a cow down for several weeks after calving last spring 1999, the farmer asked a man from the Glens to look at her, he incised the tail, and inserted garlic and she was up the next day!'

County Tyrone: 'Not garlic, but an onion slice was placed under the 'worm' ligament on the udder side of the tail root...it acted as an irritant and was probably a descendent of the garlic practice' . . . . 'I have observed a mixture of soot and garlic being placed onto a cut made in the tip of a recumbent cow's tail and then bandaged. . . I have not seen it used for about a year. The cow in question had obturator paralysis and among other things that were tried were mustard blister to the sacral spine and a charm of some kind'. . . .

County Dublin: 'For poor thriving cows, in the dark, approach cow's hind end. Grip tail, incise apply chopped garlic and wrap incision site with red flannel which was left on for seven days, improvement was expected in three weeks' . . . .

County Galway: Known as the *péist*/worm in the tail or *Ruher (rua) péist* . . . a few centimetres was slit above the hair line of the tail and garlic and soot inserted, the skin was sewn over or covered with a cloth...the objective was to get rid of the 'worm in the tail'. . . .

Q. 4 Have you ever encountered the concept of the evil/bad eye or 'blinking' as a supernatural influence in diseases of animals?

Reports that this belief is still held were received from counties Donegal, Tyrone and Limerick. The majority of the reports related to incidents that occurred between 40 and 50 years ago, as illustrated by the following accounts:

County Donegal: 'A stranger can come into the yard and by looking over the byre door can cause a cow to get sick. This cow becomes "blinked". The cure for a blinked cow is to drench her with a dose of garlic and soot'.

County Kildare: 'I was called to a cow with post-parturient haemoglobinuria and the owner's wife said to me, "I don' t care how good a vet you are, no matter what you do that cow is going to die . . . the evil eye has been put on her. I found a smear of grease on the shed door this morning, put there by a neighbour." In this case, the cow was successfully treated using a blood transfusion'.

County Limerick: 'In East Limerick, I had the experience of treating a sick sow. One of the onlookers asked me to go outside the house in which the animal was. I did so and was told that I was

wasting my time that a *piseog* had been placed on the sow by someone unfriendly to the owner, I took no notice and proceeded to treat the case . . . quite often a *piseog* was placed in the form of a curse and the outward sign of such activity was notified by placing a number of eggs in the hay in the haybarn, well buried in the hay, to be discovered only as the hay was being forked'. . . .
County Tipperary: 'Frequently encountered . . . *piseogs* . . . eggs found in the hay, aborted fetuses left on neighbours land . . . one old man told me that he had seen a neighbor woman trailing a hair spancil on his land on May eve—this was designed to cause his animals harm'. . . .
County Down: 'I was asked to certify that I had failed to cure a horse because of the fact that it was bewitched and a solicitor was consulted to establish a case.'.

COLLABORATE: Divide into groups and discuss any traditional remedies that you know about. How did you learn them? Do they work? How do you balance folk medicine and scientific medicine in your own health practices?

EXPLORE: Why do you think that veterinary folklore has gone unstudied? Many people rely on their folk knowledge before they have the opportunity to call in the professionals, so why wouldn't we study that folk knowledge?

EXPLORE: Ranchers and farmers in Ireland have diverse local terminology for animals and the diseases and conditions that afflict them. What local agricultural terminology are you familiar with? How easily do you think someone from a different region would be able to understand your terminology? What value, if any, do you think local dialects have for the populations that use them?

Agrarian Fertility Beliefs

Ancient beliefs and rituals are one type of folklore that usually sounds like folklore to most people—exotic, strange, uninformed, and outdated. Interestingly, many ancient practices continue on into modern times, with or without the knowledge of their original purposes. In the following passage from his famous 1922 work The Golden Bough, *anthropologist James Frazer discusses a long-standing tradition with early roots: the May Pole. Frazer describes how springtime traditions like the May Pole were at one time performed in order to ensure crop fertility and general vitality. If you've ever picked flowers on May Day, you've participated in the evolution of an agrarian fertility ritual that is hundreds of years old.*

The Golden Bough: A Study in Magic and Religion

In spring or early summer or even on Midsummer Day, it was and still is in many parts of Europe the custom to go out to the woods, cut down a tree and bring it into the village, where it is set up amid general rejoicings; or the people cut branches in the woods, and fasten them on every house. The intention is these customs is to bring home to the village, and to each house, the blessings which the tree-spirit has in its power to bestow. Hence the custom in some places of planting a May-tree before every house, or of carrying the village May-tree from door to door, that every household may receive its share of the blessing. Out of the mass of evidence on this subject a few examples may be selected.

Sir Henry Piers, in his *Description of Westmeath*, writing in 1682 says: "On May-eve, every family sets up before their door a green bush, strewed over with yellow flowers, which the meadows yield plentifully. In countries where timber is plentiful, they erect tall slender trees, which stand high, and they continue almost the whole year; se as a stranger would go nigh to imagine that they were all signs of ale-sellers, and that all houses were ale-houses." In Northamptonshire a young tree ten or twelve feet high used to be planted before each house in May Day so as to appear growing; flowers were thrown over it and strewn about the door. "Among ancient customs still retained by the Cornish, may be reckoned that of decking their doors and porches on the first of May with green boughs of sycamore and hawthorn, and of planting trees, or rather stumps of trees, before their houses." In the north of England it was formerly the custom for young people to rise a little after midnight on the morning of the first of May, and go out with music and the blowing of horns into the woods, where they broke branches and adorned them with nosegays and crowns of flowers. This done, they returned about sunrise and fastened the flower-decked branches over the doors and windows of their houses. . . .

On the Thursday before Whitsunday the Russian villagers "go out into the woods, sing songs, weave garlands, and cut down a young birch-tree, which they dress up in woman's clothes, or adorn with many-coloured shreds and ribbons. After that comes a feast, at the end of which they take the dressed-up birch-tree, carry it home to their village with joyful dance and song, and set it up in one of the houses, where it remainds as an honoured guest till Whitsunday. On the two intervening days they pay visits to the house where their 'guest' is; but on the third day, Whitsunday, they take her to a stream and fling her into its waters," throwing their garlands after her. In this Russian custom the dressing of the birch in woman's clothes shows how clearly the tree is personified; and the throwing it into a stream is most probably a rain-charm.

In some parts of Sweden on the eve of May Day lads go about carrying each a bunch of fresh birch twigs wholly or partly in leaf. With the village fiddler at their head, they make the round of the houses singing May songs; the burden of their songs is a prayer for fine weather, a plentiful harvest, and worldly and spiritual blessings. One of them carries a basket in which he collects gifts of eggs and the like. If they are well received, they stick a leafy twig in the roof over the cottage door. But in Sweden midsummer is the season when these ceremonies are chiefly observed. On the Eve of St. John (the twenty-third of June) the houses are thoroughly cleansed and garnished with green boughs and flowers. Young fir-trees are raised at the doorway and elsewhere about the homestead; and very often small umbrageous arbours are constructed in the garden. In Stockholm on this day, a leaf-market is held at which thousands of May-poles (*Maj Stänger*), from six inches to twelve feet high, decorated with leaves, flowers, slips of coloured paper, gilt egg-shells strung on reeds, and so on, are exposed for sale. Bonfires are lit on the hills, and the people dance round them and jump over them. But the chief event of the day is setting up the May-pole. This consists of a straight and tall sprucepine tree, stripped of its branches. "At times hoops and at others pieces of wood, placed crosswise, are attached to it at intervals; whilst at others it is provided with bows, representing, so to say, a man with his arms akimbo. From top to bottom not only the 'Maj Stäng' (May-pole) itself, but the hoops, bows, etc., are ornamented with leaves, flowers, slips of various cloth, gilt egg-shells, etc.; and on the top of it is a large vane, or it may be a flag." The raising of the May-pole, the decoration of which is done by the village maidens, is an affair of much ceremony; the people flock to it from all quarters, and dance round it in a great ring. Midsummer customs of the same sort used to be observed in some parts of Germany. Thus in the towns of the Upper Harz Mountains tall fir-trees, with the bark peeled off their lower trunks, were set up in open places and decked with flowers and eggs, which were painted yellow and red. Round these trees the young folk danced by day and the old folk in the evening. In some parts of Bohemia also a May-pole or midsummer-tree is erected on St. John's Eve. The lads fetch a tall fir or pine from the wood and set it up on a height, where the girls deck it with nosegays, garlands, and red ribbons. It is afterwards burned. . . .

In Swabia on the first of May a tall fir-tree used to be fetched into the village, where it was decked with ribbons and set up; then the people danced round it merrily to music. The tree stood on the village green the whole year through, until a fresh tree was brought in next May Day. In Saxony "people were not content with bringing the summer symbolically (as king or queen) into the village; they brought the fresh green itself from the woods even into the houses: that is the May or Whitsuntide trees, which are mentioned in documents from the thirteenth century onwards. The fetching in of the May-tree was also a festival. The people went out into the woods to seek the May (*majum quaerere*), brought young trees, especially firs and birches, to the village and set them up before the doors of the houses or of the cattle-stalls or in the rooms. Young fellows erected such May-trees, as we have already said, before the chambers of their sweethearts. Besides these household Mays, a great May-tree or May-pole, which had also been brought in solemn procession to the village, was set up in the middle of the village or in the market-place of the town. It had been chosen by the whole community, who watched over it most carefully. Generally the tree was stripped of its branches and leaves, nothing but the crown being left, on which were displayed, in addition to many-coloured ribbons and cloths, a variety of victuals such as sausages, cakes, and eggs. The young folk exerted themselves to obtain these prizes. In the greasy poles which are still to be seen at our fairs we have a relic of these old May-poles. Not uncommonly there was a race on foot or on horseback to the May-tree—a Whitsunday pastime which in course of time has been divested of its goal and survives as a popular custom to this day in many parts of Germany." At Bordeaux on the first of May the boys of each street used to erect in it a May-pole, which they adorned with garlands and a great crown; and every evening during the whole of the month the young people of both sexes danced singing about the pole. Down to the present day May-trees decked with flowers and ribbons are set up on May Day in every village and hamlet of gay Provence. Under them the young folk make merry and the old folk rest.

In all these cases, apparently, the custom is or was to bring in a new May-tree each year. However, in England the village May-pole seems as a rule, at least in later times, to have been permanent, not renewed annually. Villages of Upper Bavaria renew their May-pole once every three, four, or five years. It is a fir-tree fetched from the forest, and amid all the wreaths, flags, and inscriptions with which it is bedecked, an essential part is the bunch of dark green foliage left at the top "as a memento that in it we have to do, not with a dead pole, but with a living tree from the greenwood." We can hardly doubt that originally the practice everywhere was to set up a new May-tree every year. As the object of the custom was to bring in the fructifying spirit of vegetation, newly awakened in spring, the end would have been defeated if, instead of a living tree, green and sappy, an old withered one had been erected year after year or allowed to stand permanently. When, however, the meaning of the custom had been forgotten, and the May-tree was regarded simply as a centre for holiday merry-making, people saw no reason for felling a fresh tree every year, and preferred to let the same tree stand permanently, only decking it with fresh flowers on May Day. But even when the May-pole had thus become a fixture, the need of giving it the appearance of being a green tree, not a dead pole, was sometimes felt. Thus at Weverham in Cheshire "are two May-poles, which are decorated on this day (May Day) with all due attention to the ancient solemnity; the sides are hung with garlands, and the top terminated by a birch or other tall slender tree with its leaves on; the bark being peeled, and the stem spliced to the pole, so as to give the appearance of one tree from the summit." Thus the renewal of the May-tree is like the renewal of the Harvest-May; each is intended to secure a fresh portion of the fertilising spirit of vegetation, and to preserve it throughout the year. But whereas the efficacy of the Harvest-May is restricted to promoting the growth of the crops, that of the May-tree or May-branch extends also, as we have seen, to women and cattle. Lastly, it is worth noting that the old May-tree is sometimes burned at the end of the year. Thus in the district of Prague young people break pieces of the public May-tree and place them behind the holy pictures in their rooms, where they remain till next May Day, and are then burned on the hearth. In Würtemberg the bushes which are set up on the houses on Palm Sunday are sometimes left there for a year and then burnt.

There is an instructive class of cases in which the tree-spirit is represented simultaneously in vegetable form and in human form, which are set side by side as if for the express purpose of explaining each other. In these cases the human representative of the tree-spirit is sometimes a doll or puppet, sometimes a living person, but whether a puppet or a person, it is placed beside a tree or bough; so that together the person or puppet, and the tree or bough, form a sort of bilingual inscription, the one being, so to speak, a translation of the other. Here, therefore, there is no room left for doubt that the spirit of the tree is actually represented in human form. Thus in Bohemia, on the fourth Sunday in Lent, young people throw a puppet called Death into the water; then the girls go into the wood, cut down a young tree, and fasten to it a puppet dressed in white clothes to look like a woman; with this tree and puppet they go from house to house collecting gratuities and singing songs with the refrain:

> *"We carry Death out of the village,*
> *We bring Summer into the village."*

Here, as we shall see later on, the "Summer" is the spirit of vegetation returning or reviving in spring.

EXPLORE: As Frazer points out, cross-cultural springtime celebrations often use many similar symbols—eggs, flowers, green branches, even the participation of the younger members of the community. How do we see these symbols still being used in our own springtime celebrations? What are the symbols that correspond with other seasons?

RESEARCH: Because Western society, in general, has moved away from individual households growing their own food, what folk rituals or beliefs, if any, are in use today in order to attempt to control things like plant growth, the weather, or even general economic prosperity?

FIELD TRIP: Attend a local seasonal festival and pay close attention to the symbols at work. What themes or messages can you uncover from the repeated images or concepts that the festival employs?

Water Witching

Sometimes, traditional practices provide more aid to us than modern innovations. In 1976, Jim Rickards was a registered nurse at Santa Rosa Memorial Hospital, a father of three, and a cattle rancher looking to buy property in Sonoma County. He found a 60-acre ranch that looked promising, but it was reputed to have no water. The following is a partial transcript of an interview, conducted by Lynne McNeill, in which Jim explains how he has used the traditional skill of dowsing (also known as water witching or water divining) to locate water on his and his neighbors' properties.

Dowsing is often done with a thin, Y-shaped tree branch, which the dowser holds in his or her hands (see Fig. 10.4). The point of the branch will dip down toward the ground when the dowser is standing over underground water. In the transcript of the interview, it is interesting to see how traditional (and perhaps magical) practices exist right alongside scientific skills and knowledge in a modern farming community. Jim, now owner of J. Rickards winery, still also works as an ICU nurse at the local hospital and, despite his acknowledged success with the practice, maintains that as a scientific thinker, he doesn't want to believe that dowsing works.

L: Can you tell me a bit about how you used a divining rod to find water on your property?

J: What happened was this. I'd been looking around for a property as a home ranch for my cattle and I found this place, but it had a reputation of no water and no perc, meaning there was no percolation in the soil for septic systems. It was the water that was the deal breaker for everyone, but as a result of that, the price of the property, the per-acre price, was much less than the going rate.

The Brignoles [a family that had planted wine grapes on the property in the early 1900s] had virtually no water. I was told by Mr. Colombano about how he had watched the Brignoles have to go down to the river and load up puncheons [barrels] of water, so the whole area has really been dry for a long time. Don't forget that in those times it was all hand-dug wells, springs, those kinds of things. The Brignoles also collected rainwater, in tanks, for their livestock. But that was all.

So in the 70s I come along and find this property and say to myself, okay, if I put the good money down, in other words, the deposit. . . . You see, I'd asked for permission to perc test it and also to drill for water, and they said yes, if I put down the deposit. So with the perc testing I put 60 test holes out, which was unusual—less than 10 is normal—however I did ultimately find a place that did perc. So I had that part done.

Now the other thing, and this is more pointed to the conversation here, was that at that time, I knew nothing of water divining or water witching, but when I got to this place up here I had a real strong sense that I wanted the drillers to drill *here*. That spot exactly, you know? I had the sense that this is what I really, *really* wanted. And when [the driller] pulls up he says, "Well, can

I do it over here instead? It's closer, it has fewer problems. . . ." And I said, "No, no. I *really* want it over there."

And you know what? He drilled, and he hit water in about 70 feet. And that well was only about 120 feet deep, a really shallow thing. And it was like, holy mackerel, look at that!

So what happened next was, now that I had a well I started building my house, and my neighbor on the back side of the mountain, by the name of Nils Cornelius, he asked me if I knew anything about water dowsing and I said no but that I wanted to learn. He says, "I'll show you, I need some help over at my place." And I said, "Sure—anything."

So he shows me how to do it, with a willow stick. The reason, by the way, that they say you use willow sticks, is because they're water-loving trees, but I think the reality of it is actually the fact that they bend easy.

I went over to his house and lo and behold, the water divining for him was just mediocre, but for me it was immediate and strong. I mean, the bark would shear off in my hands because it would be so strong! And we did, in fact, find a spring. We dug it out and guess what? Of all things it was an old cistern well! It had been buried over the years and it was, in fact, their water source. We fixed it and put it back together again and bingo, they had a year-round spring.

Now Nils had subsequently moved away, and I was talking one time at work, at the hospital with a physician I know, just kind of joking about doing water divining and so forth, and he says, "Well, you know, I have this property over in Knight's Valley, and I'm wondering if you would go out and take a look at it." And I said, "Well . . ."

My traditional statement is this: I'm a man of science. I truly want to believe that [dowsing] doesn't work. I've refined my technique so that I really can't be biased, at least, I don't think so, and I'm always hoping that it won't work, but it does. Every time.

Anyway, so I went over there [to Knight's Valley] and I marked a couple spots and they drilled and lo and behold, they got 30 gallons a minute! And he said, "What do you want to be paid for it?" And I said, "Nothing—you don't need to pay me for this." And so he gave me a case of wine.

Now, the water I had drilled here on my own property was . . . I don't know. It was brackish. Not brackish in the salt-water sense, but it had lots of iron and manganese in it, so it wasn't the best in the world for drinking. So I decided I would take my new skills and try to find another spot.

As I went up the hill, I noticed that there were several ups-and-downs, ups-and-downs, ups-and-downs [from the divining rod] as I was walking straight up the hill behind my house. I got the idea that perhaps what I was seeing was lenses of water as I went up, so the next thing I did was I had a driller come, a side-hill well driller. You know those pipes that run into freeways? Those are side-hill wells. They drill way into the ground that way, and if there's any water there, it'll come out. Some are very productive—*very* productive. A famous one here, down the road in Geyserville, produces something in the neighborhood of 50 gallons per minute!

Anyway, so I get this driller and he starts drilling his well into the side of the hill, and *wow*. Every 50 feet or so as the well went in, more and more water would come out as we're hitting those lenses of water. Pretty soon we had so much water pressure that it actually blew the ground out! Once the pressure was released, it dropped to about 20 gallons per minute of wonderful, really beautiful clean water.

Now, I told you that I tried to make myself as neutral as possible, right? And you know, there's been talk that dowsers will take clues from the vegetation around them, or how things look [to determine where water is]. In order to avoid that what I do is I do it with my eyes closed.

L: Cool!

Well, not so cool if you walk off a ledge or step into a hole! So nowadays what I do is I have to have somebody with me to guide me. If I'm going to go someplace and do it, I'll have that person or somebody else with me to make sure I don't walk off a cliff. Because I keep my eyes tightly closed.

Now the sticks, often, are really, really, well they *twirl* in your hand. Like I said, I hold them so tightly that often the bark is shorn off, and sometimes, if there are little branches and things like that, they'll actually bite into my hands, because I hold that thing to tightly. But remember: I don't *want* it to work. It's not going to slip in my hand. But sometimes they break, they pull so hard. They snap in half.

L: Is that a sign of lots of water?

I don't know. There are dowsers that can tell by the pull how much water there is, how deep, all those kinds of things. I don't make that kind of claim. I don't have that experience.

L: I remember being at your house talking about divining rods and using metal ones rather than willow. What are the different styles? Does one work better than another?]

Some people will use brass welding rods. You know what a welding rod looks like? Well, they use those, and just bend the ends into square handles. Well, I didn't have any of those so I used hangers. Metal hangers. To me, there's no difference, no difference at all in the response. I get the same results, but the only time I use hangers is when I can't find a willow stick. You do need a fresh one, because it bends. With a willow stick it points down for water. With the rods, they'll cross in front.

L: Do you have any sense of how or why it works?

I think it's a thing in some people. My experience is this: some people can do it and some can't. However, if I grab a hold of somebody's wrist, I can make it work.

L: So it's a transferrable quality.

Yeah. Again, it's strange that way. And some people can do it, some people can't. Blaine [the wine-maker] helped me the other day, but his response was fairly weak. I'm not sure what it is. I think you have to have . . . I don't know. I don't know why I can do it and other people can't.

FIGURE 10.2. A dowser at work, from Pierre le Brun, *Histoire critique des pratiques superstitieuses* (1733–1736). Dowsing (whether for water, metal, precious gems, or even people) dates back to at least the early 1500s. While there is no scientific explanation for it, many people swear by it as a technique for understanding the landscape.

 Research: Can you find any scientific explanation for water witching? Is there any official documentation that it works or explanation of how it works? Why do you think the practice of dowsing for water has lasted for over 500 years?

 Collaborate: Pair with a classmate, find a Y-shaped branch, and try dowsing for water on your campus. Does it work for you? Do you feel as though you are controlling the movement of the branch, or do you feel like the branch is moving on its own? Get in small groups afterwards and compare you and your partner's experience with that of your other classmates. Was there anyone who was naturally better at it than others?

Rumor and Legend

One of the most actively circulating forms of folklore today is the urban legend, or, as folklorists prefer to call them, contemporary legends (as neither the circulation nor the subject of these legends is strictly "urban"). As a genre of folklore, contemporary legends tend to reveal a society's anxieties—we see themes like violence, safety, crime, politics, and morality cropping up in the legends and rumors we tell each other. These are all subjects that worry us, and we share, promote, debate, and dispute legends like the one below to both express and reinforce our feelings about the issues that arise. Because contemporary legends are so prevalent, websites like Snopes.com and FactCheck.org (the source of the information here) have cropped up to help separate the facts from the fiction. The original circulating legend is included, exactly as it appeared—errors retained—in many people's inboxes, in the "full question" section below.

Illegal Backyard Garden?

Posted on March 27, 2009

Q: Would a new bill in Congress make my backyard organic garden illegal?

A: A House bill proposes to split the Food & Drug Administration, creating a separate entity to oversee food safety. It's aimed at food sold in supermarkets and doesn't say anything about organic gardening, pesticides, farmers' markets or that tomato plant in your backyard.

FULL QUESTION

Hello friends and fellow citizens,
BEWARE THE FOOD POLICE! HR 875/S425
IT WOULD NATIONALIZE FARMING- DESTROY ORGANICS- EVEN ATTACK
YOUR PRIVATE GARDEN!

I just stumbled on some pretty disturbing legislation coming out of the Congress of the United States. The bill is HR 875 and it's labeled as the Food Safety Modernization Act of 2009. At first glance it didn't seem like much. However, there are several, including exposing some pretty scary legislation enclosed in the bill.
In the midst of the financial crisis, it seems that these initiatives are sliding in under the radar. Many people are not even aware of them—
It is imperative that you look into this immediately and with extreme scrutiny as our heath and well-being are threatened!!! If this bill passes, you can say goodbye to organic produce, your

Sources: 111th Congress, 1st session. H.R. 875.
Rep. Rosa DeLauro (D-Conn). "DeLauro Assails Full-Scale Breakdown of Food Safety System and Introduces New FDA Reform Legislation," press release, 4 Feb. 2009.
Food & Water Watch. Background on H.R. 875, accessed 26 March 2009.
Farm-to-Consumer Legal Defense Fund. HR 875 – The Federal Take-Over of Food Regulation, 13 March 2009.
Farm-to-Consumer Legal Defense Fund. Flawed Food Safety Bills in Congress, accessed 26 March 2009.

Local Farmer's market and very possibly, the GARDEN IN YOUR OWN BACKYARD!!!!!
Things we are finding in the bill:

* Effectively criminalizes organic farming but doesn't actually use the word organic.
* Effects anyone growing food even if they are not selling it but consuming it.
* Effects anyone producing meat of any kind including wild game.
* Legislation is so broad based that every aspect of growing or producing food can be made illegal. There are no specifics which is bizarre considering how long the legislation is.
* Section 103 is almost entirely about the administrative aspect of the legislation. It will allow the appointing of officials from the factory farming corporations and lobbyists and classify them as experts and allow them to determine and interpret the legislation. Who do you think they are going to side with?
* Section 206 defines what will be considered a food production facility and what will be enforced up all food production facilities. The wording is so broad based that a backyard gardener could be fined and more.
* Section 207 requires that the state's agriculture dept act as the food police and enforce the federal requirements. This takes away the states power and is in violation of the 10th amendment.
  The bill is monstrous on level after level—the power it would give to Monsanto, the criminalization of seed banking, the prison terms and confiscatory fines for farmers, the 24 hours GPS tracking of their animals, the easements on their property to allow for warrantless government entry, the stripping away of their property rights, the imposition by the filthy, greedy industrial side of anti-farming international "industrial" standards to independent farms—the only part of our food system that still works, the planned elimination of farmers through all these means.

I encourage you to look into this immediately and help remove this bizarre piece of legislation.

FULL ANSWER

Talk about Internet hysteria. This bill, H.R. 875, introduced by Rep. Rosa DeLauro (D-Conn.), has sparked chain e-mails, blog postings and other exclamation-point-filled rants (like the one above), claiming that the legislation targets organic farmers, benefits manufacturers of genetically engineered seeds, and threatens to uproot backyard vegetable gardens across the country. It doesn't.

DeLauro introduced H.R. 875, called the Food Safety Modernization Act, on Feb. 4, and it was promptly referred to House committees. There's no indication as to when it may be brought to the floor for consideration, despite what some blog posts maintain. The stated purpose of the bill is "to establish an agency within the Department of Health and Human Services to be known as the 'Food Safety Administration,' " which would oversee food safety and labeling in the U.S., creating a single government entity in charge of preventing food-borne illnesses. DeLauro's press release announcing the legislation, introduced after the peanut butter salmonella outbreak in the U.S., said that "FDA would be split into an agency responsible for food safety (the Food Safety Administration) and another responsible for regulation of drugs and devices. This move creates an agency solely focused on protecting the public through better regulation of the food supply."

The bill has 41 cosponsors and has been endorsed by major food and consumer safety organizations, including the Center for Science in the Public Interest, Consumer Federation of America, Consumers Union, Food & Water Watch, and The Pew Charitable Trusts. Food & Water Watch is a nonprofit organization that advocates for clean water and safe food and is headed by a woman who used to work for Public Citizen, the consumer group founded by Ralph Nader. It has posted a fact sheet on H.R. 875 on its site, disputing rumors about "food police."

The legislation stipulates that the new FSA (Food Safety Administration) would set safety regulations for food establishments and "food production facilities" and would be able to inspect such facilities. Its regulations also would pertain to imported foods. The e-mail posted above and others say that the definition of "food production facility" is so broad that it could include backyard gardens. The bill says: "The term 'food production facility' means any farm, ranch, orchard, vineyard, aquaculture facility, or confined animal-feeding operation." It seems quite a stretch to think that anyone's personal vegetable patch would be considered a "farm, ranch or orchard." First Lady Michelle Obama showed no signs of concern last week as she broke ground on a sizable 1,100-foot garden plot on the White House lawn. Organic, of course.

The e-mail above argues that DeLauro's bill "[e]ffectively criminalizes organic farming but doesn't actually use the word organic." We're not sure how exactly a bill would criminalize something it doesn't mention, but the e-mail is correct in that the word "organic" is nowhere to be found. Another Internet posting more alarmingly claims: "Bill will require organic farms to use specific fertilizers and poisonous insect sprays dictated by the newly formed agency to 'make sure there is no danger to the public food supply.' " But the quoted phrase isn't in this bill. Nor is there any mention of chemical versus organic fertilizers or "poisonous insect sprays," or, for that matter, pesticides in general.

The only mention of fertilizers we could find was this, requiring that the FSA create regulations to: "include, with respect to growing, harvesting, sorting, and storage operations, minimum standards related to fertilizer use, nutrients, hygiene, packaging, temperature controls, animal encroachment, and water." The idea that "fertilizer use" would not include organic fertilizers is pure speculation well beyond what the legislation calls for.

Also, organic farming is regulated by the U.S. Department of Agriculture, under its "National Organic Program," not the FDA.

And It Gets Even More Hysterical

E-mails and blog postings claim that the agricultural giant Monsanto will benefit greatly from the bill; some say the often-protested company was the main lobbyist, and still others say DeLauro's husband "works for Monsanto." He doesn't.

DeLauro's spouse, Stanley Greenberg, is chairman and CEO of Greenberg-Quinlan Research Inc., a public issues research and polling firm. The company does surveys. And public relations work. Monsanto was one of the firm's clients. Greenberg is a pollster, not a lobbyist or a Monsanto employee, and he just released a memoir on his life as a pollster to five world leaders, including Bill Clinton and Nelson Mandela.

Also, there is nothing in the bill about "GPS tracking" of animals, as the e-mail above states, and not a peep about "seed banking."

Small Farm Concern

Small farmers, however, may well have concerns about this bill. Food & Water Watch's fact sheet acknowledges that there's always a worry that government regulation of food production will adversely affect small farms, which can't absorb the possible costs of abiding by regulation as easily as big food producers can. "The dilemma of how to regulate food safety in a way that prevents problems caused by industrialized agriculture but doesn't wipe out small diversified farms is not new and is not easily solved," the site says. It goes on to say that other bills, not H.R. 875, that have been introduced could create problems for small operations, such as one that requires electronic record-keeping and registration fees with the FDA.

Another group called the Farm-to-Consumer Legal Defense Fund, which supports "sustainable farming and direct farm-to-consumer transactions," raises several concerns about DeLauro's legislation and how it could affect small farms and in particular, producers of raw milk, which the FDA has declared to be unfit for consumption. But the group states that "much of what has circulated the internet is not accurate," and nowhere in its criticism of the legislation does it say organic farming would be outlawed or home gardeners would face regulations.

We suppose in the grand realm of all that's possible, or more likely a futuristic B movie, federal bureaucrats could decide that public safety calls for inspections of every backyard garden in the nation, leading everyday citizens to surreptitiously cultivate tomato plants in a closet with a sunlamp, lest they get busted by the cops. But we kinda doubt it.

—by Lori Robertson
Full disclosure: The author has an organic vegetable garden.

EXPLORE: What societal anxieties are being expressed or represented in this legend? Why do you think the legend continues to circulate despite being almost entirely untrue? Are there any symbolic or metaphorical truths depicted here instead? Legends often incorporate and perpetuate stereotypes; this is one of the reasons that they are so pernicious—they often match up with what people expect or assume to be true. What stereotypes are reflected in this legend?

RESEARCH: Search online to find other actively circulating urban legends. Had you heard any of them before? We often don't initially hear legends as legends—they are presented to us as "news" or "inside information." Can you find any legends that you didn't realize were legends? Why did you find them believable?

WRITE: Compose an e-mail that you think might make a good urban legend. Choose a topic that's currently on people's minds and create a provocative message about it. What qualities does your e-mail need to feature in order to get your rumor or legend circulating? What balance of provocation and believability is needed to get people to pass along your message? Share your e-mail with a classmate and see if they feel you have created something plausible.

❧ CHAPTER ELEVEN ❧

Farms, Food, and Film

In this chapter, you will read about farms and food and farms and film, and you'll be asked to write about food as well as a film. At first, the pairing of food and film may seem an odd choice, but many of the documentary films about farming focus on food.

Food in Literature

Literature is filled with wonderful scenes that feature food. Nora Ephron writes compellingly about the power of the lowly spud in *Heartburn* (1983), the barely fictionalized story of her marriage to Watergate reporter Carl Bernstein. When she's in love, then it's *Potatoes Anna*, a dish that takes much labor and is perfect for just two people. But when there's a romantic breakup, the only food that will make Rachel, the protagonist, feel better is mashed potatoes. Each chapter of the novel tells a story but also includes a recipe that exemplifies the theme.

> Nothing like mashed potatoes when you're feeling blue. Nothing like getting into bed with a bowl of hot mashed potatoes already loaded with butter, and methodically adding a thin cold slice of butter to every forkful. The problem with mashed potatoes, though, is that they require almost as much hard work as crisp potatoes, and when you're feeling blue the last thing you feel like is hard work. Of course, you can always get someone to make the mashed potatoes for you, but let's face it: the reason you're blue is that there *isn't* anyone to make them for you. As a result, most people do not have nearly enough mashed potatoes in their lives, and when they do, it's almost always at the wrong time.
>
> For mashed potatoes: Put 1 large (or 2 small) potatoes in a large pot of salted water and bring to a boil. Lower the heat and simmer for at least 20 minutes, until tender. Drain and place the potatoes back in the pot and shake over low heat to eliminate excess moisture. Peel. Put through a potato ricer and immediately add 1 tablespoon heavy cream and as much melted butter and salt and pepper as you feel like. Eat immediately. Serves one.

Ephron's love affair with food is perhaps most apparent in the film *Julie & Julia* (2009), a film that she wrote and directed that features parallel stories of a food blogger and the chef who changed the way America eats—Julia Child.

For nonfiction focused on food, no one can touch Calvin Trillin, called the "Walt Whitman of American eats," who writes eloquently about food, whether that is the "chicken wars" between Chicken Mary's and Chicken Annie's south of Kansas City or crayfish at Breauxbridge, Louisiana. His three food books—*American Fried; Alice, Let's Eat;* and *Third Helpings*—form what is known as *The Tummy Trilogy*. No pretentious restaurants for him—which he satirizes as *La Maison de la Casa*

Continental Cuisine; show him the best roadhouse barbecue in the region, and he's happy. In his *Feeding a Yen,* a collection of essays that had been published in *The New Yorker,* where he is a staff writer, he ponders how he can get one of his favorite dishes, *posole,* to Manhattan:

> After just a couple of months in New Mexico, I myself had been inspired to hatch a scheme for creating a steady source of quality *posole* in Manhattan. *Posole* is made by boiling corn kernels in a lime solution (lime as in limestone, not lime as in the juice you have in the Margaritas you drink while you're waiting for your *posole*) and then drying them. It is often served in a bowl as a sort of stew, with the addition of pork or chicken and chiles. It has an earthy taste, and a texture that can make you forget your troubles. In Northern New Mexican homes, *posole* is traditionally served during the Christmas season. My restaurant scheme was based on the desire to eat it every day of the year.

It's always helpful to have a stocked cupboard or refrigerator when reading Trillin as he writes prose that makes the reader smell the cooking.

One mystery writer, Paige Shelton, has used farmers markets for the setting of her series, which includes *Farm Fresh Murder* and *Crops and Robbers.* She also has a country cooking school murder series, which includes titles such as *If Bread Could Rise to the Occasion.* Another series set in Blossom Valley by Staci McLaughlin begins with *Going Organic Can Kill You.* These mystery series indicate how established the farm movement has become. What is the connection to farms in these books and essays? As Wendell Berry puts it, "eating is an agricultural act." Food cannot be divorced from the farms from which it comes.

Farms and Food

Everyone can connect to farms through food. But farms have not always held the allure that they do now. Michael Pollan, author of *The Omnivore's Dilemma* and *The Botany of Desire* says that when he started "writing about agriculture in the late '80s and '90s, I quickly figured out that no editor in Manhattan thought the subject timely or worthy of his or her attention, and that I would be better off avoiding the word entirely and talking instead about

FIGURE 11.1. Bumper Sticker of the American Farmland Trust

food, something people then still had some use for and cared about, yet oddly never thought to connect to the soil or to the work of farmers" (xii).

In the twenty-first century, people are increasingly interested in food: where it comes from, whether it's "real" or not, how much it cost in transport to reach the stores, whether the laborers who harvested it receive a fair wage, if it is grown in a sustainable way. Part of the sustainable philosophy concerns the overuse of fossil fuels and their limited future use. As a result, the distance produce must travel is a worry. Many are interested in eating in a way that doesn't destroy soil, pollute, or treat animals inhumanely. Eating well can be coupled with good stewardship of the planet. Slow Food—the opposite of fast food—is an organization started in Italy in 1989 to honor traditional production methods and dining that emphasize flavor and good food. Process trumps product. If you prefer a garden fresh tomato to a store-bought one, then you have an idea about the meaning of Slow Food. (See this website http://www.slowfood.com/ for more information on the international organization. USA Slow Food has a website, too.) According to founder Carlo Petrini, "Slow Food unites the pleasure of food with responsibility, sustainability, and harmony with nature." Slow Food's instigators felt that fast food meant fast life, the ruination of traditions, and the demise of the family farm. "Slow Food USA envisions a world in which all people can eat good food that is good for them, good for the people who grow it, and good for the planet." As Wendell Berry puts it, "Do unto those downstream as you would have those upstream do unto you." Fittingly, the logo for Slow Food is a snail.

Other food movements includes the work of Alice Waters, chef of Chez Panisse in Berkeley, California, who advocates that excellent dining means eating food that is grown locally in a sustainable way and is the freshest available for the season. That means if peaches are not in season, they won't be on the menu. She also is a proponent of organic food production that does not use herbicides or pesticides for healthier people and planet. In addition to her award-winning cuisine, Waters is responsible for the Edible Schoolyard project in which schoolchildren learn about and grow their own lunchroom food. Children may not realize the sources of their food. Does hamburger come from a pig? Is bread made from cotton? After all, children see that both bread and cotton are white. As Barbara Kingsolver notes in *Animal, Vegetable, Miracle,* some children are surprised that carrots come from the ground dirty and muddy while some adults don't realize that potatoes are an underground crop. Waters also introduced the concept of locally sourced food to colleges, most notably at Yale. Many other higher education institutions have joined in, some sponsoring student organic farms or gardens while others host community gardens for students on unused land.

Many restaurants have adopted a farm-to-table philosophy, originated at Chez Panisse, such as Founding Farmers in Washington, D.C. Also called farm-to-fork or pasture-to-plate, these restaurants purchase as much of their food as possible directly from farmers, helping maintain sustainable agriculture and ensuring the freshest food for their patrons. *Locavore* approaches mean that food is not transported far, saving fossil fuels, and that chemicals do not have to be used for those long hauls. Some restaurants, such as the one at Robert Redford's Sundance Ski Resort, started their own farms to ensure supply and quality. Even farm-to-glass events celebrate using locally grown farmers market ingredients in cocktails. Yet another concept is SOLE food—food that is *s*ustainable, *o*rganic, *l*ocal, and *e*thical. An *ethicurean* is an epicurean who focuses on food produced ethically.

Community supported agriculture (CSA) is yet another idea that promotes the value of locally grown food, whether that is on the hoof, from herb gardens, or foraged. "Real food, real farmers, real community" sums up the philosophy of CSAs in which people buy shares of food from farmers, which assures the farmer of customers and also dictates how much should be produced to meet the needs of those customers. (See http://www.localharvest.org/csa/.) In a CSA, the consumer and the farmer share risks equally. The consumer typically pays up front for a season's worth of goods so that the farmer can concentrate on production during the busy days of summer. But things can go wrong. Floods, drought, or frost may reduce the expected yield. That shared risk is what gives participants a sense of "community," according to Local Harvest, which maintains a directory of farmers markets and CSAs. Another attribute of a CSA is that the weekly basket may include unfamiliar foods—kohlrabi, garlic scapes, parsnips—and the principle of "use everything" means varying what is put on the table. Celebrations include Farmers Market Week in August and Eat Local Week in October.

Other organizations such as FarmAid, American Farmland Trust, and Homegrown.org advocate for connections to agriculture. Homegrown.org is "A gathering place for celebrating the "culture" in agriculture and sharing skills like growing, cooking and food preservation." American Farmland Trust offers its bumper stickers—No Farms, No Food—to alert people to the danger of losing family farms.

In a later chapter, you'll look more closely at the "New Romanticism" of farming, including urban farming and the back-to-the-farm movement. Wendell Berry's essay, "The Pleasures of Eating," addresses how anyone can connect with farms through eating.

"The Pleasures of Eating" by Wendell Berry

Many times, after I have finished a lecture on the decline of American farming and rural life, someone in the audience has asked, "What can city people do?"

"Eat responsibly," I have usually answered. Of course, I have tried to explain what I mean by that, but afterwards I have invariably felt there was more to be said than I had been able to say. Now I would like to attempt a better explanation.

I begin with the proposition that eating is an agricultural act. Eating ends the annual drama of the food economy that begins with planting and birth. Most eaters, however, are no longer aware that this is true. They think of food as an agricultural product, perhaps, but they do not think of themselves as participants in agriculture. They think of themselves as "consumers." If they think beyond that, they recognize that they are passive consumers. They buy what they want—or what they have been persuaded to want—within the limits of what they can get. They pay, mostly without protest, what they are charged. And they mostly ignore certain critical questions about the quality and the cost of what they are sold: How fresh is it? How pure or clean is it, how free of dangerous chemicals? How far was it transported, and what did transportation add to the cost? How much did manufacturing or packaging or advertising add to the cost? When the food product has been manufactured or "processed" or "precooked," how has that affected its quality or price or nutritional value?

Most urban shoppers would tell you that food is produced on farms. But most of them do not know what farms, or what kinds of farms, or where the farms are, or what knowledge of skills are involved in farming. They apparently have little doubt that farms will continue to produce, but they do not know how or over what obstacles. For them, then, food is pretty much an abstract idea—something they do not know or imagine—until it appears on the grocery shelf or on the table.

The specialization of production induces specialization of consumption. Patrons of the entertainment industry, for example, entertain themselves less and less and have become more and more passively dependent on commercial suppliers. This is certainly true also of patrons of the food industry, who have tended more and more to be mere consumers—passive, uncritical, and dependent. Indeed, this sort of consumption may be said to be one of the chief goals of industrial production. The food industrialists have by now persuaded millions of consumers to prefer food that is already prepared. They will grow, deliver, and cook your food for you and (just like your mother) beg you to eat it. That they do not yet offer to insert it, prechewed, into our mouth is only because they have found no profitable way to do so. We may rest assured that they would be glad to find such a way. The ideal industrial food consumer would be strapped to a table with a tube running from the food factory directly into his or her stomach.

Perhaps I exaggerate, but not by much. The industrial eater is, in fact, one who does not know that eating is an agricultural act, who no longer knows or imagines the connections between eating and the land, and who is therefore necessarily passive and uncritical—in short, a victim. When food, in the minds of eaters, is no longer associated with farming and with the land, then the eaters are suffering a kind of cultural amnesia that is misleading and dangerous. The current version of the "dream home" of the future involves "effortless" shopping from a list of available goods on a television monitor and heating precooked food by remote control. Of course, this implies and depends on, a perfect ignorance of the history of the food that is consumed. It requires that the citizenry should give up their hereditary and sensible aversion to buying a pig in a poke. It wishes to make the selling of pigs in pokes an honorable and glamorous activity. The dreams in this dream home will perforce know nothing about the kind or quality of this food, or where it came from, or how it was produced and prepared, or what ingredients, additives, and residues it contains—unless, that is, the dreamer undertakes a close and constant study of the food industry, in which case he or she might as well wake up and play an active an responsible part in the economy of food.

There is, then, a politics of food that, like any politics, involves our freedom. We still (sometimes) remember that we cannot be free if our minds and voices are controlled by someone else. But we have neglected to understand that we cannot be free if our food and its sources are controlled by someone else. The condition of the passive consumer of food is not a democratic condition. One reason to eat responsibly is to live free.

But if there is a food politics, there are also a food esthetics and a food ethics, neither of which is dissociated from politics. Like industrial sex, industrial eating has become a degraded, poor, and paltry thing. Our kitchens and other eating places more and more resemble filling stations, as our homes more and more resemble motels. "Life is not very interesting," we seem to have decided. "Let its satisfactions be minimal, perfunctory, and fast." We hurry through our meals to go to work and hurry through our work in order to "recreate" ourselves in the evenings and on weekends and vacations. And then we hurry, with the greatest possible speed and noise and violence, through our recreation—for what? To eat the billionth hamburger at some fast-food joint hellbent on increasing the "quality" of our life? And all this is carried out in a remarkable obliviousness to the causes and effects, the possibilities and the purposes, of the life of the body in this world.

One will find this obliviousness represented in virgin purity in the advertisements of the food industry, in which food wears as much makeup as the actors. If one gained one's whole knowledge of food from these advertisements (as some presumably do), one would not know that the various edibles were ever living creatures, or that they all come from the soil, or that they were produced by work. The passive American consumer, sitting down to a meal of pre-prepared or fast food, confronts a platter covered with inert, anonymous substances that have been processed, dyed, breaded, sauced, gravied, ground, pulped, strained, blended, prettified, and sanitized beyond resemblance to any part of any creature that ever lived. The products of nature and agriculture have been made, to all appearances, the products of industry. Both eater and eaten are thus in exile from biological reality. And the result is a kind of solitude, unprecedented in human experience, in which the eater may think of eating as, first, a purely commercial transaction between him and a supplier and then as a purely appetitive transaction between him and his food.

And this peculiar specialization of the act of eating is, again, of obvious benefit to the food industry, which has good reasons to obscure the connection between food and farming. It would not do for the consumer to know that the hamburger she is eating came from a steer who spent much of his life standing deep in his own excrement in a feedlot, helping to pollute the local streams, or that the calf that yielded the veal cutlet on her plate spent its life in a box in which it did not have room to turn around. And, though her sympathy for the slaw might be less tender, she should not be encouraged to meditate on the hygienic and biological implications of mile-square fields of cabbage, for vegetables grown in huge monocultures are dependent on toxic chemicals—just as animals in close confinements are dependent on antibiotics and other drugs.

The consumer, that is to say, must be kept from discovering that, in the food industry—as in any other industry—the overriding concerns are not quality and health, but volume and price. For decades now the entire industrial food economy, from the large farms and feedlots to the chains of supermarkets and fast-food restaurants has been obsessed with volume. It has relentlessly increased scale in order to increase volume in order (probably) to reduce costs. But as scale increases, diversity declines; as diversity declines, so does health; as health declines, the dependence on drugs and chemicals necessarily increases. As capital replaces labor, it does so by substituting machines, drugs, and chemicals for human workers and for the natural health and fertility of the soil. The food is produced by any means or any shortcuts that will increase profits. And the business of the cosmeticians of advertising is to persuade the consumer that food so produced is good, tasty, healthful, and a guarantee of marital fidelity and long life.

It is possible, then, to be liberated from the husbandry and wifery of the old household food economy. But one can be thus liberated only by entering a trap (unless one sees ignorance and helplessness as the signs of privilege, as many people apparently do). The trap is the ideal of industrialism: a walled city surrounded by valves that let merchandise in but no consciousness out. How does one escape this trap? Only voluntarily, the same way that one went in: by restoring one's consciousness of what is involved in eating; by reclaiming responsibility for one's own part in the food economy. One might begin with the illuminating principle of Sir Albert Howard's *The Soil and Health*, that we should understand "the whole problem of health in soil, plant, animal, and man as one great subject." Eaters, that is, must understand that eating takes place inescapably in the world, that it is inescapably an agricultural act, and how we eat determines, to a considerable extent, how the world is used. This is a simple way of describing a relationship that is inexpressibly complex. To eat responsibly is to understand and enact, so far as we can, this complex relationship. What can one do? Here is a list, probably not definitive:

1. Participate in food production to the extent that you can. If you have a yard or even just a porch box or a pot in a sunny window, grow something to eat in it. Make a little compost of your kitchen scraps and use it for fertilizer. Only by growing some food for yourself can you become acquainted with the beautiful energy cycle that revolves from soil to seed to flower to fruit to food to offal to decay, and around again. You will be fully responsible for any food that

you grow for yourself, and you will know all about it. You will appreciate it fully, having known it all its life.

2. Prepare your own food. This means reviving in your own mind and life the arts of kitchen and household. This should enable you to eat more cheaply, and it will give you a measure of "quality control": you will have some reliable knowledge of what has been added to the food you eat.

3. Learn the origins of the food you buy, and buy the food that is produced closest to your home. The idea that every locality should be, as much as possible, the source of its own food makes several kinds of sense. The locally produced food supply is the most secure, freshest, and the easiest for local consumers to know about and to influence.

4. Whenever possible, deal directly with a local farmer, gardener, or orchardist. All the reasons listed for the previous suggestion apply here. In addition, by such dealing you eliminate the whole pack of merchants, transporters, processors, packagers, and advertisers who thrive at the expense of both producers and consumers.

5. Learn, in self-defense, as much as you can of the economy and technology of industrial food production. What is added to the food that is not food, and what do you pay for those additions?

6. Learn what is involved in the best farming and gardening.

7. Learn as much as you can, by direct observation and experience if possible, of the life histories of the food species.

The last suggestion seems particularly important to me. Many people are now as much estranged from the lives of domestic plants and animals (except for flowers and dogs and cats) as they are from the lives of the wild ones. This is regrettable, for these domestic creatures are in diverse ways attractive; there is such pleasure in knowing them. And farming, animal husbandry, horticulture, and gardening, at their best, are complex and comely arts; there is much pleasure in knowing them, too.

It follows that there is great displeasure in knowing about a food economy that degrades and abuses those arts and those plants and animals and the soil from which they come. For anyone who does know something of the modern history of food, eating away from home can be a chore. My own inclination is to eat seafood instead of red meat or poultry when I am traveling. Though I am by no means a vegetarian, I dislike the thought that some animal has been made miserable in order to feed me. If I am going to eat meat, I want it to be from an animal that has lived a pleasant, uncrowded life outdoors, on bountiful pasture, with good water nearby and trees for shade. And I am getting almost as fussy about food plants. I like to eat vegetables and fruits that I know have lived happily and healthily in good soil, not the products of the huge, bechemicaled factory-fields that I have seen, for example, in the Central Valley of California. The industrial farm is said to have been patterned on the factory production line. In practice, it looks more like a concentration camp.

The pleasure of eating should be an extensive pleasure, not that of the mere gourmet. People who know the garden in which their vegetables have grown and know that the garden is healthy and remember the beauty of the growing plants, perhaps in the dewy first light of morning when gardens are at their best. Such a memory involves itself with the food and is one of the pleasures of eating. The knowledge of the good health of the garden relieves and frees and comforts the eater. The same goes for eating meat. The thought of the good pasture and of the calf contentedly grazing flavors the steak. Some, I know, will think of it as bloodthirsty or worse to eat a fellow creature you have known all its life. On the contrary, I think it means that you eat with understanding and with gratitude. A significant part of the pleasure of eating is in one's accurate consciousness of the lives and the world from which food comes. The pleasure of eating, then, may be the best available standard of our health. And this pleasure, I think, is pretty fully available to the urban consumer who will make the necessary effort.

I mentioned earlier the politics, esthetics, and ethics of food. But to speak of the pleasure of eating is to go beyond those categories. Eating with the fullest pleasure—pleasure, that is, that does not depend on ignorance—is perhaps the profoundest enactment of our connection with the world. In this pleasure we experience and celebrate our dependence and our gratitude, for we are living from mystery, from creatures we did not make and powers we cannot comprehend. When I think of the meaning of food, I always remember these lines by the poet William Carlos Williams, which seem to me merely honest:

> There is nothing to eat,
> seek it where you will,
> but the body of the Lord.
> The blessed plants
> and the sea, yield it
> to the imagination intact.

Activities

EXPLORE: Wendell Berry in his essay "The Pleasures of Eating" suggests seven ways a person can be more connected to food. How many of these fit you? Would you add others to the list?

COLLABORATE: What foods give you pleasure? As a group, make a list of your favorite foods and then tally them. What are the top three foods that receive the most mentions?

WRITE: Keep a food journal for one week, noting what you eat and at what times. Also note who prepared the food, and if possible, how far the food traveled to get to you. At week's end, note patterns that you see from an analysis. Do you admire certain food habits? Are there any habits you want to change? Did you learn anything about yourself from this recording and analysis?

WRITE: Visit a restaurant that features a sustainable or organic theme such as one that has a philosophy of *pasture-to-plate* or *tip-to-tail* dining. Order a varied array of dishes and then write a restaurant review. Your audience may be users of a website such as TripAdvisor, Yelp, or Urban Dining, or a local or student newspaper. Research the criteria for restaurant reviews before writing yours.

WRITE: Write a textual analysis or a review a cookbook that features a farm-to-table philosophy (e.g., *Chefs on the Farm*). Textual analysis means that you read the words of the book with a rhetorical eye. Is there a persuasive element? Explanations? An awareness of audience? How is the cookbook formatted to be appealing? You may pick one recipe that exemplifies the philosophy behind the cookbook and use it as an organizing principle.

WRITE: Choose a recipe that has meaning for you. It may be one you know from family tradition or from travels or some other memory. Reproduce the recipe or menu at the top of your essay. Some options for reacting to the recipe/menu: 1) reflect on the importance of this recipe or menu in your personal life and its meaning to you; 2) analyze how this recipe reflects a new approach to eating as exemplified by community supported agriculture (CSA), the organic food movement, or another approach; 3) describe how this recipe or menu exemplifies traditions of eating that are not necessarily appropriate for a healthy lifestyle; or 4) analyze in relationship to our overall course theme.

Sample Essay
Guah (Scrapple Recipe)
Source: Sophia Hoehns Taylor Kinkead (early 1900s)

This recipe is made when a hog is butchered. The pork that is used is generally the parts left over that cannot be cut, wrapped, and packaged in a logical way; this includes pig's feet, brains, or perhaps the head—although more on headcheese to follow. The meat is either chopped or ground for the final assemblage.

Recipe:
    Cover pork with water and cook until meat pulls away from bones. Cool. Save the broth.

    Mix 2 cups cornmeal with 2 cups of cold water.
    Put 3 cups of broth from the hog in a pot with the shredded meat.
    Add the cornmeal mixture.
    Stir constantly.
    Add red pepper and sage to taste.
    Put in 9 x 13 container (Pyrex) and let chill and set.
    Can either be eaten simply sliced or fried.

Background information: On a farm, it's important that all parts of the butchered animal are used, what some contemporary restaurants call "tip to tail" cuisine. For my family, hog butchering meant not only the actually cutting up of the meat but also the processing of various parts, such as rendering lard in a large black kettle hung from a tripod over a fire in the yard. Because butchering must be done in fall, we all dressed in our cool weather coats, one of us designated to stir the lard as it boiled with a long wooden stick reserved just for that purpose. I can clearly recall my mother in an old plaid coat of my father's and a cap with the ears pulled down stirring away. Once the fat was cooked, then the chunks were placed in a press. As the pressure was put on the fat chunks, the liquid came out a spout in the bottom, which passed through a clean white cloth as a filter and into a container. Presto! Lard for cooking chicken later in the winter and for making the crust of fruit pies. The leftover pork in the press became cracklings, chewy chunks of pork not to be confused with chitlings (the small intestines of the pig).

The common term for what my family called "guah" is scrapple. This recipe has been in my family from my grandmother's time. Sophia Hoehns Taylor Kinkead was the second wife of my grandfather, he having lost his first wife, Alice Belle to tuberculosis, and she having lost her first husband to a farm accident. Note her maiden name, which is German, and which leads to an ethnic source for this recipe. Scrapple is commonly associated with the Pennsylvania Dutch, who were not Dutch at all but Germans who were confused with Dutch when they noted that they were "Deutsche." Although scrapple in our home was usually fried and served plain, it may be dotted with butter, served with eggs, or topped with syrup or applesauce.

What about headcheese? The difference between Scrapple and Headcheese is that in the latter, no cornmeal is added. The meat is simply taken from the bone when cooked, and then it is pressed into a loaf pan, where it naturally gels, for cutting and eating in slices. I must say that as a child, I had a much easier time eating the entire hog than I would today when my tastes have gotten more finicky, but I am definitely glad that I had the experience of seeing the process from hoof to table.

WRITE: The assignment above asks you to analyze and reflect on a single recipe. In this assignment, you are asked to do the same kind of analysis but on an entire menu. Again, this may be a set of dishes from a traditional family feast (e.g., Thanksgiving or another holiday) or a menu that you found intriguing (e.g., a tasting menu from a fine dining restaurant). Include the menu in your essay. A sample essay follows.

Sample Essay
Slow Food in Northern Utah

In a fall 2006 issue of the Logan *Herald Journal*, a story about a Slow Food Utah dinner held in Richmond, Utah, at Rockhill Creamery, a farm that specializes in artisan cheeses and includes on its websites photographs of its named cattle caught my attention. See http://www.rockhillcheese.com/ for more information on "Hearty cheeses from hardy cows" or visit them at the Gardeners' Market or the Saturday market at their Richmond site.

The menu sounded fabulous. Amateur (but passionate about food) cooks joined together to create a menu that paired cheeses of Rockhill Creamery with a fall menu of Cache Valley products, including honey from Willow Valley Apiary, Lau Family Farm beef, and vegetables from Tveit Gardens in Mendon. I determined at that moment to become a member of Slow Food so that I would get an invitation to the next biennial dinner to be held in 2008. Yes, two years means delayed gratification, but what gratification! I should note that I am a cheese snob. My preference runs to French cheeses, but I also like a good Gouda, Fontina, or aged cheddar.

Was the wait worth it? Take a gander at this menu that appears below.

Do five courses sound like a lot of food? Perhaps not, when one begins nibbling on hors d'oeuvres at 3:30 in the afternoon and punctuate courses with visits to the creamery to see where the cheese is produced and to meet The Girls, six Swiss Brown dairy cattle who produce the milk that results in Dark Canyon Edam and Wasatch Gruyere. Our servers were often familiar: a faculty member in Nutrition and Food Sciences, the head of the Cache Study on Aging. All were volunteers who believe in the maxim "eat slowly, buy thoughtfully." We sat down to first courses and dinner about 7 pm at tables scattered around the lawn, glorified by colorful flowers and bushes. This late in September, wraps were important as the sun went down.

Our chefs, perhaps amateur--although that certainly did not show in the sophisticated dishes presented to us--demonstrated a notable preference for Italian cuisine with *gnudi* (a variation on gnocchi) and *Pizzoccheri*, neither of them familiar to us. In fact, these were the highlight of the meal for us, and it was difficult to choose just a couple with the variation exemplified in the 9 separate dishes.

Dessert, which featured polenta, normally considered a side dish, was served about 8:30 p.m. Definitely slow food, but it was shared with others at our table with good conversation, often about the philosophy of slow food itself: to consume and patronize whenever possible local foods that do not rely on chemical, long-haul transportation, or multiple processing. Instead, this was food often picked or produced that day for immediate enjoyment.

Was the wait and investment in an international organization that promotes serious attention to food and its production worth it? You bet.

MENU
Slow Food Utah At Rockhill Creamery
September 28, 2008

APPETIZERS:

❖ Rustic Torta (stuffed with chard, raisins, walnuts)
  ➤ *Rockhill Creamery featured cheese: Desert Feta*

❖ Arancini (breaded apple-risotto balls, with Slide Ridge Wildflower Premium Estate Honey)
  ➤ *Rockhill Creamery featured cheese: Snow Canyon Edam (Reserve)*

❖ Roasted Pear Crostini drizzled with Slide Ridge Mountain Mahogany Private Reserve honey
  ➤ *Rockhill Creamery featured cheese: Zwitser*

FIRST COURSES:

❖ Heirloom Tomato Sampler: Kellogg's Breakfast, Isis Candy, Paul Robson, Red Pear served with grilled ciabatta
  ➤ *Rockhill Creamery featured cheese: Young Dark Canyon Edam*

❖ Gnudi (creamy cheese dumplings with squash blossoms)
  ➤ *Rockhill Creamery featured cheese: Wasatch Mountain Gruyere (Reserve)*

❖ Pizzoccheri (homemade buckwheat pasta served with potatoes, cabbage & sage butter)
  ➤ *Rockhill Creamery featured cheeses: Young Gruyere & Farmhouse Gouda Reserve*

MAIN COURSE:

❖ Braised Lau Family Farm Lamb Shanks: accompanied by mashed butternut squash, roasted beets & multi-color green bean/red pepper/corn medley

CHEESE PLATE:

❖ Served with cantaloupe, Slide Ridge Jean Louise Chamomile Signature Gourmet Honey, and Saba
  ➤ *Rockhill Creamery featured cheeses: Snow Canyon Reserve & Farmhouse Reserve Gouda*

DESSERT:

❖ Polenta Pound Cake (topped with anise-spiked peaches, blackberries, raspberries & crème fraiche)

Fresh local produce provided by:
First Frost Gardens
USU Student Organic Farm
Cache Valley Farmers

Farms and Film

In this section, two types of films will be discussed: documentary and dramatic. The first is a non-fiction approach while the second tells a story.

Documentary Films

A documentary film literally documents a topic. In that sense, it is like nonfiction. This genre of film may have a more difficult time finding an audience (and funding), but documentaries are increasingly popular. The length of a documentary may vary from a few minutes to time generally allotted to feature films.

With increasing attention to food production, environmental awareness, and healthy living, films about agriculture are in the ascendency. *Food, Inc.* (2008) exposes corporate farming as unhealthy for all concerned; it was a finalist for an Academy Award. *Super Size Me* (2004) traces an individual for 30 days who eats only at a fast food restaurant, gaining almost 25 pounds. *King Corn* (2007) details the odyssey of two college friends who move to Iowa to grow an acre of corn, revealing in the process the extent of industrialization in farming and the pervasiveness of corn, not only as food, but as fuel. *The Real Dirt on Farmer John* (2005) explores how one farmer turns unconventional. *Troublesome Creek: A Midwestern* features a farm in financial trouble, as does *The Farmer's Wife*.

Dramatic Films

A dramatic film is also called a *narrative film* as it tells a story. For instance, the classic comedy *The Egg and I* (1947) features a pair of newlyweds who are novice farmers. Likewise, *Ma and Pa Kettle* films of the 1950s demonstrate how apparent country bumpkins may have much knowledge; the pair first appeared in *The Egg and I*. But farm films may have serious topics, too, such as threats—the danger of losing the farm in difficult economic times as in *Country*; tangled and troubled relationships in *Desire Under the Elms* and *A Thousand Acres*, or natural disaster as in *The River*. *Fast Food Nation* (2006) takes a nonfiction source and turns it into a satirical movie about the "dark side" of American fast food.

Films with Discussion Questions

Documentary:
The Real Dirt on Farmer John (2005). According to the film's website, this award-winning documentary film is the "epic tale of a maverick Midwestern farmer. An outcast in his community, Farmer John bravely stands amidst a failing economy, vicious rumors, and violence. By melding the traditions of family farming with the power of art and free expression, this powerful story of transformation and renewal heralds a resurrection of farming in America."

<u>Discussion Questions</u>:

- The film often visually recreates and reinterprets Grant Wood's painting *The American Gothic* (see Visual Rhetoric chapter for more on this painting). What are the filmmakers suggesting with these references to the painting? Is the film "gothic" in any way (you may want to look up the "gothic" tradition in art and literature to find out the characteristics of this approach).

- Identify humorous scenes in the film and discuss how this humor is created here and how it functions to advance the film's main themes.

- Discuss what the film has to say about the community-supported agriculture (CSA) movement. What are the perceived benefits of being a CSA member? Consider both real and intangible benefits. How do these benefits relate to ideals discussed thus far? As you discuss, consider Farmer John's slogan, "Know your farmer. Know your food."

- John Peterson thinks of himself as both a farmer and an artist. Discuss the importance of "farmer as artist" in the film. How is farming a creative act, and how do our perceptions of farming change when we think of it as an art?

- Discuss the notion of *community* in the film. Sometimes Farmer John is at odds with community, and sometimes he is at the center of a community. What does this film suggest about a farmer's relationship to community? Consider aspects such as John's neighbors, his mother's vegetable stand, and the scenes of violence and accusations. Also consider the symbolic significance of the barn raising at the film's end, especially in terms of the cultural function that barn-raisings have historically served in rural communities (see http://amishamerica.com/what-happens-at-an-amish-barn-raising/ or watch the films *Seven Brides for Seven Brothers* or *Witness*).

- Farmer John's farm website at angelicorganics.com includes a section on additional writings by John Peterson under the titles *I Didn't Kill Anyone Up Here* and *Glitter and Grease*. Discuss these short works and relate them to the film.

Dramatic Film:

A Thousand Acres is a 1997 film starring Jessica Lange, Michelle Pfeiffer, and Jason Robards, based on the 1991 novel of the same name, which won both the National Book Critics Award and the Pulitzer Prize for Fiction. A modern retelling of Shakespeare's *King Lear*, the tragic story focuses on a successful Iowa farm family. When the Cook family patriarch decides to pass the running of the farm on to his three daughters and their families, it sets off a chain of events that reveals dark family secrets and the destructive nature of unbridled ambition.

<u>Discussion Questions</u>:

- Do you think that Larry Cook "loves" the land? What is his attitude about his farm and about the occupation of farming? Does he believe in the Jeffersonian ideal of farming?

- Are farming and the *business* of farming the same thing in this film? What kind of power does farming give the characters in this film? Discuss whether or not that is unusual in terms of what you've encountered in this class before before.

- What kind of a narrator is Ginny? Is she a trustworthy narrator? How would the novel have been different if it had been narrated by one of the other characters?

- Ginny declares, "A farm abounds with poisons, though not many of them are fast-acting." The novel, too, abounds with poisons—both literal and symbolic. Discuss the poisons in the novel, where they come from, and how they affect characters. Once you've discussed how the poisons have affected the characters' bodies, consider how other intangible things have been poisoned, like mind, spirit, humanity, morals, and relationships.

- Discuss Jess Clark's character. Is he likeable? When? What makes him unlikeable? Do his attitudes about agriculture influence your feelings about him? Why does Smiley resist making Jess's ideas for organic farming the "easy answer" to the problems she portrays? Are his ideas about organic methods sound and realistic?

- If you had to describe Rose's character with only one word, what would that word be? What if you could describe her with only ten words—what behaviors sum up her character? Discuss whether you sympathize with Rose through the novel. What actions does she do that influence your opinion?

- The novel and film are set during the farm crisis of the 1980s. How is that timeframe important as a setting in the film?

- Jane Smiley has said that she was influenced in the writing of this book by the Shakespearean play *King Lear*. If you have read and remember that play, discuss what similarities and differences you see with the Shakespearean play.

- Early in the novel on which the film is based, Ginny says, "However much these acres looked like a gift of nature, or of God, they were not. We went to church to pay our respects, not to give thanks." Why is this quote important? What are the consequences of this attitude in this story?

- In the long history of tragedies in this family, discuss what you think was the first catalyst. What was the root cause of this family's problems? While there is one important and heinous sin in their past, is that necessarily the first sin or the first cause of problems? Are there other events or attitudes that set the chain of reaction into motion?

- Read Smiley's novel and consider what changes the director of the film made to the story. Films, of course, typically leave out some of the narrative as a matter of limited time—but are there plotlines or scenes this film left out that surprised you? Discuss whether or not you think the actors were true to what you read in the book. Are there ways that the actors' portrayals seemed different from your ideas about the characters? Are there ways that they helped you better understand the book or the characters? Would you have cast other actors in any of these roles? If so, who and why?

Writing about Films

Writing about a film is in some ways similar to writing about literature. The same elements come into play: themes, plot, character, conflict, structure. A film has special considerations that the printed page does not: lighting, editing, acting, directorial decisions, cinematography, composition or *mise en scene*. Instead of bibliographic information for a book, the film review includes the following information: title of the film, director, date of release, country, and running time. It may also include a brief cast list and note of any awards garnered. An important concept in the film review is a *spoiler*. Generally, key plot points are not mentioned that give away the ending. If such information is deemed essential, then generally *[spoiler alert]* is noted so that readers may choose to stop reading.

The late Roger Ebert is the undisputed master of film reviews, recognized by a Pulitzer Prize in 1975, the first movie critic to be so honored, and the only one for more than 25 years. His reviews seem to come from a trusted friend, and sometimes they exhibit his dry wit.

Review of *The Biggest Little Farm*
by Evelyn Funda

Documentary, 92 minutes, 2018
Directed and produced by John Chester and distributed by Neon Films

The Biggest Little Farm is a feature-length film about the southern California farm that John and Molly Chester buy and restore according to biodynamic methods that emulate how natural eco systems work. John is a five-time Emmy-winning filmmaker who has filmed wildlife projects around the world, so it is no surprise that the film recently won the 2019 Critic's Choice Award for cinematography or that it has been recognized for people's choice awards at film festivals around North America. But it isn't merely visually appealing or yet another film about the back-to-the-land movement's "good life." It is about the messy, frustrating complexity of farmlife that can lead either to perfect harmony or utter disaster. Coexisting with the diversity on their farm is, says John, "a delicate dance" where "the dance might be familiar but the partners are always changing."

The film begins with a flash-forward as one of the major California fires threatens their farm. Molly is frantically packing to evacuate their home while John is trying to move livestock to safety. From the potential disaster of the fires, the story moves back to 2010 and to Molly's long-held desire to leave urban life and live on a farm with orchards, gardens, and livestock. As award-winning illustrator Jason Carpenter's animations show the couple bouncing along on the back of a grinning pig through a picturesque landscape, both Molly and John sheepishly admit that their dream was like something out of a children's book. Think something like Margaret Wise Brown's classic The Big Red Barn.

Their reality, however, begins on a 200-acre neglected, monoculture farm about an hour north of Los Angeles, where the farm's soil is so compacted and sterile that a shovel won't even break the surface. Over the next eight years, with the help of quirky biodynamics pioneer Alan York acting as mentor, they create an integrated system of composting, cover crops, and crop rotation that builds soil fertility. They introduce a wide variety of farm animals whose "poop is our gold" because it reintroduces necessary microorganisms into the soil. With these methods, they transform the hillsides into a thriving "fruit basket" with 75 varieties of stone fruit trees, bountiful gardens, and a Noah's ark full of farm animals. By year seven, they estimate that they produce and sell more than 500,000 pounds of food.

In keeping with a main thread of the film, the animals are portrayed like characters from a children's book, with Todd, their rescue dog, taking the male lead as a wise soul. When a pregnant sow named Ugly Betty arrives at the farm, the Chesters mercifully rename her Emma and allow her the freedom to root through the pastures, overturn her watering trough, and defy pig stereotypes by being a picky eater. Soon Emma gives birth to a remarkable litter of seventeen healthy piglets. When those piglets grow up and are hauled off the farm (to an unspecified but undeniable fate), the void in Emma's life is filled by an unlikely bond (think Charlotte's Web) with a tattered rooster who had been rejected by the farm flock. Aptly named Mr. Greasy, his kinship with Emma is so close that John begins to make jokes that her second litter of piglets resembles her boyfriend in their coloring.

But I did say this was not a simple story of the good life, didn't I?

There is plenty of death and destruction in the film that is handled in more direct ways than the fate of Emma's offspring. After her first litter, Emma gets mastitis and very nearly dies. Local coyotes regularly massacre their flocks of chickens and ducks. Thousands of starlings peck at ripening stone fruit, and in their first year of harvest, they lose 70% of their crop. Finding shelter in the ground cover planted in their orchards, thousands of snails denude their citrus trees. Gophers kill hundreds of their stone fruit trees by eating their roots. Raising over 200 different crops or animals by year four, according to York's eco diversity advice, John nevertheless realizes that "Every step we take to improve our land," John laments, "seems to just create a perfect habitat for the next pest."

But perhaps the most devastating blow is when during that same year, their mentor and dear friend dies from a form of aggressive cancer. Left without his counsel in the face of all of these failures, John and Molly try to make sense of Alan's advice. He had told them it would take time for the farm to create an "equilibrium" within the system of diversity, but then they would be able to farm "without an extraordinary power of effort…. Complexity and diversity all supporting each other" in a "self-perpetuating, self-regulating simplicity." But how?

Activities

VIRTUAL FIELD TRIP: Take a visit to the Rural Route Film Festival; some of its films have farm themes. http://ruralroutefilms.com/

VIEWING AND WRITING: Choose a film to view that focuses on farm as a major theme. Write a review of the film; a sample is provided below. The format of a film review is much like a book review, providing important production information, a summary, and an analysis. Make sure that your focus is on how farms, farming, and farm people are depicted.

Sample Film Review

Wild River (1960)
Director: Elia Kazan
USA
Running time: 110 minutes
Awards: Nominated in the Berlin International Film Festival; Designated in 2002 to be included in the National Film Registry (Library of Congress)

Summary:
The Tennessee Valley Authority (TVA) was created by federal act in 1933 to help modernize one of the poorest areas of the United States and provide electricity. It might be described as a "backward" area with a lack of up-to-date agricultural methods and a high rate of illiteracy. The creation of an abundant source of electricity and power meant that some 15,000 families, many of them farm families, were displaced by the floodwaters that covered their land.

In 1960, director Elia Kazan looked at this massive modernization project through the lens of nature and the environment in his film *Wild River* starring Montgomery Clift as the TVA employee who is trying to get matriarch Jo Van Fleet to leave her land as he also romances with granddaughter Lee Remick, a widow with two young children. The screenwriter adapted the work of Borden Deal's *Dunbar's Cove* and William Bradford Huie's *Mud on the Stars* for the script. It was filmed on location near Chattanooga, Tennessee.

The rich bottomland of the farms that will be underwater are shown sympathetically, and the river and green hills look idyllic—until the viewer sees the tree stumps, which anticipates the clearing of those green hills for the coming dam and its reservoir. The panorama shots give a sense of what will be lost. The close-ups focus on the characters, particularly on the face of elderly landowners such as Mrs. Garth, who is reluctant to leave her farm. It is Clift's job to convince her. The script exposes the conflict between individual rights and the common good. In US law, eminent domain allows property to be taken—even without the owner's consent.

In addition to the themes about wilderness, property rights, and romantic conflict, a subplot focuses on the role of African Americans and the anger of the town when Clift hires them to work on the federal project. Remember that these are the earliest days of Civil Rights, and this is The South.

In the end, Mrs. Garth capitulates, but it is clear that leaving the land will mean her death. Remick and Clift admit their attraction and marry in spite of the fact that he has been an instrument of destruction to the family. One of the final shots is of them flying away with the camera looking down on the encroaching waters that are covering the Garth property.

Analysis:
At the time of the TVA, citizens were probably more willing to accept without question federal decisions such as the creation of a powerful electricity source. By 1960, however, questions had begun to arise about "common good" initiatives. In point of fact, the Corps of Engineers seemed to be on a mission to leave no river undammed. Or, perhaps that is better put as undamned. The actors portray the powerful emotions of conflict and romance in low-key but effective performances. Which side is right? That is left for the viewer to determine, but it is clear the effects on people and land. A later film, *Deliverance*, (1972) about four men on a wild river that will disappear when the dam is finished in Georgia, recalls some of the themes of Kazan's film: conflict of property rights; modernization; inbred and illiterate poverty-stricken communities. A brief scene that reveals a church cemetery being excavated and moved provides insight into the impact of such dam projects. The inclusion of both of these films by the Library of Congress in its film registry indicates their powerful messages of the importance of land and property rights.

A Sample of Farm Films

Documentary Films

As We Sow (2002)

Betting the Farm (2013)

Broken Limbs (2004) about apple farms in Washington State.

Death on a Factory Farm (2009)

Dirt: The Movie (2009)

A Farm Story with Jerry Apps (2013)*:* Jerry Apps remembers farm life in the 1930's and '40's when he was growing up on a small Midwestern dairy farm. The portrait of a farm boy's childhood in Waushara County is told through personal memories and photos from the Wild Rose community. He describes the party-line telephone and the neighbors who listened in on every conversation. In the days before mechanization and rural electrification, the help of neighbors was essential for farming. Apps is the author of several book titles, including these: *Limping through Life: A Farm Boy's Polio Memoir; Letters from Hillside Farm; Rural Wit and Wisdom: Time-Honored Values from the Heartland; Garden Wisdom.*

Farmageddon (2011): Tells the story of families on small farms battling government regulations of their farm products.

Fed Up!: Genetic Engineering, Industrial Agriculture and Sustainable Alternatives (2002)

Food Fight (2008)

Frankensteer (2005)

The Garden (2008), the touching story about a garden established on unused land that brings together a community but then is destroyed by developers.

Harvest of Fear. (2009) FRONTLINE and NOVA explore the intensifying debate over genetically-modified (gm) food crops. Interviewing scientists, farmers, biotech and food industry representatives, government regulators, and critics of biotechnology, this two-hour report presents both sides of the debate, exploring the risks and benefits, the hopes and fears, of this new technology.

A Changing Harvest (2013)

Our Daily Bread (2005, German)

The Lexicon of Sustainability is a series of short films dedicated to defining and explaining terms such as *free range, forage, pasture management, backyard pollinators,* and the *edible schoolyard*. Watch these films and more at this website: http://www.lexiconofsustainability.com/

Heat and Harvest: Impact of Climate Change on California (2012) http://science.kqed.org/quest/series/heat-and-harvest/

The Farmer's Wife (1998), a film by David Sutherland, centers on the passionate, yet troubled, marriage of Juanita and Darrel Buschkoetter, a young farm couple in rural Nebraska facing the loss of everything they hold dear. The film is in three parts and was one of PBS's most popular films on record. http://www.pbs.org/wgbh/pages/frontline/shows/farmerswife/

Forks Over Knives (2011) advocates a low-fat, plant-based diet for healthy living.

Farm Boy (2006)

Food Fight (2009)

Food Matters (2008)

Fresh: New Thinking about What We're Eating (2009)

Fridays at the Farm (2006)

The Garden (2008)

Guns Germs, and Steel (2005): Based on Jared Diamond's book of the same name, the first episode of this film focuses on how agricultural advancement around the world impacted social advancement in various cultures.

Heart and Soil (2008)

Jimmy's GM Food Fight (2008)

Ingredients: The Local Food Movement Takes Root (2009)

My Father's Garden (1996)

The Natural History of the Chicken (2000) profiles various types of chicken owners.

Natural World: A Farm for the Future (2009), is set in Devon, England.

A River of Waste: The Hazardous Truth about Factory Farms (2009)

Rooftop Farm: A Farm Grows in Brooklyn (2013)

Save the Farm (2011)

Sustainable Table: What's on Your Plate? (2011)

To Make a Farm (2013), a Canadian film directed by Steven Suderman (2013)

Troublesome Creek: A Midwestern (1995): An Iowa family restructures their farm during the Farm Crisis of the early 1990s. The story is told from the point of view of the adult daughter who had left the farm years earlier.

Truck Farm (2011)

Victorian Farm and *Edwardian Farm* (2009)

Dramatic Films

Babette's Feast (1987)

Cold Comfort Farm (1995)

Country (1984)

Eat Drink Man Woman [1994, Japanese]; *Tortilla Soup* (2001) is the Latina version.

The Egg and I (1947)

The Informant (2009), directed by Steven Soderburgh and starring Matt Damon, is about price fixing in corn industry.

Kitchen Stories (2003, Sweden)

The Land Girls (1998) and *Land Girls* (2010) are both films about women in the British Women's Land Army. The 2010 film was a PBS series.

The Last Farm, Icelandic 16 minute film (2004) that won an Academy Award.

Ma and Pa Kettle series (1949)

The Milagro Beanfield War (1988)

Rebecca of Sunnybrook Farm (1938)

The River (1984)

Seven Brides for Seven Brothers (1956): Musical film that features a barn-raising.

Sweet Land: A Love Story (2006): Set in post-WWI Minnesota, this film focuses on the romance of a feisty German, mail-order bride and her Norwegian husband as they battle prejudice and hard times.

Temple Grandin (2010)

Wild River (1960)

Witness (1985). The witness to a murder and a police officer hide out in an Amish farming community.

CHAPTER TWELVE

Farms and Popular Culture

FIGURE 12.1. Missouri Corn Palace display in the Palace of Agriculture at the 1904 World's Fair. The "corn temple" structure was 65 ft tall with a dome that was 125 ft in circumference. The temple used 1,000 bushels and consisted of 50 different shades of corn and was often used as a lounge and a meeting place. Photograph by the Official Photographic Company, 1904. Missouri Historical Society Photographs and Prints Collections. NS 20614. Courtesy of the Missouri Historical Society, St. Louis. https://mohistory.org/collections/item/resource:146833

> "I got passion for my plants, and I ain't afraid to show it, show it, show it, show it."
> –Peterson Brothers' "I'm Farming and I Grow It" (parody song)

What Is Popular Culture?

Popular culture is comprised of the ideas, productions, programs, and phenomena that emerge from a culture's mainstream media. Generally considered to appeal to a broad base of the population, pop culture is distinguished from folklore mainly by the means of transmission. Whereas folk culture relies on person-to-person or word-of-mouth communication, popular culture often has the power of mass broadcast or publication behind it. Magazines, television shows, films, posters, even YouTube videos are examples of the popular culture we access on a daily basis. In this chapter, you will challenge your understanding of the word *text*, expanding it to include nonverbal representations. The root of the word *text* is the Latin *textere*, which means *to weave* (this is the root of the word, *textiles*, too). If we think of the cultural products below as weaving together diverse images, contexts, ideas, and language, we can see that even nonverbal culture can be read like a text.

Agriculture at World's Fairs

World's fairs are international expositions that bring together cultures and highlight national achievements. Part entertainment, part display of national pride, and part effort to educate visitor about different cultures, World's fairs typically demonstrate the hopes and desires of their own times as well as offer utopian dreams of the future. They often lasted as long as six months and became popular vacation destinations.

For instance, nearly 20 million people visited the 1904 World's Fair in St. Louis, Missouri, where the approximately 18-acre Palace of Agriculture was one of the highlights. There, various states used their agricultural products with an almost patriotic zeal as the medium for elaborate displays. California had the 12-foot high Great Prune Bear of Sacramento, while North Dakota displayed a life-sized statue of Teddy Roosevelt on his horse sculpted entirely out of butter. As the host state for the fair, Missouri's booth was the most ornate and extravagant, with its 40-foot tall Corn Palace (pictured at the beginning of this chapter); life-size Indian Maiden and Harvest Queen made entirely out of corn, with corn silk hair, corn husk clothes, and clover seed "embroidery"; and a 15' x 35' mural of a quaint farm scene rendered entirely out of corn, grain, and grasses by a French Canadian artist F.D. Fortier. You can see more of the 1904 Fair at http://www. lyndonirwin.com/1904agri.htm.

The 1939 World's Fair in New York, on the other hand, had as its theme "Building the World of Tomorrow." Gone were the exhibits that portrayed the farm as quaint. Instead, the 1939 exhibits did more to highlight industrial, scientific, technological and artistic advancements than to inspire visitors with displays of abundant and beautiful farm products. In response to the *New York Times* prediction in 1938 that in the future laboratories, rather than farms, would supply our nation with "an entirely synthetic supply," the New York Fair included a display of a fully electrified farm, the futuristic "Rotolactor" (a cross between a milking machine and a merry-go-round for cows), and another display that asked "Will the Chemist's Flask do the Work of 1,000 Farms?" The fair's organizing committee stressed that the event's theme should be to "demonstrate that supercivilization that is based on the swift work of machines, not on the arduous toil of men." (See Helen A. Harrison's *Dawn of a New Day: The New York World's Fair, 1939–40* and Eva Jochowita's "Feasting on the Future: Foods of the World of Tomorrow at the New York World's Fair of 1939–1940").

 COLLABORATE: Imagine that you've been appointed to the committee planning the agricultural exhibition for an upcoming world's fair. Keeping the above history in mind, plan out the goals of your agricultural exhibit. What is your theme and creative vision? What exhibits will you aim for and what will they look like? Who will be your audience? Will your exhibits entertain, educate, express national pride, or offer a message about the future of farming?

Crop Circles

From World's Fair events, let's move to a more supernatural look at farming and popular culture. Crop circles, considered both a form of cereal art and possible evidence for the existence of alien life, gained notoriety in the late 1970s but have been reported as early as 815, in Lyon, France. Crop circles are a unique cultural phenomenon in that the farm itself becomes the medium of art, the canvas upon which a design is created.

The following article for *National Geographic News*, written by Hillary Mayell, was published August 2, 2002.

"Crop Circles: Artworks or Alien Signs?"
By Hillary Mayell

Mel Gibson's new film, Signs, is reviving public interest in the phenomenon of crop circles. It would be unfair to reveal what it is that's scaring Mel so badly in the world of movies.

In the real world, the battle to explain the formations is a torrid wrestling match between artists and people who believe in otherworldly influences.

Are the circles an emerging art form: agrarian graffiti, large-scale land art that will be written about in future art history texts as the most remarkable artistic innovation to emerge from the 20th century? Or are they the result of UFO landings or mysterious messages from extraterrestrials?

The most curious aspect of the sometimes vitriolic debate is the fact that each group needs the other.

Depending on what you believe, crop circle artists make most, if not all, the formations. But without the mystery and the otherworldly possibilities, would anyone be paying attention?

FIGURE 12.2. *The Mowing-Devil, or, Strange News Out of Hartford-shire.* [London?] 1678. Title page. Folger Shakespeare Library Call#267-885q. Used by permission of the Folger Shakespeare Library.

Crop Circles' English Roots

Crop circles first appeared in the fields of southern England in the mid-1970s. Early circles were quite simple, and simply appeared, overnight, in fields of wheat, rape, oat, and barley. The crops are flattened, the stalks bent but not broken.

Wiltshire County is the acknowledged center of the phenomenon. The county is home to some of the most sacred Neolithic sites in Europe, built as far back as 4,600 years ago, including Stonehenge, Avebury, Silbury Hill, and burial grounds such as West Kennet Long Barrow.

As the crop circle phenomenon gained momentum, formations have also been reported in Australia, South Africa, China, Russia, and many other countries, frequently in close proximity to ancient sacred sites.

Still, each year more than a hundred formations appear in the fields of southern England.

In 1991, Doug Bower and Dave Chorley came forward and claimed responsibility for the crop circles over the past 20 years or so, and the battle between artists and other-world believers was engaged.

"I think Doug Bower is the greatest artist of the 20th century," said John Lundberg, a graphic design artist, Web site creator, and acknowledged circle maker. Bower's work has the earmarks of all new art forms, "pushing boundaries, opening new doors, working outside of the established mediums," Lundberg continued.

His group, known as the Circlemakers, considers their practice an art. Lundberg estimates that there are three or four dedicated crop circle art groups operating in the United Kingdom today, and numerous other small groups that make one or two circles a year more or less as a lark.

Circlemakers now does quite a bit of commercial work; in early July, the group created a giant crop formation 140 feet (46 meters) in diameter for the History Channel. But they also still do covert work in the dead of night.

Evolving Art of Crop Circles

Formulating a design and a plan, from original concept to finished product, can take up to a week. "It has to be more than a pretty picture. You have to have construction diagrams providing the measurements, marking the center, and so on," said Lundberg. Creating the art is the work of a night. Lundberg said that for an artist, being a crop-formation artist is an interesting place to be.

"You think about art in terms of authorship and signature," he said. But circle makers never claim credit for specific formations they created. "To do so would drain the mystery of crop circles," he explained. "The art form isn't just about the pattern making. The myths and folklore and energy [that] people give them are part of the art."

Over the last 25 years, the formations have evolved from simple, relatively small circles to huge designs with multiple circles, elaborate pictograms, and shapes that invoke complex nonlinear mathematical principles. A formation that appeared in August 2001 at Milk Hill in Wiltshire contained 409 circles, covered about 12 acres (5 hectares), and was more than 800 feet (243 meters) across.

Two phenomena appear to be pushing the evolving art.

To combat a widely promulgated theory that the circles were the result of wind vortices—essentially mini-whirlwinds—crop artists felt compelled to produce ever more elaborate designs, some with straight lines to show that the circles were not a natural phenomenon, said Lundberg. The other impetus is true of all art forms: Artists influence one another, and designs evolve in response to what has been done before.

Crop Circles: An Opposing View

Adamantly opposing the crop-circle-as-art-form position are the "croppies"—researchers of the paranormal and scientists seeking to explain the formations as work that could not possibly be the result of human efforts.

The phenomenon has spawned its own science: cereology. Some believers are merely curious, open to the existence of paranormal activity and willing to consider the possibility that at least some of the circles were created by extraterrestrial forces. At the extreme end are what Lundberg calls the "Hezbollah" of believers.

Exchanges between acknowledged circle makers and cereologists can be vitriolic in the extreme. But in a curious way, the two groups need one another.

The believers propel and sustain interest in the work, beating the drums of extraterrestrial activity on Earth and keeping crop formations in the news. They can also be quite vocal in their denunciations of the admitted artists, charging that they are con men, liars, and agents in government disinformation campaigns.

Lundberg's group has been vilified as Team Satan; its members have received stacks of hate mail, and over the years there have been attacks on their cars and property.

Skeptics in the media (including this author) are also considered dupes, either too ignorant or narrow-minded to understand an otherworldly phenomenon or active participants in a government conspiracy to keep the masses uninformed.

Still, the vast majority of croppies are just people with alternative belief systems.

"I think it's a little more played out over here [in the United Kingdom]," said Lundberg. "People are more familiar with the whole phenomenon."

Wiltshire's New Economy: Crop Circle Tourism

While the relationship between crop artists and cereologists is uneasy, the relationship between artists and farmers is mutually beneficial. Farmers provide the canvas, the artists bring in the tourists. The crop circle season extends from roughly April to harvesting in September, although the best time to make a circle is in mid to late June. When still immature, wheat rises back toward the sun, making a circle look brushed rather than flattened, said Lundberg.

How do the local farmers feel waking up to find an entire field of wheat flattened? Crop circles pump millions of pounds into the Wiltshire economy, said Lundberg. The circles are a major tourist attraction, spawning bus tours, daily helicopter tours, T-shirts, books, and other trinkets.

The circles draw people who believe the formations have a unique energy. They visit the formations as a sort of spiritual Mecca, to meditate, pray, dance, and commune with worldly spirits. Farmers frequently charge a small fee or have a donation box for people who want to enter the circles.

"In 1996 a circle appeared near Stonehenge and the farmer set up a booth and charged a fee," said Lundberg. "He collected 30,000 pounds (U.S. $47,000) in four weeks. The value of the crop had it been harvested was probably about 150 pounds ($235). So, yeah, they're happy."

On the question of whether all such circles are human made, Lundberg is perched firmly on the fence. "I don't care," he said. "I have an open mind. It would be great if people could view circles as an art form. But really, to me, as long as they're well made and well crafted, anyone can believe whatever they want to believe."

RESEARCH: Do a Google image search for crop circles and consider the range of designs and forms that you find. If crop circles are an art form, what do you think they say about the artist and the culture?

Farmers' Markets

The variety of ways to look at farming through a popular culture lens is infinite. Farmers' markets have been around longer than crop circles, but they declined precipitously in the twentieth century. In the past two decades, the number of farmers' markets has grown sharply due to a cultural desire to "Know Your Food, Know Your Farmer" (the motto of John Peterson, featured in the film *The Real Dirt on Farmer John*). According to the USDA, direct sales of food products from farmers to individual consumers rose nearly 50% between 2002 and 2007, and by August of 2013, over 8,000 farmers' markets existed in the US, an increase of 36% since 2008 alone. Writers like Michael Pollan, Barbara Kingsolver, Alice Waters, and Jamie Oliver have helped popularize farmers' markets by drawing attention to the need for a more organic, natural, wholesome, and local food culture.

From The Farmers' Market Book: Growing Food, Cultivating Community
Jennifer Meta Robinson and J.A. Hartenfeld

Based on an ancient hallmark of society, farmers' markets today sate a hunger not calculated in the FDA's recommended daily allowances. They incorporate patterns of community and exchange that feed us deeply. The recent resurgence of farmers' markets nationwide signals a desire among many for a sense of authenticity and locality that is not found in the high-tech supermarket experience. Buying local potatoes with traces of soil from a grower who still has the same dirt on his boots apparently provides a kind of sustenance not accounted for in the latest nutritional pyramid.

Markets may seem at first nostalgic or idealistic, but the props and atmosphere of each come out of the present time and place, as fresh and diverse as those allow. Food assumes the role of the main character, but upon closer examination, we see something less tangible. At farmers' markets, an individually felt, but cooperatively generated experience plays out on a human scale. Different classes, races, neighborhoods, religions, and backgrounds meet to exchange food, yes, and also language, music, recipes, news information, and ideas. In the marketplace, both our dependence on each other and our independence, our similarities and our differences comes into focus. A market creates intersecting trading zones where histories, social groups, and cultures reinforce, share, and challenge. Some of the players arrive as vendors and some as customers, but the exchange goes both ways and through all the senses. Through the purposeful, life-sustaining, and often surprisingly engaging exchanges of the market, people come to know each other as more than assumptions and stereotypes. Eye to eye, out from behind the screens, we take on responsibility and accountability for the stories we tell.

Farmers' markets bring traditions together with current lifestyles. They help us to envi-

> For many customers, a market "symbolizes the city as it ought to be," sharing the mantle of honesty, health, and hearth idealistically associated with rural life. The colors, vitality, and festiveness of the market serve to "glamorize" the produce, as one customer put it, "seducing" customers into buying and into returning. But that should not be taken to mean that a market is all and always good. Nor is it a nostalgic remnant of a simpler time, if that ever existed. Instead, it is a living performance, with all the complexities contemporary life allows for. Unlike the uniformity of corporate marketing, farmers' markets allow for dissent, diversity, contradiction, and conflict. –Robinson and Hartenfeld

sion both rural and urban lives that can be satisfying and viable in the modern world. Growers have one foot in the agricultural methods and know-how of centuries past and the other in some of the most influential innovations of recent times. Some try to wrestle the juggernaut of progress toward sustainability. Some are eager to try the next great invention. Many lessen the vagaries of weather, markets, and health with jobs off the farm as newspaper reporters, medical doctors, janitors, university professors, graphic artists, store clerks, truck drivers, carpenters, language teachers, or any of countless other more reliable occupations. But inevitably, all try to make a place in contemporary society for the timeless concerns of growing produce and husbanding the land.

FIGURE 12.3. Poster from Salt Lake City Farmers Market, 2002. Illustration by Greg Newbold — www.gregnewbold.com

The customers, too, hail from as many professions as nations as the locality provides. Their interest in what they eat and where it comes from is keen. Their quest—for fresh food, favorite varieties, and assorted produce ever earlier or later in the season—drives the vendors to learn more, do more, and risk innovation. Customers may be interested in hunting for their grandmothers' bleeding heart plants or adding to their granddaughter's herb garden. At least a few are willing to try a potent new goat cheese or choose of their looks. On the whole, customers are willing to weave the contrarian pace of the farmers' market into their buys lives.

Market sales are one to one. In 1910, a third of the population of the United States was farmers living on farms. Ninety years later, less than 1 percent work in agriculture, fishing, forestry, and hunting combined. Even among those few, most do not live on the land they work. The trend seemed unstoppable, what Wendell Berry calls a "catastrophe now virtually complete." Along the way, retail farmers' markets languished, until they had mostly disappeared from the United States by the mid-1960s, like family farms, casualties of corporate farming and global food market experiments. Those that did survive presented a hybrid of anachronism and oasis. Since the 1970s, however, the number of people producing food for sale at farmers' markets has grown. By 2004, more than 3,700 farmers' markets were operating in the United States, growing in number by nearly 50 percent during the previous ten years. And some 19,000 growers sold their produce only at farmers' markets. As people find contemporary culture increasingly homogenized, superficial, and rootless, many look to farmers' markets for good food and a sense of community.

Markets present the possibility of common ground for a diverse society. Their very regularity (usually weekly) makes them more intimate and socially complex than other

"Farmer's markets are an important public face for agriculture."

—Secretary of Agriculture Tom Vilsack

public events. While farmers' markets obviously present opportunities for growers and customers to participate in a commercial exchange, something bigger often compels both sides against the national tide of convenience, uniformity, and brand appeal. Take, for example, the Waltham, Massachusetts, farmers' market at which customers line up in an empty lot where a dozen vendors display their wares. On one particular market day, no one seemed deterred by a rather loud band that had set up in front of the brick wall of an adjacent building. The customers, like the vendors, were apparently regulars. At one stand, a blind man stood while his raspberries and lettuce were bagged. His German shepherd guide dog alertly watched a little Pomeranian across the way. As the men began to pay for this produce, he told the vendor he felt he was forgetting something and asked what else she had. She rattled off "arugula, lettuce, onions, tomatoes, soap, and patty-pan squash." Yes, he said, it was the squash he had forgotten and could he get a pound of that. She held out a sample so that he could be sure. He took it in his hands and declared it good. As she was making his change, he commented that he could always find her stall because of the cinnamon in her soap. He liked that smell, he said. He would see her next week, he said, then corrected himself. No, he would be away. And she wished him a safe trip.

Or consider the questions wildly out of touch with how things grow. One summer Saturday, a Bloomington, Indiana customer soberly asked a vendor selling garlic braids how he got the garlic to grow that way; other customers routinely ask a flower farmer at the same market how long it takes to cut flowers to grow roots or whether the flowers of perennial plants will come back the same color every year. Such exchanges are humorous, but they also require special care and respect. Opportunities to teach and to learn, they open conversations that cannot occur in the supermarket aisles over a box of genetically patented mashed potatoes grown and processed a thousand miles away. IN a sense, such questions are crucial ones. How do plants grow? By what human effort? What of their character is attributable to nature and what to human nature? What choices and trade-offs so they represent? What would it mean to make these choices sustainable?

Farmers' Market Posters

Posters advertising farmers' and gardeners' markets are intended to communicate several messages: eat fresh, meet your neighbors, shop local, relieve stress, know the producers, return to heritage, support local craft, and have fun. Artwork ranges from photographs to graphic design—sometimes humorous, sometimes calling on patriotism. Take a look at the representative posters on the next page.

FIGURE 12.4. Posters by New York Farm Bureau, Inc., nyfb.org. Poster photos copyright Larry LeFever, Grant Heilman Photography, Inc.

RESEARCH: Do a Google image search for additional farmers' market posters. What themes emerge from the visual rhetoric of the posters you find?

FIELD TRIP: Find out whether or not your local community has a farmers' market, and plan a time to stop by. Observe what sort of actions and interactions are taking place around you. How do people interact with each other? With the food? With the surrounding city or geographical space?

EXPLORE: Seek out information about farmers' markets in different locales: urban, suburban, and rural. How does the aesthetics of the farmers' market adapt to these different settings? How do the posters for those markets reflect their unique settings, and what do the posters for those markets say about community identify?

The Peterson Brothers' Musical Parodies

Another aspect of popular culture can be found in music. In June of 2012, three Kansas farm brothers became an overnight sensation when their first farm music video went viral on YouTube. Entitled "I'm Farming and I Grow It," the Peterson brothers' video is a parody of "I'm Sexy and I Know It," the 2011 hit by the duo LMFAO. The Peterson parody video was followed in December 2012 with "Farmer Style (Gangnam Style)" and then in June 2013 with "A Fresh Breath of Farm Air," which parodies the song from "The Fresh Prince of Bel-Air." As of late 2013, these three videos have combined total of nearly 25 million views. Watch the three YouTube videos that made Greg, Nathan, and Kendal Peterson famous, and then use the following prompts to analyze them as you would analyze other texts.

Peterson Farm Brothers

WWW.PETERSONFARMBROTHERS.COM
Link to their videos:
https://petersonfarmbrothers.com/videos/
Their YouTube channel:
https://www.youtube.com/petersonfarmbros

PETERSON FARM BROTHERS

The Peterson Brothers' truck features the lyric that made them famous. In front of the truck, pictured from left to right: Greg, Nathan, and Kendal Peterson.

EXPLORE AND CONSIDER: The Peterson brothers' videos are part of a growing "agvocacy" movement, which uses media proactively to represent modern agriculture. Citing specific lines or moments in the videos, discuss the many ways that they advocate for the "noble farmer" ideal. Discuss how the videos are produced (the effects, camera angles, scenery, etc.), and how those elements enhance the "agvocating" effect. Thematically link the Peterson brothers' message to the main ideas about American farming you have seen elsewhere in this class; for instance, do their ideas seem to be in line with those of Thomas Jefferson?

WRITE: These three videos function as parodies. The word parody actually comes from a Greek word that means "mock song." It is a type of literary trope that uses the structure of another work of art and imitates and reshapes it in a humorous way, often by exaggerating characteristics of the original work. To be effective, the original work must be sufficiently recognizable; therefore, it closely engages in a kind of dialogue with the original work's theme, subjects, style, and/or characters. Although having a comic effect, parodies may aim to make a serious point; often they have a political or social message or criticism about significant ideologies or beliefs. Consider how the Peterson brothers' videos fulfill the characteristics of parody by answering the questions that follow.

- How do the Peterson brothers reshape the original famous songs?
- How effective is their use of humor in getting across a serious message?
- What is their serious message? Is there any social or political agenda behind these songs?
- How do their parodies respond to the original content of these song; are they making some kind of thematic criticism of the original content?
- Are there other ways that they are using the rhetorical form of parody?

- In general, what characteristics must original songs have to make them good targets for parody?

COLLABORATE: In small groups, write your own parody song, either on a farm-related topic or on a school-related topic. Then, if you dare, perform your parody for your class.

RESEARCH: The Peterson brothers have given several interviews that can be found online. They have also assisted in the production of other parody videos that you can find on YouTube. Find these and ask yourself if they offer any new insight into these parody videos.

RESEARCH: Before the Peterson brothers made their parodies, another popular series of YouTube parodies entitled "The Meatrix" (2003) won more than a dozen major film and web awards and were translated into 30 languages. "The Meatrix Trilogy" is considered one of the most successful online advocacy campaigns to date. See http://www.themeatrix.com. Watch the videos about factory farms and discuss how they functions as parody. Compare and contrast their approach to the Peterson brother videos. Also consider where this video falls on the spectrum between "agvocacy" and "agvitism"?

Farm Aid

Willie Nelson was participating in the 1985 Live Aid benefit concert for famine victims in Africa when fellow musician Bob Dylan said, rather offhandedly, that it would be great to have some kind of similar aid available for American farmers in danger of losing their livelihoods. So it was that the idea of Farm Aid born. With Nelson's friends Neil Young and John Mellancamp on board, Nelson organized the first of the yearly concerts later that same year. Of special significance was the Farm Aid Concert of 2001, which was performed just 18 days after 9/11. Renamed "A Concert for America," the event suggested that American farmers were cornerstones of strength in the nation's time of need. The organizers were negotiating a very difficult position of seeking funds for the Farm Aid cause while the country's attention was turned toward New York City. Consider, for instance, how well the concert's rhetoric dealt with the sensitive topic, especially in the rhetoric of the transitions between acts or as performers move in and out of the songs. At one point, Neil Young came out to the stage wearing a baseball cap that read "FDNY," the emblem of New York City firefighters. "I just made a new friend backstage," he said. "Jim Lenox from Ladder 37 of FDNY is here, taking his first day off. He's been there since the first day." Farm Aid urged television viewers and concert goers to contribute to the Fund for World Trade Center Green Market Farmers set up to help relocate five farmers' markets in lower Manhattan shut down by the terrorist bombings on September 11. These were just some of the ways that Farm Aid tied the farm cause to the events in New York.

> "Willie [Nelson] said many times in interviews, 'We're not having another concert.'"
> —Carolyn Mugar, Farm Aid Executive Director

> "When Farm Aid was started, it was a time in America when everybody was feeling very charitable—Hand Across America, Live Aid, this aid, that aid. And twenty years later, we're the only people still doing it." —John Mellencamp

> (From *Farm Aid: A Song for America*, ed. by Holly George-Warren)

For more on Farm Aid and the 2001 concert, see the MTV news story: **http://tinyurl.com/FarmAid01a** and **http://tinyurl.com/FarmAid01b**.

Martina McBride's "Independence Day"

In the folklore chapter of this book, you learned the importance of context to understanding meaning. The 2001 Farm Aid concert provides an excellent example of the notion that context is everything. Watch Martina McBride's Farm Aid performance of her song "Independence Day." Then, consider this in contrast with her performance of the same song at "The Grand Ole Opry 80th Anniversary Celebration at Carnegie Hall," filmed in November of 2005, and the original music video that was released in 1993.

McBride's performance at Farm Aid 2001: https://www.youtube.com/watch?v=5Q3LyECse3g

McBride's original music video released in 1993 (this version won the Country Music Association's award for best video in 1994): https://www.youtube.com/watch?v=4VPpAZ9_qAw

McBride's performance at the Carnegie Hall Celebration of the Grand Ole Opry, 2005: https://www.youtube.com/watch?v=DX6a3NO2LYw

© Ebet Roberts

Neil Young's "Don't Cry No Tears"

Neil Young sings "Don't Cry No Tears" at Farm Aid 2001: https://www.youtube.com/watch?v=6zxrSw7Ah_I (see especially his speech at 3:40).

© Ebet Roberts

EXPLORE: How do McBride's performances differ in these various contexts, and how do these contexts change the message of the song, especially in terms of the 2001 performance?

 EXPLORE: Follow the link to Neil Young's comments between sets. How does he negotiate the shift in rhetorical circumstances when Farm Aid is unexpectedly over-shadowed by September 11th?

 FIELD TRIP: Go to the Farm Aid website, explore the various links and stories, consider the visual rhetoric of the site, and explore the issues of nostalgia, politicizing the farm, patriotic rhetoric, and any other relevant issues.

 RESEARCH: Look up the lyrics to John Mellencamp and George Michael Green's "Rain on the Scarecrow," which was written shortly before the very first Farm Aid in 1985. Analyze the lyrics as you would analyze a poem.

FarmVille

Social network games are yet another aspect of popular culture. FarmVille is one of a number of farm-themed simulation games available today. As of Fall 2013, the game had nearly 40 million likes on Facebook, and it is one of the ways that people today are engaging with the idea and practice of farming. Players can plow, plant, and harvest crops as well as care for their farm animals. Managing a farm in a game setting means that players may not have to rise at dawn to milk cows or muck out the barn.

FIGURE 12.5. Screen shot of FarmVille

VIRTUAL FIELD TRIP: Play at least one hour of one of the farm-related simulation games available online or on various gaming platforms (such as FarmVille, Farm Town, 3rd World Farmer, Big Farm, Farming Simulator). You can play many of these games for free through Facebook or through gaming websites.

Be prepared to discuss in class the experience of playing.

- Was playing the game fun, addictive, annoying, or something else?
- How is the game you chose advertised?
- How does it describe itself?
- Describe the target audience of the game, and what clues led to your conclusions?
- What is the objective of the game and what do you have to do?
- Do you know how popular the game is?
- Does the game seem to have an agenda; in other words, does it work to persuade you to think about the occupation of farming in a certain way?
- Compare and contrast the methods of farming in the game you chose to some other representation of the farming experience represented elsewhere in this textbook. For instance, is FarmVille like the Country Life Commission or Kittredge's "Owning it All"? Is it based on a Jeffersonian model or an agribusiness model?
- What function in society do these popular games serve?

❦ CHAPTER THIRTEEN ❦

Visual Rhetoric of Farms

What Is Visual Rhetoric?

Part of our cultural competence includes knowing what iconic images mean. When we as creators recognize that certain iconic images represent particular ideas to our audience, we no longer need to explicitly articulate that message. Visual rhetoric becomes a kind of shorthand or hyper-language. By manipulating images and drawing upon recognizable elements, the creator can bring a whole new set of meanings to bear on the message, enriching and complicating the message.

For instance, look at the image on this page. By itself, the word *farmer* likely evokes certain ideas, images, and associations that we have discussed in this book. By now, you may associate the word with the Jeffersonian ideal of the yeoman farmer, in addition to any previous associations you had prior to reading this book. The image on the right, however—which features the exact same text as the image on the left—communicates much more. In this case, the original Superman symbol conveys messages of superior strength, invincibility, heroism, morality, patriotism, integrity, and middle-American values.

Through visual rhetoric, the creator can simply insert the single word *farmer* into the iconic image or logo and tie the farmer figure in with the superhero ideas that the image itself communicates. This intertextuality creates a layering of messages. If someone comes from a culture where Superman is not a familiar character (like the visiting Martian from Chapter One, for instance), the image on the right might not make sense at all. Therefore, as with written and oral rhetoric, visual rhetoric requires the successful interplay of the specific relationships of message, audience, and cultural awareness.

Art and the Farm through the Ages

Agriculture is an ever-present theme in visual arts—painting, drawing, photography, printmaking, sculpture, and architecture. Chapter Three depicts a medieval drawing of laborers in the field. The sculptural monument in the photograph is from an Italian village, celebrating and honoring the farmer, a village that is popular for agritourism. On the other hand, the grim painting "The Man with the Hoe" by Jean-Francois Millet inspired Edwin Markham to write a poem of the same name: "Bowed by the weight of centuries he leans /

FIGURE 13.1. Monument honoring farmers in Bevagna, Umbria, Italy. Photo: Joyce Kinkead.

Upon his hoe and gazes on the ground, / The emptiness of ages in his face." Van Gogh's "The Potato Eaters" is yet another dark painting showing the difficult lives of those who farm.

A more contemporary view of art and farming is evident at Gibbs Farm in New Zealand, which places monumental abstract sculptures on farmland stocked with animals. (See http://gibbsfarm.org.nz/). Here, a "Beltie" cow may graze next to a concrete block pyramidal art installation while sheep scamper up the sides of the artwork. Nebraska features Art Farm and a sculpture pasture (see www.artfarmnebraska.org). Old Frog Pond Farm & Studio is located in Massachusetts. Chris Jaworski is a sculptor who assembles steel components from antique agricultural equipment and tools that he has rescued from his own family farm or from tractor graveyards. Less permanent sculptures may be crafted from butter, as seen at state fairs and farm shows.

Photography

"Knee-high by the fourth of July" is a popular saying in rural areas referring to an informal measurement of crops used to gauge the growth of wheat or corn from one year to the next. In early rural photography, there was a similar, often-used visual motif. In order to offer perspective, people were placed in the middle of a field of grain or corn. The individual in the picture was not importantin fact, very often they weren't even identified by name. Instead, they were there to give a sense of scale.

The photo on the next page by J. E. Stimson of a mother and child is reminiscent of innumerable classic paintings that have been done over the centuries. Look at the detail at the right and you might think she looks like a "Madonna of the wheat field." However, according to the photo's title, "Red Cross and Turkey Red Wheat, Dry Grown, U.S. Experiment Station, Newcastle, WY, 1903," we should be focusing our attention not on the woman but on the wheat, which were among the best varieties for the West because of winter hardiness and resistance to disease and drought. Neither the woman nor child ever was identified in any of Stimson's papers that are now housed in the Wyoming Archives. They are used, instead, to indicate the vigor of the crop and therefore the success of the Experiment Station's testing.

FIGURE 13.2. J. E. Stimson, "Woman and Child, Red Cross and Turkey Red Wheat, Dry Grown, U.S. Experiment Station, Newcastle, Wyoming, 1908." J. E. Stimson Collection #2298, Wyoming State Archives, Department of State Parks and Cultural Resources.

Similarly, you can see the use of human and horse figures for perspective in this photograph from the Carey Act region of Southern Idaho that was taken by Clarence E. Bisbee, circa 1910. Here, the message was that although the field had been in sagebrush a short time before, irrigation had made the land very productive very quickly.

FIGURE 13.3. Clarence Bisbee, "Fourth Year in Rotation of Oats Grown on Al Page Ranch, 71 Bu. per Acre," Clarence E. Bisbee Collection, Twin Falls Public Library. Courtesy of the Twin Falls Public Library.

In this 1887 photo below taken by Solomon D. Butcher in Custer County, Nebraska, the Hilton family is posed in their farmyard. Often settlers like the Hiltons were posed in front of their sod houses, but in this case, Butcher reported, Mrs. Hilton was adamant that they not be photographed in front of their house. She wished to send copies of the picture to friends and family in the East, and she did not want to be seen living in a dirt house. She did insist, however, on having her prize possession, a pump organ, hauled into the yard for the photo to demonstrate that their homestead was not entirely lacking in cultural sophistication.

FIGURE 13.4. David Hilton family near Weissert, Custer County, Nebraska, ca. 1887. Photo by Solomon Butcher. Nebraska State Historical Society.

 RESEARCH: Either search through family photos for a rural photograph or go to an archive and ask to see local photo collections of rural areas. After you've chosen a photo, "read" it by considering the following:

- Look closely at the photo and enumerate its important details (consider obvious things, like a pump organ in a pasture, and also subtle things, like how a hat is cocked on a man's head).
- Discuss why you think those details are in some way revealing.
- Are there any details that seem ordinary at first but upon reflection, reveal something deeper about the photo?
- Does there seem to be a message communicated the photo, something that either the photographer or the people in the photo are trying to suggest? In what ways are they effective in sending that message?
- Do you think there are any revealing details in the photo that undermine or contradict that message?

Victory Garden Posters

During World Wars I and II, government propaganda emphasized that "Food is a Weapon." US farmers left for military service, which meant a labor shortage in agriculture; meanwhile, farmland in Europe became battlegrounds. The wartime rationing at home of commodities such as flour, dairy products, and sugar meant that more food could be diverted to soldiers and allies. While our boys were fighting over there, citizens at home were urged address the food shortages by becoming soldiers in the Victory Garden movement to "Sow the Seeds of Victory" which would "insure the fruits of peace." You could "do your bit" by "keep[ing] the home soil turning," an obvious pun on popular World War I song "Keep the Home Fires Burning."

An effective civic morale booster, Victory Gardens (also known as "war gardens") gave lay-farmers, including women and children, a feeling of empowerment and a sense that they too could contribute to the war effort in tangible ways. Gardeners were performing a patriotic service for the country, even if they weren't wearing a uniform. The food they produced offset the pressure on transportation systems, which were busy shipping munitions to Europe, and if citizens at home didn't need to buy food, they had more money to buy war bonds to fund the war effort.

The Department of Agriculture issued a 20-minute film about victory gardens that claimed, "A Victory Garden is like a share in an airplane factory. It helps win the War and pays dividends too. . . . Each [garden is] a health insurance policy, a dooryard savings bank, each a vitamin mine from which you can take stuff more precious than silver or gold. But remember what Grandpa says, 'No work, no garden.' . . . No work, no spuds. No work, no turnips, no tank, no flying fortress, no victory. Bear that in mind, all you victory gardeners, and work for victory!" You can see this film at https://archive.org/details/victory_garden. Even superheroes got into the act when Superman, Batman, and Robin were pictured on the front of a Marvel comic planting a Victory Garden.

For those who had little experience gardening, the USDA distributed pamphlets to train the urban population in what to sow. Vacant lots were commandeered for the war effort, and victory gardens were planted on rooftops, in parks, baseball fields, and schoolyards. They sprung up in posh neighborhoods of New York City, on the grounds of Golden Gate State Park, the Boston Commons, and even at the White House, where Eleanor Roosevelt, despite her husband's protests, instructed gardeners to take up the front lawn and replace it with a victory garden. In World War II, nearly 20 million Americans participated in the Victory Garden movement and supplied upwards of 40% of the produce in the US. They hung victory garden posters in their windows or planted a US flag in their garden along side the peas and potatoes.

EXPLORE: Discuss as a class the visual rhetoric of the posters on the next page. What kinds of symbols are they using? What kind of feeling do they evoke? Who are their audience?

RESEARCH: Do an Internet search for additional Victory Garden or War Garden posters. Bring an image to class and be prepared to discuss it, using the same questions above.

FIGURE 13.5. "Sow the seeds of Victory!" Artist James Montgomery Flagg (1877–1960), lithograph, 1917. Library of Congress.

FIGURE 13.6. "Helping Hoover in Our U.S. School Garden," American Lithographic Co., 1919. Library of Congress, Prints & Photographs Division, Washington, DC.

FIGURE 13.7. Uncle Sam says, "Garden to Cut Food Costs." Lithograph, A. Hoen & Co., Baltimore, 1917. Courtesy LOC.

FIGURE 13.8. "War Gardens for Victory—Grow Vitamins at Your Kitchen Door." Published between 1939 and 1945. Copyright by J. H. Burdett, director, National Garden Bureau.

FIGURE 13.9. "Join the United States School Garden Army—Enlist Now." Artist Edward Penfield. Published by American Lithographic Co., New York, ca. 1918.

"My Victory Garden"

by Ogden Nash
(published in *House and Garden* magazine in November 1943)

Today, my friends, I beg your pardon,
But I'd like to speak of my Victory Garden.
With a hoe for a sword, and citronella for armor,
I ventured forth to become a farmer.
On bended knee, and perspiring clammily,
I pecked at the soil to feed my family,
A figure than which there was none more dramatic-er.
Alone with the bug, and my faithful sciatica,
I toiled with the patience of Job or Buddha,
But nothing turned out the way it shudda.

Would you like a description of my parsley?
I can give it to you in one word--gharsley!
They're making playshoes out of my celery,
It's reclaimed rubber, and purplish yellery,
Something crawly got into my chives,
My lettuce has hookworm, my cabbage has hives,
And I mixed the labels when sowing my carrots;
I planted birdseed--it came up parrots.
Do you wonder then, that my arteries harden
Whenever I think of my Victory Garden?

My farming will never make me famous,
I'm an agricultural ignoramus,
So don't ask me to tell a string bean from a soy bean.
I can't even tell a girl bean from a boy bean.

 FOR FURTHER READING: Read about World War I "War Gardens" in *The War Garden Victorious, Its War Time Need and Its Economic Value in Peace*, (1919) by Charles Lathrop Pack, Director of The National War Garden Commission. The book is available as an e-book at http://www.earthlypursuits.com/WarGarV/WarGardTitle.htm

Women's Land Army

During both World Wars and on both sides of the Atlantic, the Women's Land Army was an important volunteer organization in which women took the place of men on family farms. More than a million American women signed up as members during World War II alone. They donned the specially designed uniforms, underwent specialized training for farm work, and then took to the fields. While promotional WLA posters asserted that, "Farm work is war work," they consistently portrayed them as cheerful, robust, vigorous women who were shown "reap[ing] the harvest of victory" in a world remarkably free of either the dirt of a farm or the death of an army battle.

FIGURE 13.10A. The Woman's Land Army of America—Training School, University of Virginia, ca. 1918. Artist Herbert Paus. Library of Congress, Prints & Photographs Division, Washington, DC.

FIGURE 13.10B. Pitch in and Help!—Join the Women's Land Army of the U.S. Crop Corps. 1944. Artist Hubert Morley. Courtesy of Hennepin County Library. Women wearing overalls with the insignia of the Woman's Land Army work on a farm, milking a cow, weeding, harvesting, and feeding chickens.

 RESEARCH: Do a Google image search for more examples of Women's Land Army posters. What themes to you find depicted? What kind of rhetorical strategies are they using to appeal to women?

California Orange Crate Labels

In the late 1800s, California citrus growers began applying paper labels to their crates of fruit. Each orchard had its own designs, and the labels were a way to distinguish the origin of the fruit as well as its quality. The earlier labels depicted more natural scenes, detailing the surrounding California countryside. Later labels took on a more commercial look and served to disguise the sometimes-harsh industry and capitalism of citriculture behind a mask of agricultural bounty

and scenic beauty. Though oranges are not native to the Americas, it's hard to find a more representative fruit for Southern California.

Crate labels sometimes included literary allusions as in Barbara Worth oranges, derived from the 1911 novel *The Winning of Barbara Worth* by Harold Bell Wright, who was the first American writer to sell a million copies of a novel. Its popularity was augmented by the 1926 film of the same name, featuring Gary Cooper in his first major film, telling the story of how California's Imperial Valley became a major agricultural center by reclamation and irrigation.

EXPLORE: In the trio of labels above from the Sunkist company, the icon of the wrapped orange indicates greater quality. What to the individuals depicted on the labels tell consumers about the relative qualities of the fruit contained within the crates? What do depictions of race and gender in the orange crate labels seem to indicate? What messages are the artists and growers attempting to send to consumers? Are they in keeping with the readings from Chapter 5 about California?

RESEARCH: Do a Google image search for more examples of orange crate labels. What themes to you find depicted? How is California (not only its oranges) being advertised to consumers?

Marilyn Monroe in a Potato Sack

It was said that Marilyn Monroe was so beautiful that she could look good in a potato sack! In 1952, Monroe took the challenge as a publicity stunt, and photographer Earl Theisen captured these images. The photos weren't widely distributed, though one was published in *Stare Magazine* that summer. Copies went to the Long Produce Co. of Twin Falls, Idaho, as well as to the Union Pacific railroad, the major transporter of Idaho potatoes.

FIGURE 13.11. Marilyn Monroe in a stylish potato sack. Photo: Evelyn Funda, 2019. Photo permission courtesy of Idaho Potato Museum.

EXPLORE: How does the visual image of the utilitarian potato sack change when it becomes a dress for a beautiful woman? Which visual image is altered more by the juxtaposition: Marilyn, or the sack?

Gee's Bend Work-Clothes Quilts

Alabama's community of Gee's Bend (pronounced "Jeez" Bend), population 300, is the poorest community of the poorest county in the nation. Located at the site of a former plantation, most of its African American residents can trace their ancestry back through tenant farmers, sharecroppers, and plantation slaves. The community is home to the Gee's Bend quilters, who fashion their art from threadbare clothes once worn by farmers working in the cotton fields. Variously referred to by their makers as "britches quilts" or "ugly quilts," the coverlets are characterized by their large blocks of color, freeform shapes, and distinctive geometric simplicity— sometimes reminiscent of rows in a field, fence posts, or the shingles on a roof. They lack the intricacies and care-

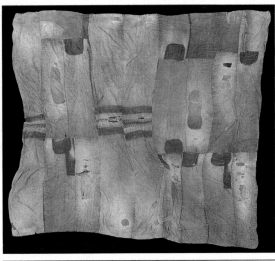

FIGURE 13.12. Lutisha Pettway, "Bars" Work-Clothes Quilt, ca. 1950. Cotton and denim, 80" x 84". The Museum of Fine Arts, Houston, Museum purchase, 2002.414.

ful piecing of many traditional quilt designs, such as the Double Wedding Ring or Cathedral Windows patterns that were stitched by middle-class women in the nineteenth century.

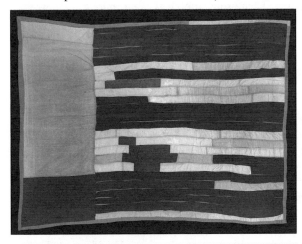

FIGURE 13.13. Emma Lee Pettway Campbell (1928–2002), Blocks and Strips work-clothes quilt, ca. 1950. Gift of Souls Grown Deep Foundation from the William S. Arnett Collection, 2014 (2014.548.43). Image copyright © The Metropolitan Museum of Art, New York, NY.

Rather than disguising the original use of their fabrics, the Gee's Bend quilters incorporate the traces of fading, tears, stains, and patches into their designs.

The Gee's Bend women began to gain attention in the 1960s. It wasn't until 2002, though, that Bill Arnett, collector of African American vernacular art, arranged for seventy of the quilts to be shown in a travelling exhibit that went to the foremost museums in Houston, New York City, San Francisco, and elsewhere. This exhibit brought the quilters critical acclaim, with art critics comparing their work to abstract painters like Mark Rothko, while others saw the quilts as a new form of primitivism, akin to the experimentations and improvisations found in the music of jazz.

However, with fame came controversy. Some art critics thought they detected a patronizing racism in the reviews, such as in art critic Michael Kimmelman's New York Times review in which he asserted, "Imagine [Henri] Matisse and [Paul] Klee... arising not from rarefied Europe but from the caramel soil of the rural South."* Meanwhile, Arnett, who had edited three books about the Gee's Bend quilters to promote their work, found himself the target of a 2007 lawsuit that claimed he had violated the quilters' copyright by licensing images of their quilts to be reproduced on items such as coffee mugs, designer scarves, and decorator items. The lawsuit raised a host of ethical questions, including whether art collectors co-opt other people's creations or promote their work.

Today, the Gee's Bend Quilting Collective offers regular weekend quilting retreats during which participants learn techniques from famed quilters China and Mary Ann Pettway. They also enjoy massages and locally sourced farm-to-table meals created by a celebrated chef. Gee's Bend quilts continue to draw broad acclaim, including when Amy Sherald cited them as inspiration for her official portrait of former First Lady Michelle Obama, which hangs in the Smithsonian's National Portrait Gallery. The lawsuit with Arnett has been settled, and the foundation he established to promote African American vernacular art is in charge of ensuring that the artists now get their fair share of licensing fees.

* Michael Kimmelman, "Jazzy Geometry, Cool Quilters," *New York Times*, November 29, 2002, sec. E, p. 33.

VIEW AND WRITE: Choose a work of visual art to analyze in a writing assignment. You may find a work in an art museum or gallery or on the helpful website www.art-stor.org. Consider the *image* of farms and farming in the work. In an essay, describe the work of art that you have chosen. Begin by including title, artist, date, artist's country, size, and material used. Insert a picture of the work of art at the top. Include important contextual information. Then using farming as a lens to look at the work, analyze why this work is important to the theme of this course.

The following essay, which is a model for this writing assignment, refers to the painting that is on the cover of this book.

Jon Anderson, USA
Cache Valley Barn: Spring
Acrylic on canvas, 1994
36" x 42"

In Hamlin Garland's story "Uncle Ethan Ripley," the elderly farmer gives in to a traveling salesman and allows him to paint the new barn with the disfiguring letters that advertise Dodd's Family Bitters. The result is particularly bitter to Mr. Ripley and even more so to his wife, who demands that the sign be painted over and hidden. Cache Valley has its own iconic barn with the advertisement "The Woman's Tonic, Dr. Pierce's Favorite Prescription." This barn, set in the idyllic landscape just south of Logan, has been the subject of many artists' paintbrushes and cameras. Jon Anderson, professor of Art at Utah State University, used the barn and its surrounding fields and mountain backdrop for a planned series of four seasons. He finished two: spring and summer. The one depicted here features the colorful greens and yellows of spring.

Acrylic paint offers bright interpretation to the fields, mountains, clouds, and sky. Massive white and purple clouds hang over the landscape, and their shadows fall on the fields. The canvas is stretched around a wooden frame so that picture extends around the sides and to the back. The style has something of a cartoon or children's book look to it with trees done as rounded bumps. The fields are done as patchwork on a quilt. In the left foreground sits the barn, its message ironic: "The woman's tonic." Just what is tonic for a woman? Is it the stimulant of working on a farm? Probably not. Might it be the landscape and environment itself? That transcendental interpretation of tonic is more likely—at least from this viewer's perspective.

Cache Valley Barn offers an idealistic look at farming and the land; the barn is set against a beautiful mountain background. No threats exist nor is hardship evident. Instead, this is an idyllic view. It harkens back to the early American notion of the farm as garden, a kind of Eden. In contrast to the "bitter" early commercialization of Uncle Ethan's barn, the Woman's Tonic barn evidences nostalgia for a simpler past.

Farms and the New Romanticism

FIGURE 14.1. MaryJane Butters harvesting corn.
Photo ©MaryJane Butters, CC BY-SA 3.0. https://commons
.wikimedia.org/w/index.php?curid=17555388.

CHAPTER FOURTEEN

Return to the Land

"How You Gonna Keep 'Em Down On The Farm"

Reuben, Reuben, I've been thinking
Said his wifey dear
Now that all is peaceful and calm
The boys will soon be back on the farm
Mister Reuben started winking and slowly rubbed his chin
He pulled his chair up close to mother
And he asked her with a grin

How ya gonna keep 'em down on the farm
After they've seen Paree'
How ya gonna keep 'em away from Broadway
Jazzin around and paintin' the town
How ya gonna keep 'em away from harm, that's a mystery
They'll never want to see a rake or plow
And who the deuce can parleyvous a cow?
How ya gonna keep 'em down on the farm
After they've seen Paree'

Rueben, Rueben, you're mistaken
Said his wifey dear
Once a farmer, always a jay
And farmers always stick to the hay
Mother Reuben, I'm not fakin'
Tho' you may think it strange
But wine and women play the mischief
With a boy who's loose with change

How ya gonna keep 'em down on the farm
After they've seen Paree'
How ya gonna keep 'em away from Broadway
Jazzin around and paintin' the town
How ya gonna keep 'em away from harm, that's a mystery
Imagine Reuben when he meets his Pa
He'll pinch his cheek and holler "OO-LA-LA!
How ya gonna keep 'em down on the farm
After they've seen Paree'?

(Songwriters Joe Young and Sam M. Lewis; music by Walter Donaldson, 1918)

Back-to-the-Land Movements

At the end of World War I when "How Ya Gonna Keep 'Em Down on the Farm" seemed prophetic about the diminishing number of farms, it would be difficult to imagine that twenty-first-century farms might be more attractive than Broadway or Paris. In fact, contemporary farmers—often young and well educated—may have studied abroad in Paris. Why is the hard life of farming increasingly attractive to them? It can be a hardscrabble, low-paying existence, just as it was in the early twentieth century. The allure lies in several factors:

- Desire for a meaningful life out of the corporate rat race
- Commitment to ecology and the environment
- Belief in health benefits of food produced in an organic, sustainable way
- Belief in the benefits of the physical activity involved in farming
- Concern for social justice, coupled with cynicism about contemporary politics and government
- Aim of unplugging from the industrial food system
- Desire to be self-reliant and autonomous
- Value hard work and its effects on family life and child development
- Desire for the sense of wonder that comes with growing food and animals
- Sense that an increased locavore movement may actually result in a living wage and a good life
- Pure pleasure of eating your own produce
- Goal of energy efficiency
- Survivalist sensibility of having food stuffs and stock
- Interest in simple food or the culinary revival of heirloom varieties
- Reliable produce provided for restaurants—which the farmers may own
- Need to "unplug" (although some farmers use social media to connect with consumers)
- Ability to create and be creative
- Aim of recapturing good memories from childhood farm days or visits
- Sense of loyalty to the land, particularly for family-owned farms over generations
- Sense of being in touch with nature and seasons
- Belief in the garden as the intersection of nature and humans and the metaphorical power of *garden* in its philosophical and aesthetic sense
- Return to a philosophy that farming is a noble occupation

In general, the back-to-the-farm movement belongs to young people who are passionate about working with their hands and heads and growing food. Young farmer nights in southeastern New England (see http://youngfarmernight.com/) offer the opportunity to network and to learn about all natural beef or processing chicken. However, not all new farmers are young. A *New York Times* article "From Boardroom to Barnyard" (http://www.nytimes.com/video/2013/07/31/fashion/100000002295379/boardroom-to-barnyard.html) profiled a corporate executive who, appalled by what she learned reading Michael Pollan's *The Omnivore's Dilemma*, traded in her stylish business suits for rough and ready outdoor work clothes. Her farm currently has 1,000 CSA customers who willingly pay $28 for a chicken raised organically and humanely.

The testimonials to the power and pleasure of living on a farm and growing food abound in a wealth of book titles. Kurt Timmermeister's *Growing a Farmer: How I Learned to Live Off the*

Land (2011) begins: "I live in a lovely place. It is a small farm, just a few acres, but it is beautiful. I created this farm over many years. . . . I never intended to be a farmer and yet it feels right. I enjoy a connection to the land, to the animals here, and I am endlessly thrilled to make food; to feed people" (11). Kristin Kimball becomes an unlikely farmer when she went from her job in Manhattan to interview a farmer about the young farmers. Although a vegetarian, she helps him butcher a hog on the first visit, as he's short-handed. Somehow they fall in love and marry, which is documented in her memoir *The Dirty Life* (2010).

> Mark and I are both first-generation farmers. The farm we've built together could be described as antique or very modern, depending on who you ask. The fertility comes from composted manure and tilled-in cover crops. We use no pesticides, no herbicides. The farm is highly diversified, and most of the work is done by horses instead of tractors. . . . We raise hogs and beef cattle and chickens on pasture, and at butchering time we make fresh and dried sausages, pancetta, corned beefs pates, and quarts of velvety stock.
>
> The food we grow feeds a hundred people. These "members" come to the farm every Friday to pick up their share of what we've produced. Our goal is to provide everything they need to have a healthy and satisfying diet, year-round.

Kimball says "farming transforms you" (5). She and others have turned away from fast food, cubicles, and TiVo for a life that is both difficult and rewarding.

A Brief History of Back-to-the-Land Movements

"Do You Want to Join the Back-to-the Farm Movement? No, You Don't" is the title of a New York *Times* article of January 29, 1911. Over a century ago, another back to the farm movement was in place, this one based in part on alleviating city congestion and addressing the concerns posed by studies like *The Country Life Commission Report*. The reason given for the negative answer in this article is that the uninitiated has little chance of success on a farm even with funding and physical strength, as expertise in farming is required to make a living. Of interest is the one positive example shared with readers, a young woman with eight acres who weekly ships to her clients a container of "luscious vegetables, poultry, and fruit; and for each hamper receives a dollar, the express being paid by the consignee."

Helen and Scott Nearing may be considered "the great-grandparents of the back-to-the-land movement," according to the *Washington Post Book World*. They left the city in 1932 for a life in the country first in Vermont, and then in Maine.

Turning around the Trend:
For the first time since World War II, the 2007 Census of Agriculture showed a modest 4% increase in the number of farms in the US in comparison to the 2002 figures. Small farms growing multiple crops accounted for most of that growth, and rather than monocrops, no single crop accounted for more than 50% of the production value on most of these farms. The kinds of crops showed a slight shift, too, as numbers for grain, oilseeds, and cattle, and hogs all went down while the numbers for fish, sheep, goats, as well as vegetables and fruits and nuts, all went up. Farm operators of these small farms tend to be younger than the previous average age, and the sector of women farming increased by 29% to over 300,000 women farmers listed as primary operator, making this the fastest-growing sector in farming. Also seeing gains were the numbers of Hispanic and Latino farmers and African-American farmers.

Their two volumes, *Living the Good Life* (1954) and *Continuing the Good Life* (1979) became guidebooks for those seeking simpler lives and wanting to be self-reliant. Likewise, Louis Bromfield, whose novel *Early Autumn* won the Pulitzer Prize in 1927 became even better known for his nonfiction work such as *Pleasant Valley* (1945) and *Malabar Farm* (1948) that celebrate organic and self-sustaining gardening where pesticides were banned. Malabar Farm State Park, near Mansfield, Ohio, continues to operate under this management style of conservation farming and sustainable agriculture.

Another period of back to the land occurred at the end of World War II, popularized by the successful book and film of the same name, *The Egg and I* by Betty MacDonald. Certainly the aftermath of a war left some feeling that perhaps they could reclaim their humanity through connecting with the land. But it was surpassed in the 1960s and 1970s by the back to basics philosophy when people turned to communal living and questioned the value of urban—and particularly suburban—life. The latter was viewed as superficial and artificial, even corrupt. Cynicism was in full swing with effects of the Watergate scandal, the Vietnam War, and the energy crisis.

In 1974, Carla Emery self-published her expansive book *The Encyclopedia of Country Living: An Old-Fashioned Recipe Book* about her family's self-sufficient life on a remote northern Idaho farm. The first editions of the book were mimeographed, assembled page by page, and distributed directly by Emery, who sold more than 45,000 copies this way before the 9th edition of the book was picked up by Bantam Books in 1977. Since then, over 750,000 copies have been sold. Part how-to book and part autobiography, *The Encyclopedia of Country Living* includes stories of personal and family struggles, Emery's self-deprecating humor, passages of philosophical manifestos and spiritual meditation—all interspersed with folk wisdom, advice on buying land and doctoring sick animals or babies, growing food organically, and recipes for everything from fried frog legs to bread. Calling land ownership a "spiritual responsibility," Emery urged her readers to "live morally and spiritually as if Jesus were coming in the next five minutes, but economically and ecologically . . . as if He won't be here for 5,000 years more." In her opening she writes:

> If you've considered moving to the country, Yes! Get out of town. Get as far into the country as you can get. Get as far away from neighbors as you can. Go where the majority is sky and earth and the animals and plants that are of it. They are nearer the Truth than you, and you'll learn and benefit by association with them. You'll be going to Reality. You'll be giving yourself a chance to escape the lures of human mythology, of all our delusions and foolishness. They breed in big cities, they flourish there far from Nature. . . . But don't move to the country in search of a notion of freedom that pictures you lying on the grass all of a fine summer's day chewing on a succession of hay straws. . . . You get freedom by giving yourself into a kind of bondage in a promise to serve. . . . The rewards are largely the spiritual cultivation that work and austerity bestow.

Contemporary publications such as *Whole Earth Catalog* and *Mother Earth News* joined environmental texts such as *Walden, Sand County Almanac* (1949) by Aldo Leopold, and the alarming *Silent Spring* (1962) by Rachel Carson, which effectively sounded the alarm about the detrimental effects of pesticides, particularly on bird populations. Earth Day is one outcome of this movement, and curbing pollution and litter came to the forefront.

Time will tell if the current 21st-century back-to-the-land movement will be successful, or if eventually the novice farmers will return to suburban/urban existence. What may differ in this movement is the addition of social media to assist. The FarmOn Foundation (farmon.com), organized by young "agricultural enthusiasts" in Canada, offers this tagline: "Farming is hard work. We get it. And we can help."

Urban Farming

Another organization committed to feeding people is Urban Farming, which is creating "an abundance of food for people in need by planting, supporting and encouraging the establishment of gardens on unused land and space while increasing diversity, raising awareness for health and wellness, inspiring and educating youth, adults and seniors to create an economically sustainable system to uplift communities around the globe." See http://www.urbanfarming.org/. The organization started in Detroit in 2005 with only three gardens and is working to have a million gardens in its registry.

Seedfolks, a 1997 children's novel by Paul Fleischmann, popularized the notion of using vacant land for gardens. In this story, Kim, a nine-year-old Vietnamese girl, plants six Lima bean seeds in a vacant lot to honor her father who was a farmer. Others in the multiethnic neighborhood begin to plant their own seeds, resulting in a baker's dozen of plots. This American Library Association Best Book for Young Adults has galvanized several communities to read it as a group and to find their own unused land that can be turned into gardens so that others can reap similar harvests and find meaning in their lives.

The South Central Farm in Los Angeles, another community garden project that took advantage of unused land, did not fare so well. Although it was a successful endeavor for twelve years, the owner of the land decided not to allow its use for production and had the garden bulldozed. A 2008 documentary, *The Garden* , tells the heartbreaking story of the garden farmers and how they tried in vain to save the garden. As of 2013, the land has still not been developed and lies fallow.

A selection from *Farm City* by Novella Carpenter ends this chapter. Carpenter farmed a vacant area adjacent to her rented property in a poor neighborhood of Oakland, California. Seemingly an unlikely farmer, she tells the often hilarious story of trying to raise livestock and grow vegetables in an urban landscape.

Rooftop gardens provide an unlikely venue for agriculture. But Brooklyn Grange grows over 40,000 pounds of organic produce in a year. It was started in 2010 by enterprising cooperative members who hauled thousands of pounds of soil up several flights of stairs to build the garden with engineers' approval. This is a type of microfarming, which may comprise a two-acre farm in the country or be as small as a patio garden.

Urban gardens are not just for lower socio-economic groups. Upscale farming projects include designer chicken coops and runs. Catalog shoppers may find such coops in the range of $500–1,500. Some feature wheels so that the chickens can be moved from location to location in order to forage for tasty bugs and seeds. Chickens who reside in these accommodations may be named charmingly—Benedict and

FIGURE 14.2. Williams Sonoma Chicken Coop and Run

Scramble, for instance. Owners get a sense of satisfaction but also eggs with bright yellow yolks, something that store-bought eggs just don't offer.

Bookshelves are populated with memoirs and advice manuals for urban gardening. Spring Warren's *The Quarter-Acre Farm: How I Kept the Patio, Lost the Lawn, and Fed My Family for a Year* (2011) relates how she established a goal of growing 75% of the food for her family of four. *The Edible Front Yard, Edible Landscaping, Edible Estates, Little House in the Suburbs, A Chicken in Every Yard*, and *Backyard Chickens* are all in this tradition—and just a few of the many books advocating for self-sufficient gardening/farming. *Urban Farms* by Sarah C. Rich and Matthew Benson (2012) offers profiles and stunning photographs of sixteen urban farms around the country. Robin Mather writes in *The Feast Nearby: How I lost my job, buried a marriage, and found my way by keeping chickens, foraging, preserving, bartering, and eating locally (all on $40 a week)* (2011)—well, what else is there to tell? The title gives away the story, except to say that she was successful by moving from Chicago back to her native rural Michigan. Jennifer Cockrall-King provides a journalist's perspective in her *Food and the City: Urban Agriculture and the New Food Revolution* (2012).

Agritourism

Dude Ranches were early entries into the agritourism business, offering *greenhorns* or *tenderfoots* the opportunity to see up close and personal what the Old West was really like—sanitized of course. If you've gone to a corn maze, picked fruit on a farm, taken a sleigh or hayride at a living history farm, cut down your own Christmas tree at a tree farm, or stayed in a farm bed-and-breakfast, you were participating in agritourism, or *agritainment*. In the dismal economic times when farms might be sold due to recession problems, the US Department of Agriculture and others sought means whereby the family farm could be saved. One of these ways was to turn farms into Disneylike places where families could enjoy "a grand day out."

The National Institute of Food and Agriculture (NIFA) offers advice through a brochure, "Adding Value to Agriculture: A Collaborative Approach Based on Agricultural Tourism." Information includes how to highlight heritage festivals and food tourism to provide a more reliable income stream than traditional farm sources, an approach that protects farmers from fluctuations in the market. Whidbey Island—a stone's throw from Seattle—hosts an annual Farm Tour Festival, which opens farms to tourists on a weekend in September.

"The Disneyland of Agritourism . . . just make sure you go hungry!!"

REVIEWED JULY 10, 2011

One can not put into words the dining experience at Sa Mandra, a Sardinian family run farm/restaurant. Set just a mile or so from the airport in Fertilia, this charming farm and all it's wonderful workers and servers draw you into their magical world, the minute you step foot on the path into the farm. Ancient farm equipment, Sardinian antiques, pottery and cooking utensils adorn the various different buildings on this farm complex. But make sure you go in there hungry, because you are about to experience mind blowing traditional Sardinian dishes served in an six course menu, including wine . . . and all for 40 euros.

. . . Boars that were roasting on a fireplace big enough for eight men to stand in side by side, pastas stuffed with the cheeses made on the farm, homemade prosciuttos and salumis that are included in an "eight" plate antipasto, delicious pastries served with homegrown seasonal fruits and wines from a nearby vineyard.

You may be groaning as the meal progresses and the platters keep coming, but you just have to taste everything, because I venture to guess you will never have a dining experience like this one ever again in you life.

I know you mother told you to clean your plate, but here is a situation where eating everything that is served to you is a physical impossibility. Not to worry though, the final course is a selection of digestiffs that the waiter encourages you to try!!!

One caveat . . . make sure you arrive there during daylight or have GPS in your auto . . . set on a winding country road, the signs are barely visible and you could find yourself in Olbia if you're not on the lookout.

The US Census of Agriculture only began tracking figures for agritourism in 2002, and according to the 2007 report, US farmers claimed agritourism income of over $500 million dollars. The types of agricultural recreation varies widely and includes farm schools for children and adults who may want to learn skills in arts and crafts, gardening, quilting, or carpentry. Other farms host family and company events, such as weddings or company picnics. In agritourism, the farm itself and the farm experience have become the product. For instance, the Roloff Farm in Oregon— made famous by the TLC reality series *Little People, Big World*—sell a bottle of their "Country Style Dirt" on their website with the guarantee that it has been "naturally washed by Oregon rain."

In Europe, agritourism is more closely related to farm stays in which getting back to nature can be an exotic outing for urban dwellers. Italy has a robust *agriturismo* enterprise, where families can engage in farm activities such as collecting eggs, making cheese, and driving dairy cattle to pasture. (See http://www.agriturismo.it/en/.) For Italians, "Agriturismo obviously means fresh air, wholesome food, the splendour of the countryside or the mountains." Take a look at the TripAdvisor review (figure) for this Sardinia-based farm Azienda Agrituristica Sa Mandra.

How *real* is an agritourism experience? Is it Disneyland in dirt? Or does it offer a meaningful experience for those who live in urban centers? States understand that agriculture can be big business even as a tourist venue. Massachusetts boasts 400 farm venues on its tourist map (http://www.mass.gov/agr/massgrown/agritourism_farms.htm). Vermont, Wisconsin, and Utah—among others—celebrate cheese tours. Forbes covered the increasing number of agritourism sites overseen by women in an article: http://www.forbes.com/sites/85broads/2012/04/30/women-farmers-are-making-bank-in-agritourism/. For many of them it's about ensuring an educational opportunity for children "who had lost all touch with the farm life that provides their daily food." In brief, it's about more than hayrides and pumpkin patches.

The Farm Girl Empire

MaryJane Butters is a back-to-the-farm proponent. She built an empire on a philosophy that adheres to organic farming and environmental activism. Her business includes catalog orders for food and farm-themed items; a magazine, *MaryJanesFarms*; overnight stays at a farm bed-and-breakfast; a FarmGirl group with a blog; Pay Dirt Farm School; organic cotton sheet sets; and books such as *Glamping with MaryJane* that promotes camping with glamor. This Utah native has lived in the Palouse country in Idaho, famous for its lentil production, since 1986. Her farm was featured in a *National Geographic* story, "A Farming Revolution" (December, 1995). The tagline of her website is "Simple Solutions for Everyday Organic." Although Butters's business is now on solid footing, at one time it was precipitously close to collapse. A 2004 *New Yorker* essay investigates the creation of the farm girl movement in the piece that follows.

"The Simple Life, Inc."

By Dana Goodyear

MaryJane Butters lives at the end of a long dirt road in the black-soil region of northern Idaho. The road, which she named Wild Iris Lane, passes through wheat fields that are spread like a green duvet and buzzed by crop dusters, and the wooden sign for MaryJanesFarm is gaily painted in Butters's thematic colors—buttermilk yellow, barn red, and forest green. The same colors beatify the goat barn and the outhouse, which until two years ago was the only toilet among the collection of small, assorted buildings on the fifty-acre farm. Butters manufactures a line of some sixty mail-order instant and quick-prep organic foods, and the farm serves as her assembly plant. Attempts to raise and process organic legumes and grains have been expensive and disappointing, and so, aside from a few herbs, she doesn't actually grow the ingredients herself. But, still, she says. "It was always my dream to be a farmer. I think of myself as a food scientist and a farmer and a good cook and an advocate of farmers. I'm really proud to call myself a farmer. I think I've earned it. I love that I'm a woman farmer, and an *organic* woman farmer."

Butters is a farmer in the same way that Martha Stewart is a housewife. One of her favorite books is "The 22 Immutable Laws of Marketing." Another is "The Fall of Advertising & the Rise of PR." Five years ago, she started *MaryJanesFarm*, an aspirational country-life magazine filled with autobiographical snippets and photographs of the farm, to sell her packaged foods and a line of rural-made goods. It now has a circulation of some sixty thousand and is available in ten thousand grocery stores and bookstores; she plans to print a hundred thousand copies of her next issue, which comes out in November. "I branded myself so people would ask, 'Who is this Mary-Jane?'" she says. "It creates a forum for me to talk about farming." So far, the most immediate and tangible dividend of her branding has been a $1.35-million deal she signed with Clarkson Potter last fall for a series of books about life on the farm, the first of which, "MaryJane's Ideabook, Cookbook, Life-book," will come out next summer.

Butters wants to "put a face to food," and on her packaging that face belongs to a smiling blue-eyed gal in Western gear, adapted from a nineteen-forties label she found at a thrift store in Oregon. Butters herself is fifty-one and petite, with long ash-blond hair that sometimes hangs in a braid all the way down her back and sometimes is swept into a wispy bun and pinned at the crown of her head. She has periwinkle-blue eyes and a heart-shaped face, and favors Capri pants, hand-stitched pastel-colored hostess aprons, and round-toed Mary Janes with eyelet appliqué and wooden soles. To describe her aesthetic, which involves the liberal use of doilies and clothespins, dropped "g"s, and anything Amish, she invented the term "farmgirl"—as in "Farmgirl is a condition of the heart." It's an expression that, she has found, is inclusive enough to stimulate the longings of both urban apartment dwellers who buy *MaryJanesFarm* at Whole Foods and rural women who buy it at Wal-Mart.

Before her book advance, Butters had been scraping by—a few years ago, she and her husband, Nick Ogle, had a combined income of eighteen thousand dollars, and were forced to lay off several employees—but now she has more than quadrupled her staff, to eighteen. She has hired another designer for the magazine, a girl Friday, and a recipe tester and food stylist. In the spring, she brought on a woman to do research and development, special events, and merchandising. More recently, Butters hired two seasonal farmhands, Austin Goodman and Erik Jacobson, to help maintain the gardens, where she grows spinach, arugula, basil, carrots, sunflowers, strawberries, asparagus, rhubarb, squash, shallots, irises, gladiolus, zinnias, peonies, lilies, sunchokes, lovage, cherries, walnuts, and Asian pears, along with her prize crop, a field of sinuous, pale-green heirloom garlic plants. For the time being, Butters is too engrossed in writing the book and taking photographs to spend much time in the garden—"me, physically, out there hoeing."

Goodman and Jacobson are both trained photographers, and often find themselves shooting the produce with one of Butters's two new digital cameras, one for still photography and one for B-roll, in the likely event that she decides to do a television show or a series of how-to DVDs. In any case, jobs at the farm are fluid. Butters doesn't hesitate to assign a graphic designer to clean the chicken coop—she thinks of it as farmgirl training—or to ask a farmhand to wallpaper it with an old-fashioned nose-gay pattern, to please the visiting editors of *House & Garden*. "So much here is about presentation and making it look beautiful," Goodman says. "So much of what she's doing is geared toward people's *ideas* of a farm." In the refrigerator of the test kitchen, eggs and vegetables often have signs posted on them saying "Photo Shoot—Do Not Eat."

One evening in early July, Butters's twenty-four-year-old daughter, Megan, arrived from Spokane with her fiancé, Lucas, and a U-Haul full of their possessions. They were moving to Kansas, where Lucas had been offered a job as a college basketball coach. Megan and her brother Emil, who is twenty and works as a mechanic in nearby Moscow, grew up on the farm, and Butters thinks they will both end up living there someday. She expects Megan to take over her business: "You know how Dear Abby kind of gave her column to her daughter? Like that." When Butters married Ogle, in 1993, he and his two sons, who are now in their twenties, stayed in their own house—a flaking white clapboard farmhouse down the road which, as Butters says, "is in serious need of some T.L.C."—and Butters and her kids stayed in theirs. "It gets toxic to sleep together every night," Butters says. "We work together on the farm every day." In more playful moods, she says, "it keeps the romance."

Butters told her kids and employees to meet in the plum pit, an open-air living room surrounded by a grove of plum trees, where she has two luxuriously bedecked beds shrouded with mosquito netting, an antique white propane stove, and some homemade camp stools arranged around a fire. (There are plastic tarps on hand, in case of rain.) She thought of the gathering as simultaneously "Meg's last night at the farm"; an opportunity to shoot a picture of happy people eating hobo dinners, for the camping chapter of the book; and a chance to test a corn-on-the-cob recipe she was working on, using bundles of rosemary for basting brushes. At dusk, she started a fire and arranged a jar of lemons, some diced green apples, little balls of ground beef from an isolated organic herd, elk sausage, zucchini, and a canister of carrots that had just been harvested from the garden. She scratched a match on a stone to light a pair of kerosene lamps—she had given the chore to someone else, who had done it wrong, allowing smoke to darken the lantern's globes and potentially ruin the shot—and instructed Julie Bell, the food stylist, to cut lengths of aluminum foil to wrap around each person's dinner before sticking it in the fire. "She feeds the idea, and I fluff it," Bell said. Butters dispatched two helpers to cut willow switches to use for s'mores, and told an assistant who was wearing a MaryJanesFarm T-shirt to cover it up with a jean jacket. "That's just shameless advertising," she said.

Butters looked through her camera, which was mounted on a tripod near the firs where the corn was grilling. She took several pictures, then stepped away and raked up some bruised peony blossoms that she'd scattered around earlier. "I thought they looked cool," she said tensely. "But they don't look cool in a photograph." They sky grew dark, and Jacobson wheeled in a big construction lamp. Then, because Butters kept saying the pictures were "too hot" and dousing the fire with water, he and another employee held a piece of white gauze over the lamp. "Mom's working, *always* working," Emil teased. Butters rolled her eyes at him. At some point, he and Megan and Lucas wandered away. It was ten o'clock before Bell said, "We need to get some of these things on the grill, MaryJane!"

"Remember, this is more about the photograph than eating—sorry," Butters said. She walked swiftly to the nearby design studio, where the magazine is produced, and looked at a few dozen pictures of the blackening corn on the computer screen.

Eventually, the kids returned to the plum pit with Ogle. They had been drinking beer and playing horseshoes in the garden. Ogle is solid and sandy-haired, with blue eyes and a perpetual sunburn. He was wearing a Hawaiian shirt, shorts, and a panama hat. "This is like a photofest over here," he said, and grazed on the raw ingredients. He started to assemble a dinner, and everyone but Butters and Jacobson followed suit; they were at the stove, where she was trying to get a picture of the finished corn, and he was holding a mirror to catch highlights. In the end, she didn't get the group shot she had wanted, because, although she had asked everyone not to eat until she was ready, no one had listened. When she disappeared into the studio again, Megan advised anyone who wanted a s'more to make one quickly, before her mom got back. Only two people dared, and the vintage picnic hamper filled with organic chocolate chips, organic graham crackers, and Bell's homemade marshmallows was returned to the test kitchen, for a later shoot.

Ogle, a taciturn sort who was brought up on the conventional farm that adjoins Butter's property, has watched with equanimity as the land has been transformed from a homestead into a stage set. "You know, it's all a work in progress," he says. "She's always been like that."

Mary Jane Butters became MaryJane three years ago, because "I couldn't brand Mary-space-Jane—the shoes and the candies had been around forever." Besides, she says, the no-space, no-apostrophe style of MaryJanesFarm was perfect for the Internet. Butters grew up Mormon in a modest house "on the wrong side of the tracks," in Ogden, Utah, with a two-year supply of food in the basement. Pictures of her happy, flaxen-haired younger self and her four happy, flaxen-haired siblings appear in every issue of the magazine. One picture of Butters, as a child of about five, wearing—what else?—Mary Janes, and sitting in a crate full of baby chicks, was on the cover of her première issue (now out of print and circulating among enthusiastic readers), and adorns a MaryJanesFarm stitching kit, which is also sold separately as a purse. She camped and fished; she helped her father, who worked for forty-some years at the American Can Company, in his garden, and her mother with preserves. They were "downwinders," in the era of aboveground nuclear testing, and Butters, who was diagnosed with a thyroid condition as a girl, remembers that sometimes when it rained the puddles would be hot. "We were drinking strontium 90 in our milk every day," she says.

When she graduated from high school, in 1971, she got a job as a secretary. She married her high-school boyfriend and was going to help put him through medical school, but was determined to avoid the situation her mother, however contentedly, had always been in: having a man provide for her. The following summer, Butters and her husband worked for the Forest Service in northern Idaho; her post was on a lookout tower, his on a timber-thinning crew. They didn't see much of each other. She read everything by Henry David Thoreau, and by the end of the summer she had decided that she wanted to have the marriage annulled.

Butters got a scholarship to the state university in Logan, Utah, and started dating a student from Chappaqua, New York. She discovered Karl Marx, and questioned the Vietnam War and the treatment of women in the Mormon Church, though she insists she didn't "hook up with a peer group that was into hairy armpits." That summer, she was hired by the Forest Service to be a wilderness ranger, and spent three months alone in the woods, twenty miles from the nearest road. (She was among the first women chosen to be rangers.) After a couple of years, she dropped out of college and enrolled in a carpentry trade school, and, in the summer of 1975, she was offered a job as the station guard at the Moose Creek ranger station, in the Selway-Bitterroot Range, on the Idaho-Montana border, one of the largest and most remote wilderness areas in the lower forty-eight. The young man from Chappaqua wanted to go with her, so she married him in his parents' living room before a justice of the peace.

At Moose Creek, Butters learned how to fell trees using hand tools. "I was this rough-and-ready woman," she says. "I was living in cabins and wearing men's clothing." She felt that she was missing something, though. "I had a dream one night that I went to this old house in the woods where these two spinster sisters had lived and died. They had left it for me to live in, and it was full of quilts and aprons and everything." She took it as a sign, and, at twenty-seven, found a job in a slightly less remote place—a ranch four hours up the Snake River, which was accessible only by boat. She brought her husband and a treadle sewing machine, planted a garden, worked as a milkmaid, and got pregnant with Megan. The primitive life did not agree with her husband, but after Emil was born, in 1983, Butters insisted that they buy the farm near Moscow. Its last occupants had been a gang of Hells Angels, who had left the outhouse overflowing and a pile of beer cans on the porch. There was no heat and no plumbing, and, before a year was up, her husband left. In her early thirties and the single mother of two young children, Butters chopped all the wood herself and washed the family's clothes in a wringer washer—a litany of hardships that are now among her fondest memories. She grew vegetables and sold them at the farmer's market, got a job as a construction worker, and, after the Chernobyl disaster, became an environmental activist. At an anti-pesticide meeting, she met a farmer who was growing a variety of garbanzo bean that required few chemicals. She says, "I went, Aha! Organic. It seems like I've always been that way, just questioning any of that—toxic politics, toxic old Mormon men." But, mostly, the food business was a way to stay home with her kids. She converted an extra room of her house into a packaging plant, designed some black-and-white labels on her computer, and started sending out samples of her homemade falafel mix and dehydrated lentils to co-ops and health-food stores.

In business, as in life, Butters's preferred mode of dispensing with enemies or obstacles is to "kill them with kindness," and she has often displayed a sort of cunning innocence. She writes to executives at rival companies and asks for guidance: "I like to call 'em up and say, 'Let's all be catalysts, let's be a success team.' We need everyone to be working to advocate organic." She thinks nothing of appealing to strangers for cash. In the early nineties, she wrote to Yvon Chouinard, the founder of the outdoor gear and clothing company Patagonia, enclosing a packet of her lentil soup and a letter asking to borrow thirty-five thousand dollars. He lent her the money, and became one of her most trusted advisers. Chouinard, who started as a manufacturer of climbing equipment and began making clothing only to support the original business, thinks Butters is very shrewd to have extended her brand to print and merchandise. But when he first met her, he said, "I was a little skeptical, because she's a little bit of a hippie, very idealistic, kind of uncompromising in a lot of ways. She was very naïve about business, basically building up her business with other people's money. I told her, 'You need to have a sense of responsibility to return these people's money.'"

In 1993, Butters incorporated as Paradise Farm Organics, and raised some capital through private-placement stock. When she needed cash again, in 1998, she decided to have what she calls a homegrown I.P.O.—she wrote the prospectus herself—and raised half a million more. She currently has sixty-two shareholders, mostly neighbors and friends in the Pacific Northwest, none of whom, she says, really expect to make any money from the venture. "You can sell hope and charge for it," she says. "That's what selling stock is." Her packaged food has typically grossed three or four hundred thousand dollars in a year, but that has usually been just enough to cover expenses, and many years the business has run at a loss. Now that she has money to spend, Butters says, "I just sort of want it to run through my hands."

MaryJanesFarm, which Butters first published in 1999, has been her most effective vehicle of persuasion yet. She sent copies to Nell Newman, Paul Newman's daughter and the co-founder and president of Newman's Own Organics, and to Lois Weisberg, Chicago's commissioner of cultural affairs. The magazine is billed as "ad-free," though Butters allows that it is really "one big ad." In it, she introduces her farm crew and publishes regular features such as "Home Safe Home," a scrapbook of alarming items about the hazards of printed toilet paper and paint, and "Every Woman Has a Story," where she profiles her rural neighbors and customers. The look is glossy, but the vision is decidedly backward, with articles extolling the pleasures of using washboards and making rope by hand. Butters applauds feats of "re-purposing," and once ran a spread on unusually shaped vegetables that could be fashioned into children's toys. The list of Essential Accessories for farmgirl style grows longer every issue: custom-made fancy hats, crocheted clothes hangers, zip-up Dansko work boots like the ones worn by MaryJane. For $58.80, beginning knitters can buy a Knitted Care Wrap kit, which includes natural cotton yarn and instructions for making bandages and sending them, via the Mormon Church, to victims of leprosy.

Butters still prefers chopping wood to any other form of exercise, but feminism—the movement that she says allowed her to live differently from the way all the women in her family had lived before—now seems myopic to her. "We thought we had to throw out all the domestic things that we love," she says. "We had to go out and be a man. That has left us depleted and missing our center."

A few years ago, Faith Popcorn, the trend forecaster, wrote to Butters, congratulating her on a "good job cocooning," and has since asked her to join the board of her think tank. Pamela Krauss, the editorial director at Clarkson Potter, sees a potential market in women in their thirties and early forties who never took home economics and don't know much about canning or cooking or sewing or planting a garden. "That generation of women is really responding to MaryJane, because they don't have those basic skills, and there is something deeply satisfying to being self-sufficient on that level," Krauss says. "There is a very large population of people who are at the point in their lives when they're changing careers, or maybe they were stay-at-home moms and their kids are in school and they're looking for something else to define their lives."

Butters, a natural teacher, has a gift for simplification, and makes it seem that everything she does is easy and attainable. Assured before a camera, she effortlessly slips into anecdotes about her Forest Service days while demonstrating how to sharpen a hoe with a handheld file. On her Web site, she has created a community modeled on the neighborliness and fellow-feeling she remembers from her Mormon childhood. In the "Farmgirl Connection" chat rooms, women with handles such as Farmgirl at Heart and JourneyWoman lend advice about comfrey poultices and homesteading, and share farmgirl resources: "These bra stories are great fun! And informative!"; "I like to purl more than knit, too"; "Does anyone know where I can get some mushroom compost?"

Butters, who subscribes to forty-six magazines—from *E* to *O*—is highly suggestible, and much of what she reads ends up in the magazine's "Newsroom" section. In sorting out exactly who she is and what she represents, Butters remains undaunted by contradictions. "I'm almost on the verge of saying, 'My brand stands for TV-free,'" she will announce, explaining that she has declined offers to do cooking shows and never returned a call from the Fox television personality Ryan Seacrest. A few hours later, though, she'll produce from her files a typed-up television pitch that proclaims: "Butters is poised to become what Suze Orman is to finance, what Deepak Chopra is to mental wellness, and what Ken Burns is to history." To her readers, she presents herself as well meaning and imperfect—deeply capable, frankly ambitious, and subject to revision.

The farm reflects Butters's restlessness and changes with her fortunes. There is a smokehouse, a woodshed, a root cellar, a wood shop, and a converted barn that houses a library and a loft, where Butters sleeps. (The original farmhouse burned down in 1996.) In August, she broke ground on an eleven-thousand-square-foot farmhouse, which will have a country store, a greenhouse, a sewing room, a dried-flower room, and a bed-and-breakfast. She says her aim is to celebrate the skills of rural people and the household crafts of women and to restore the dignity of the family farm: "I'm going to create the new face of agriculture." This spring, she put up five wall tents, permanent structures with wooden floors, wood-burning stoves, and feather beds, where people can go on "organic safaris," for as much as a hundred and seventy dollars a night. The price includes a breakfast of fresh eggs you gather yourself or Butters's packaged oatmeal, and allows you to pitch in with whatever farmwork interests you. She plans to build a forty-to-sixty-cow dairy and a new chicken coop, "a real elaborate, fancy one." She imagines renting the farm out for organic weddings—even funerals. When Ogle suggested they get Webcams at the farm, the first thing Butters said was "Well, then we really couldn't pee outdoors anymore!" The next was "Are other people doing it?"

The American organic movement began as a creature of the publishing industry. In the early nineteen-forties, J. I. Rodale, who had made a small fortune in electrical equipment, read about the compost experiments of the English botanist Sir Albert Howard. Rodale had had a lifelong interest in health and nutrition; as the son of a Lower East Side grocer, he had often been made to eat tinned meat from his father's shop, and blamed his bad eyesight and other health problems on an inadequate diet. Inspired by Howard's claims about the connection between soil health and human health, Rodale started the magazine *Organic Farming & Gardening*. By the nineteen-sixties, when the hippies decided to go back to the land, Rodale was considered a prophet, the publication had a circulation of more than half a million, and the agricultural research facility he established in Emmaus, Pennsylvania, was a place of pilgrimage. In 1971, Rodale suffered a heart attack on the Dick Cavett show and died; that same year, Alice Waters opened Chez Panisse, in Berkeley, which was soon another place of pilgrimage among people who could afford to be obsessed with sustainable, local, seasonal food. Maria Rodale, the granddaughter of J. I. and the founding editor of *Organic Style*, a new life-style and shopping magazine, says that Waters transformed organic culture from a "fascist health movement" into a pleasure.

Although organic food still represents less than two percent of the American food sector, it is growing at a rate of twenty per cent a year, compared with two to five per cent for the overall food market. Maria Rodale says that the renewed mass interest is the result of Waters's effect on gourmet sensibilities and the food scares (alar apples, mad-cow disease) that started in the late eighties. But the growth of the organic market has made it irresistible to multinational corporations, and the sense of hope that was palpable in the late eighties and the nineties—that organic food could save the family farm—is souring. Marion Nestle, a professor of nutrition at New York University and the author of "Food Politics," says that, because people are willing to pay more for food labeled "organic," we now have "what is essentially a two-class system—this high-end, expensive organic food and the mass-marketed other kind, which is much cheaper. The food companies that are publicly owned have to grow, and that forces them to try to figure out where they're going to expand, so they're all pushing into organics, because that's where the new money is."

In sixty years though, no one has been able to prove that there is a nutritional benefit to eating organic food, and the movement, often fractious, continues to be a collection of loosely affiliated idealists and profiteers. In that spirit, Butters counts both J. I. Rodale, whose mission was health, and Waters, who intends to bring about social change through cooking, as heroes, and borrows as needed from their philosophies. With perhaps unintended irony, she calls a weeklong, three-thousand-dollar apprenticeship program she conducts "the Pay Dirt Farm School" in honor of Rodale's 1945 treatise on earthworms and compost. But Butters is not an experimental farmer (she has no patience for academics or research or test plots), an accomplished cook ("All I've ever had is maybe the 'Joy of Cooking'"), or a true practitioner of local, sustainable food production (her business, after all, is mail order); she is, like Martha Stewart, a marketer. "Martha broke incredibly important ground," Butters says. "She took what women do in their homes and gave it validity. She took domesticity and put it on a platter—a silver platter." For Butters, whose product is nineteen-fifties-style packaged food, closer in sensibility to Betty Crocker cake mix, the ideal audience is the Wal-Mart shopper. To reach such shoppers, at a time when organic food still costs thirty-five per cent more than conventionally grown food, she must knock organic from its specialty-food pedestal. "I think it's important to put organic food to the left of somebody and to the right of somebody, and it doesn't have to be a religious gourmet thing," she says.

The centerpiece of her campaign is an invention formerly known as the Tarte Tian™. In the fourth issue of the magazine, Butters described a moment when she was preparing the dish in Chicago in front of thirty-five people, including Oprah's chef, and realized "I'm not French." When she got home, she changed the name to BakeOver™. The BakeOver™ is an organic, do-it-yourself, one-skillet meal—skillet available in MaryJanesFarm, for $24 to $37, depending on the size, along with a special ovenproof handle that must be bought separately for $9.50. The preparation is basic—"I swear to you, my food is truly elegant AND easy," Butters writes in the magazine—and amounts to sautéing fruits or vegetables in the skillet, making a crust by adding water and butter to any one of Butters's bread or brownie mixes, and baking the whole thing for twenty minutes. "I say to mainstream people who have never eaten organic and are overwhelmed by Whole Foods and the price, 'Here's how you can do organic,'" she says. "I teach them to go into the grocery store and go straight to the vegetables and then to the meat and dairy and avoid the whole middle section of the store." They will save money, she says, so long as they stock their pantries with her mixes, which cost around five dollars for a two-serving packet. That way, she tells people, "you're never going to not have an ingredient." It's also a time-saver. "For people who just don't have time, at least it's fast food that's good for you," she says.

The promotional copy for the Pay Dirt Farm School says that it is "one part culinary school," and the BakeOver™ is a mainstay of the curriculum. A few nights after Megan's farewell hobo dinner, three students—a loan officer from New Orleans, who, with her husband, had just bought a farm fifty miles from the city; a single woman from Great Falls, Idaho; and a career counselor from Osnabrück who is the German translator of the *Times* best-seller "Wishcraft: How to Get What You Really Want"—stood in rapt attention in the test kitchen as Butters described the principles. "This is recipe-free, this idea," she said. "You're going to be doing the same thing every night, but the versatility is far greater than pizza." She told them that night's version would be Thai, with frozen shrimp. "I looked in the freezer today and I had some frozen corn, so we'll throw that in," she said, and set the women to work chopping red bell peppers. Next she showed them how to make dough from her johnnycake mix and roll it out on a floured countertop. "You can be really informal with this," she said, shaping the dough into a precise circle by tracing around the bottom of a skillet with a knife. "I just had an extra pan here, so I made it all perfect." She stood at the stove, pigeon-toed, sautéing the peppers, the corn, and the shrimp in the skillet, and sprinkled in a little dried coconut milk and chili powder. After covering the mixture with dough, she put the skillet in the oven. Twenty minutes later, she flipped it onto a plate, and cut each of the apprentices a generous wedge of the heavy, sweet, quiche-like cake. "Gorgeous," the German woman said.

Butters encourages people to eat a BakeOver™ for every meal, as a main course and as dessert. She knows a couple in Moscow who eat nothing else. Not long ago, four "farm wives" came for a lunch tour, at thirty-five dollars a head. "One woman said, 'MaryJane, I am so hooked on your BakeOver™ idea. It's all I do anymore. I do it every night with whatever's in my crisper,'" Butters recalled. After learning that several of her employees were on the South Beach Diet, she has started to think about a twenty-one-day meal plan based on the BakeOver™.

Butters's latest invention, which she will introduce in the book, is the ChillOver™, a Jell-O inspired dish that uses Japanese seaweed extract instead of the "ground-up animal hooves and things" that constitute gelatin. With the ChillOver™, she hopes to emulate Jell-O's success. "It was this worthless food, and then they did this marketing blitz and suddenly, everybody's eating it every day," she said. She plans to "do a little box, just like Jell-O," and introduce a line of ChillOver™ molds: one in the shape of a chicken and another in the classic fluted style.

Butters herself doesn't often eat the packaged foods she sells. "I'm more of a salad person," she said. The foods can be more sophisticated and appealing than ordinary instant fare—the Organic Lebanese Peanut Bulghar is made with currants, curry, and sea salt; the Organic Ginger Sesame Pasta uses orange peel and soybean miso—but they tend to be high in calories and carbohydrates. Ogle's consumption of them, so regular that she named an instant mashed-potato dish Nicks' Organic Couch Potatoes, causes her some concern. "I'm like, 'Nick, you've gotta eat a salad. You can't have mac-and-cheese three days in a row!'" Nonetheless, she is proud that her foods don't have "preservatives or fillers or weirdnesses." And the fact that even she equates her products with fast food is somewhat beside the point: Butters believes it's just better for you to eat food from a small farm, handled by someone you can call up on an 800 number—even if much of the food doesn't actually come from her farm, and she no longer has time to answer the phone.

Over the July 4th weekend, more than twelve hundred people came to the farm for the first Market Day, which Butters hopes to make a monthly event. Twelve venders, with names like Rustique and the Farm Chicks™ (Butters helped them to get trademarked), set up stalls of attractively deteriorated bedsteads and moldering quilts and last century's arithmetic primers in a four-thousand-square-foot white tent that had been erected at the far end of Butters's land. There was folk music, a recitation by a poet-farmer, a wool-spinning demonstration, and a strawberry-shortcake stand, where Julie Bell sold four hundred shortcakes and three hundred cookies, using sixty-six pounds of MaryJanesFarm organic buttermilk biscuit mix.

On the first morning, Butters hung a banner that said "FARM" in pale-blue letters, with the phrase "American Rural Made" superimposed in red, across the back of a 1963 white Ford truck with woven-hemp awnings, below which she had displayed some handmade Christmas stockings. Goodman, whose jobs for the day were trash collection and photography, was taking pictures of Butters as she secured the banner. "Could you work slower?" he asked. "Could you fuss with that again?" Butter's female employees wore farmgirl attire, with the aprons and the Mary Janes, and operated a booth where they sold straw Breton hats with black grosgrain ribbons, similar to one Butters has appeared in many times in her magazine. Next to the MaryJanesFarm booth was a blackboard that welcomed everyone and said, in small chalked letters, "Be sure to say hi to Nick!"

After excusing herself to put on her apron and gather her thoughts, Butters appeared in a fitted white cowgirl shirt with a red ribbon tied at the neck; a full red skirt with a pattern of leaping horses, covered by a diaphanous black apron; and chunky white earrings from an estate sale.

Her hair was in a bun, and she was wearing pink lipstick. Meeting visitors on the road down to the tent—people on their way to pick their own scapes and berries, or those wanting to see the plum pit, a good number of them now wearing Breton hats—she said graciously, "And who are you? And how did you hear about us? Do you have a farm?" She urged them to have some strawberry shortcake, which was going to pay for the whole event, since it had been marked up four-fold, to four dollars. At the tent, she signed magazines. She picked up children so that their parents could take her picture with them, and posed in her 1981 Mercedes, which, the day before, Emil had finished painting the color of her fingernails, O.K. Coral. The car will be run on biodiesel, a sustainable fuel made from mustard seed grown on the farm, and on the doors Emil had stenciled "Powered by homegrown fuel. MaryJanesFarm" in an elegant font chosen by one of the designers.

"People were doin' the whole celebrity thing," Butters said afterward. "It feels funny, but I guess I have to get used to it for when I go on book tour." She said she was exhilarated, and very happy with the kinds of people who showed up—like the ladies from Oakesdale, Washington, about an hour away, who are planning on making a MaryJane doll, with earrings and a bun, and overalls and work boots and nineteen-fifties clothing. ("You know, the woman who made American Girl never even did an ad on TV, and she sold to Mattel for seven hundred million dollars," Butters said. "So people like dolls.") She was pleased that they were "rural people, mainstream people," she said. "And there were some real farmers, who said, 'What are you doing with that mustard seed?'" She told them about a grant she'd received from the state of Idaho that paid for a twenty-thousand-dollar oil press; she was going to mount it on a trailer and bring it to their farms so that they, too, could make their own fuel. "I know that they've been fed the wrong food and the wrong information, and I want to approach them slowly, come to them where they are," Butters said later. "I want them to feel safe, and then I can plug certain things."

Butters knows that the projection of security and the rootedness and domestic harmony will always be her farm's most important asset. She saw that again on Market Day. "People wanted to go to a farm, reconnect with that, see what a farm does, what a farm is," she said. "The U-Pick thing was a hit, the music, being outside in a beautiful setting, the hay bales in the field. Totally like Disneyland reinvented. It was a whole family event—even old people were here! So I really see it now. My vision's very clear. This is a farm. This is agritourism. People want to experience a farm, even for a day like this." She now has utter confidence that she is onto something big. "After this weekend," she said, "I definitely think this is a farm."

EXPLORE: Visit the website for MaryJaneFarms: http://www.maryjanesfarm.org/. What are your impressions of the present-day condition of the enterprise, a decade or more after the publishing of this essay?

COLLABORATE: Within a group of two or three, discuss the title of this essay, "The Simple Life, Inc." What are the multiple meanings of this title?

WRITE: You are given a chance to interview MaryJane Butters. Your goal is to ask how her business operations differ now from that depicted in this 2004 essay. Develop a list of questions for the interview, keeping in mind good interview principles: to be respectful of the person, to give them meaningful questions, and to provide a final product that informs people and is significant. Review the MaryJaneFarms website to ensure that you are knowledgeable about the current state of business. Test your interview questions on a partner in a role-playing exercise. Revise the questions as needed. Then write the updated version of this essay, drawing on your analysis of the website. Your group might even consider interviewing MaryJane or an associate for real!

VIEWING: A photo essay communicates through pictures. Pick a theme related to farms (e.g., working hands, barns, corn) and take several photographs. Then organize them to be shared. *MaryJane Farms Magazine* sometimes includes photo essays, and you might actually submit your final product.

RESEARCH: Butters is quoted near the end of the article, "Totally like Disneyland reinvented. It was a whole family event—even old people were here! So I really see it now. My vision's very clear. This is a farm. This is agritourism." How is the Disneyland metaphor appropriate for this venue? What is meant by *agritourism*? Do some research about agritourism sites and choose one to three agritourism locales that you would like to visit. Then plot your itinerary. Share with others and compare the various options.

RESEARCH: Online resources from the USDA and state and extension agencies offer plenty of advice to farmers wanting to tap into agritourism dollars. Find and read 1–2 resources from these agencies; also consider the article on MaryJane's farm as your class sets up a debate in which one side argues for the benefits of agritourism (both to the community, culture, and the individual farmer) while the other side argues the disadvantages of agritourism and considers the charge that these events are little more than "Agri-Disney."

Farm City: The Education of an Urban Farmer
Novella Carpenter

Novella Carpenter calls herself the "child of back-to-the-land hippies" who had a farm in Northern Idaho. She studied journalism under Michael Pollan at University of California, Berkeley, and his thematic and stylistic influence is evident in her memoir *Farm City*, which challenges how we think of farms in America. Unlike Kingsolver and Kilmer-Purcell who exchange the city for the countryside, *Farm City* is about *staying* in the city to farm. Can you be a "farmer," Carpenter asks, if you live near the center of Oakland, a city with the highest murder rate in the country, at the end of a dead end street in a ghetto, and you plant your crops on squatted land within the sound of Bay Area's BART commuter line? The answer is a resounding yes.

PART I
TURKEY

CHAPTER ONE

I have a farm on a dead-end street in the ghetto.

My back stairs are dotted with chicken turds. Bales of straw come undone in the parking area next to my apartment. I harvest lettuce in an abandoned lot. I awake in the mornings to the sounds of farm animals mingled with my neighbor's blaring car alarm.

I didn't always call this place a farm. That didn't happen until the spring of 2005, when a very special package was delivered to my apartment and changed everything. I remember standing on my deck, waiting for it. While scanning the horizon for the postal jeep, I checked the health of my bee colony. Honeybees buzzed in and out of the hive, their hind legs loaded down with yellow pollen. I caught a whiff of their honey-making on the breeze, mixed with the exhaust from the nearby freeway. I could see the highway, heavy with traffic, from the deck.

I noticed that three bees had fallen into a watering can. As their wings sent out desperate ripples along the water, I broke off a twig from a potted star jasmine and offered it to the drowning insects. One bee clambered onto the stick and clung to it as I transported her to the top of the hive. The next bee did the same—she held fast to the twig like a passenger gone overboard, clutching a lifesaver. Safe atop the hive, the two soggy bees opened their wings to the morning sunlight. Once dry and warm, they would be able to fly again.

Just to see what would happen, I lifted the final rescuee to the entrance of the hive instead of the top. A guard bee stomped out from the dark recesses of the brood box. There's always one on vigil for disturbances, armed and ready to sting. As the guard bee got closer to the wet one I braced myself for a brutal natural history lesson.

The waterlogged bee started to right herself as she waved a soggy antenna. Another guard bee joined the first, and together they probed the wet bee. She couldn't have smelled of their hive anymore, which is how most bees recognize one another. Nonetheless, the guards began to lick her dry.

"Hey! Hey!" a voice yelled.

I peered down to the end of our dead-end street.

A new car, a silver Toyota Corolla, had arrived on 28th Street the night before, probably the victim of a joyride—Corollas are notoriously easy to start without a key. Local teenagers steal them and drive around until they run out of gas. Already the car had lost one wheel. By nightfall, I predicted, it would be stripped completely.

Amid the jumble of abandoned cars and trash and the shiny Toyota Corolla, I made out the figure of the man who was yelling. He waved vigorously. Bobby.

"Morning, sir!" I called and saluted him. He saluted back.

Bobby lived in an immobilized car. He switched on his television, which was mounted on top of one of the other abandoned cars. An orange extension cord snaked from a teal-colored house at the end of the block. The perky noise of Regis and Kathie Lee joined the sound of the nearby traffic and the clattering trundle of the San Francisco Bay Area's subway, BART, which runs aboveground next to the highway.

Just then, a monk came out of the Buddhist monastery across the street from my house and brought Bobby a snack. The monks will feed anyone who is hungry. Next to the fountain in their courtyard there's a giant alabaster statue of a placid-faced lady riding a dragon: Kuan Yin, the goddess of compassion. My bees loved to drink from the lotus-flower-filled fountain. I often watched their golden bodies zoom across 28th Street, at the same height as the power lines, then swoop down behind the temple's red iron gates.

The monk who handed Bobby a container of rice and vegetables was female, dressed in pale purple robes, her head shaved. Bobby took the food and shoved it into a microwave plugged in next to the television set. Nuked his breakfast.

I heard the clattering sound of a shopping cart. A can scrounger. Wearing a giant Chinese wicker hat and rubber gloves and carrying a pair of tongs, she opened our recycling bin and started fishing around for cans. She muttered to herself in Chinese, "Ay-ya."

I watched as Bobby jogged over to her. I had never seen him run before. "Get out of here," he growled. His territory. She shook her head as if to say she didn't understand and continued fishing. Bobby butted her with his belly. "I said *get*," he yelled. She scurried away, pulling her cart after her. Bobby watched her retreat.

Then, when she was almost around the corner, as if he felt bad, Bobby put his hands to his mouth and yelled, "I'll see you at the recycling center!" Just a few blocks away, the center paid cash by the pound for metal. Chuckling to himself, Bobby glanced up at me on the deck and flashed me a mostly toothless smile.

This place, this ghetto of Oakland, California, brings out the best and the worst in us.

Bored of waiting around outside, I headed back inside my apartment. A fly strip dangled from the ceiling, and ripped feed bags piled up near the door. A black velour couch my boyfriend and I found in the street sagged in the corner.

I guess the neighborhood brings out the best and worst in me, too. Sure, my chickens lay eggs—but the flock has spawned an occasional rooster that crowed loudly and often, starting at 4 a.m. Bees do result in honey and wax and better pollination—but they have also stung people from time to time. The garden: verdant cornucopia on one hand, rodent-attracting breeding ground on the other.

I flopped onto the couch and read the chalkboard tally that hung near the door:

4 chickens
30,000 bees [approximately]
59 flies
2 monkeys [me and my boyfriend, Bill]
That tally was about to change.

A long-debunked scientific theory states that "ontogeny recapitulates phylogeny." Basically that means that the order of development in an embryo indicates its evolutionary development— for example, a human embryo first looks like a fish because we evolved from fish. When Bill and I first moved from Seattle to Oakland, I was reminded of that theory, because somehow we ended up re-creating our old life in the exact same order as we had created it in Seattle. The first year in Oakland, we built the garden; the second year, we got the honeybees and then the chickens. In this, our third year of development, it was time to evolve to the next level.

Out of the corner of my eye, I watched through the window as the postal jeep turned down our street and pulled to a stop in front of our house. A man dressed in wool shorts hopped out, holding an air-hole-riddled box in his arms. I bounded downstairs. My neighbor Mr. Nguyen, who lived one floor below me, was sitting outside on the porch, smoke and steam from his morning cigarette and Vietnamese coffee wafting up together in the crisp spring air. In his sixties, Mr. Nguyen dyed his graying hair black, wore button-down dress shirts, and was surprisingly sprightly. He set down his coffee, stubbed out his cigarette, and walked into the street with me to receive the package.

The postal worker made me sign an official-looking piece of paper before he would hand me the box. It peeped when I opened it.

It was filled with puff balls. Fuzzy yellow ducklings called out desperately with their orange bills. Long-necked goslings squawked, and fluffy multicolored chicks peeped. Three odd-looking chicks with an unattractive pimple of skin atop their heads gazed up quietly from the box.

The delivery guy shook his head in disbelief. I could tell he had questions. Were we not in the city? Wasn't downtown Oakland only ten blocks away? Who is this insane woman? Is this even legal? But years of working for the government had, perhaps, deadened his curiosity. He didn't look me in the eye. He didn't make a sound. He just jumped back into his postal jeep and drove away.

Mr. Nguyen giggled. For the last few years he had happily observed— and participated in— my rural-urban experiments. He knew poultry when he saw it: he had been a farmer in Vietnam before enlisting to help the Americans during the war. "Oh, yes, baby chicks," he said. "Ducks." He pointed a cigarette-stained finger at each species. "Goose." His finger paused at the pimpled heads. He looked at me for a hint.

"Baby turkeys?" I guessed. I had never seen a baby turkey either.

Mr. Nguyen raised his eyebrows.

"Gobble-gobble. Thanksgiving?"

"Oh, yes!" he said, remembering with a smile. Then he grimaced. "My wife make one time."

"Was it good?" I asked. I knew that his wife, Lee, was a vegetarian; she must have made an exception for Thanksgiving.

Mr. Nguyen shook his head vigorously. "No, tough. Too tough. Very bad." I thought he might spit.

I closed the lid, and the peeping stopped. Mr. Nguyen went back into his apartment, returning to the blare of a Vietnamese-language television show.

In the middle of 28th Street, I held the box of poultry and waterfowl. The abandoned ghetto where we lived had a distinct Wild West vibe—gunfights in the middle of the day, a general state of lawlessness, and now this: livestock.

I glanced at the invoice connected to the box: "Murray McMurray Hatchery," it read. "1 Homesteader's Delight." I didn't think about it at the time, but looking back on it, I realize that "Homesteader's Delight" does have a rather ominous ring to it.

Every second-rate city has an identity complex. Oakland is no different. It's always trying to be more arty, more high-tech, more clean than it is able.

O-Town is surrounded by overachievers. The famously liberal (and plush) Berkeley lies to the north. The high-tech mecca of Silicon Valley glimmers to the south. Just eight miles west via the Bay Bridge is San Francisco—so close, but the polar opposite of Oakland. SF is filled with successful, polished people; Oakland is scruffy, loud, unkempt.

I've always chosen uncool places to live. I guess it's because I was born in Idaho, rivaling only Ohio as the most disregarded state in the union. Then I lived in a logging town in Washington State whose big claim to fame was a satanic cult. By the time I moved to Seattle (living in the boring Beacon Hill neighborhood), the uncool, the unsavory, had become my niche. When I went traveling and someone warned me—speaking in low tones, a snarl to her lips—not to go to Croatia or Chiapas or Brooklyn, I tended to add the place to my itinerary immediately.

"Whatever you do, don't go to Oakland," a stocking-cap-clad guy at a Seattle barbecue told me when I confessed that I was going to check out the Bay Area on a long road trip/quest to find a new place to live. I made a mental note to check it out.

Bill and I took three months to explore the candidates. At his insistence, we brought our cat. Bill's a tough-looking guy, with shaggy hair and a strut like he's got two watermelons under his arms. His voice is Tom Waits gravel from years of smoking. He might resemble a Hells Angel, but he's really just a love sponge who spends a great deal of time cuddling with our cat. We hit all the cities we thought we might like to live in: Portland (too perfect). Austin (too in the middle of Texas). New Orleans (too hot). Brooklyn (too little recycling). Philly and Chicago (too cold).

But Oakland—Oakland was just right. The weather was lovely, a never-ending spring. There was recycling and a music scene. But what really drove me and Bill away from the clean and orderly Seattle and into the arms of Oakland was its down-and-out qualities. The faded art deco buildings. The dive bars. Its citizenry, who drove cars as old and beat-up as ours.

Because of inexperience and a housing shortage, Bill and I wound up sharing a ramshackle house in the Oakland hills with a pack of straight-edge vegan anarchists. They wore brown-black clothes, had earth names like Rotten, and liked to play violent computer games in large groups in the common room. Sober.

At first I thought it was cute that anarchists had rules. No alcohol. No dairy products. No meat. Then the paradox started to chafe.

Forced by the strict house regulations, Bill and I would have to rendezvous in our travel-worn van in order to take nips off a contraband bottle of wine, gorge ourselves on banned cheese products, and remember the good old days when we oppressed chickens in our backyard in Seattle. And we plotted our uprising.

One night I unearthed an apartment listing on Craigslist that would set us free. I found it during video game night at the house, surrounded by a pack of anarchists in our living room. While they fired imaginary guns on their computer screens, I clandestinely scanned the ad for the apartment. It was reasonably priced and in downtown Oakland. Feeling subversive, we went for a tour the next day.

The first thing we noticed when we came down from the verdant hills into the flatlands—also known as the lower bottoms—was the dearth of trees. Gray predominated. Bill drove, his coffee brown eyes nervously scanning the scene. We passed one green space huddled under a network of connecting on-ramps. A basketball court, some shrubs. It was called Marcus Garvey Park. No one was there, even on an early summer day.

What was happening was liquor stores. Captain Liquor. Brothers Market. S and N. One after another. The surrounding restaurants were mostly fast-food chains: a Taco Bell, Carl's Jr., Church's Chicken. One variety store caught my eye. Its handmade sign used no words, just images: a pair of dice, socks, eggs, toilet paper. Life's necessities. It reminded me of the little roadside *tiendas* in Mexico. It was the third world embedded in the first.

The houses, though dilapidated, had clearly once been lovely homes: elaborate Victorians next to Spanish Mission bungalows, Craftsman cottages, and vintage brick apartment buildings. They were chipped, charred, unpainted, crumbling. Beautiful neglect.

As we cruised the neighborhood we took stock of our potential neighbors. A man wearing a head scarf was singing as he swept garbage out of the gutter in front of his liquor store. A group of old men sat in lawn chairs in front of their apartment building. A blond woman with scabs on her face limped along the street, pausing to ask for spare change from the young black kids on the corner. The kids wore enormous white T-shirts and saggy pants; they counted their bills and stood in the middle of traffic, waving small plastic bags at prospective customers. Clearly a rough crowd.

All these people out on the street—they were characters I had never met in Seattle, or in our more suburban house in the Oakland hills. I was curious, and yet I had to admit it: they scared me. Could I really live here? Walk around the streets without worrying about getting mugged?

The place was a postcard of urban decay, I thought as we turned down 28th Street. Cheetos bags somersaulted across the road. An eight-story brick building on the corner was entirely abandoned and tattooed with graffiti. Living here would definitely mean getting out of my comfort zone.

We came to a stop in front of a gray 1905 Queen Anne. Like almost every other house in the Bay Area, it had been divided into apartments. The place for rent was the upstairs portion of the duplex. Bill and I surveyed the house. The paint was peeling; a bougainvillea sagged in the side yard. It was a dead-end street, stopping at what was once the grass playground of an elementary school.

Bill pointed out that a dead-end street is a quiet street. He had once lived on one in Orlando and got to know all his neighbors. It made things intimate, he said. Just then, a dazzling woman with cropped platinum hair and platform boots peeked out of her metal warehouse door and beckoned us over to her end of the street.

"My name's Lana," she said. "Anal spelled backward." Bill and I exchanged looks. She stood behind her chain-link fence, a 155-pound mastiff at her side. A robed Buddhist monk emerged from the house next door. He and Lana waved. He disarmed his car alarm—the danger of the 'hood trumps even karma—and drove away. Lana gazed at the retreating car and said, "The old monk used to make me bitter-melon soup when I was sick."

Lana told us, in her high, funny voice, that she had lived on "the 2-8" for fifteen years. "It's not bad now," she assured us. "A few years ago, though, I had people running over my roof, firing machine guns. Now it's like Sesame Street." She shook her head.

Lana then pointed at each of the houses and described its inhabitants: a white family she called the Hillbillies in the teal house, a black mom with two kids in the stucco duplex, an apartment house filled with Vietnamese families who wanted to live near the temple. An abandoned building with a sometime squatter. An empty warehouse that no one knew much about. As we took leave of Lana she invited us to Blue Wednesday, a salon for artists and performers she held every week.

"She seems interesting," I said as we walked back to get our tour of the apartment. Our landlords had arrived in their gold BMW.

"We should move in," Bill said, running his fingers through his shaggy dark hair. He didn't even need to see the apartment.

Our soon-to-be landlords were an African couple with socialist tendencies. They led us upstairs for a tour of the bright little apartment. Hardwood floors. A tile-lined fireplace. A backyard. A living room with a view of a 4,500-square-foot lot filled with four-foot-tall weeds. The landlords didn't know who owned the lot, but they guessed that, whoever they were, they wouldn't mind if we gardened there. We gaped at the enormous space. It had an aspect that would guarantee full sun all day. In Seattle we tended what we thought was a big backyard vegetable garden, but this lot—it was massive by our standards. It sealed the deal.

Bill and I grinned on our way back to our hovel in the hills with the vegan anarchists, still giddy from too much California sunshine and the prospect of a new home.

A few weeks later, when we moved into our new apartment, we discovered that our neighborhood was called GhostTown, for all its long-abandoned businesses, condemned houses, and overgrown lots. The empty lot next to our house was not rare: there was one, sometimes two, on every block. And through the vacant streets rolled GhostTown tumbleweeds: the lost hair-pieces of prostitutes. Tumbleweaves.

The day we moved into GhostTown, a man was shot and killed outside a Carl's Jr. restaurant a few blocks away. We drove past the crime scene—yellow caution tape, a white sheet with a pair of bare feet poking out. We heard on the radio that Oakland had been named number one—it had the highest murder rate in the country. When we drove by later, the body was gone and the business of selling hamburgers and soda had resumed. That night, the not-so-distant crack of gunfire kept me up.

Because of the violence, the neighborhood had a whiff of anarchy—real anarchy, not the theoretical world of my former roommates. In the flatlands, whole neighborhoods were left with the task of sorting out their problems. Except in the case of murder, the Oakland police rarely got involved. In this laissez-faire environment, I would discover as I spent more time in GhostTown, anything went. Spanish-speaking soccer players hosted ad hoc tournaments in the abandoned playfield. Teenagers sold bags of marijuana on the corners. The Buddhist monks made enormous vats of rice on the city sidewalk. Bill eventually began to convert our friends' cars to run on vegetable oil. And I started squat gardening on land I didn't own.

As I fiddled with the door to our apartment, the new box of fowl tucked under my arm, I recognized that I was descending deeper into the realm of the underground economy. Now that I had been in California for a few years, I felt ready for what seemed like the next logical progression, something I had never dared in the soggy Northwest.

Meat birds.

I felt a bit nuts, yes, but I also felt great. People move to California to reinvent themselves. They give themselves new names. They go to yoga. Pretty soon they take up surfing. Or Thai kickboxing. Or astral healing. Or witch camp. It's true what they say: California, the land of fruits and nuts.

In Northern California one is encouraged to raise his freak flag proudly and often. In Seattle my mostly hidden freak flag had been being a backyard chicken owner, beekeeper, and vegetable gardener. I got off on raising my own food. Not only was it more delicious and fresh; it was also essentially free.

Now I was taking it to the next level. Some might say I had been swept up by the Bay Area's mantra, repeated ad nauseam, to eat fresh, local, free-range critters. At farmer's markets here—and there is one every day—it isn't uncommon to overhear farmers chatting with consumers about how the steer from which their steaks were "harvested" had been fed, where their stewing hens ranged, and the view from the sheep pen that housed the lamb that was now ground up and laid out on a table decorated with nasturtium blossoms. Prices correspond with the quality of the meat, and Alice Waters assures us that only the best ingredients will make the best meals. But as a poor scrounger with three low-paying jobs and no health insurance, I usually couldn't afford the good stuff.

Since I liked eating quality meat and have always had more skill than money, I decided to take matters into my own hands. One night, after living in our GhostTown apartment for a few years, I clicked my mouse over various meat-bird packages offered by the Murray McMurray Hatchery Web site. Murray McMurray sold day-old ducks, quail, pheasants, turkeys, and geese through the mail. They also sold bargain-priced combinations: the Barnyard Combo, the Fancy Duck Package, the Turkey Assortment.

These packages, I had thought, might offer a way to eat quality meat without breaking the bank. But I had never killed anything before. Blithely ignoring this minor detail, I settled on the Homesteader's Delight: two turkeys, ten chickens, two geese, and two ducks for $42.

I bought my poultry package with a click of the mouse and paid for it with a credit card. It was only after the post office delivered the box that I realized one can't just buy a farm animal like a book or CD. What I now held in my hands was going to involve a hell of a lot of hard work.

My first task was to install the birds in a brooder, a warm place where they could live without fear of catching cold or encountering predators. I carried the box o' birds upstairs and set it next to the brooder I had hastily built the night before. "Built" might be a strong word—my brooder was a cardboard box lined with shredded paper, with a heat lamp suspended above it and a homemade waterer inside.

The hatchery advised that the chicks would be thirsty from their twenty-four-hour journey in a box. So the first order of the day was to dip the birds' beaks into a dish of water and teach them to drink on their own.

I picked up my first victim, a little yellow chick covered in a soft, downy fuzz, and held her tiny pink beak up to the homemade waterer. It consisted of a mason jar with tiny holes drilled into the lid; when the jar was turned upside down into a shallow dish, capillary action allowed only a bit of water to dribble out and pool in the dish. Amazingly, the chick knew just what to do. She sipped up a beakful of water, then tilted her head back to swallow. The mason-jar waterer glugged, and more water seeped out.

I released her into the cardboard-box brooder, and she wandered over for another sip of water. Then she realized she was alone. She peeped and stumbled around the shredded newspaper looking for her companions. The fowl still in the postal box, strangely silent since I'd placed it on the living room floor, suddenly went wild when they heard her peeps.

So I reached into the box for another chick and worked quickly. Without fail, each victim peeped in distress. The others then chirped in solidarity. All ten finally installed, the chicks quieted down. Exhausted from their journey and my manhandling, they mounded into a fluffy pile under the circle of warm light and took a nap.

Bill stumbled out of our bedroom wearing his boxer shorts, his hair mussed. Not a morning person, he glanced at the baby birds like they were a dream, then headed for the bathroom.

While the chicks slept, I had to educate the dim little turkey poults. They looked like the chicks but with bigger bones and that strange pucker of skin on top of their heads, which I later learned would develop into a turkey part called the snood. Their demeanor was reminiscent of chicks that had done too much acid.

It took the first turkey poult three firm dunkings before it got the hang of drinking water. The poult resisted when I put its beak into the dish, craning its head away, struggling in my hand like a hellcat. Finally, exhausted from struggling, its head went lax and drooped until it dropped into the water dish, where it discovered—surprise!—water, and drank greedily. The other two (the hatchery had sent me an extra poult and an extra duckling, probably as insurance against death by mail) were no different. After I released them, the poults poked around the brooder, gentle and cautious. Eventually they waddled over and joined the puff pile of chicks.

The downy, almost weightless ducklings and goslings drank deeply, using their bills to slurp up large amounts of water. When I set them into the brooder, they waded their big orange feet into the water dish and splashed around. Water hit the side of the box and splattered the sleeping chicks, who awoke and began to peep in protest. Sensing that this might be a disastrous species intersection, I lugged out an aluminum washtub and set up a separate brooder with extra water, a towel, and a bright warm light for the waterfowl.

The baby birds were home, warm and safe. The chicks scratched at their yellow feed just like our big chickens out back did. Sometimes they would stop midscratch and, feeling the warmth of the brooder light, fall asleep standing up. The puffy gray goslings curled their necks around the yellow sleeping ducklings. A Hallmark card had exploded in my living room.

I called my mom. A brooder box full of fowl was something that woman could appreciate. She had once been a hippie homesteader in Idaho.

"Listen to this," I said, and held the phone near the brooder box. A hundred little peeps.

"Oh my god," she said.

"Three turkeys, three ducks, two geese, and ten chickens," I crowed. I watched the chicks and poults moving around the brooder—pooping, scratching, pooping, pecking, pooping.

"Turkeys! Do you remember Tommy Turkey?" she said.

I didn't, but the photo in our family album had stuck with me: my older sister, Riana, in a saggy cloth diaper being chased by the advancing figure of a giant white turkey. Tommy. My mom told us about Tommy every time we got out the old photo album from the ranch days.

"Well, he was mean as hell, and he would chase you guys. . . ."

I looked out the window while my mom described the smokehouse she and my dad had built. Bill had made it downstairs, where he was out front tinkering with our car. His legs peeked out from underneath our dilapidated Mercedes as he rolled around amid the street's numerous Swisher Sweet cigar butts. I had warned him about my meat-bird purchase, and he had been excited about the prospect of homegrown meat, but now that he saw the baby birds—fragile, tiny—he seemed a bit skeptical.

Tommy grew to be an enormous size, my mom said, and as back-to-the-land hippies, she and my dad had been very pleased. They didn't encounter any predator problems that year, and butchering him was a cinch. But disaster did hit: the smokehouse burned to the ground while they were smoking the turkey.

"Oh, no," I groaned.

"Life was like that," she said glumly. I felt sorry for her. My mom's stories usually involve some heroic hippie farm action. I hadn't heard this part of the story before, but I knew bad things had happened. My parents' marriage had dissolved on the ranch in Idaho, after all—my dad too much the mountain man, an uncompromising nonconformist; my mom isolated and bored.

Her voice brightened. "Even though the smokehouse burned down, we did manage to salvage the turkey."

"What do you mean?" I asked.

"We dug through the charred wood, and there it was, a perfectly cooked turkey. I brushed off all the cinders and served him for dinner." She paused and smacked her lips, a noise that was repellent to me as a teenager but now filled me with hope. "It was the best turkey I've ever had," she declared. We said our goodbyes, and I hung up the phone.

I glanced into the cozy chick brooder. The chicks slept on their mattress of shredded pages from the *New York Times*. Their fuzzy bodies slumbered on snatches of color ads for watches, a stern op-ed about pollution in China, the eyebrows of a politician. I had to remind myself that though they were cute, these baby birds would eventually become my dinner. Thanksgiving, in particular, was going to be intense. I imagined the killing scene: a butcher block, an ax, three giant Tommy turkeys I had known since poulthood. I wasn't sure if I could bring myself to do it.

But the conversation with my mom left me emboldened for my foray into killing and eating animals I had raised myself—this urge was clearly part of my cultural DNA. I wondered if this would prove that I could have it both ways: to sop up the cultural delights of the city while simultaneously raising my own food. In retrospect, though, I wonder why I thought my experience would be any less disastrous than my parents'.

The next day, following the suggestions of a homesteading book from the 1970s, I swabbed the baby birds' butts with Q-tips. The long flight in a box can cause digestion problems for the chicks—namely, pasted vents. Which is a fancy way of saying blocked buttholes. So I dutifully wetted them down, plucked dried matter from their bottoms, and felt terrible when I had to tug off whole chunks of downy feathers. I wasn't satisfied until all their parts looked pink and healthy.

After morning chicken-butt detail, I sat in my kitchen and surveyed our squat garden. All the east-facing windows of our apartment overlook the lot, which after the past few years had been transformed into a vegetable and fruit-tree garden. I could see that the collards were getting large and that the spring's lettuce harvest promised to be a good one. Even from inside, I could see some mildew forming on the pea vines.

It was going to be a remarkable year; I could sense it. If my life in Oakland was a developing embryo, with this meat-bird addition, it was as if a fishlike creature had suddenly sprouted wings. . . .

A word about my backyard: Don't entertain some bucolic fantasy. In the middle of it, Mrs. Nguyen's exercise bike sat on a bare patch of dirt. The landlord had installed a rusty metal shed at the foot of the stairs a few years earlier, and it now held all the things we and the Nguyens wished we could get rid of. A shattered mirror lay between the fence and the shed.

In the very back of the yard was the chicken coop Bill had built from pallets in what had been a large dog run made with sturdy chain link fencing no overgrown with weeds and volunteer trees. Abutting this chicken area was an auto-repair shop/junkyard, which hosted two does: a pale brown pit bull and a dark-eyed Rottweiler mix. A forklift often zoomed around the repair shop, dodging rusting transmissions and barrels of god knows what. A little beyond the autoshop, you could see downtown Oakland's non-descript skyline. . . . Not exactly a country idyll. . . .

People from the neighborhood harvesting food from my garden is a common sight. There's Lou, a stooped man who helps himself to the lush crop of greens in the winter; a mute lady who carries a plastic sack into the garden and doesn't stop harvesting lettuce until that bag is swollen—or until I open the window and call down at her, "OK! That's enough! Leave some for everyone else!"

Some of the harvesters are annoying. One year, an unidentified person stopped by for what he thought was onions and picked some of my young garlic instead, then abandoned the small bulbs on the ground. In response, I made a little handwritten sign that said GARLIC, NOT ONIONS, READY IN JULY! and another, near a collard-greens patch, saying "DON'T PICK <u>ALL</u> THE LEAVES OFF THE PLANT. These signs aren't necessarily effective. They just fade and get buried by a pile of wood chips in the fall. But I feel the need to instruct nonetheless.

A simple solution would be to snap a padlock on the gate. Then again, I'm a trespasser myself—I don't lease or rent the verdant lot, so I'd feel like a hypocrite telling others to stay away.

EXPLORE: Carpenter refers to California as a place where people go to reinvent themselves, and she mentions that her neighborhood is like the wild west and that her poultry comes in the "Homesteader's Delight" package. Consider and be prepared to discuss how her story fits in with the historical patterns of farming that we've seen thus far in this text. Also consider how this story paints a radically different picture of the American farm.

EXPLORE: Using GPS or another map finder, locate Carpenter's urban farm and take note of what surrounds GhostTown Farm.

WRITE: Take either a pro or con stance regarding city farms and write a letter to the editor of the local newspaper. Within your group, share your letters and then delineate the arguments for each side.

RESEARCH: Will everyone in a neighborhood feel positively about city farms? What are the ordinances in your city or town regarding keeping farm animals?

FOR FURTHER READING: Want to read more of Novella Carpenter's stories about urban farming? Check out her blog GhostTown Farm at http://ghosttownfarm. wordpress.com/. How does a blog differ from a book? Have you ever considered writing a blog, or do you have one already? What are the conventions of a blog?

FOR FURTHER READING: In the explanatory material at the beginning of this chapter, several book titles about urban farming or farming are mentioned. Choose one of these or another that is similar; read it and write a review appropriate for *Mother Earth News*.

FOR FURTHER READING: Many farm-focused books use the calendar year to organize the story. Barbara Kingsolver uses a March-to-March timeline in *Animal, Vegetable, Miracle*. Likewise, Sue Hubbell's *A Country Year: Living the Questions* begins and ends with "Spring." Terra Brockman's *The Seasons on Henry's Farm: A Year of Food and Life on a Sustainable Farm* is divided into 52 chapters, one for each week of the year, with the overarching sections labeled as the cycles of the moon: Hunter's Moon, Long Night Moon, Old Moon, Sap Moon, and so forth. Choose a book to read that is structured by the calendar. Write a literary analysis essay of the book.

 WRITE: In Barbara Kingsolver's *Animal, Vegetable, Miracle,* daughter Camille Kingsolver is responsible for providing the recipes and menus over the various seasons in this book. If you were to catalog a list of recipes and menus for the year, what would you include?

 WRITE: Your local library has asked you, because of your expertise with farm literature, to prepare a guide to books that focus on urban farming. Select at least ten books, skim them, and then develop an annotated bibliography. The books might focus on urban farming in general or more particularly on raising chickens or planting gardens. Put the final version in a format that will be useful to the library, which might be a brochure, posters, or an oral presentation.

Additional Resources

Farming looks mighty easy when
your plow is a pencil, and you're a
thousand miles from the cornfield.

—Dwight D. Eisenhower
Address at Bradley University
25 September 1956

❦ APPENDIX A ❦

Major Projects to Consider

Here you will find suggestions for major projects that might be considered as culminating assignments for a term spent investigating the literature and culture of farms and farming.

Searching for Ceres: The Roman Goddess Ceres represents agriculture and fertility. She is often portrayed with a sheaf of wheat. Her daughter Persephone was famously stolen by Hades and taken to the Under World.
> **Option One**: Find an image of Ceres and in an essay offer a description of the work of art along with your analysis of its meaning.
> **Option Two**: Find several images of Ceres and, placing them in chronological order, analyze and reflect on how her image has changed over centuries of time.

The Farm Bill: The Farm Bill is an important, but often contentious, piece of federal legislation. Briefly summarize the content of the farm bill and why it is controversial. Then, using a minimum of three texts that you have read in this class, argue for or against funding the Farm Bill.

Reflective Essay: Write a formal reflective essay in which you also synthesize your reading and viewing over the term, drawing from examples in the texts and the fine arts. What images of rural life, particularly farm life, have evolved over time? What are our current perceptions of an agricultural life? How has this course changed your perceptions?

Memoir: A genre to explore is *memoir*, which is literary nonfiction that focuses on reminiscences of scenes from a person's life. In that sense, it is autobiographical. Thoreau's *Walden* (1854) is a memoir. Read a memoir and in an essay demonstrate how it meets the criteria of memoir. Or, read two memoirs, one by a woman, and one by a man. Does gender influence memoir? How are they alike? How do they differ? There is a wealth of titles to choose from in memoir: Ivan Doig's *This House of Sky*; Kristin Kimball's *The Dirty Life*; David Grene's *On Farming and Classics*; Catherine Friend's *Hit by a Barn*; Joel Salatin's *Family Friendly Farming*; William Alexander's *The $64 Tomato*; E. B. White's *One Man's Meat*; Novella Carpenter's *Farm City*; Betty MacDonald's *The Egg and I*; Anne Barclay Priest's *Trafficking in Sheep*; and Brad Kessler's *Goat Song*. Goodreads.com has a helpful list of farm memoirs.

International Farm-themed Books: This book has focused largely on farms in, the United States. How do books set in other countries differ? Perhaps one of the very best known farm-themed books of all time is Pearl S. Buck's *The Good Earth*, set in pre-revolutionary China. It continues to be a fascinating story of one family's relationship with the land. Other books set beyond the shores of the USA include Rosina Lippi's *Homestead* (Austrian fiction, multi-generational); Donald Hall's *Romanian Furrow* (nonfiction); Park's *Land* (epic novel set in Korea); Olive Shreiner's *The Story of an African Farm*. Read a book set in a country other than the US. Write an essay in which you compare and contrast the book to one you have read that is set in the US. Are there similar themes? What are the relationships of the characters?

Nonfiction Farm Books: Richard Rhodes's *Farm: A Year in the Life of an American Farmer* tracks the course of events on an Iowa Farm, focusing on one family. Rhodes is the author of the Pulitzer Prize–winning book, *The Making of the Atomic Bomb*, and is a master at investigating and writing about diverse topics, such as Hedy Lamarr, the movie bombshell who was also an inventor. His *Hole in the World* is about his own childhood at the hands of abusive parents and how being sent to live on a farm was his salvation. One option: read *Farm: A Year in the Life of an American Farmer* and write a literary analysis. Another option: note that many of the farm books focus on "a year" timeline, including *Animal, Vegetable, Miracle* by Kingsolver and Sue Hubbell's *A Country Year: Living the Questions*. Skim several "year" books and write an essay about why this timeframe is particularly suited to writing about life on a farm.

Whodunit? Surprised to find that mysteries may be set on farms? The mystery genre is an ever-popular one, and for good reason as readers try to guess the outcome before all is revealed. Read one or more mysteries set on farms and prepare a book talk recommending farm-themed mysteries. Here are some titles that might get your started: *The Pig Did It* (the first of a trilogy of pig-themed mysteries set in Ireland by Joseph Caldwell); *Three Bags Full* (follow literate sheep— they've been read to on a daily basis by their shepherd—as they solve a murder in this mystery by Leonie Swann); *Going Organic Can Kill You* (one of the Blossom Valley series by Staci McLaughlin); *Farm Fresh Murder* (a farmers' market mystery) by Paige Shelton; *Mystery Ranch* (a classic by Max Brand that adds the Western genre to the mystery).

Radio Interview: Imagine that you host a 30-minute author interview show, and you have just been told by the station manager that you have the opportunity to interview the author of a book that focuses on farming. Choose a book (e.g., *Weeds: A Farm Daughter's Lament; The Dirty Life; This House of Sky*) and read it. Identify two to three passages that you'd like the author to read on air. Prepare a list of ten questions to ask the writer.

Book Group/Library: Because you are an expert on "Farm Literature," your book group or local library has asked you to compile a recommended reading list. Begin by developing an annotated bibliography that includes the author, title, publication date, and a brief summary for each book. You might also give your personal rating. Then develop a Guide to Farm Literature in an appropriate format, such as a print brochure, a slide presentation, or a poster.

Extended Definition: Book-length extended definitions on sugar (*Sugar Changed the World* by Aronson and Budhos) and salt (*Salt: A World History* by Kurlansky) as well as essays on wheat and soil ("Wheat" by Richard Rhodes in his *The Inland Ground*; "Our Good Earth" by Charles Mann in *National Geographic*, September 2008) demonstrate how one item or part of a farm may be given in-depth analysis. Mimi Sheraton chose to follow the trail of Bialy rolls (*The Bialy Eaters,*

2002), and in so doing, uncovered the devastation wrought through genocide and the Holocaust. Choose one topic to explore in an essay. Extended definition makes use of history, comparison and contrast, examples, process, negative definition, as well as other approaches to form a cohesive whole.

Poking Fun: One scene in the satiric TV show *Portlandia* which pokes fun at people who are very organic- and eco-minded, features a couple at a restaurant who want to order dish but relentlessly interrogate their waitress about how the bird was raised. The waitress provides the chicken's complete, full-color dossier. (To watch, see this URL: http://www.hulu.com/watch/208808.) Cartoonists also poke fun at the same theme. *The New Yorker* cleverly includes such cartoons; for instance, one by Edward Koren features farmers with a calf in a baby carriage with the caption "We raise our beef humanely" or David Sipress's picture of one cow saying to another, "Do you ever ask yourself 'humanely raised' for <u>what</u>?" Choose a medium—for example, a poster, script, cartoon, or story—and create a work that satirizes the organic, sustainable, locavore, back-to-the-farm movement.

From One Medium to Another: Sometimes one work will inspire another work in yet another medium. Take for instance Andrew Maxfield, a composer who found inspiration in Wendell Berry's work, particularly his poetry, and set the words to music. (See http://wendellberrymusic.com/.) His musical compositions not only celebrate Berry's work but also contribute to the work of The Berry Center, a nonprofit organization that supports sustainable agriculture. Are you inspired by work that you have read in this *FARM* book? Might you consider using a text from this book to create another work, perhaps in another medium, such as sculpture, music, or writing? Consider how an artist interprets a text to create another work.

Saving the Family Farm: A recurrent theme in literature and other works about the farm is the danger of losing the land because of financial woes or weather disasters. Mardi Jo Link's *Bootstrapper* (2013) tells the story of how a single mother tries to preserve the northern Michigan farm where she and her three sons live. The films *Country* and *The River* also depict farms in danger of being lost. The organization Farm Aid was founded in 2001 to help farmers hold onto their land. Originally thought to be a one-time concert, Farm Aid continues, as the economic crisis for farmers never went away. Explore this theme of saving the family farm in an analytical essay that draws together several texts—literary, film, and visual art.

Edible Education: Edible Education 103: Telling Stories About Food and Agriculture is a Fall 2012 course at UC Berkeley, Graduate School of Journalism and College of Letters and Science. The course is moderated by Michael Pollan, a Knight Journalism Professor at UC Berkeley and author of *The Omnivore's Dilemma* and other works. Fifteen lectures are available online at this site: http://www.cityfarmer.info/2012/12/18/edible-education-103-at-uc-berkeley-course-lead-by-michael-pollan/
What can be done to make the food system healthier, more equitable, and more sustainable? What is the role of storytelling in the process? Listen to a lecture in the series. If you were to be asked to deliver a lecture in this course, what topic would you address? Write the script for that lecture, including illustrations.

Barn Again: The American barn is a familiar icon and one that often provokes an emotional response. The Smithsonian organized a traveling exhibition of *Barn Again! Celebrating an American Icon* (2003) and developed educational guides. Although barns increasingly are disappearing or falling into disrepair, they remain an important symbol in American culture. Doug Mottonen did research on barns in Utah to write his *If Barns Could Talk*. Barns can figure in any number of assignments as they truly do have stories.

- Are there barns in your community? Is there an opportunity to conduct a local history project on one or more? Barns can be a window onto a community's past.
- Find and read the poem "Barn Fever" by Peter Davison, which calls the barn "an emblem of the past." How does this poem tell a history?
- Some communities feature their historic barns in driving tours for field trips. See http://www.bearriverheritage.com/DrawAboutUs.aspx for two examples, one *Historic Barns of Northern Utah* and the other *Historic Barns of Southeastern Idaho*. Might you develop a similar driving tour of historic barns for your area? **National Agricultural Library of USDA**: http://www.nal.usda.gov/. The History, Art, and Biography section of the National Agricultural Library has interesting features, including the Thomas Jefferson correspondence collection and a fine image and picture collection of past and contemporary work. Choose one of its holdings and describe it in a brief essay, noting its importance and why it should be archived.

Farm blogs: A list of farm blogs can be found at http://farmerbloggers.com/followfarmer/index.html, but many others can be found on the Internet. Analyze the blog rhetorically. You may choose to focus on a specific aspect of the blog. For instance at MaryJane Farms, you might choose to analyze the videos on the website, perhaps looking at her as a farmgirl version of Martha Stewart, using farming as a lifestyle. You may want to use the term *vlog*, which is a video blog.

Theorizing the Farm: Theorize the farm by recognizing ways in which farming serves a cultural function in our society. You may think of it as a fill-in-the-blank to the following statement: Farming culturally represents an act of _____. List these, providing a paragraph discussing each of your "theories" that suggests a "so what," and *specifically* points to where you saw it in class discussions, readings, or research. The questions and prompts below should help you recognize these cultural functions.

Questions and Prompts for "Theorizing the Farm" Exercise:
- What are the metaphors we use for farming?
- What symbols (literal things representing an idea) do you recognize in any cultural discussion of farming?
- Where do we use other rhetorical devices in our discussion of farming, such as overstatement and hyperbole (exaggeration)? Do we ever personify aspects of farming in surprising ways? Does our language about farming ever use *metonymy* (i.e., "The pen is mightier than the sword" means that written language is greater than warfare) or *synecdoche* (i.e., a part of something is used to represent the whole, as when we refer to "the crown" to mean a king or "All hands on deck!" as an order for sailors)
- What meaning or purpose does farming give our lives?

- What relationship does farming suggest between humans and the land or the things a farmer does? People tend to conceive of our human association to farming by thinking of it in terms of human relationships. For instance, do we see the act of farming as paternal, maternal, fraternal, or other? What other human relationships come into play here?
- What stories, myths, tall tales, or legends do we associate with farming repeatedly or seem at the heart of our cultural thinking about farming?
- What kind of language do we use to talk about farming? Where do we use loaded language—that language that appeals to emotion rather than logic?
- How do we conceptualize the various acts associated with farming (planting, tending, and harvesting, for instance)?
- What does it mean to be successful as a farmer? What innate qualities does a good farmer have? What powers? What does being successful at farming prove?
- By contrast, what does it mean to be a failure as a farmer? What essential things does that mean the farmer lacks?
- Farming seems to have *cultural* as well as personal/individual significance. Why is farming a notion linked to our cultural identity? Why does it seem to be important to us as a country? In what ways does American farming seem to differ from agriculture anywhere else in the world?
- Are there notions about farming that are shaped by issues of gender, spirituality, politics, patriotism, popular culture, etc.?

Farm Journal: Organize your own Farm Journal that is part research, part reflection and meditation, part visual creation, part theoretical exploration, and wholly an interdisciplinary project. The object of the assignment is for you to consider how far ranging are our cultural notions about farming. Record your own ponderings about how farming is conceptualized. At the beginning of the term, set up some kind of portfolio, loose leaf notebook, PowerPoint document, regular blank journal, or scrapbook where you can gather additional materials related to this subject. Work on this project throughout the semester. You may arrange these materials in any way you wish. However, your journal must have the following:

☐ **Cover and Preface**. Decorate a cover or opening page that reflects some important aspect of the topic; provide a preface(at least two single-spaced pages of approximately 600 words) that discusses the choices you made for your cover and how and why it accurately reflects what is inside and what kinds of conclusions you've drawn. Your cover should make a statement about what you've learned over the term. The preface should also act as an introduction to the contents of your journal, perhaps by talking about the process of collecting these materials and/or an overview of the general insights gained from the chosen materials.

☐ **Collect and Reflect—Contemporary**. Collect contemporary materials related to the subject of farming. This could be a letter to the editor in the newspaper about local farms, the text of a television news story about the recently passed Farm Bill, a farmer's daughter joke you recently heard, the lyrics of a new country western song, and so on. For the most part, these will probably be primary materials. You should gather a *minimum of five* documents in this category; make sure these documents are properly cited in your journal.

Reflect: Then, for at least three of these materials, write a short reflection/meditation. The objective here is to choose some topics from your farm journal and ruminate on in some extended way. Each reflection/meditation should be about a page long (about 350 words). Use these ideas to probe more deeply into a topic: analyze the rhetoric of a document (visual rhetoric of photo or painting, perhaps, or the rhetoric of a letter to the editor or lyrics to a song). Apply what you've learned to new materials you are putting into your farm journal; compare and contrast your Farm Journal materials with the literature you read.

☐ **Collect and Reflect—Historical**. Collect historical materials related to the farm. Do research into primary materials. Look at *The Farmer's Wife* magazine, for instance, and examine/copy the covers or the advertising. Interview a retiring farmer. Find out something about the beginning of the John Deere Company. Read an interview with Thomas Hart Benton or find the works of some other artist from the past. Research some interesting fact about a food or crop, mirroring Michael Pollan's approach (the cultural history of the banana, for instance). Gather a *minimum of five* documents in this category; properly cite these documents in your journal.

Reflect, as above, on at least three of those materials. Each reflection/meditation should be about a page long (about 350 words). Your reflection should be a well-written, unified essay with a good sense of a thesis.

Married to the Farm? Gary Nabhan, is a food and farming activist. He proposes that farmers renew their vows to be good stewards of the land. Following are the vows he proposes:

> *I, (name), a gardener, farmer, seed saver, and eater,*
> *wish to renew our sacred vows*
> *to take care, love and serve*
> *the astonishing diversity of life on this earth.*
> *Through sickness and in health* (I bet you knew that line was coming*),*
> *in times of crisis and times of joy,*
> *to sow the seeds of food justice,*
> *to sow the seeds of food security,*
> *to sow the seeds of food democracy,*
> *to sow the seeds of true food sovereignty,*
> *through our own actions and our own eating patterns*
> *so that we may all eat what we have truly sown.*
> *I reaffirm our covenant with this earth,*
> *to humbly be one more way that seeds themselves regenerate into more seeds to nourish all of us.*
> *Love one another and go and sow in peace.*

Source: http://garynabhan.com/i/archives/2249

Nabhan uses vows of marriage altering the prose to suit his purpose. If you were to revise a text to fit a farming theme, what would that text be, and for what purpose? Try your hand at creating an appropriate text as Nabhan does.

The Grange Movement: Officially known as the National Grange of the Order of Patrons of Husbandry, the Grange is a community organization that encourages farmers to organize in order to promote the well-being of agriculture in politics. Founded in 1867, it functions as an advocacy group. One of its accomplishments is rural free mail delivery. What do you know about the Grange? Does your community have a Grange that presses for the causes of farmers? Conduct research on the Grange and focus on one topic of interest that results in a researched paper.

Farmer vs. Rancher: The classic film *Shane* (1953), from the book of the same name by Jack Schaefer, pits cattle rancher against homesteader. View the film or read the book. Then find two to three other films or books with similar themes of farmer vs. rancher. Write a researched essay that explores this important conflict.

❧ Appendix B ❧

Glossary

Literary Terms

bildungsroman. A story about the building of someone's character, often a coming of age story.

characterization. The creation and development of the people in a story.

conflict. A struggle a character must overcome.

foreshadowing. The use of clues to suggest something that is going to happen.

genre. The type or kind of prose or poetry.

intertextuality. Comparing texts to find similarities in styles, topics, and themes.

irony. A twist of fate in which the results of action are not the expected ones.

metaphor. Figurative language in which dissimilar items are likened to each other.

mood. The feeling a reader gets from a story. This is related to *tone.*

novel. A work of fiction.

plot. The events that occur in a story.

point of view. First person point of view uses *I* while second person point of view, which is used rarely, uses *you*; third person point of view relies on people's names, as in "Jesse saw the accident."

protagonist. The main characters in stories, usually the one with which readers identify. *Antagonists* oppose the protagonist.

setting. Where and when the action takes place.

style. The way in which a story is written in contrast to what it is about.

symbolism. A person, place, event, or object that carries deeper meaning than simply the literal meaning.

theme. The central idea that the author conveys.

Farm Terms

agriculture. The process of growing crops as well as their distribution.

agrarian. The social and political philosophy that holds rural life can shape ideal social values. In Jefferson's time, an agrarian economy was conceived as essential to the public good.

agribusiness. The business of agriculture that includes wide range of modern food production, including seed suppliers, processing plants, retailers. Also known as "corporate farming," this term refers to large-scale farming operations that may include vertical or horizontal conglomerates. This term is often used in contrast to "family farm."

almanac. An annual publication that is laid out in chronological order—a calendar for the year. Its purpose is to predict the weather and offer advice to farmers for planting. It also includes the phases of the moon along with times for sunrise and sunset. One of the most famous almanacs was Ben Franklin's *Poor Richard's Almanack*.

barbed wire. Invented in 1874, barbed wire features sharp points and restrains livestock.

booster. A Booster promotes a community or organization, and boosterism was particularly common in the settlement of the Midwest and West with sometimes outlandish claims made in order to attract settlers. Sinclair Lewis' significant novel *Main Street* includes boosterism as a theme.

CAFO. The acronym for "Concentrated Animal Feeding Operation," a highly intensive and industrialized method used in factory farm/agribusiness operations that includes feeding lots and poultry and hog confinement buildings.

Century Farms. Term applied to farms that have been in continuous operation by a single family for 100 years or more. Although some states tracked century farms since the Depression, a renewed recognition of century farms occurred in the late 1970s and during the Farm Crisis.

conglomerates. Businesses that hold vested interest in various points along food's path to consumer. They include vertical (businesses that have vested interest in multiple points along the path from field to fork) and horizontal conglomerates (monopolies of the same farm categories, i.e., owning several hog farms under different names).

Country Life Commission. President Teddy Roosevelt, belonging that rural America is the backbone of the nation, organized this Commission in 1908 to ensure that country life was attractive and that people did not depart for cities.

Dawes Act of 1887. This is also known as the "Indian Homestead Act." The act divided reservation land into privately owned lots of 160.

DDT. Latin name is *dichlorodiphenyltrichloroethane*. This chemical is the best known of those developed after World War II for agricultural applications. The chemist who developed it received a

Nobel Peace Prize in 1948; however, it was found to have serious and disastrous impact on environment and human health and was banned from use in 1972.

economies of scale. A business term based on idea that cost advantages are greater the larger a company becomes.

ethicurean. "Chew the right thing." People who are ethicureans eat sustainable, organic, local, and ethical food.

exurb. Unlike city or suburbs, this area lies beyond the suburbs, and is typically inhabited by those sufficiently wealthy to live a more rural lifestyle.

factory farms. Farms in which livestock or their products (e.g., eggs) are raised in high-density areas, such as feed lots or confinement buildings, which provide for maximum production but have been criticized for inhumane environment.

Farm Crisis of 1980s. Economic disaster caused by numerous farm policies, overproduction, and farm debt; led to significant increase in farm foreclosures and bankruptcies, bank closures, rural community decline, and a increase in suicide rate among farmers.

Genetically Modified Organism (GMO). Altering an organism—plant or animal—through genetic engineering. In agriculture, GMOs may result in an effort to increase production.

gentry. These people of the Middle Ages held land and estates. They were of a high social class but may not be of the nobility. In Colonial America, landed gentry evolved into the notion of gentleman farmer, who farms mainly for pleasure rather than for profit.

"Get Big or Get Out!" Belief expressed by two Secretaries of Agriculture, Benson and Butz, that the future of farming did not lie with small, family farms; instead, they believed, agribusiness was the best approach.

Grange. An advocacy group founded in 1867 that promotes the cause of farmers, The National Grange of the Order of Patrons of Husbandry seeks economic well being of agriculture through political activism.

Green Revolution. The effort to take agribusiness approaches globally in order to ensure international food security, a term that was first used in the 1960s.

Homestead Act. Enacted in 1862 by President Lincoln, the Homestead Act gave applicants land, *homesteads*, for little or no money, and helped settle the western and Midwestern lands.

Hooverville. Named after President Herbert Hoover, these shanty towns were built by homeless tenant farmers during the Great Depression.

husbandry. Cultivating crops and breading and raising livestock are the province of husbandry, and it's expected that scientific principles will be applied to the process.

industrial farming. Featuring economies of scale to achieve maximum profit, this type of farming provides much of the food available in supermarkets.

Jethro Tull. Before the rock group with this name, Jethro Tull (1674-1741) was an English agricultural pioneer who perfected a planter that dropped seeds in neat rows as well as a horse-drawn hoe.

John Deere. A blacksmith, John Deere (1804-1886) revolutionized the plow by manufacturing them in steel with a moldboard shaped differently than the standard. The result was "the plow that broke the plains" and allowed the Midwest to be settled.

land-grant college. Created by the Morrill Act of 1862, institutions of higher education were established by funds granted through land in each state. Their purpose was to provide education to the sons and daughters of the industrial classes, which includes farming.

locavore. Deemed the 2007 Word of the Year by *New Oxford American Dictionary,* refers to a person who prefers to eat food produced locally, food that has not been transported long distances.

Manifest Destiny. The belief that American settlers had a divine right to explore and expand throughout the continent.

microfarmng. Small farming, such as growing vegetables in patio containers in an urban setting, farming on a city lot, or acre plus farming.

mono-cropping. The practice of intensively growing only on crop in a field, which makes harvesting easier, but also makes the crop more susceptible to disease and pest infestation, as happened with the Irish Potato Famine of the late nineteenth century. Polyculture or mixed cropping are the opposite.

open range. Cattle and sheep are allowed to roam widely in open range grazing.

organic. Foods that are produced by organic methods that limit or prohibit pesticides and chemical applications. Certification is by a strict set of measures. An alternative for farmers is Certified Naturally Grown, which is less restrictive.

pastoral tradition. Focuses on an ideal, rural landscape that includes admiration for nature and an emotional response to the land. A pastoral landscape, for instance, is aesthetically pleasing even if artificially developed.

penny auctions and nickel auctions. A form of protesting farm foreclosures first during the Great Depression and later during the Farm Crisis of the 1980s in which banks were blamed for robbing farmers of livelihood during difficult economic times; referred to a solidarity among auction goers that no one would bid more than a penny or nickel, thus ensuring that banks couldn't profit from farmer's misfortune.

plantation system. Agricultural system in Antebellum South that separated slaves from white "planters" or owners in a complicated hierarchy based on race and skills. Sugar and tropical fruit plantations are also found in the Hawaiian Islands and coffee plantations are found around the world.

permaculture. A method of ecological design that creates spaces patterned after natural ecosystems that don't require human input to thrive. It is a design concept to mimic natural ecosystems.

ranching. The practice of ranching focuses primarily on raising grazing livestock. Unlike traditional farms, ranches are often large, due to the arid land in the West where they tend to be located.

rurban. A residential area where some farming occurs.

rural area. Not urban, this is an area located outside cites and towns, typically with low population.

Rural Electrification Act (REA). Passed in 1936, this act brought electricity to rural areas and improved the quality of life.

Rural Free Delivery (RFD). This act, promoted by The Grange, meant that mail was delivered to rural homes.

serfs. In feudal times, these peasants were in the lowest class, attached to the land, and required to perform labor for the owner.

sharecropping and tenant farming. Systems in which the farmer does not own the land he or she farms, prevalent in the South after the Civil War; also found in other areas of the US. Historians sometimes call sharecropping and tenant farming in the South "slavery-in-kind."

short-handled hoe. Used by migrant workers, the hoe forced workers to stoop in the fields all day, which had crippling, life-long effects for the workers. Cesar Chavez called it a "symbol of suffering" for migrant workers.

subsistence farming. A type of farming in which farmers grow only enough food to feed themselves and their families.

sustainable agriculture. Using principles of ecology, this type of agriculture focuses on quality of life in addition to environmentally sensitive production.

transcendentalism. Espoused by Emerson and Thoreau early in the nineteenth century, transcendentalism is a philosophy that focuses on nature, particularly nature as a key to spirit. It also calls for people to be self-reliant and independent.

urban millennium. Refers to the global population shift in which more people lived in urban areas than in rural; thought to have happened in 2007.

USDA. The United States Department of Agriculture is the government department responsible for leadership on food, agriculture, natural resources, rural development, and nutrition issues. A Condensed History of American Agriculture 1776–1999 can be found at this site: http://www.usda.gov/documents/timeline.pdf.

Victory Gardens. Campaign during World Wars I and II in which the public was encouraged to grow some of their own food as a show of patriotism and support for the troops. Victory Garden campaigns often argued that "Food is a Weapon" that could help win the war; thus, all citizens could "do their bit" in the war effort.

Women's Land Army. World War I and II war campaigns to have women assume farm jobs while men were off at war. This was one way that allowed women to participate in the war effort.

yeoman farmer. Independent farmer who owned a small acreage and was directly involved in day-to-day running of his farm. He also took on civic obligations and was respected in the community as being honest.

APPENDIX C

List of Literature with Farm Themes

The following list is a brief enumeration of books with farming themes. Searches on the Internet will yield many, many more, including such classics as Ole Edvart Rolvaag's *Giants in the Earth,* Erskine Caldwell's *Tobacco Road,* and Rachel Carson's seminal *Silent Spring.*

Author Last	Author First	Title
Allen	Will	*The Good Food Revolution: Growing Healthy Food, People, and Communities*
Amos	Evelyn E.	*Life in the Upper Country: The Diary of Evelyn E. Amos 1948-1957*
Azarian	Mary	*A Farmer's Alphabet*
Azarian	Mary	*The Four Seasons of Mary Azarian*
Beame	Hugh	*Home Comfort: Stories and Scenes of Life on Total Loss Farm*
Berry	Wendell	*Three Short Novels*
Berry	Wendell	*A World Lost*
Blew	Mary Clearman	*All But the Waltz: Essays on a Montana Family*
Blew	Mary Clearman	*Lambing Out and Other Stories*
Blunt	Judy	*Breaking Clean*
Brox	Jane	*Clearing Land: Legacies of the American Farm*
Buck	Pearl S.	*The Good Earth*
Butler	Anne M. & Ona Siporin	*Uncommon Common Women: Ordinary Lives of the West*
Butters	MaryJane	*MaryJane's Ideabook, Cookbok, Lifebook: For the Farm Girl in All of Us*
Cather	Willa	*My Ántonia*
Cleaveland	Agnes Morley	*No Life for a Lady*
Cronin	Doreen	*Click, Clack, Moo*
Doig	Ivan	*This House of Sky: Landscapes of a Western Mind*
Doig	Ivan	*Dancing at the Rascal Fair*
Downing	Michael	*Perfect Agreement*
Frazier	Craig	*Stanley Goes for a Drive*
Friend	Catherine	*Hit by a Farm: How I Learned to Stop Worrying and Love the Barn*
Greene	David	*Of Farming & Classics*
Greenwood	Annie Pike	*We Sagebrush Folks*
Gulliford	Andrew	*America's Country Schools (3rd ed.)*
Hall	Donald	*The Man Who Lived Alone*

Hall	Donald J.	*Romanian Furrow*
Hall	Donald	*String Too Short to be Saved: Recollections of Summers on a New England Farm*
Harris	Bill	*Barns of America*
Harrison	Jim	*Farmer*
Heaney	Seamus	*Death of a Naturalist*
Hein	Teri	*Atomic Farmgirl: Growing Up Right in the Wrong Place*
Howard	Manny	*My Empire of Dirt: How One Man Turned His Big-City Backyard into a Farm*
Hubbell	Sue	*A Country Year: Living the Questions*
Janik	Carolyn	*The Barn Book*
Jordan	Teresa	*Riding the White Horse Home: A Western Family Album*
Kalish	Mildred Armstrong	*Little Heathens: Hard Times and High Spirits on an Iowa Farm During the Great Depression*
Kerr	Norwood Allen	*The Legacy : a Centennial History of the State Agricultural Experiment*
Kidd	Sue Monk	*The Secret Lives of Bees*
Kingsolver	Barbara (et al.)	*Animal, Vegetable, Miracle: A Year of Food Life*
Klamkin	Charles	*Barns: their History, Preservation, and Restoration*
Kline	David	*Great Possessions: An Amish Farmer's Journal*
Knadler	Jessie	*Rurally Screwed: My Life Off the Grid With the Cowboy I Love*
Kohl	Edith Eudora	*Land of the Burnt Thigh*
Larson	Jean Rehkamp	*The Farmhouse*
Larsson	Carl	*A Farm*
Laskas	Jeanne Marie	*Fifty Acres and a Poodle: A Story of Love, Livestock, and Finding Myself on a Farm*
Laxalt	Robert	*Sweet Promised Land*
Lee	David	*Day's Work*
Lee	David	*The Porcine Canticles*
Leffingwell	Randy	*John Deere: A History of the Tractor*
Lippi	Rosina	*Homestead*
Logsdon	Gene	*The Contrary Farmer*
Logson	Gene	*The Mother of All Arts: Agrarianism and the Creative Impulse*
Logsdon	Gene	*The Pond Lovers*
Masumoto	David Mas	*Epitaph for a Peach: Four Seasons on my Family Farm*
McCorkindale	Susan	*Confessions of a Counterfeit Farm Girl: A Memoir*
Meyers	Kent	*The Witness of Combines*
Mohin	Ann	*The Farm She Was*
Morgan	C.E.	*All the Living*
Moynihan	Ruth B. (et al., ed.)	*So Much to be Done: Women Settlers on the Mining and Ranching Frontier*
Nabhan	Gary Paul	*Enduring Seeds: Native American Agriculture and Wild Plant Conservation*
Nichols	Beverley	*Down the Garden Path*

Owens	William A.	*This Stubborn Soil: A Frontier Boyhood*
Parisi	Philip	*The Texas Post Office Murals: Art for the People*
Peck	Robert Newton	*A Day No Pigs Would Die*
Peck	Robert Newton	*A Part of the Sky*
Perkes	Sid	*Lettie*
Perrin	Noel	*Third Person Rural: Further Essays of a Sometime Farmer*
Perrin	Noel	*First Person Rural*
Perrin	Noel	*Second Person Rural*
Pollan	Michael	*The Botany of Desire*
Pollan	Michael	*The Omnivore's Dilemma*
Pritchard	Forrest	*Gaining Ground: A Story of Farmers' Markets, Local Food, and Saving the Family Farm*
Ralston	Jeannie	*The Unlikely Lavender Queen: A Memoir of Unexpected Blossoming*
Rhodes	Richard	*Farm: A Year in the Life of an American Farmer*
Rhodes	Richard	*The Inland Ground: An Evocation of the American Middle West*
Salatin	Joel	*Everything I Want to Do Is Illegal: War Stories from the Local Food Front*
Sandoz	Mari	*Old Jules*
Siebert	Diane	*Heartland*
Sloane	Eric	*An Age of Barns*
Smiley	Jane	*A Thousand Acres*
Smiley	Jane	*Moo*
Spragg	Mark	*Where the River Change Directions*
Sprigg	June	*Shaker Design*
Steinbeck	John	*The Pastures of Heaven*
Stewart	Elinore Pruitt	*Letters of a Woman Homesteader*
Stratton	Joanna L.	*Pioneer Women: Voices from the Kansas Frontier*
Sykes	Hope Williams	*Second Hoeing*
Walker	Mildred	*Winter Wheat*
Weaver	Will	*Sweet Land: New and Selected Stories*
West	Kathleene	*The Farmer's Daughter*
White	E.B.	*Charlotte's Web*
Williams	Miller (ed.)	*Ozark, Ozark: A Hillside Reader*
Woginrich	Jenna	*Barnheart: The Incurable Longing for a Farm of One's Own*
Wright	Harold Bell	*The Winning of Barbara Worth*
Wroblewski	David	*The Story of Edgar Sawtelle*

🐓 Appendix D 🐓

Permission and Plagiarism Agreements

I give my instructor, _____, and the _____ Department

at _____(college name):

(Mark *one* of the following choices.)

☐ Permission* to use any writing that I produce as part of this course as a model for writing in future classes. **You may use my name.**

☐ Permission* to *anonymously* use any writing that I produce as part of this course as a model for writing in future classes. **You may not use my name.**

☐ **No permission**** to use any writing that I produce as part of this course for any purpose other than grading.

ALSO

I, _____, pledge that my work this semester is my own original work.

Signed: _____ **Date:** _____

Name (Printed): _____

Permanent Address: _____

E-mail: _____

* Permission may be rescinded for a particular assignment by writing a note to the instructor stating that permission is rescinded.

** Permission may be granted for a particular assignment by writing a note to the instructor stating that permission is granted.

Acknowledgements

While the topic of farming and literature is not widespread in college curricula (although we believe it should be, particularly at land grant institutions), some sources have been helpful in developing our original classes that became the inspiration for this reader.

- "The Poetics of Farming from Hesiod to the San Joaquin," a freshman seminar offered by Julia Major, University of California at Davis (2004).
- "Agriculture and the American Midwest," a freshman · course offered by Michael Kowalewski (associate professor of English) and Mary E. Savina (professor of Geology), Carleton College. Featured in a *Chronicle of Higher Education* "Syllabus" article of 17 November 2000.
- Ag in the Classroom, Project Director Debra Spielmaker, Utah State University.

Our thanks also to the following:

- Garrison Keillor for his suggestion of Joyce Sutphen and her poetry centered on farm themes.
- Ruth Ann Gregory of Warsaw, Missouri, for her folklore sayings about weather.
- Jon Anderson, professor emeritus of Art, for his *Cache Valley Barn*.
- Andrew McAllister, photographer, for his work capturing the cover image.
- Kolbie Astle of USU for her found poem from *What I Saw and How I Lied*.
- Jaqueline Pelzer for her assistance on orange crate labels.

Colleagues in the Department of English: Christine Cooper-Rompato, associate professor of English, and Phebe Jensen, professor of English, for their assistance in identifying medieval and Shakespearean literature exemplifying farming themes. Lisa Gabbert, associate professor, for her assistance with folklore and farming, particularly festivals. Rosa Thornley for permission to use her sections of her master's thesis on shivaree traditions and for suggesting Gee's Bend quilts. And to Rosa Thornley and Bonnie Moore for investing in teaching the course. Rebecca Sanders for her assistance in manuscript preparation. And particularly to Jeannie Thomas, head of the department, for her unflagging support and advice.

From Utah State University administration, we thank Dean John Allen, Chief of Staff Sydney Peterson, Provost Noelle M. Cockett, and President Stan L. Albrecht.

Additionally, we appreciate the wonderful students who have been participants in the creation of our "Farm Lit" courses.

Finally, we are grateful to our families for their love and support. A book project necessarily takes time away from them.

Proceeds from sales of this book benefit students' projects in the Department of English at Utah State University. Additionally, the authors contribute to sustainable agriculture projects. Please support these efforts by purchasing new copies of *FARM*.

About the Authors

Joyce Kinkead, distinguished professor of English at Utah State University, grew up on a farm near Warsaw, Missouri, where the family settled in the Little Tebo (Thibaut in the original French) Bottom in 1832, led by Milton Kinkead and his wife Jane Blanton Kinkead, who traveled from Kentucky. A member of the Limestone Pals 4-H Club, she worked at the MFA Exchange and Feed Store while in high school, and then completed her collegiate studies. She is a scholar in composition and rhetoric, but her reading of "Under the Lion's Paw" during junior high and of *Main-Travelled Roads* during college instilled a desire to teach a course in literature of the farm. In 2013, she was named Utah Professor of the Year by CASE and the Carnegie Foundation.

Evelyn I. Funda was born in 1960 in the small rural town of Emmett, Idaho, which is the main setting for her agricultural memoir *Weeds: A Farm Daughter's Lament*. Funda explores her three-generation farming experience there, where her Czech immigrant family spent their lives turning a patch of sagebrush into cropland and where she was a member of the Busy Bees 4-H Club. Today, Funda is an associate professor of American literature at Utah State University. She has published extensively on the literature of Willa Cather, and her creative nonfiction has appeared in literary magazines, including *Prairie Schooner.*

Lynne S. McNeill earned her PhD in folklore from Memorial University of Newfoundland, and is the author of the introductory textbook *Folklore Rules*. Her interests in folklore range broadly: from Bigfoot to pig roast parties, cats to *Little Red Riding Hood*, Internet memes to ghost hunting. She is active in the American Folklore Society and the International Society for Contemporary Legend Research, and she serves as the reviews editor for the journal *Contemporary Legend*. She has appeared on Animal Planet and the Food Network, and has been a guest on public radio's RadioWest.